Patrick Francis Moran

Essays on the origin, doctrines, and discipline of the early Irish Church

Patrick Francis Moran

Essays on the origin, doctrines, and discipline of the early Irish Church

ISBN/EAN: 9783742858696

Manufactured in Europe, USA, Canada, Australia, Japa

Cover: Foto ©Lupo / pixelio.de

Manufactured and distributed by brebook publishing software (www.brebook.com)

Patrick Francis Moran

Essays on the origin, doctrines, and discipline of the early Irish Church

ESSAYS

ON THE

ORIGIN, DOCTRINES, AND DISCIPLINE

OF

The Early Irish Church.

BY

THE REV. DR. MORAN,

VICE-RECTOR OF THE IRISH COLLEGE, ROME.

DUBLIN:
JAMES DUFFY, 15, WELLINGTON-QUAY;
LONDON: 22, PATERNOSTER-ROW.
1864.

TO

THE MOST REVEREND DR. JOSEPH DIXON,

Archbishop of Armagh, Primate of all Ireland, etc.

WHEN about to present to the public the following Essays on the origin, doctrines, and discipline of the ancient Church of Ireland, I felt irresistibly inclined to connect them in some way with the ancient See over which you preside, and to place them under the protection of the successor of St. Patrick, to whose labours we owe the blessings of the true religion, which I have been endeavouring to defend.

When investigating the ancient records of our country, everything tended to inspire me with veneration for Armagh, the centre from which the word of truth went forth to all Ireland—the See founded by our apostle, and the principal theatre of his labours, to which he bequeathed the fullness of his authority—a See for which the blessing and prayers of its founder have secured, through the lapse of so many centuries, a succession of prelates illustrious for zeal, piety, and knowledge, and their labours in propagating and defending the faith. The praises of your predecessors, St. Celsus and St. Malachy, are known to all; who, repairing the ruins of the temple, occasioned by Danes and other northern barbarians, restored and preserved the purity, integrity, and beauty of religion. What shall I say of the illustrious archbishop Dowdal, who, at a later period, and in difficult times, whilst filling the primatial chair, unawed by regal power and secular persecution, nobly defended the rights of Christ's Church against the tyranny of Henry and Edward, and the violence and perfidy of pretended reformers, proving himself worthy of the dignity in which he had been confirmed by apostolic authority? Nor is the learned Waucop less worthy of our admiration, who, acting for the Holy See, contributed so much to check the growth of heresy in Germany; and whilst holding the see of Armagh, assisted with the other bishops of Christendom in Trent, in illustrating the faith, defining its dogmas, and condemning those who sought to alter or corrupt it, and cutting them off as rotten branches from the mystic vine. And would not the constancy, patience, and other virtues of Dr. Creagh, who was doomed to pine away for many years in the horrors of a fetid prison, because he was faithful to his trust; and of the illustrious Dr. Plunket, the last martyr in the United Kingdom, be sufficient to shed lustre upon the annals of any Church?

But it would be too long to pass in review the other glories of Armagh, or to dilate on the wonderful providence with which St. Patrick has watched over his See. Suffice it to say, that it has given to the Church of God a long and unbroken line of prelates and martyrs—true lovers of Ireland and its ancient faith; and that it is now occupied by one whose virtues, learning, meekness and zeal render him equal to any of his most distinguished predecessors, whilst he surpasses them in the courage with which he has determined to raise up, even in the midst of the poverty of our country, a Church in honour of St. Patrick, which will reflect lustre upon all Ireland, and excite the admiration of future generations.

Filled with these sentiments for the primatial see of Ireland, and its present occupier, I take the liberty of dedicating to your Grace, and placing under your patronage, the Essays now going forth to the public; which, though not worthy of your acceptance, I present as an humble testimony of my sincere respect and veneration for your exalted virtues and high station.

Your very humble devoted servant,
P. F. MORAN.

Irish College, Rome,
 15th April, 1864.

PREFACE.

The following Essays have been written with the view of illustrating the origin of the Irish Church, and showing that the doctrines which she held in the earliest ages of her existence were the same as those which, after a lapse of more than fourteen centuries, she now professes.

Founded with the blessing and sanction of Christ's Vicar on earth; connected from the beginning with the rock of Peter, and participating in its solidity, our Church has been ever zealous in promoting the blessings of true religion, giving, at the same time, to the world the noblest examples of courage, devotedness, and fidelity, in preserving the sacred deposit of the faith committed to her by St. Patrick.

Immediately after the conversion of our country, it became distinguished for a love of learning and a missionary spirit, and was known as the island of saints and sages: in later times, when the storm of persecution swept over the land, when Catholic property was confiscated, when education was prohibited, when those who were faithful to the old religion were driven into exile, or cast into prison, or doomed to purple the scaffold with their blood, such was the constancy and heroism of our forefathers in professing the true faith, and suffering for the cross of Christ, that they acquired for our island the name of the *martyred* nation of the West.

This constancy in adhering to her religion is Ireland's greatest glory—a peerless privilege, which every true lover of his country should be anxious to defend and preserve.

We have lost our property, our commerce, our independence, but our religion could not be rooted out; so that our illustrious poet Aubrey de Vere could truly sing of Ireland in one of his beautiful poems lately published—

> "But fixed as fate her altars stand;
> Unchanged like God, her faith;
> Her Church still holds, in equal hand,
> The keys of life and death."*

To contribute, however feebly, to illustrate the ancient faith of Ireland, and to encourage our people to imitate the glorious examples of their fathers, was the only object of the writer in compiling the Essays now about to be presented to the public.

The first Essay treats of the origin of the Irish Church, and of the labours of SS. Palladius and Patrick. Evidence the most incontrovertible is alleged to show that our apostle derived his authority from Rome, and founded our Church with the sanction of Christ's Vicar on earth, whilst the arguments in favour of a contrary opinion, brought forward by Usher and others in past times, and by the learned Dr. Todd in a late work, are proved to have no foundation. The reader of the Essay will find that the ancient monuments of our country, our liturgies, our penitentials, as well as the deeds of our fathers, all unite in extolling the dignity of the Apostolic See, and proving that Ireland always acknowledged the supremacy of Rome.

The second Essay treats of the blessed Eucharist, and shows the profound devotion of our ancient writers to that holy Sacrament, in which our Divine Lord manifested the excess of His love for mankind, leaving to us His body and blood, with His soul and divinity, to strengthen us in our pilgrimage through this valley of tears.

The third Essay treats of the Blessed Virgin. The praises attributed to her by our ancient writers, in strains as eloquent as those of St. Bernard, show that they had nothing in common with modern heresy and infidelity, which appear to delight in assailing the most noble of all

---

* Aubrey de Vere, Inisfail, etc. p. 21

creatures, imitating the example of the serpent cursed by God, that bites at the heel by which it is crushed.

To these dissertations we have added several Appendices, which treat of important matters connected with our civil and religious antiquities. In some of the canons which we have collected, the reader will admire the wisdom with which the Church, without using violence or interfering with the rights of others, brought about the abolition of slavery;* whilst some extracts which we have been able to make from old Irish manuscripts in Rome, show how much mistaken were Dr. Todd and others in their remarks on the disciplinary laws of our Church regarding the celibacy of the clergy.†

We now commit the humble results of our researches to the public, trusting that what we have written may tend to promote a study of Irish antiquities, to exalt the name and glory of our country, and above all to strengthen and increase among our people the true faith, which is the victory that overcometh the world.

* See Appendix No. III. p. 264-268.
† See Appendix No. VI. p. 304.

			ERRATA.		CORRIGE
Pag.	12,	lin. 10,	Analius,	.	Auxilius.
,,	24,	,, 4,	history,	.	history and Acts.
,,	60,	,, 20,	6,	.	46.
,,	61,	,, 27,	remarks,	.	marks.
,,	77,	,, 5,	last,	.	last lost.
,,	80,	,, 25,	keeping,	.	heaping.
,,	85,	,, antepen.	a never,	.	an ever.
,,	108,	,, 5,	dato,	.	dabo.
,,	111,	,, 26,	pectalicus,	.	petalicus.
,,	129,	,, 14,	cousarum,	.	causarum.
,,	176,	,, antepen.	Jones,	.	Jonas.
,,	179,	,, antepen.	som,	.	some.
,,	193,	,, 27,	Yeolmkill,	.	Y Colmkill.

As the Author, residing in Rome, had not an opportunity of seeing the proof sheets, if there be other mistakes, he trusts that the reader will not hold him responsible for them.

ESSAY
ON
THE ORIGIN OF THE IRISH CHURCH,
AND
ITS CONNEXION WITH THE HOLY SEE.

THE close union of the Irish Church with the See of St. Peter, during the past three centuries of persecution, has justly been regarded as the source of that heroic fortitude which her children displayed in defence of the Catholic faith. Rome watched over Ireland with maternal care,—strengthened her in her weakness,—consoled her in her trials,—welcomed to a secure asylum her exiled children,—corrected her in her faults,—and rejoiced with her in her many triumphs.

In the days of Ireland's glory, when peace and piety smiled upon our country, and the Christian religion poured out its blessings with no unsparing hand upon the sons of St. Patrick, not less dear to our island was the chair of St. Peter—not less close were the bonds which united her with the See of Rome; and her poets and her sacred writers may be said to vie with the modern panegyrists of Catholic faith, in extolling the prerogatives of that central see of the Catholic world.

That our connexion with the Holy See, from which so many spiritual blessings have been derived, and especially the preservation of our faith, the most precious of all treasures, was originally established by St. Patrick, has been the universal belief of Irish Catholics during the lapse of fourteen hundred years. Hence, their love and gratitude towards St. Patrick, are only equalled by their devotion and attachment to the see of Peter—the source of their spiritual life.

Among Irish Protestants, however, the feeling is different. Though it cannot be said that they have manifested much respect for the name or labours of St. Patrick,* yet they have occasionally claimed him as their own; and in order to show that his views were conformable to theirs, they have not hesitated to assert that he received no sanction for his mission from Rome, and that he established a church in Ireland something like the Irish Anglican Church, hostile to, or at least independent of, the successors of the Prince of the Apostles.

Since the days of the learned Usher, this theory has been repeatedly proposed, and arguments of every kind have been employed to render it popular, and to give it at least the semblance of plausibility.

The object of the present essay is to pass in review the early records of our ecclesiastical history, as far as they are connected with this subject, and to show that no fact can be more clearly established by the weight of historical evidence, than the original connexion of the Irish Church with Rome, the seat and centre of all spiritual jurisdiction.

Abundant materials for our undertaking are supplied by the classical works of Father Colgan, the Bollandists, and Dr. Lanigan. It is not necessary to add, that we avail ourselves of the valuable publications of Dr. Todd, Dr. Reeves, Dr. Petrie, the late lamented O'Donovan and O'Curry, and others, whose laborious and impartial researches have contributed very much to illustrate the origin and the antiquities of our Church. We have also drawn largely on the documents which are preserved in the libraries of Italy and other parts of the continent.

The question before us is one of great interest, national and religious: we shall discuss it on its intrinsic merits, and decide it by the mere authority of historical records and critical arguments. We cannot, however, be cold or indifferent when

---

* At the time of the Reformation, the last resting-place of St. Patrick was profaned, and his remains disturbed. His celebrated crozier, called the Staff of Jesus, was burned in Dublin.—(See Dr. Todd's St. Patrick, p. 329, note.) Irish Catholics, on the other hand, like loving children, cherish with unbounded respect the name of their father in the faith, and have erected innumerable churches under his invocation, at home and abroad.

attempts are made to sully the lustre of the Catholic Church in Ireland, or to deprive us of the glorious traditions of him to whose labours we owe the knowledge of the Gospel, being reminded by St. Paul to venerate the memory of our apostle, and to defend the doctrines he has handed down to us: "Fratres, mementote præpositorum vestrorum qui vobis locuti sunt verbum Dei, quorum intuentes exitum conversationis, imitamini fidem."— St. Paul, Heb. xiii. 7.

In the present essay (Part I.) we shall treat of St. Palladius, and of the labours of St. Patrick, and his mission from the Holy See; and then refute (Part II.) various theories laid down in modern times, in regard to our apostle or the origin of our Church. We shall also (Part III.) collect various passages of our earliest writers, to illustrate the doctrine of the ancient Church of Ireland on the supremacy of the Pope.

PART THE FIRST.

CHAPTER I.

MISSION OF SAINT PALLADIUS.

St. Palladius sent to Ireland by St. Celestine in 431.—Palladius as deacon held a high place in Rome.—Ireland called Scotia.—St. Palladius founds some churches in Wicklow, but fails in his mission: he dies in Scotland.

UNTIL the pontificate of Pope Celestine, Ireland was not numbered amongst Christian islands. Some of her children had, no doubt, already given their names to Christ, and scattered congregations here and there may have assembled to preserve, as best they could, the blessings of the faith which had been granted to them; as yet, however, no apostle had visited her shores— no sun had risen to dissipate the clouds of paganism, nor did her hills and valleys as yet echo with the glad tidings of redemption.

St. Prosper, who held a high post in the Roman Church,

published, about the year 434, a brief chronicle, in which he registered under each successive year some few of the leading facts connected with its history. It is in the year 431, during the consulship of Bassus and Antiochus, and whilst the bishops of the Christian world were assembled at Ephesus to solemnly proclaim the exalted dignity of the Mother of God, that he thus records the first mission from the Apostolic See for the conversion of our island:

"Ad Scotos in Christum credentes ordinatur a papa Cœlestino Palladius et primus episcopus mittitur."*

"Palladius was consecrated by pope Celestine, and sent as the first bishop to the Irish believing in Christ."

This mission of St. Palladius to the Irish shores, bearing the light of faith, and with it the bonds of union with the Apostolic See, is one of the few points of our history on which all historians are now agreed. The authority of Prosper is such as none can controvert; and the words of his testimony are so clear, that they allow no room for hesitation or doubt. A few remarks will therefore suffice to illustrate the passage we have cited.

But little is known of the early career of St. Palladius. One other short notice in the chronicle of Prosper† comprises all the information that can be gleaned concerning him:

"Agricola, a Pelagian, son of Severianus, a Pelagian bishop, corrupted the churches of Britain, by insinuation of his doctrine; but through the instrumentality of Palladius, the deacon, pope Celestine sends Germanus, bishop of Auxerre, in his own stead (*vice sua*), to root out heresy, and direct the Britons to the Catholic faith."

The simple title of Palladius in the former extract, and the epithet, *The Deacon*, given to him in the words just cited, imply that he was well known to the Romans, for whom Prosper was writing, and held the office of deacon in the Roman Church. The Irish writers, and especially Muirchu-Maccu-Mactheni, in the Book of Armagh, supply all the explicit evidence we could desire on

---

* Vetustiora Latinorum Scriptorum Chronica, by Thomas Roncallius, Padua, 1787, tom. i. p. 520.
† Ibid.

that head; for they expressly style him deacon and chief-deacon of St. Celestine. This was a post of high honour and responsibility in the Roman Church. Many of the early pontiffs were elected to the popedom from being deacons of Rome; and during the vacancy of the see or the captivity of the pontiff, the whole administration of affairs devolved on them. Even two centuries later than the period of which we now treat, when archbishop Tomian of Armagh, and other Irish prelates, addressed a letter to Rome on the Paschal Question, the reply, which was written during the vacancy of the See, bears the names* of "Hilary, archdeacon, guardian during the vacancy of the Apostolic See," and "John the deacon," who was, moreover, pope-elect, and soon after ascended the papal throne as John IV.

Thus, in his office of deacon of Rome, Palladius was entitled to represent to the pope the wants of the Christian Church, and his solicitations in favour of Britain were sure to meet with a favourable response. His subsequent mission, as first evangelizer of our island, is quite in accordance with his high dignity in Rome, and with the views of the Holy See, which ever attached the greatest importance to the bringing of the Gospel light to pagan nations.† The example of pope Gregory at once recurs to mind, who, though bearing the burden of the Church of Rome, would

---

* Labbe, tom. v. Concilior; Usher Syllog. Epp., No. ix.; Bede, Hist. Eccl., ii. 19.

† From the earliest days of Christianity, the Roman pontiffs have occupied themselves with the conversion of pagan nations, and continue to do so to the present time, carrying out the commission given to them in the person of St. Peter by Christ, to feed his lambs, and to feed his sheep. St. Innocent the First, writing to Decentius in the year 402, refers to this fact: "Is it not known to all," says he, "that the things which have been delivered to the Roman Church by Peter, the Prince of the Apostles, and preserved ever since, should be observed by all; and that nothing is to be introduced devoid of authority, or borrowed elsewhere? Especially as it is manifest that no one has founded churches for all Italy, the Gauls, Spain, Africa, and the interjacent islands, except such as were appointed priests (or bishops) by the venerable Peter and his successors." "Cum sit manifestum in omnem Italiam, Gallias, Hispanias, Africam, et Siciliam, insulasque interjacentes, nullum hominem instituisse ecclesias, nisi eos quos venerabilis Petrus aut ejus successores constituerunt sacerdotes." (Ap. Coustant.) All the northern nations of Europe were converted by missionaries sent by Rome; and at present any progress made in converting the heathen is due to the successors of St. Peter The missionaries sent by Protestant societies or churches produce no effect.—See Marshall's excellent work, "Christian Missions: their

fain go in person to renew the Gospel-seed in the wasted plains of Albion.

Some reader unacquainted with the records of Ireland in her first ages of faith, may be surprised at seeing *Scotia* marked by St. Prosper as the field of Palladius' apostolate. However, in the fifth century Ireland was the only country known by the name of *Scotia*. This was at one time a matter of angry discussion; but at length all controversy has ceased. The researches of the Scottish antiquaries themselves, and their open acknowledgment of the fallacy of the opinion which referred that name to modern Scotland, have set this question at rest for ever.* We shall, therefore, on this head, merely remark with Dr. Todd, that "whoever reads the works of Bede and Adamnan, will not need to be informed that, even in their times, *Scotia* meant no country but Ireland, and *Scoti* no people but the inhabitants of Ireland."†

As regards the result of the mission of Palladius, his preaching was not destined to bear much fruit, or gather the inhabitants of our island into the fold of Christ. The following extracts contain all that is known of his missionary labours in Ireland.

The life of St. Patrick in the Book of Armagh, written by Muirchu-Maccu-Mactheni before the year 700, relates that—

"Palladius, archdeacon of Pope Celestine, Bishop of Rome, and 45th successor of St. Peter in the Apostolic See, was ordained and sent to convert this island, lying under wintry cold. But he was unsuccessful, for no one can receive anything from earth unless it be given to him from heaven; and neither did these fierce barbarians receive his doctrine readily, nor did he himself wish to remain long (transigere tempus) in a land not his own; wherefore, he returned to him who sent him. On his way, however, after passing the first sea, having begun his land journey, he died in the territory of the Britains.—Liber Armac. fol. 2, ap. Petrie, Essay on Tara, R.I.A. xviii. pag. 84; Todd's St. Patrick, p. 288.

Agents, their Method, and their Results," London, second edition, 1863. The solicitude of the Roman Pontiffs extended itself even to the temporal wants of remote churches. Eusebius (lib. iv. c. xxviii. Eccl. Hist.) gives a letter of St. Dionysius of Corinth, written in A.D. 176, which bears ample testimony to this fact.

* Pinkerton's Enquiry into the History of Scotland, vol. ii. p. 261; Chalmer's Caledonia, vol. i.; Innes' Civil and Eccl. Hist. of Scotland, etc.
† Todd's St. Patrick, p. 282.

The scholiast on St. Fiacc's hymn, of which we shall have occasion to speak hereafter, further informs us that Palladius landed in Hy-Garrchon, the present Wicklow, and thence penetrated to the interior, where he—

"Founded some churches, viz., *Teach na-Roman*, or house of the Romans, *Killfine*, and others. Nevertheless he was not well received by the people, but was forced to sail around the coast towards the north, until he was driven by a tempest to the land of the Picts, where he founded the church of Fordun; and there he is known by the name of Pledi."— Ap. Colgan, Tr. Thaumat. p. 5.

Another ancient record, known as the Vita Secunda, gives some additional details:—

"The most blessed Pope Celestine ordained bishop the archdeacon of the Roman Church, named Palladius, and sent him into the island of Hibernia, giving to him relics of the blessed Peter and Paul, and other saints; and, moreover, the volumes of the Old and New Testaments. Palladius entering the land of the Scots, arrived at the territory of the men of Leinster, where Nathi Mac Garrchon was chief, who was opposed to him. Others however, whom the divine mercy had disposed towards the worship of God, having been baptized in the name of the sacred Trinity, the blessed Palladius built three churches in the same district— one which is called *Kill-fine* (i.e., church of Finte: perhaps the present Dunlavin), in which, even to the present day, he left his books received from St. Celestine, and the box of the relics of SS. Peter and Paul, and other saints, and the tablets on which he used to write, which, in Irish, are called from his name, *Pallere*—that is, the burden of Palladius, and are held in veneration; another was called *Teach-na-Roman*, the house of the Romans; and the third, *Domnuch-ardech* (Donard, near Dunlavin), in which repose the holy companions of Palladius, viz., Sylvester and Salonius, who are still honoured there. After a short time Palladius died at Fordun, but others say that he was crowned with martyrdom there." Ap. Colgan, Tr. Thaumat. p. 13.

We shall conclude our extracts with the narrative of the Vita Quarta, whose author is supposed to be St. Aileran, and which seems to have been compiled about the middle of the seventh century. After mentioning the consecration of Palladius by Pope Celestine, it thus continues:—

"When, therefore, Palladius arrived in the territory of the Lagenians, he began to preach the word of God. But as the Almighty had not predestined the Irish people to be brought by him from the errors of heathenism to the faith of the holy and undivided Trinity, he remained there only a few days. Nevertheless some few did believe through him; and in the same district he founded three churches, one of which is called *Church-Finte* (Ecclesia Finte), in which, to the present day, are preserved his books received from St. Celestine, and a box with the relics of the blessed apostles Peter and Paul and other saints, and the tablets on which he used to write, which are called from his name, in Irish, *Pallad-ir*, and are held in great veneration. Another church was built by the disciples of Palladius, and is called the *House of the Romans*. The third is the church which is called *Domnach-arda*, in which are the holy companions of Palladius, viz., Silvester and Solinus, whose relics, after some time, were carried to the island of Boethin,* and are there held in due honour. But St. Palladius, seeing that he could not do much good there, was anxious to return to Rome, and migrated to the Lord in the region of the Picts. Others, however, say that he was crowned with martyrdom in Ireland."—(Ap. Colgan, Trias Thaumat., p. 38.)

CHAPTER II.

GENERAL SKETCH OF SAINT PATRICK'S HISTORY.

Early life of St. Patrick.—His captivity and liberation.—He studies at Lerins in France.—Visits Rome a first time.—Accompanies St. Germanus to Britain.—Sent a second time to Rome.—Consecrated bishop in France.

No doubt can be entertained as to the due claim of St. Patrick to be *the Apostle* of our island; and it is equally certain that we are indebted under God to his missionary labours for the conversion of our country to the Christian faith. Now, it is to Rome that the most ancient of our Christian monuments point, as the source

---

* This island belongs to the townland of *Inishboyne*, not far from Arklow, county Wicklow. It derived its name from St. Boethin, who flourished in the beginning of the seventh century. The monastery there was plundered and destroyed about the year 774, as the Annals of Ulster (ad h. a.), and the Four Masters (ad an. 770), attest. Thus we have in this passage an intrinsic proof that this life of St. Patrick was not written later than the eighth century. We have also an argument that the Vita Secunda, just cited, was written at least before the relics of SS. Sylvester and Solinus were transferred to Inis-Boethin, and hence cannot be later than the year 600: for it expressly records of Donard, "in qua sunt sancti viri de familia Palladii, Sylvester et Salonius *et ibi honorantur*".— Ap. Colgan's Tr. Th., p. 13; Todd, p. 297.

whence St. Patrick derived his spiritual mission; they attest with one accord that his preaching amongst us bore impressed on it the seal and sanction of the Vicar of Christ.

Whilst as yet in boyhood, and living with his parents in the vicinity of Boulogne,* Patrick was led a captive to Ireland, and sold there as a slave to a chieftain named Milchu. Being by divine interposition freed from captivity, in his twenty-second year, he resolved to dedicate himself to the service of God. It was the famous monastery of Marmontier, half a league from Tours, and as yet replete with the perfume of the virtues of its great founder, St. Martin, that he chose as the preparatory school for his missionary career. Thence, after a few years, he journeyed on to the island of Lerins, to perfect himself still more in piety and learning. Lerins was at this time styled the *insula beata*,† and holy men from every part of Christendom flocked thither as to a blessed sanctuary and silent retreat. The founder of this great school of literature and virtue, St. Honoratus, was still living;‡ and contemporaries

---

* Much has been written about the birth-place of St. Patrick. In the "Confession" it is merely stated that his family had a farm near the town *Bonavem Taberniæ*, and that he himself was made captive there. (Todd, St. Patrick, pag 362.) Another passage fixes this town in *Armoric Letha* (ibid. 361); and Lanigan well proves that it was not far from the present Boulogne-sur-Mer. (Ec. Hist. i 92 seqq.) But was St. Patrick born in this same place? The most ancient authority, *i.e.* St. Fiacc, mentions *Nemthur* as the place of our saint's birth. But what town is indicated by this name? The Vita Secunda identifies *Nemthur* and *Campus Taburnæ*. The Vita Tertia makes the same statement, as also the Vita Quarta (cap. i.). This would seem to prove that *Nemthur* was the name of the place near *Bonavem Taberniæ* where St. Patrick was made captive. Probus further writes, that he had ascertained as a matter of certainty that the *Vicus Bannave Taburniæ regionis* was situated in *Neutria*. It is resting on these authorities that many writers refer the birth-place of St Patrick to Armorica. On the other hand, the scholiast on Fiacc's hymn tells us that Nemthur was the same as *Alcluida*; and the Tripartite Life repeats the same statement. It does not, however, follow from this, as Ussher and many others to the present day assert, that he was born at Alcluaid in Scotland, now called Dumbarton. Perhaps the Vita Quarta gives us the key to reconcile the apparently conflicting statements, as it not only identifies Nemthur with the Armoric Bonavem, but adds (cap. i.), that this town was *in regione Strato-clud*, or Alcluid.

† St. Hilarius in Vit. St. Honorati, cap. 17, ap. Bolland. in tom. ii. Januarii; also S. Eucherius, De Laude Eremi, pag. 342, seqq. See The Monks of the West (vol. i. pag. 463, seqq.), by Montalembert, for an eloquent description of this monastery.

‡ He died in 428.

with our apostle in its hallowed retreat, were St. Hilary of Arles, St. Eucherius of Lyons, St. Lupus of Troyes,* and the author of the golden Commonitorium, Vincent de Lerins.

From the biographies of our saint we may gather, that from Lerins he proceeded to Rome, and represented to the Holy Father the spiritual darkness which hung over our distant island. Italy, however, was still distracted by the barbarian invasions, and the time marked by Providence for Patrick's apostolate had not yet come; he therefore returned once more to Gaul, and devoted himself anew to the study of the science of the saints, under the guidance of Germanus, the great Bishop of Auxerre.

We have already seen how, in the year 429, at the solicitation of the deacon of the Roman Church, missionaries were sent into Britain to combat the growing errors of Pelagius. St. Germanus of Auxerre was appointed special legate of Rome, by the Pontiff Celestine; his associate was St. Lupus of Troyes, and amongst those chosen to accompany them in their sacred expedition, was the friend and disciple of these holy men—our own apostle St. Patrick. Thus was he not only trained for his future apostolic labours in communion with Rome, but his first spiritual triumphs were also won under the guidance of the legate of the Holy See.

Whilst these holy missionaries were rooting out heresy in Britain, St. Palladius was destined to combat paganism in our island. No sooner was this intelligence conveyed to Germanus than he fixed his eyes on Patrick, as one who was specially suited to be associated in this sacred enterprize, and who, by his acquaintance with the language and inhabitants of Ireland, seemed prepared by Heaven itself to be harbinger to it of the blessings of faith. The first care of our apostle was to secure the blessing of Christ's Vicar for his new career: "St. Patrick," writes Probus, "poured forth to God the following prayer:† 'O Lord Jesus Christ, lead

---

* He was appointed bishop of Troyes in 427.

† This prayer of St. Patrick is evidence of the faith in the supremacy of the See of Peter, which he professed. Whilst other bishops are restricted to a certain territory, and cannot exercise authority beyond its limits, the Pope alone, as successor of St. Peter, has jurisdiction over the

me, I beseech thee, to the seat of the holy Roman Church, that, receiving authority there to preach with confidence Thy sacred truths, the Irish nation may, through my ministry, be gathered to the fold of Christ.' And soon after, being about to proceed to Ireland, this man of God, Patrick, went, as he had wished, to Rome, the head of all churches, and having asked and received the apostolic blessing, he returned, pursuing the same road by which he had journeyed thither."*

St. Patrick was accompanied to Rome by a holy priest named Segetius, who was instructed by Germanus to attest the virtues of our apostle, and to represent him as "a strong husbandman, well suited for the culture of the harvest of the Lord." St. Celestine, no doubt, offered but little opposition to a proposal which was thus urged by one in whom he placed such unbounded confidence as Germanus; and everything induces us to receive, as having foundation in historic truth, the long-received tradition of Rome, that the assistant clergy of Pope Celestine *all declared, of one accord, that for the mission to the Irish people, no one was so well suited as St. Patrick;* whilst they, at the same time, declared him to be "a man of religious life and sanctity, of angelic aspect, adorned, moreover, with heavenly wisdom, and enriched with every virtue."†

whole world, can send missionaries to every region, and establish new dioceses in countries which had never previously received the yoke of the Gospel. Hence the anxious desire of St. Patrick to obtain jurisdiction from him. Before the days of St. Patrick, St. Athanasius, by appealing to Pope Julius, and St. John Chrysostom to Innocent the First, acknowledged the authority of the Holy See Whilst our apostle Patrick was preaching the Gospel, the great St. Leo (epist. 14, ap. Baller), in a letter to Anastasius, bishop of Thessalonica, thus beautifully explains the nature of the primacy : "Vices nostras ita tuæ credidimus caritati (Anastasius was the Pope's representative) ut in partem sis vocatus solicitudinis, non in plenitudinem potestatis." Then he adds : "De qua forma, episcoporum quoque orta est distinctio, et magna ordinatione provisum est, ne omnes sibi omnia vindicarent, sed essent in singulis provinciis singuli, quorum inter fratres haberetur prima sententia, et rursus quidam in majoribus urbibus constituti, solicitudinem susciperent ampliorem, per quos ad unam Petri sedem ecclesiæ universalis cura conflueret et nihil usquam a suo capite dissideret." As the church is one sheepfold, one kingdom, one body, it was necessary that it should have one head, from which all spiritual jurisdiction should be derived.

* Probus in Vita S. Patricii ; ap. Colgan, Tr. Thaum. p. 49 ; also, Opp. Bedæ, tom. iii. edit. Basil, 1563.

† Officium Canonic. Lateranen. Antiquiss. printed in 1622. It would

It was only a short time before the death of pope Celestine that St. Patrick thus secured the blessing of the Apostolic See for his future labours in our island. Without delay he journeyed back to Auxerre, to his friend and patron, St. Germanus; and as he thence hastened towards the western coasts, to the vineyard assigned for his spiritual toil, two disciples of Palladius bore to him the tidings of that bishop's death, "whereupon," adds his biographer, "he bent his way to a neighbouring bishop, St. Amatorex,* and having received episcopal consecration at his hands, set out, accompanied by Apalius, Iserninus, and some others, for the Irish shores, in the summer of the year 432.

CHAPTER III.

ST. PATRICK'S CONNEXION WITH ST. GERMANUS.

Documents which prove that St. Patrick was the disciple of St. Germanus, papal legate: St. Fiacc, Muirchu-Maccu-Mactheni, Eric, Irish Nennius, Probus, and many other writers, attest this fact.

We have thus endeavoured to weave into a concise narrative the chief facts connected with St. Patrick's mission to our island. In regard to many of the minor details, conflicting narratives may be found in the ancient lives of our apostle; but the whole tradition of the Irish Church, from the fifth to the twelfth cen-

---

he interesting to compare the character of St. Patrick, and his preparations for his mission to Ireland, with the life and character and preliminary career of Drs. Brown, Curwin, and Loftus, Bale, Staples, etc., the first propagators of the Reformation in Ireland, who were corrupt, rapacious, and cruel.— See introduction to History of Archbishops of Dublin, by Dr. Moran, ch. i. p. 36; ch. iv. p. 97.

* The Book of Armagh, fol. ii., styles this bishop *Amatorex*, "a wonderful man and chief bishop;" and subsequently calls him *Matorex*, "a holy bishop." The other lives of St. Patrick generally call this bishop *Amator*. Who this bishop was, is a puzzle to our saint's biographers. (See Colgan, Tr. Thaumat, p 9, note 34; Lanigan, i. 200; Todd, 318.) In such a matter of uncertainty, it may be lawful to hazard a conjecture, that the Irish writers indicated by that name the see of St. Lupus of Troyes. Whilst the Irish lives all conspire in referring to this *Amatorex* and Germanus the chief part, after Celestine, in sending St. Patrick to our island, the old Latin treatise on the Irish liturgy refers it to the representations of Lupus and Germanus.

tury, without a dissentient voice, attests the two main facts: 1. That St. Patrick was trained for his future apostolate under the guidance of the papal legate, St. Germanus; and 2. That his mission to the Irish nation was sanctioned by the blessing of the Roman pontiff, St. Celestine.

We shall give a few of the early documents which illustrate these two cardinal points of all our Christian history:

St. Fiacc, first bishop of Sletty, which was once a remarkable town, situated not far from Carlow, on the banks of the Barrow, is the author of a hymn in the Irish language, in praise of St. Patrick.* From being a pupil of the Druidical bard Dubtach, he became a disciple of our apostle, and under his guidance preached the faith throughout the greater part of the present territory of Leinster. St. Patrick (Tirechan thus writes in his annotations, preserved in the Book of Armagh) conferred the degree of bishop upon him; so that he was the first bishop that was ordained among the Lagenians, and Patrick gave a *cumtach* (*i. e.*, a box or case) to him, with a bell and a *menstir*, and a crozier, and a *felire;* and he left seven of his people with him.†

This authentic witness as to the history of his great master, leaves no doubt as to St. Germanus having prepared our apostle for his future missionary career. He thus writes:

> "The angel Victor sent Patrick over the Alps;
> Admirable was this his journey—
> Until he took his abode with Germanus,
> Far away in the south of *Letha*.

> "In the isles of the Tyrrhene sea he remained:
> In them he meditated;
> He read the canon with Germanus,
> This, histories make known."‡

---

* Ware, De Script. Hiberniæ, lib. i. cap. 1; Colgan, Trias Thaum., p. 7; Curry, Lectures, p. 342 seqq.; Lanigan, Eccl. Hist., i. 80.

† Petrie, Round Towers, p. 333; Irish Glosses, by Stokes, I.A.S., 1860, p. 103. Some of these ecclesiastical presents seem to have been subsequently bequeathed by St. Fiacc to his church. The Vita Tripartita writes: "Ecclesiam edificavit primo S. Fiechus in loco qui ex ejus nomine Domnach-Fiacc, postea appellata est, eique reliquit sacram supellectilem, cymbalum nempe ministeriale, epistolas Paulinas, et baculum pastoralem."—(Ap. Colgan, Tr. Th. p. 152.)

‡ See the original text in Colgan, Tr. Th. p. 1: Curry's Lectures, p. 503: Whitley Stokes' Irish Glosses, I.A.S. p. 125. This ancient poem of St. Fiacc is preserved in the Liber Hymnorum, of which one MS. of

From this passage we learn that St. Germanus was chosen by St. Patrick for his spiritual master; and reference is made to earlier written records which attested the same fact. What these records may have been, it is now impossible for us to determine. It seems probable, however, that St. Patrick himself left to his disciples some record of his pilgrimage. Thus, in the Book of Armagh, which Dr. Graves has with so much skill proved to have been transcribed in the year 807,* are preserved the *Dicta Sancti Patritii*, one of which partially, at least, illustrates the words of St. Fiacc :—

| "Timorem Dei habui ducem itineris mei per Gallias atque Italiam etiam in insulis quæ sunt in mari Tyrrheno.† | "The fear of the Lord was guide of my journey through Gaul and Italy, and to the islands which are in the Tyrrhene Sea." |

The next document we shall refer to, is the sketch of St. Patrick's life, written by *Muirchu-Maccu-Mactheni*, which is also preserved in the Book of Armagh. This writer assisted at the famous ecclesiastical convention known as the Synod of Adamnan, presided over by Flann Febhla, the Abbot of Armagh, in 697.‡ His brief notice of St. Patrick is addressed to St. Aidus, Bishop of Sletty, who assisted at the same synod, and whose death is recorded in the Annals of Ulster in 699.§ In the preface he states, that many had hitherto endeavoured to present an accurate narrative of the past events of sacred history: his own father, Cogitosus, was perhaps the only one who had safely steered amidst the rocks and whirlpools of this dangerous course : he himself, however, " with little skill, without any certain guide, with frail memory,

---

the ninth or tenth century, is extant in Trinity College, Dublin, and another of the same age in the College of St. Isidore, Rome.

* Proceedings of Royal Irish Academy, November 30, 1846

† Liber Armacan. fol. 9, cited by Usher in his Primordia, and by Petrie, Essay on Tara Hill, p. 35. The word *Letha*, used by St. Fiacc, was often used to indicate *Italia*.—(See Curry's Lectures, p. 502-4 ; Irish Nennius, I.A S. 1848, p. 69.) The ancient gloss in the MS. of the Liber Hymnorum, in Trinity College, Dublin, adds on this passage, "*i.e. Italia in qua fuit Germanus.*" -Ap. Curry, loc. cit.

‡ The decrees of this synod are preserved in the Burgundian Library, Brussels, No. 2,324 —See Colgan, Act. SS. p. 382. Reeves' Adamnan, pref. p. 2, and 179.

§ In the end is also added, "Hæc pauca de sancti Patritii peritia et virtutibus, Muirchu-Maccu-Mactheni, dictante Aidæco Slebtiensis civitatis episcopo, conscripsit."—Liber Armac. fol. 20.

humble ideas, and barbarous style, but with most upright intention, in obedience to the command, and through reverence for the piety and authority of Aidus," undertakes "to cull here and there some few from the many deeds of St. Patrick."* The first chapters of this memoir of our apostle, thus written before the close of the seventh century, are unfortunately lost. The titles, however, of the lost chapters still remain ;† and one of these makes known to us that the sixth chapter referred "to St. Patrick's journey into Gaul, where, having found Germanus, he remained with him."‡ Moreover, the second folio retains quite sufficient to attest the connection of our apostle with the holy Bishop of Auxerre:—

"The Angel Victor announced to him that the time was come when he should go forth with evangelic net, to gather in those fierce and barbarous nations, for whose instruction God had destined him. . . . When, therefore, the opportunity presented itself, he set out, strengthened by the aid of Heaven, to undertake the missionary career for which he had been long prepared : and Germanus sent with him a holy priest named Segetius, that he might be at the same time, a companion and a witness ; for as yet he had not received from St. Germanus the episcopal consecration."§

Amongst the Cottonian manuscripts there was one containing a short, but very ancient, treatise on the liturgy as used in the Irish

---

* Quoniam quidem, mi Domine, Aide, multi conati sunt ordinare narrationem, utique istam, secundum quod Patres eorum et qui ministri ab initio fuerunt sermonis, tradiderunt illis, sed propter difficillimum narrationis opus diversasque opiniones et plurimorum plurimas suspiciones, numquam ad unum certumque historiæ tramitem pervenerunt. Ideo ni fallor juxta hoc nostrorum proverbium, ut deducuntur pueri in ambitheatrum in hoc periculosissimum et profundum narrationis sanctæ pylagus (sic) turgentibus proterve gurgitum aggeribus inter acutissimos carubdes per ignota æquora insitos a nullis adhuc lintribus excepto tantum uno Patris mei Cognitosi (sic) expertum atque occupatum, ingenioli mei puerilem remi cymbam deduxi. Sed ne magnum de parvo videar fingere, pauca hæc de multis S. Patricii gestis, parva peritia, incertis auctoribus, memoria labili, attrito sensu, vili sermone sed affectu piissimo, caritatis etiam sanctitatis tuæ et auctoritatis imperio obediens carptim gravatimque explicare aggrediar."—Lib. Armac. fol. 20.

† Book of Armagh, fol. 20.

‡ "De inventione sancti Germani in Galliis et ideo non exivit ultra."
—See these titles of the lost chapter, in Petrie, Essay on Tara, p. 87.

§ "Visitavit (angelus) dicens ei adesse tempus ut veniret et evangelico rete nationes feras et barbaras ad quas docendas miserat illum Deus ut piscaret. . . . . Opportuno ergo tempore imperante comitante divino auxilio cæptum ingreditur iter ad opus in quod olim præparatus fuerat utique evangelii : et misit Germanus seniorem cum illo, hoc est Segitium presbyterum ut testem comitem haberet quia nec adhuc a sancto domino Germano in pontificali gradu ordinatus est."—Liber Armac. fol. 2.

Church. Ussher merely describes it as "written before the time of Bede;"* but Spelman,† when publishing it in his British Councils, adds, that the manuscript itself belonged to the seventh century. This curious treatise makes St. Mark the author of the Cursus Scotorum, or Irish liturgy, and adds:—

"In after times it was used by the most blessed Cassianus, who was associated with the blessed Honoratus, in the monastery of Lerins. After him, blessed Honoratus, its first abbot, and St. Cesarius, bishop of Arles, and the blessed abbot Eucherius, who was in the same monastery, used this liturgy; and with them in that monastery were blessed Lupus and Germanus, who, in conformity with their rule, sang the same liturgy, and through their saintly life attained the most exalted episcopal dignity. They subsequently preached to the Britons or Scots, as the life of St. Germanus of Auxerre, and the life of St. Lupus testify; and they spiritually trained up and nourished with sacred learning the blessed Patrick, whom, being consecrated bishop, they, by their commendation, elevated to the chief episcopate of the Scots and Britons."‡

Thus we trace St. Patrick once more to Lerins, and to the school of St. Germanus.

Eric, author of the life of St. Germanus, was himself numbered amongst the clergy of Auxerre: he flourished, moreover, at the time of Charles the Bald, when France was inundated with a number of learned and holy men from the schools of Ireland.§ Hence he was acquainted alike with the traditions of Ireland and with those of the church of St. Germanus. He, moreover, appeals to earlier monuments regarding our apostle, as attesting the facts which he records:—

"As the discipline of children redounds to the glory of their father, I have deemed it opportune to briefly commemorate one, and one the most illustrious of the many children whom St. Germanus brought forth to Christ, and instructed in the doctrines of faith. I mean Patrick, who, as the history of his life records, was the chief apostle of Ireland, and spent fourteen years under the most holy tutorship of Germanus, and

---

* Ap. Lanigan, i. 62. † Concilia, etc., i. p. 167.
‡ Spelman, loc. cit.; Usher, Primord., p. 840; Wilkins, Concil. Magnæ Brit., vi. p. 741. We shall give this curious tract in full, with some remarks, in the appendix.
§ Eric himself writes: "Quid Hiberniam memorem contempto pelagi discrimine, pene totam cum grege philosophorum ad nostra littora migrantem."—Epist. ad Carolum Calvum, præf. ad act. S. Germani.

drank in no small share of learning regarding the heavenly Scriptures, at the very source of this rich fountain."*

This testimony is surely one of great weight in confirming the proposition which we have laid down. It proves that three hundred years from the death of St. Patrick, the panegyrists of the great apostle of Auxerre made his tutorship of our saint a theme of eulogy; it proves that St. Patrick was reckoned amongst the most remarkable of the saints who went forth from his school of sanctity; it proves that the written memorials of our apostle attested the spiritual bonds which united him with St. Germanus.

The learned Franciscan, John Colgan, published in his Trias Thaumaturga a commentary on the hymn of St. Fiacc, full of interesting details regarding the various facts which are there commemorated. Much has been said about intrinsic arguments as to its date and importance. Such arguments, however, often receive their colouring from the preconceived opinions of those who propose them. For us it at present suffices to remark, that the most skilful of our Celtic philologists refer its language to the seventh or eighth century, whilst, as Petrie remarks, itself is preserved in MSS. *which cannot be later than the ninth*.† This scholiast thus commemorates the connection of our apostle with St. Germanus:—

"Germanus was bishop of a city called Auxerre, and Patrick applied himself to study under his guidance . . . . It happened that Germanus came to Britain to root out the Pelagian heresy, and he came accompanied by Patrick, and many others; and he unceasingly laboured to root out that heresy, until intelligence was brought to him that his own city had begun to be infected with it Then he and Patrick returned to France, and applied themselves to combat the same pestilential errors."‡

---

* "Et quoniam gloria Patris in suorum clarescit moderamine filiorum, e multis quos in Christo filios, in religione creditur habuisse discipulos, unius tantum ejusdemque famosissimi, castigata brevitate sufficit inseri mentionem. Patricius, ut gestorum ejus series prodit, Hiberniæ peculiaris apostolus regionis, sanctissimo ejus discipulatui xviii. addictus annis non mediocrem e tanti vena fontis in Scripturis cœlestibus hausit eruditionem."—Lib. i. cap. 2. sec. 21; AA. SS. Julii, tom. vii. The numeral xviii., which is found in the printed text, is a clerical error for xiiii.

† Essay on Tara, p. 71.

‡ Tr. Thaumat. p 5. Colgan thus speaks of the author of these scholia: "Scholiastes hic Fieci scripsit partim Latine, partim Hibernice præfationem sive argumentum operi S. Fieci præfixum, et scholia in idem opus, in margine adnotata, et ipsa codicis vetustate pæne exesa et ex parte

He then goes on to state that, in a city where their preaching was unsuccessful, Germanus took counsel with our apostle as to the course they should pursue: St. Patrick answered, "Let us for three days observe a rigorous fast at the city gates; and then let us leave the matter in the hands of God." This counsel was followed, and their preaching was crowned with complete success. In the subsequent commentary, too, the scholiast more than once returns to this subject of the connection of St. Patrick with Germanus; of his having learned from that holy man "Sacros canones, omnesque ecclesiasticas disciplinas;" and in fine, of St. Germanus having sent Patrick to Celestine, and given him as a companion the priest Segetius, who was to bear testimony to his merit and virtues.

The Irish Nennius, published by the Irish Archæological Society, in 1848, is not a mere translation of the old British author. In everything connected with Ireland, it is an original independent work, generally based on the authentic records of our country. After detailing, at considerable length, the history of St. Germanus, it thus briefly sketches the career of St. Patrick:—*

"At this time Patrick was in captivity in Erin with Miliuc; and at this time Palladius was sent to preach in Erin. Patrick went to the south to study, and he read the canon with Germanus. Palladius was driven from Erin, and he went and served God in Fordun in Mairne. Patrick came to Erin after studying, and baptized the men of Erin. To describe the miracles of Patrick to you, O men of Erin! were to bring water to a lake: they are more numerous than the sands of the sea, and I shall therefore pass them over, without giving any narrative of them just now."

We now come to the lives of St. Patrick published by Colgan and the Bollandists, all of which attest the same fact, of St. Germanus having been the spiritual tutor and guide of our apostle.

The Vita Secunda, judged by Colgan to have been written

obliterata. Author videtur antiquitatum patriæ longe peritus, et satis vetus qui ut dicemus videtur floruisse circa annum 580, vel saltem ante sæculi sexti finem."—(Loc cit. p 7.) Ussher, too, in his Primordia, reckons these scholia as holding the place of a distinct and most ancient life of St. Patrick—Primordia, etc., p. 827, seqq.

* Irish Nennius, I. A. S., 1848, pag. 107.

by a disciple of St. Patrick in the sixth century, and bearing intrinsic evidence, as Dr. Todd remarks, of his having used very ancient materials in its composition, devotes its 22nd chapter to the training of St. Patrick by Germanus :—

"Crossing over the British sea, he sought a certain most holy man, remarkable for his zeal in the cause of faith, the head of the church of Gaul, the bishop of Auxerre, by name Germanus ; with him he remained for a considerable time, like Paul at the feet of Gamaliel, in humble submission and obedience, and with a fervent mind applied himself to the study of wisdom and of the Scriptures. .... It was in the island of Lerins that Patrick was instructed by Germanus. He was then thirty years of age ; for thirty years he was under the guidance of Germanus, and for sixty years did he preach to the Irish." [*]

The Vita Tertia is even more full in its details. In a heavenly vision he was instructed to proceed to foreign parts, and lay in a store of sacred learning: "he went therefore to the most wise Germanus, who in the city of Auxerre was honored by all the bishops of Gaul, and remained with him for four years, studying and fulfilling the Scriptures, being a virgin both in body and mind." From Auxerre he proceeded to Lerins (insula Tamerensis) ; and "having spent nine years there, Patrick wished to proceed to Rome, the head of all churches, whither the Christians resorted from all

---

[*] Ap. Colgan, Tr. Th. pag 13. The island of Lerins is in this passage and in many other documents called *insula Aralanensis*. The thirty years' study of St. Patrick, under St. Germanus, have been a great puzzle to the modern biographers of our saint. They are, nevertheless, mentioned in nearly all the old Irish documents. It was in 418 that St. Germanus was chosen by St. Amator bishop of Auxerre. Before that time he was engaged in some of the highest civil and imperial offices ; so we cannot suppose that he received any disciples before the year 418. Now, how is this to be reconciled with the thirty years tuition of St. Patrick, and with the date of St Patrick's mission to Ireland, which was in 432 ? Some writers with Colgan (loc. cit. pag. 30, n. 18) endeavour to explain it, by supposing that Germanus may, many years earlier, have taught St. Patrick the rudiments of secular learning ; others pass to the extreme of hypercriticism, and reject the whole statement as a mere invention of the writers themselves. Dr. Todd (St. Patrick, 319. note i) concludes from it that there are *insuperable difficulties* to reconcile it *with the facts of history*. Perhaps, however, the statement of the ancient writers is historically true, and that it only implies that St. Patrick for thirty years looked to St. Germanus as his spiritual guide. It certainly cannot mean that he was for thirty years living with him ; for during this period they describe St. Patrick as visiting Lerins and Rome, etc. Now from 418 till St. Germanus' death was precisely thirty years ; and hence the statement of these ancient lives had its origin in the fact, that even after St. Patrick's arrival in Ireland, he looked still to St. Germanus for counsel and spiritual guidance.

parts of the world. This was approved of by St. Germanus, who sent with him a venerable priest named Segetius, as a witness to his religious career.'*

The life attributed to St. Aileran by Colgan, and which bears internal evidence of having been written before the year 774,† repeats the same narrative. It moreover adds, that St. Germanus received Patrick with the greatest honour (summa cum veneratione); Lerins was the name of the island where he was under the direction of Germanus; and thirty years was the period during which he followed his guidance. Whilst with Germanus, our apostle was favored with an angelic vision, summoning him to evangelize our island; and the news of Palladius' death having been received, "St. Germanus sent Patrick to Rome for the apostolic license; for this was required by the ecclesiastical law."‡

Probus, in his invaluable life of our saint, states, that when setting out for Rome, he tarried for some time with Germanus, submitting himself in all things to his guidance—"in patience, obedience, charity and chastity, in sanctity of heart and soul: preserving his virginity in the fear of the Lord, and living in goodness and simplicity during the whole period of his mortal career." During his sojourn with Germanus, he was often favored with angelic visions; and being admonished that the time was come for him to hasten to the theatre of his missionary labours, St. Germanus sent with him as a companion and a witness, the holy priest Segetius."§

In the Leabhar Breac, there is preserved a fragmentary ancient life of our apostle; it too briefly commemorates, that "Patrick went to learn wisdom and religion in the south-east of Italy, to the bishop Germanus."‖

The Vita Tripartita, published in Latin by Colgan, had not its due weight assigned to it till it was discovered, in the ancient

---

* Ap. Colgan, Tr. Th. p. 23. † See ante p. 7-8.
‡ "Misit ergo S. Germanus B. Patricium Romam ut cum Apostolicæ Sedis episcopi licentia ad prædicationem exiret: sic enim ordo exigebat."—Ap. Colgan, loc. cit. p. 39.
§ Ap. Colgan, loc. cit. p. 48.
‖ See the original Irish text with some remarks, published by I. A. S. Tribes and Customs of Hy-Fiachragh, by O'Donovan, 1844, pag. 413.

Irish language, in the British Museum in 1849.* Colgan, relying on ancient testimonies and other arguments, had referred this life of our apostle to the sixth century; and Curry, after diligently examining the Irish text, concludes: " As far as my judgment and my acquaintance with the idiom of the ancient Gaelic language will bear me, I would agree with Father Colgan's deductions."† St. Evin is supposed to be its author: he was founder of the old monastery, which with the name gave origin to the town of Monasterevan; and hence he is invoked by Ængus, in his Festology, as "the fair saint from the banks of the Barrow."‡ According to this very ancient record, St. Patrick in a vision heard the voices of the Irish youths from the wood of Fochlut, calling on him to go and preach to them. Guided by the angel Victor, he resolved first to apply himself to sacred science, and placed himself under the guidance of St. Germanus: " This bishop was most illustrious by birth, and dignity, and life, and learning, and ministry and miracles; from him Patrick received the successive degrees of the ecclesiastical orders." Not satisfied with having spent many years under the holy guidance of so great a master, Patrick "resolved to visit the see of St. Peter, who was endowed with the firmness of the rock, that thus he might the more fully learn the canonical practices of the holy Roman Church, and have his own career blessed by the apostolical authority. Having disclosed this matter to Germanus, this holy bishop approved of his sacred resolve, and gave him the servant of Christ, Segetius, as a companion, and a witness of his unblemished life."§

We have now brought the first part of our enquiry to a close, and if historical evidence can bear with it any force of persuasion,

---

* See a very interesting history and analysis of this ancient life, in Curry's Lectures, pag. 345, seqq.
† Curry, Lectures, pag. 350.
‡ Ængus' Festology, ad 22 Dec.; ap. Curry, loc. cit.
§ Sedet animo Patricii sedem sancti petere Petri in petra fundati et S. Romanæ ecclesiæ canonicis institutis uberius imbui cupiens auctoritate apostolica et actus suos roborari. Cum antem quod corde conceperat, enodasset B Germano, approbavit sanctum ipsius propositum S. Germanus adjungens ei Christi servum Segetium presbyterum itineris socium, laboris solatium, sanctæ conversationis testem idoneum.—Colgan, Tr. Thaumat. p. 70.

we rest assured that the authorities produced in the preceding pages will convince any unprejudiced reader, that it was the universal tradition of our country, even from its earliest ages of faith, that St. Patrick was prepared for his missionary labours in Ireland, under the guidance of the legate of the Holy See, the great bishop of Auxerre, St. Germanus.

CHAPTER IV.

ST. PATRICK'S MISSION FROM ROME.

St. Patrick's Mission from Rome proved by St. Patrick's proverbs, St. Columbanus, St. Ultan, the Leabhar Breac, St. Eileran, Marianus Scotus, St. Prosper, and others.

WE now proceed to the second point of our inquiry, in which we assert that our apostle's sacred expedition to our island was undertaken with the approval and sanction of the Vicar of Christ and successor of St. Peter.

Many of the passages which have just been cited from our early writers, whilst they connect our apostle with St. Germanus, represent him, too, as united with Rome, the head and centre of the Catholic world. Indeed this may be viewed as a corollary from what has been already proved; and as St. Patrick received his religious training from Germanus, we may at once conclude that his mission to our island bore impressed upon it the seal and sanction of the Vicar of Christ. Hence, many of the most learned of our Protestant writers have admitted as indubious this mission of St. Patrick from Rome. Petrie, though questioning many other matters connected with our apostle, looks on this as a fact in attesting which all the ancient records conspire. Ussher, too, lays down this connexion with Rome as a primary principle for explaining other matters of controversy.† To remove, however, the scruples of those who are accustomed to regard as

---

* Essay on Tara, p. 92.
† A Discourse on the Religion anciently professed by the Irish: Dublin, 1815. p. 84.

unsupported by historic evidence those facts which are endeared to the popular tradition of our country, we shall briefly present some of the chief monuments which prove that St. Patrick was commissioned by Rome to preach the Gospel in our island.

St. Patrick himself, in one of those beautiful proverbs called the *Dicta Sancti Patritii*, preserved in the Book of Armagh, refers to the See of Peter as the source whence the sacred truths of faith were brought to us; and takes occasion from this remark to exhort his spiritual children to be ever faithful to the Church of Rome:

"De sæculo requissistis ad Paradisum, Deo gratias: ecclesia Scottorum immo Romanorum; ut Christiani ita et Romani sitis."

These words are undoubtedly obscure; but still, considering the connexion of the members of the whole passage, it admits of no meaning but the following:—

"Thanks be to God: you have passed from the kingdom of Satan to the city of God; the church of the Irish is a church of Romans; as you are children of Christ, so be you children of Rome."*

It was less than a hundred years from the death of St. Patrick, when Columbanus erected for himself and his companions a few rude huts in the gloomy forests of Burgundy. His fame for wisdom and miracles soon attracted disciples around him; in a few years the continent was filled with his monasteries, and he is deservedly ranked amongst the apostles of France, Switzerland, and North Italy. Before he set out on his missionary career, he had, for fifty years, assiduously devoted himself to sacred learning in our island: he conversed with those who had been themselves disciples of St. Patrick, and he enriched his mind from the abundant stores which were gathered together in the great monastery of Bangor. Now, this illustrious ornament of our island in the sixth century, when sketching on the continent the character of his countrymen, declared that "the Irish are the scholars and disciples of Rome;" and, addressing the Roman pontiff, he adds:

* Liber. Armacan. fol. 9.

"The Catholic faith is held unshaken by us as it was delivered to us by you, the successors of the holy Apostles."*

St. Ultan of Ardbraccan was one of the first writers who reduced to order the history of our apostle, and comprised them in a regular life.† This saint is commemorated by Ænghus on the 4th of September—

> "Great is the happiness of the children
> Around Ultan of Ard-Breccain,"‡

which words allude to the parental care with which he provided for those infants whose mothers had been cut off in the plague of 656. The Four Masters, and our other authentic annals, fix his death, at a very advanced age, in 657.§ The loss of his life of our apostle has been partly compensated, by the many extracts from it made by his own disciple, St. Tirechan, which are preserved in the Book of Armagh. In one place Tirechan speaks of himself as belonging to a family specially dedicated "to God and St. Patrick:"∥ elsewhere he is expressly styled the *alumnus vel discipulus* of St. Ultan; and it is added, that the memoirs of St. Patrick which he compiled were extracted from the book, or written at the dictation, of his master: "Tirechan episcopus hæc scripsit ex ore vel libro Ultani episcopi."¶ Thus we may justly conclude that this work of Tirechan was written before the death of St. Ultan. The fact of its being preserved in the Book of Armagh,** which was transcribed, as we have seen, in the year 807,

---

* "Toti Heberi sumus, ultimi habitatores mundi . . . Sed fides sicut a vobis primum sanctorum scilicet apostolorum successoribus, tradita est inconcussa tenetur."—Epist. ad Bonifac. IV. Biblioth. PP. Gallandi, xii. p. 352.

† He is expressly commemorated as such in the MS. Irish Tripartite Life, in British Museum, pp. 9 and 39; conf. Curry, Lectures, etc., p. 607-8.

‡ See the original Irish quatrain of Ænghus in Martyrol. of Christ's Church, I.A.S. 1844, pref. p. lxxiv.

§ The Four Masters say he was 180 years of age: the Calendar of Donegal says he died in his 189th year.

∥ See Todd, St. Patrick, p. 444-5.

¶ Confer. Curry's Lectures, p. 608.

** For many interesting details about the Book of Armagh, see Westwood, Palæographia Sacra.

adds still more weight to its statements, as it proves how important and accurate a record it was esteemed even at that early date. The chief scribe of Armagh, named Ferdomnach, is supposed to have transcribed these writings from the original copies into this Book of Armagh; and Dr. Graves has judiciously remarked,* that "the annotations of Tirechan were evidently becoming illegible at the time that Ferdomnach's copy of them was made. This is sufficiently indicated by notes in the margin, which show that the scribe found it difficult to read the manuscript from which he was transcribing."

It is in the following concise, but singularly expressive, terms that this ancient writer attests the mission of St. Patrick from pope Celestine:—

"Decimo tertio anno Theodosii Imperatoris a Cælestino episcopo, papa Romæ, Patricius episcopus ad doctrinam Scottorum mittitur qui Cælestinus xlv. episcopus fuit a Petro Apostolo in urbe Roma.

"Palladius episcopus primo mittitur qui Patricius alio nomine appellabatur, qui martyrium passus est apud Scottos ut tradunt sancti antiqui.

"Deinde Patricius secundus, ab angelo Dei, Victor nomine, et a Cælestino papa mittitur cui Hibernia tota credidit, et qui eam pene totam baptizavit."†

"In the thirteenth year of the emperor Theodosius, the bishop Patrick was sent by Celestine, bishop and pope of Rome, to instruct the Irish. This Celestine was the forty-fifth successor of St. Peter in the city of Rome.

"Bishop Palladius was first sent, who was also called Patrick by a second name, and he was martyred among the Irish, as the old saints have said.

"Then the second Patrick was sent by the angel of God, Victor, and by pope Celestine: all Ireland received his teaching, and nearly all of it was regenerated by him in baptism.

The Leabhar Breac is described by Petrie as "the oldest and best Irish manuscript relating to Church history now preserved, or which perhaps the Irish ever possessed."‡ Professor Curry more than once commends it in his Lectures, as "of great interest and importance," and presenting "the chief collection of religious

---

* On the date of the Book of Armagh: by Rev. Charles Graves; Proceedings of R.I.A. vol. iii., Nov. 30th, 1846.

† Liber Armacan. fol. 16; ap. Petrie, Tara, p. 85; Transactions of R.I.A. vol. xviii. part 2nd, 1837.   ‡ Ibid. p. 74.

compositions," which are extant in the Gaelic language.* Amongst the other treasures which it contains, is an ancient tract on the life of our apostle, written in Irish, which abounds with references to continental events, and to the earlier writers of our island;† and expressly attests the mission given by pope Celestine to Palladius and Patrick to preach the Gospel in Ireland :—

"We ought to know at what time Patrick, the holy bishop and chief instructor of the Irish, began to come to Ireland to preach and baptize, and to resuscitate the dead, and to cure all diseases, and to banish all the demons from Ireland, and to sanctify and consecrate, and to ordain and bless, and to contest and triumph; for the Apostle says: I have fought a good fight, etc. The year, therefore, that Patrick came to Ireland was the four hundred and thirty-third from the Incarnation, in the ninth year of the reign of Theodosius, king of the world, and in the first year of the episcopacy of Sixtus, the coarb (*i.e.* successor) of Peter, and in the fourth year of the reign of Leoghaire Mac Niall, at Tara, and in the sixtieth year of his own age : and for sixty years he baptized and instructed the men of Erin, as Fiacc says :

> He preached for three score years
> The crucifixion of Christ to the tribes of the Feni.

And here is the character given by Heleran of Patrick, at the time when he brought an account of him to Clonard :

> Meek and great was the son of Calphurn,
> A vine-branch laden with fruit . . . . .

Palladius was sent by pope Celestine with a gospel for Patrick to preach it to the Irish. This was the four hundred and first year from the crucifixion of Christ.‡ In the year after this, Patrick went to preach in Ireland, Ætius and Valerius being consuls. It was in this year that Sixtus assumed the supremacy of Rome after Celestine, and it was the fourth of the reign of Leoghaire son of Niall, at Tara."§

Thus this ancient tract corroborates the former evidence, and, in its own singular form of expression, represents our apostle as com-

---

* Lectures, p. 352 seqq.

† Having mentioned the death of St. Patrick, the writer adds a series of the subsequent principal events, the last of which is the death of king Conchobhar of Tara, and Artri, abbot of Armagh, both of whom, as we learn from the Annals of Ulster, died in 832. This fixes the date of the composition of this tract.

‡ The Irish writers generally place the crucifixion in the year 31 of the present era. This date is also assigned in the tract which we are citing, a little further on, as may be seen in Petrie, Tara, p. 80.

§ The whole of this curious tract is given by Petrie, in his Essay on Tara, p. 74 seqq.

missioned by pope Celestine, through Palladius, to evangelize our island.

The verse from St. Eileran, given in this passage, is also cited by Æughus in his Festology, on the 17th of March. St. Eileran receives from our Irish writers the epithet of *the Wise*—" Eileranus sapiens ;" and, according to the Four Masters, died in 664. He was abbot of Clonard, and, besides a life of St. Patrick, was author of a Latin treatise on the genealogy of our Saviour, and of a beautiful Irish litany, extracts from which were first published by the late Professor O'Curry. It is to him that Colgan attributes the life known as the Vita Quarta; and in it we find thus registered the blessing of pope Celestine granted to our apostle :—

"St. Germanus* sent the blessed Patrick to Rome, that thus he might receive the sanction of the bishop of the Apostolic See to go forth and preach; for order so requireth. . . . And Patrick, having come to Rome, was most honourably received by the holy pope Celestine ; and relics of saints being given to him, he was sent into Ireland by that pontiff."†

* St. Germanus could not have acted otherwise without putting himself in opposition to the doctrines and practices of the Church of Gaul. St. Ireneus, bishop of Lyons, the disciple of Polycarp, who received his doctrines from St. John, in the second century writing of the Church of Rome, says: "Ad hanc ecclesiam propter potiorem principalitatem necesse est omnem convenire ecclesiam, hoc est, eos qui sunt undique fideles, in qua semper ab his, qui sunt undique, conservata est ea quæ est ab apostolis traditio." (Lib. iii. c. 3, adv. hær.) St. Zozimus, who was pope at the time of St. Germanus, thus writes (Epistola 5a) to all the bishops of Gaul : " Jussimus præcipuam, sicuti semper habuit, metropolitanus episcopus arelatensium civitatis in ordinandis sacerdotibus teneat auctoritatem ; viennensem, narbonensem primam et secundam provincias ad pontificium suum revocet. Quisquis vero posthac contra apostolicæ sedis statuta, et præcepta majorum, omisso metropolitano episcopo, in provinciis supradictis quemquam ordinare præsumpserit, vel is, qui ordinari se illicite sciverit, uterque sacerdotio se carere cognoscat." A little afterwards, all the bishops of the province of Tarracon, complaining of the uncanonical ordination of a bishop, thus address pope Hilary : "Proinde nos Deum in vobis penitus adorantes ad fidem recurrimus apostolico ore laudatam, inde responsa quærentes unde nihil errore, nihil præsumptione, sed pontificali totum deliberatione præcipitur. . . . Quæsumus sedem vestram, ut quid super hac parte observari velitis, apostolicis afflatibus instruamur." Instructed in a school which held such doctrines, St. Patrick must have been devotedly attached to the Holy See. Certainly he transmitted to his disciples an unbounded devotion to the successors of St. Peter.

† Misit ergo ut præfati sumus, Sanctus Germanus, beatum Patricium Romam, ut cum Apostolicæ Sedis episcopi licentia ad prædicationem exiret ; sic enim ordo exigebat. Igitur per mare Tyrrhenum navigando transivit. . . . Perveniente vero illo Romam, a sancto papa Cælestino honoritice est susceptus, et traditis sibi sanctorum reliquiis ab eodem papa Cælestino in Hiberniam missus est.—Colgan, Tr. Thaumat. p. 39.

We have already seen how the scholiast on the hymn of St. Fiacc attested the connection of St. Patrick with the bishop of Auxerre. He is equally minute in detailing the subsequent events of our apostle's life, preparatory to his Irish mission:

"When Patrick had applied himself to the study of the canons, and other ecclesiastical learning under Germanus, he told Germanus that he had often, in vision, heard the voices of infants from the place called *Caille Tochlaide*, inviting him to go and aid the Irish Germanus replied to Patrick: Go, therefore, to the successor of St. Peter, that is, to Celestine, that he may authorize you; for this privilege belongs to him Patrick, therefore, went to pope Celestine; but he did not sanction his design, for he had already sent Palladius to Ireland to evangelize it. . . . Patrick, however, admonished Germanus a second time of the visions with which he was favoured; wherefore, Germanus sent back Patrick a second time to Celestine, accompanied by Segetius, who should give attestation in his name. Celestine hearing of the death of Palladius, said: No man can receive anything on earth, save he to whom it is given from above. Then Patrick was consecrated by the permission of Celestine and of Theodosius the younger, who was the king of the world. It was Amatorex that consecrated him; and Celestine, it is said, did not live more than one week after the ordination of Patrick. Pope Sixtus succeeded him, and in the first year of his pontificate, Patrick came into Ireland. He, too, most favourably regarded Patrick, and gave to him a portion of the relics of SS. Peter and Paul, together with many books."*

It will be sufficient to briefly refer to the other lives of St. Patrick, all of which repeat the same fact, of his having received the mission from pope Celestine to preach the Gospel in Ireland. Thus, the Vita Secunda, after describing the deeds of Palladius, adds: "Patrick was sent by the same pope into Ireland."† The third life is equally explicit: "Patrick, by the command of pope Celestine, returned to this island."‡ The words of Probus have been already given in the preceding narrative (page 10): he commemorates the prayer breathed by our apostle, that Heaven might conduct him to Rome, the head of cities; and he adds that

---

* Apud Colgan, loc. cit., p. 5. The phrase, *in conspectu Celestini et Theodosii*, can only mean *with the countenance or sanction of*, etc. This Latin phrase is often thus used by the writers of the iron age.

† Patricius ab eodem papa Cælestino in Hiberniam transmissus, etc.—Ap. Colgan, Tr. Thaumat. p. 13.

‡ Tunc S. Patricius ex imperio papæ Cœlestini reversus est ad hanc insulam.—Ibid. p. 23.

this prayer was heard; "and St. Patrick having asked for and received the apostolic blessing," hastened to his spiritual labours in our island. In fine, the Tripartite Life thus writes:

"The angel Victor admonished Patrick that he was commanded by God to proceed to Ireland, and preach to them the faith of Christ. . . . . In obedience to the angel's admonition, and to the divine command, Patrick resolved to visit the see of Peter—the mistress of faith, and the source of every apostolate; that thus his journey and preaching might be strengthened and consecrated by its authority. He made known this design to Germanus, who, approving of it, sent with him the priest Segetius as a companion, and a witness of his spotless life. . . . Wherefore, the intelligence of the death of Palladius being received, the divinely pre-ordained mission, and the conversion of the Irish nation was, by the apostolical authority, committed to Patrick. Celestine, with the approval of Germanus and Amatorex (the Roman), ordained him bishop, and gave to him the name of Patrick."*

These ancient lives, in many of the details, are found to vary; but all conspire in attesting the one great fact of St. Patrick's mission having been sealed by the supreme authority of the Vicar of Christ. The lives of some of our other saints are equally explicit, when referring to this early union of our Church with Rome. For instance, the life of St. Kiaran, which is much extolled by Ussher,† thus commemorates St. Patrick's apostolate:

"The glorious archbishop Patrick being sent by pope Celestine, came over to Ireland, and by God's grace converted the leaders, chiefs, and people to Christ: and all Ireland was filled with the faith and baptism of Christ."‡

St. Eric of Auxerre was not content with describing the preparation made by our apostle for his future mission, under the guidance of Germanus; he further relates the blessing given to his apostolate by the Roman pontiff, St. Celestine. Patrick, he says, drank in the heavenly truths from the holy bishop of Auxerre; "and as Germanus saw him magnanimous in religion, eminent for

---

* Colgan, Tr. Thaumat. p. 122-3.
† Primordia; Dublini, 1639, p. 790.
‡ Deinde gloriosus archiepiscopus Patricius missus a Cælestino papa venit in Hiberniam qui Dei gratia reges, duces, principes, populosque ad Christum convertit: et tota Hibernia repleta est fide et baptismo Christi." —Ibid.

virtue, strenuous in the sacred ministry, and thinking it unfit that so strong a husbandman should be listless in the culture of the harvest of God, he sent him to holy Celestine, the pope of the city of Rome, accompanied by his own priest, Segetius, who might bear testimony of ecclesiastical probity in his regard at the Apostolic See. Being thus approved by its judgment, leaning on its authority and strengthened by its blessing, he journeyed to Ireland, and being given to that people as their chosen apostle, he illustrated the whole nation at that time, indeed, by his preaching and miracles, as he continues at the present day to do, and will continue for ever to illustrate it by the wonderful privileges of his apostolate."*

Earlier than St. Eric was the holy bishop Marcus, who, after devoting himself for many years to the practice of virtue in the Irish monasteries, illustrated the north of Italy† by his learning and piety. His Historia Brittonum was written in the year 822, and was long regarded by British writers as a sort of text-book for the history of their country.‡ In it he introduces a short sketch of the life of our apostle, which we may justly regard as embodying the narrative of the most authentic records of the Irish Church:—

"Under divine guidance Patrick was instructed in the sacred Scriptures, and then he went to Rome and remained there a long time, studying, and being filled with the Holy Ghost, learning the holy Scriptures and the sacred mysteries. And whilst he was there applying himself to these pursuits, Palladius was sent by Pope Celestine as first bishop to convert the Irish to Christ; but God, by some storms and signs, prevented his success; and no one can receive aught on earth unless it be given to him from above. This Palladius, returning from Ireland to Britain, died

---

* "Ineptum ducens (Germanus) robustissimum agricolam in Dominicæ segetis torpere cultura ad sanctum Cælestinum urbis Romæ papam per Segetium presbyterum suum, eum direxit : qui viro præstantissimo probitatis ecclesiasticæ testimonium apud Sedem ferret Apostolicam. Cujus judicio approbatus, auctoritate fultus, benedictione denique roboratus Hiberniæ partes expetiit, gentique illi proprie datus apostolus, tum quidem eam doctrina et miraculis, nunc quoque et in perpetuum mirificis apostolatus sui illustrat privilegiis."—Ericus, loc. cit. lib. i. cap. 2, ap. Bolland. Julii vii. p. 258.

† Mabillon's Acta SS., tom. vi., ad an. 884. Eckhard, Casus S. Galli; Pertz's Monumenta Germanica, vol. ii. p. 78.

‡ See Introduction to Irish Nennius, p. 18, for a full and interesting account of this writer and his work..

there in the land of the Picts. The death of bishop Palladius being known, the patricians Theodosius and Valentinian being the Roman rulers, Patrick was sent by pope Celestine, the angel of God, Victor, accompanying, guiding, and assisting him, and by bishop Germanus, to convert the Irish to the belief in the holy Trinity."*

It now remains to notice the ancient and most authentic of our annalists who, whilst fixing the arrival of St. Patrick in our island as the great starting point of the Christian era in our history, without a dissentient voice, derive his mission from the Holy See. Thus, the Four Masters write : " St. Patrick was ordained to the episcopacy by the holy pope Celestine, the first who commissioned him to come to Ireland and preach, and give to the Irish the precepts of faith and religion."† The Annals of Innisfallen also record that " Patrick came from Rome bishop into Ireland, and devoutly preached here the faith of Christ."‡ The Annales Senatenses, better known as the Annals of Ulster, thus begin :—

"Anno ab Incarnatione Domini, 431, Palladius ad Scotos a Cælestino urbis Romæ episcopo, ordinatur episcopus, Ætio et Valeriano coss. Primus mittitur in Hiberniam ut Christum credere potuissent, anno Theodosii 8vo.

"Anno 432. Patricius pervenit ad Hiberniam ix. anno Theodosii junioris; primo anno episcopatus Sixti, 42di. episcopi Romanæ Ecclesiæ : sic enumerant Beda et Marcellinus et Isidorus in Chronicis suis ; in 12°. anno Leoghaire Mac Neill . . . . . .

"Anno 439. Secundinus, Auxilius, et Iserninus mittuntur episcopi ipsi in Hiberniam in auxilium Patricii."§

In the year from the Incarnation of our Lord 431, Palladius was by pope Celestine ordained bishop of the Irish, Ætius and Valerianus being consuls. He was the first that was sent to Ireland that they might be converted to Christ. This was in the eighth year of Theodosius.

In the year 432, Patrick came to Ireland in the ninth year of Theodosius the younger, and first of the episcopacy of Sixtus. Sixtus was the forty-second bishop of Rome, as Bede, and Marcellinus, and Isidore reckon in their chronicles. This was in the twelfth year of Leoghaire, son of Niall.

* "Historia Brittonum edita ab anarchoreta Marco ejusdem gentis sancto episcopo." Ex codice Vatic. Sæc. decimi. This work was published in 1819, in London, by W. Gun ; but his MS. seems to have been full of inaccuracies.

† Four Masters, by O'Donovan, ad. an. 432.

‡ Ap. O'Conor, Rerum Hibernic. Script. vol. ii. p. 95. See an interesting account of these Annals in Curry's Lectures, p. 75, seqq.

§ Petrie's Essay on Tara, p 82 ; Curry's Lectures, p. 90, seqq.

In the year 439, Secundinus, Auxilius, and Iserninus, were sent bishops into Ireland to assist St. Patrick.

Dr. Petrie, when citing the first portion of this entry, has fallen into a singular mistake, and thence taken occasion to undervalue the testimony of these annals. Authorities, he says, are appealed to, viz., Bede, Marcellinus, and Isidore, as evidence of St. Patrick's mission; "but unfortunately no passages relating to Patrick's mission are found in any printed edition or manuscript copy of the works referred to."* This, indeed, if true, would be a singular inaccuracy of these annals; their reference, however, to other authors has no connection with St. Patrick's mission. It was a debated point amongst our Irish annalists, as it is indeed amongst historians to the present day, what was the precise number of popes from St. Peter to Sixtus. Some reckoned St. Clement merely as a coadjutor of St. Peter; others regarded Anacletus as not distinct from Cletus. In the passages already cited we have seen how pope Celestine was styled, by Tirechan and the author of the Tripartite Life, the forty-fifth pope. Hence the Ulster annalist, having given his opinion that St. Sixtus was the forty-second pope, cites as references for this opinion, Bede, Marcellinus, and Isidore; but he does not cite them, as would be wholly contrary to the custom of our annalists, in regard to domestic events, as an authority for the arrival of St. Patrick in our island: this event he absolutely records in the ninth year of Theodosius, the first of pope Sixtus, and the twelfth of king Leoghaire.†

Even the Irish annalists, who on the continent won an illustrious name for themselves and their country, were not forgetful of the event which brought the blessings of Catholic faith to our island. Marianus Scotus, whose Irish name was Maelbrigte (*i.e.* servant of Brigid), was born in Ulster in 1028. He had for his master the famous Tighernach of Boirche, coarb of St. Finnian in the monas-

---

* Petrie's Tara, pag. 82.
† The present Annals of Ulster give the reading xlii. episcopi. See Curry and Petrie as above: we suspect, however, that this is an error of the copyist for xlv. Similar mistakes abound in the ancient manuscripts.

tery of Moville.* In 1052 he assumed the monastic habit in Ireland, and four years later he entered the Irish monastery of St. Martin at Cologne. Being ordained at Wurzburg in 1059, he embraced the austere life of a recluse, and was immured for ten years at Fulda. He thence removed in 1069 to Mentz, where he pursued the same penitential course, and in complete seclusion worked out his great chronicle of the world. "This work (says Reeves) is the most elaborate historical production of the middle ages, and has always enjoyed the highest encomiums of the learned."† The autograph of this chronicle, with Marianus's own signature, is preserved in the Vatican, and has been accurately printed by Pertz, in the Monumenta Historica Germaniæ.‡ It is thus that this illustrious Maelbrigte chronicles the mission of St. Patrick to Ireland:—

"In the eighth year of Theodosius, Bassus and Antiochus being consuls, Palladius was ordained by pope Celestine, and sent as first bishop to the Irish believing in Christ. After him was sent St. Patrick, who, being a Briton by birth, was consecrated by pope St. Celestine, and sent to the archiepiscopate of Ireland. There, during sixty years, he confirmed his preaching by signs and miracles, and converted the whole island to the faith of Christ."

Thus we have endeavoured to lay before the reader some of the chief, direct, and positive arguments which render historically certain that St. Patrick, when coming to gather in the Irish nation into the fold of Christ, bore with him, solemnly impressed on his apostolate, the seal and sanction of the Vicar of Christ. The indirect testimony of Prosper should, however, have of itself sufficed to convince any unbiassed mind of the truth of our assertion. St. Prosper, in his work against Cassian, written whilst Sixtus

* See Annals of Four Masters, ad. an. 1061 and 1098. Lanigan errs when making him successor of St. Finnian of Clonard.—(Eccl. Hist. iii. 446.) Others confound him with the great annalist Tighernach O'Braoin, who was abbot of Clonmacnois. Marianus himself, however, in the autograph copy of his annals, styles his master Tighernach of Boirche, the district now called Mourne.

† Wattenbach's Papers on the Irish Monasteries in Germany; Leipzig, 1856; translated by Dr. Reeves, p. 13, note q.

‡ Tom vii. pag. 481, seqq. Fac-similes of the original MS. are given, with an elaborate critical apparatus, by Professor Waitz.

D

was Pope, between the years 433 and 440, thus claims for St. Celestine the conversion of Ireland:—

"Whilst that pope (he says) laboured to keep the Roman island (Britain) Catholic, he caused also the barbarous island to be gathered to the fold of Christ, by ordaining a bishop for the Irish."*

The first words refer to the mission of St. Germanus to Britain, which freed that country from the infection of the Pelagian heresy; the subsequent words attest that Ireland was, at the time he wrote, a Christian nation, and that this blessing was borne to our island by another mission from pope Celestine. This surely cannot refer to the unsuccessful preaching of Palladius, and can only be understood of the mission of St. Patrick, who was the chosen one in the counsel of God, to be the dispenser to our island of the blessings of redemption.

---

* "Ordinato Scotis episcopo dum Romanam insulam studet servare Catholicam, fecit etiam barbaram Christianam."—Prosper contra *Collatorem*, cap. 41. It is published in the appendix to St. Augustine's works, tom. x. part 2, p. 196. A passage of this work in which he says that St. Augustine addressed a letter to Xystus, then, indeed, a simple priest, but now pope, *tunc Presbyterum Xystum, nunc vero Ap. Sedis Pontificem*, proves that it was written during the pontificate of Xystus, who succeeded St. Celestine in 432, and died in 440.

ESSAY

ON

THE ORIGIN OF THE IRISH CHURCH,

And its Connexion with the Holy See.

PART THE SECOND.

MODERN THEORIES REGARDING SAINT PATRICK.

THE remarks made in the past chapters will probably have sufficed to convince every unprejudiced mind, that St. Patrick embarked on his missionary career with the sanction and blessing of the Vicar of Christ. Many theories, however, have been put forward from time to time, conflicting more or less with this undoubted fact; and hence, in order that its truth may be placed in clearer light, we shall briefly pass in review the chief systems invented by these modern theorists to throw doubt on the mission of our glorious apostle.

CHAPTER I.

Theory of Dr. Ledwich, that St. Patrick never existed, refuted.

DR. Ledwich, in a work entitled "The Antiquities of Ireland," vindicated to himself the unenviable claim of being the first and only universal sceptic as to the life and history of St. Patrick. In one sweeping proposition he rejects altogether the existence of the saint, resting this theory on the gratuitous assumption, that St. Patrick was unknown to and unmentioned by any writer previous to the ninth century.

This foolish theory will not detain us long. All the Christian traditions of our country are clustered around the memory of St.

Patrick. Our hills, and islands, and streamlets, and fountains re-echo his name. Every monument that traces the line of separation between Christianity and paganism in Ireland, rests for its basis on his existence. And hence, even should we suppose the assumption of Dr. Ledwich, as regards the silence of our early records, to be true, yet it would not suffice to warrant the conclusion which he would fain deduce from it.

That assumption, however, is wholly at variance with truth. The writers of the ninth century that commemorate St. Patrick, refer to the earlier writers of his life. In the eighth century, Ængus, in his Felire, thus marks the feast-day of our saint:

> "The blaze of a splendid sun,
> The apostle of stainless Erin,
> Patrick, with his countless thousands,
> May he shelter our wretchedness."*

The Irish "Collection of Canons" existing in MSS. of the eighth century, contains decrees enacted by St. Patrick. Litanies preserved in continental MSS. of the same century, as well as in the famous Stowe Missal, of at least the same period,† rank him amongst our patrons. Alcuin celebrates him as "Scotorum gloria gentis;" and a hymn in honour of St. Brigid, transcribed before the close of the eighth century, mentions amongst the titles of her praise, that she was the disciple of St. Patrick—*alumna Patricii*, and had as her bulwark of defence his powerful patronage—*opima Patricii patrocinia*.‡

In the seventh century, the monuments are still more numerous that commemorate our glorious apostle. Thus, St. Adamnan speaks of a holy bishop who was "*Sancti Patricii Epi. discipulus.*"§ What shall we say of the many records of our saint, preserved in the now famous Book of Armagh. Two of its chief monuments, composed in the seventh century, by Maccutheni and Tirechan,

---

* See Curry, Lectures, etc., p. 368 ; and Petrie, Essay on Tara, p. 89.
† See the paper read by Dr. Todd before the R.I.A., June 23rd, 1856, on the Ancient Irish Missal, etc., p. 33.
‡ Mone, Hymni Med. Æv., iii. 241 ; Reeves' Early Irish Caligraphy, p. 29.
§ Reeves' Columba.

appeal to earlier sainted bishops of our island as their vouchers and the sources of their narratives. The antiphonary of Bangor, composed before the year 691,* presents the hymn of St. Secundinus in his honour, and entitles it, "Hymnus S. Patricii Magistri Scotorum." St. Cummian Fota, who died in 661, has left a hymn in honour of the apostles, ably edited by Dr. Todd,† from the Liber Hymnorum; its sixteenth strophe is devoted to our apostle Patrick:

"Patricii Patris obsecremus merita,
Ut Deo digna perpetremus opera."

St. Cummian Albus, abbot of Iona, in his life of the founder of that great monastery, commemorates at the very outset, "St. Patrick, the first apostle of Ireland." St. Cuimin of Connor lived at the same time, and in his Irish poem "on the characteristic virtues of the Irish saints,"‡ one verse is devoted to the fasting of "Patrick of Ardmacha's city, the son of Calphurn." The year 634 was rendered remarkable by the letter of the abbot of Durrow on the Paschal Question ;§ in it, one of the arguments to prove the antiquity of the Roman cycle, is precisely its having been used by "Patritius papa noster."

In the sixth century, we find St. Patrick's name registered by the hand of St. Columba himself. This great apostle of the Picts, in the precious copy of the Gospels‖ which he transcribed, terminates his labour by breathing a prayer to "the holy bishop Patrick." The hymn of St. Fiacc, commemorating some of our apostle's deeds, bears intrinsic evidence of great antiquity, and even its scholia, being written in the most ancient Gaelic of the Brehon laws, were judged by Usher to belong to the sixth century. The same judgment was passed by Eugene Curry on the Vita Tripartita of our saint, attributed by Colgan to St. Evin.¶ And yet

---

* Conf. Lanigan, Eccl. Hist. i. 59, seq.
† Lib. Hym. fasc. i. p. 77.
‡ Translated by Curry, and edited by Dr. Kelly, in Martyrology of Tallaght, pag. 161.
§ Usher, Sylloges Epp. ep. 11.
‖ Conf. Reeves' Columba, pag. 242 and 327 : Westwood Palæogr. Sac. ; O'Conor, Script. Rer. Hib. 1-182 ; Lhuyd, Archæolog. p. 242.
¶ Curry, Lectures, etc. p. 386.

what shall we say, when St. Fiacc refers to still earlier written records regarding St. Patrick: and St. Evin not only cites such documents, but also registers customs and proverbs which had their origin in his deeds and teaching. Some of the earlier records thus referred to, are still happily preserved. Such is the hymn of St. Secundinus, addressed to St. Patrick whilst yet living:* it is thus referred to in St. Fiacc's hymn:—

> "The hymn which was sung to thee whilst living,
> Will be a protecting lorica unto all."†

Surely such evidence as this, is more than sufficient to attest the historical reality of our apostle. But still, supposing that none of this evidence was at hand, the writings of St. Patrick; his "Confessio"; the "canons" which he enacted; his letter to Coroticus; the prayer or "lorica," which he composed, to say nothing of his other writings, all which are now admitted, and proved to be the genuine composition of our saint,‡ are such monuments as render the fact of St. Patrick's existence as certain to many of the present generation, as is the fact of the existence of the great Dr. Ledwich himself.

CHAPTER II.

Theory of Sir William Betham, that St. Patrick lived long before the year 432.—Theory of Usher, that Ireland possessed a hierarchy before the days of St. Patrick.

THE second theory passes to the other extreme, and is equally paradoxical; its appearance in the literary world is due to the fantastical imagination of Sir William Betham. "The truth is," writes this author, "as will be shown in the following pages, that the first apostle of Ireland, Patrick, the Roman-Briton, introduced

---

* Lib. Hymn. fascic. i. etc. p. 11.
† Colgan, Trias Thaumat. pag. 3. This passage is not happily translated by Todd, Hymn, pag. 33.
‡ See excellent remarks on some of those writings of our apostle in Todd's St. Patrick, 425, seqq.

Christianity into Ireland *centuries* before the year 430, and Palladius was truly sent to the Scots *believing in Christ, i.e.,* a nation of Christians," etc.*

Strange enough, the author of this theory appeals to the Book of Armagh, which was then a sealed book to Irish readers: and yet, in that very Book of Armagh, the year 432 is marked for the mission of St. Patrick, the Roman emperor Theodosius is named as then in the eighth year of his imperial authority, and pope Celestine is commemorated as the occupant of St. Peter's See.† Elsewhere in the same book, St. Patrick's arrival in Ireland is placed subsequent to the death of Palladius, the archdeacon of Celestine.‡ And yet this book was appealed to as evidencing that the mission of St. Patrick took place centuries before the year 430!

Another authority appealed to is that of Prosper, who describes Palladius as sent to *the Scots believing in Christ.* But surely it is strange that Sir William did not remark, that in the very same sentence, Prosper styles Palladius *the first bishop* destined to our shores: " Palladius primus epus. mittitur." Hence the anchorite Marcus, in his Historia Brittonum, when paraphrasing this passage of Prosper, describes Palladius as sent *ad Scotos convertendos ad Christum.* Undoubtedly, St. Patrick did not find our island *a nation of Christians*, as his own writings sufficiently attest; and yet, all the monuments of our history link together the names of Patrick and Germanus of Auxerre,§ and Celestine of Rome, and Leoghaire of Ireland.‖ How, then, can our apostle and *his nation of Christians*, be assigned to a period earlier by centuries than the year 430?

The formula used by Prosper in his chronicle—*ad Scotos in Christo credentes*—may, perhaps, seem strange to some of our

---

* Betham's Antiquarian Researches, p. 248.
† Maccuthenus, ibid. fol. 2.
‡ Tirechan in Lib. Armac. fol. 16, ap. Petrie, Essay on Tara, p. 85.
§ St. Germanus was appointed bishop in 418. See his life, by a contemporary, Constantius, in A.A. SS., Julii vii., p. 213, seqq.
‖ Leoghaire, the son of Niall of the Nine Hostages, became monarch of Ireland in 428 or 429, as all our annalists are agreed.—See Petrie, Tara, p. 28, seqq.

readers. There is much in the recent work of Dr. Todd* to explain this passage, and prove that there existed before the time of our apostle, scattered converts in our island. The life of a holy Irishman, disciple of St. Germanus of Auxerre, will also illustrate this point.† He was son of an Irish prince, and received the light of faith from Germanus in Britain, in 429. Returning to Ireland, his friends and retainers listened to his exhortations, and gladly received at his hands the waters of baptism. It is more than probable that there were many such cases throughout our island; and surely St. Germanus made known to the pontiff, St. Celestine, the happy tidings of some rays of faith having thus shone upon our pagan country, and prayed him to send a bishop to guide these neophytes, and entirely conquer and consolidate the new spiritual kingdom thus opened to the missionaries of our faith. This is the only meaning that the contemporary monuments permit us to assign to the words of St. Prosper.‡

THEORY OF DR. USHER.

The learned Usher, whose opinion was adopted by Harris, to omit a host of subsequent superficial writers, defended as a favourite theory, that the Irish Church already possessed a hierarchy when Palladius and Patrick were destined to our shores; and SS. Ailbe, Declan, Ibar, and Kieran were ostentatiously put forward as predecessors of these missionaries in the episcopate of Ireland.

This theory, however, has found no followers since the time of Lanigan, so clearly did he reveal its inconsistency and falsehood; and Dr. Todd has placed in still clearer light the arguments of this best of our ecclesiastical historians.

---

* St. Patrick, p. 189, seqq.

† Acta SS., Maij, tom. i. p. 259. Eric of Auxerre mentions a certain *Michomeris*, an Irishman, who followed St. Germanus on his return to Auxerre.—Acta SS., Julii, tom vii. p. 256.

‡ The other sophistical reasons put forward by Betham, in defence of his theory, may be seen well refuted in D'Alton's Essay on the Antiquities of Ireland, Dublin, 1830, p. 193.

St. Ailbe's death is recorded by our annalists in 527.* St. Declan is described in the life to which Usher refers, as having survived St. Ailbe, and as having had for his contemporaries St. Colman of Cloyne, who died in the year 600; St. Dimma Dubh, who was bishop of Counor, and died in 658; and St. Ultan, who, as we have seen (p. 24), died in the year of the great mortality, in 657. There is an ancient Irish verse preserved on these two saints, which proves that in our early Church they were not looked on as predecessors of St. Patrick:

> "Humble Ailbe is the Patrick of Munster,
> With all due honour;
> Declan is the Patrick of the Desii:
> The Desii are with Declan for ever."†

St. Ibar's death is found registered between the year 500 and 504, in all our annalists; and Tirechan, in his annotations, preserved in the Book of Armagh, expressly names St. Ibar as one of the bishops consecrated by our apostle St. Patrick. St. Kieran's life admits of still less controversy: he was a disciple of St. Finnian in the famous school of Clonard, which was founded in 540; and amongst his contemporaries were St. Ciaran of Clonmacnois, St. Ruadhan of Lodhra, and St. Brendan of Birr; all of whom are reckoned in the second order of our saints, and died about the middle of the sixth century.

It would be easy to add other arguments which refute this once fashionable theory. Palladius, as we have just seen, is styled by his contemporary Prosper, and by Bede, "the first bishop of the Irish." Our own apostle, too, was evidently unacquainted with these his saintly predecessors; for towards the end of his earthly career, full of gratitude to God for the abundance of His mercy to our island, he thus exclaims:

> "How has it come to pass in Ireland, that those who never had any knowledge of God, and hitherto worshipped only idols and abominations,

---

* This is the date in the Annals of Tighernach, Annals of Ulster, Annals of Innisfallen. The date of 541 is given by the Four Masters; but it may have been another saint of the same name, whose death is also recorded in 541 by the Annals of Ulster.

† Usher, Primord., p. 866; Todd, St. Patrick, p. 219.

should be lately become the people of the Lord, and are called the children of God? The sons of Ireland and the daughters of its chieftains now appear as monks and virgins of Christ."*

We shall not, however, dwell on these arguments, but we shall rather remark, that the facts recorded in the lives of these saints, corroborate more and more what has been proved in the preceding chapter, that, forsooth, Rome was universally regarded as the source whence the blessings of faith were borne to our island; and furthermore, that our apostle St. Patrick received from Rome his mission for the apostolate of Ireland.

An extract from St. Kieran's life, regarding St. Patrick, has been already cited; and from other passages produced by Usher, we learn that St. Kieran devoted himself to religious pursuits in Rome for twenty years, till he was ordained there and sent as bishop " ad annunciandam fidem in Hibernia."†

St. Ailbe is also said to have been sent by his master, St. Hilary, to the Roman pontiff. He went thither accompanied by fifty holy men, all natives of Ireland, and having remained for more than a year in Rome, he was consecrated bishop by the pope, and sent to evangelize our island.‡

St. Ibar, too, in the Annals of Innisfallen, is described as " coming from Rome a bishop into Ireland." As for Declan, he is said to have met in Rome his future friend and fellow-labourer, St. Ailbe; and, some years after the departure of this saint for his missionary labours, " was consecrated a bishop, receiving from the pope a special commission to return to his own country and evangelize the Irish people."§ When journeying towards our island, he met with St. Patrick, who was proceeding from Gaul to Rome, to prepare himself for the apostolate of Ireland. It was in Rome, too, that St. Kieran was said to have received the prophetical announcement from St. Patrick, that the bleak *Saighir* would become a great city, springing up around the monastery of Kieran.‖

---

* Confess. S. Patritii in fine.
† Usher, Primord., p. 512; O'Conor, Rerum Hib. SS. ii. p. 12.
‡ Ibid. § Todd, p. 209. ‖ See Todd, ibid. p. 200, seqq.

CHAPTER III.

Dean Murray's theory, that St. Patrick had no mission from Rome, examined.

The late Protestant dean of Ardagh, having prepared for the task by writing an "Introduction to the Study of the Apocalypse," and other similar works, turned his attention to the history of the Irish Church, and as the result of his researches, published to the world, "Outlines of the History of the Church in Ireland," which, under the improved title of "Ireland and her Church," was published a second time in 1845.* The reader will naturally expect some novel theories from such a writer; and, indeed, should he have the patience to peruse a few pages of dean Murray's work, he will meet with them beyond all his expectations. As regards St. Patrick, he candidly enough admits his existence,† but qualifies this admission by rejecting as groundless the mission of our apostle from Rome. The whole reasoning on which this theory rests, is thus condensed by the learned dean: "While the papal (*i. e.*, foreign) writers make Palladius the first apostle, and take no notice of Patrick, the Irish make Patrick the first, and take no notice of Palladius."‡

We shall take no notice of his subsequent foolish remarks on the *corruptions* of Rome. Suffice it to say, that Dr. Todd, with more candour, acknowledges, in his late work, that in the fifth century, *at least*, such corruptions could not be found in the Roman Church.§ We shall rather inquire into the truth of the assertion so boldly hazarded by the worthy dean.

Is it true, then, that the foreign or papal writers take no notice of St. Patrick? is it true that the Irish writers consign to oblivion the name of Palladius?

As regards the Irish writers, we have seen that St. Tirechan

---

* Ireland and her Church, by the Very Rev. Richard Murray, D.D., dean of Ardagh, second edition, London, 1845, introd. p. 7.
† Ibid. p. 20.   ‡ Ibid. p. 22.   § Pref. page 6.

mentions both Palladius and Patrick;* that the scholiast of Fiacc gives us the acts of Palladius as well as those of our apostle;† that, in a word, Muirchu-Maccu-Macthenus, the Leabhar Breac, the Annals of Ulster, and the various Irish lives of our saint, expressly commemorate as well St. Palladius as St. Patrick, as commissioned by pope Celestine to evangelize our island.

The other member of dean Murray's assertion is equally inconsistent with truth. Many foreign writers might easily be produced who expressly commemorate our apostle and eulogize his labours. Bede, in his Martyrology, and Alcuin, though Saxons,‡ refer to him as the apostle of our island. Eric of Auxerre gives full details of his relations with Rome. The venerable monk of Gemblours, Sigebert, further adds: "Pope Celestine sent to the Irish believing in Christ, Palladius as first bishop. After whom to the same, by the same, was sent Patrick, a Briton by birth, the son of Concha, sister of St. Martin of Tours; his baptismal name was *Suchat*, which was changed by St. Germanus into *Magonicus*, and again into that of Patrick by pope Celestine, by whom he was consecrated the archbishop of the Irish. Remarkable for his miracles, and holiness, and preaching, during sixty years, he converted the whole island of Ireland to the faith of Christ."§ Similar passages from Giraldus Cambrensis (whom dean Murray regards as one of the first introducers of *Romanism* into Ireland), and John of Tinmouth, may be seen in Usher, page 845. We shall merely cite the words with which Ricemarch describes the mission of St. Patrick to our island:—

"Patrick, skilled in the language and doctrine of Rome, accompanied by a train of virtues, and consecrated bishop, set out for the country from which he had fled before."

And after a little while he registers an angelic announcement made to our apostle:—

---

* Liber Armacan, fol. 16. † Vid. sup., p. 4.
‡ It is curious how, even in these early centuries, the Saxon writers entertained a jealousy of their Irish neighbours. See a remarkable example in the chronicle of the eighth century, published by Card. Maij, Spicileg. Roman, vol. ix. p. 120.
§ Chronicon Sigeberti ad an. 431, edited by Vossius in 1627.

"The Lord has made you ruler of the island of the Irish, which as yet has not received the word of truth. To that island you are to devote your labours—there has God fixed your abode; you will there become illustrious by miracles and virtues, and you will subjugate the whole nation to the sweet yoke of the Gospel."*

These passages will suffice to prove how repugnant to historical truth is the statement of dean Murray. He seems, indeed, to have been led into error by the silence of Prosper, and Bede in his Chronicle, and some other historians of Rome. For their omission of an historical fact, however, they alone are responsible; and their silence cannot surely justify the sweeping assertion of the learned dean. Prosper, as we have already remarked, merely commemorates one or two distinctive facts of each successive year. The connection of Palladius with Rome, and his mission, being the first destined to our pagan island, justified that writer in commemorating it in 431. When Prosper was writing in 434, perhaps the intelligence had not as yet reached Rome of St. Patrick's success, to justify the special commemoration in the following year. At all events, the death of Celestine, and the election of Sixtus, were events quite sufficient to mark the year 432. As for Bede, he mentions St. Patrick in his Martyrology. In his Chronicle, however, which is very brief, he commemorates only such events as have special reference to Britain. Fordun, in his Scoto-Chronicle, acts in the same way. Speaking of the reign of the Pictish king, Durst, he says: "During whose reign bishop Palladius was sent by pope Celestine to teach the Scotch, who, however, had long before received the faith of Christ." Thus he takes the words of Prosper and applies them to Scotland, and omits all mention of Ireland and St. Patrick. The Irish translator of this chronicle was evidently not pleased with the omission; and in the passage just referred to, omits all mention of Scotland and Palladius, substituting in its stead the simple commemoration: "In the nineteenth year of his reign, holy bishop Patrick arrived in Ireland."†

---

* Ricemarchi ap. Usser. Primord., p. 843.
† See Irish Nennius, I.A.S., 1848, p. 161.

CHAPTER IV.

Some opinions of Dr. Lanigan and Dr. Petrie examined and refuted.

THE most illustrious name on the roll of ecclesiastical historians of Ireland is that of Rev. John Lanigan. His critical remarks have contributed more than those of any other writer to illustrate the early life of our apostle. When fixing his death, however, he abandoned the straight road of facts, and wishing to establish a favourite theory,* he involved in inextricable confusion the missionary labours of St. Patrick.

He therefore fixes the death of our apostle in the year 465, and rests this opinion on three arguments—

1. The statements of some writers who commemorate *about that time* the death of *Sanctus Patritius senior*.

2. The chronicle of Marianus Scotus, which limits our apostle's preaching to forty years.

3. The Annals of Innisfallen, which place the death of St. Patrick precisely in the year 465.

I. The existence of an Irish saint of the name Patrick, and characteristically designated Sen-Patrick, or Patrick senior, was a very problematic question in the time of Dr. Lanigan. It is now, however, a matter of certainty; and the remarks of Petrie† have well proved that he was a native of our island, who, having been for some time tutor of our apostle, had received from him in return the light of faith, and proceeding to Glastonbury, was famed for his virtues and miracles, and died there in 457. He is thus commemorated in the Festology of Ængus, on the 24th of August:—

> " The glory of the people of Glastonbury,
> As fame has handed down to us,
> Is Sen-Patrick, leader of the hosts,
> The meek tutor of our patron."

---

* Ecclesiastical Hist. of Ireland, vol. i. pag. 361, seqq.
† Essay on Tara, pag. 69-73.

The Annals of Connaught* expressly commemorate his death in 457; and what is more important, the annotations of Tirechan, in the Book of Armagh, confirm the same date. Thus, then, the first statement which Dr. Lanigan's theory rests on, has no reference to our apostle St. Patrick.

II. As regards our famous annalist *Marianus*, his text, as known at the time of Lanigan, recorded the preaching of St. Patrick, in our island, *per* xl. *annos*. So well known, however, is the inaccuracy of copyists in regard to the numerals, that this passage, unsupported by other evidence, should be unhesitatingly supposed an error for *lx. annos*, especially as Marianus records the arrival of St. Patrick in Ireland in 432, and his death in 493. The autograph of Marianus is happily still preserved in the Vatican library, and was accurately edited by German antiquarians within the past few years. Now in this autograph manuscript we find written in full, by Marianus' own hand, "*per annos sexaginta*," so that so far from Marianus giving any countenance to Dr. Lanigan's theory, he fully corroborates the concurrent testimony of all our annalists, that our apostle terminated his earthly pilgrimage in the year 493. The ancient Irish quatrain, cited under this year by Tighearnach, as also by the Four Masters and other writers of our history, is thus translated by Petrie:—

> "From the birth of Christ, a pleasant period,
> Four hundred above fair ninety,
> Three noble years after that
> To the death of Patrick, chief apostle."†

III. The third argument is equally unfounded. The Annals of Innisfallen, as cited by Lanigan from Harris' MSS., recorded "Quies Patricii, 16 kalendas Aprilis, anno 432, a passione Dni." Whence Dr. Lanigan argued, that as our Saviour died in the year 33, the date assigned to St. Patrick's death in the Annals of Innisfallen corresponds to the year 465. We have seen, however, that

---

* "Anno ccccvii. dormitatio S. Senis Patricii Episcopi Glosoniensis Ecclesiæ."—Annals of Connaught, ap. Petrie, loc. cit. pag. 69. It is curious that Usher, quoting this passage, gives the numerals ccccliv., which was probably the reading of his MS.—Primord. pag. 895.
† Loc. cit. 88.

the Irish annalists place the death of our Saviour in the year 31, so that even admitting the accuracy of Dr. Lanigan's text, the year 465 could not be proved from it. However, the ancient copy of the Annals of Innisfallen, cited by Petrie, reconciles the whole passage with the other authentic annals, for it prefixes the date* cccclxxxxiii.; and further adds, in the same year with the death of St. Patrick, "quies Meic Cuilnid Luscai." Now, as we learn from the Annals of Ulster and Tighearnach, the holy bishop of Lusk, MacCullen, died about the year 495; hence we may conclude, that the incidental date *from the death of our Lord* should be 462, which, according to the Irish computation, coincided with the year 493 of our era.

THEORY OF DR. PETRIE.

George Petrie, Esq., whose zeal in the promotion of the study of our national antiquities, has elicited the applause of all lovers of our literature, in one of the most remarkable of his essays,† presented to the public, not indeed as a matter of certainty, but rather as a probable conjecture, a novel theory regarding our apostle.

Having sufficiently proved that besides the Patrick characteristically styled *the Apostle* of our island, there was another saint of the same name, distinguished by the designation of Sen-Patrick, or Patrick senior, who died in 457, Petrie proceeds to remark:—

1st. That the acts of these two saints have been so blended together by our ancient writers, that it is no longer possible to say what belongs to *the apostle* Patrick.

2nd. That *the apostle* Patrick of the Irish writers, was possibly no other than the Palladius of the Roman authorities.

1. As regards the first point of this theory, Petrie brings forward no argument to prove that the acts of the two saints Patrick were actually blended together by our ancient writers. It is merely from the similarity of name, he judges, that such a confusion is possible; and hence, that the reader must remain in suspense, unable to

---

* Conf. Petrie, loc. cit pag. 90. He prints the text, indeed, *cccclxxxviii.*, but this is evidently a copyist's mistake for *cccclxxxxiii*.

† "On the History and Antiquities of Tara Hill," by George Petrie, Esq., published from the Transactions of R. I. A., in Dublin, 1839.

decide to which of the Patricks each individual fact is to be referred. But let us take a somewhat similar case. It is only within the past few years that the learned Dr. Reeves satisfactorily established the claim of our country to number an *Augustine* amongst its ecclesiastical writers; and proved, moreover, that the tract entitled "De Mirabilibus Sacræ Scripturæ" was his production. Now, would we not be deemed sceptical were we to thence conclude, that the facts connected with the great Augustine's life were doubtful, and that we should pause before deciding to which of the Augustines each individual fact was to be referred?

It is precisely so in the case of our own apostle. The existence of fifty other Patricks could not be said to interfere with his characteristics and historic personality,—indeed, there is scarcely an historic personage on record whose individuality can be said to be more clearly defined than is that of the great St. Patrick. All the ancient documents of our history agree, in assigning the apostolate of our island to one who had at first been led a captive to its shores; who subsequently prepared himself for his sacred mission under the guidance of St. Germanus; who was often divinely aided in his difficulties and trials by the angel-guardian of our country, St. Victor; who, in 432, was commissioned to enter on his holy apostolate; who, in fine, after sixty years of unwearied toil and penitential deeds, passed to an eternal reward. Surely, with such characteristics emphatically assigned to him by a series of writers, from the fifth century to the present time, St. Patrick's history must be said to be endowed with an individuality which none can controvert, and which a similarity of name can nowise destroy. It is precisely to such a Patrick that all our ancient writers assign a mission from the Holy See, to bear the Gospel-light to the Irish shores.

2. The second part of Petrie's theory is even weaker than the preceding one: and hence, though Dr. Todd, in his late work on St. Patrick, eagerly adopted many of the other principles of Petrie, he, nevertheless, deemed it necessary to abandon altogether this groundless hypothesis.

Indeed, the dignity enjoyed by Palladius in the Church of Rome cannot easily be reconciled with the career of our apostle, Patrick. The office of deacon of Rome was second only to that of the pontiff. The popes in these early ages were frequently chosen from their rank, and the temporal concerns of the Holy See were all confided to their care. Now, that St. Patrick occupied so influential a position, was wholly unknown to his contemporary panegyrists, as well as to the numerous writers of his life.

Again, it was through the influence of Palladius, that St. Celestine sent Germanus and his companions to Britain, to root out the spreading evil of Pelagianism. Now, one of the humble associates of Germanus in that expedition—so humble, indeed, that all the continental writers of St. Germanus' acts leave his name unregistered in connection with his mission to Britain—was the future apostle of our island.

But it is unnecessary to pursue this line of reasoning, since all our ancient writers, whilst presenting the characteristics of St. Patrick, define also the distinctive features of Palladius. All of them are agreed in defining with precision the year in which each of these prelates received his mission from Rome: they record the names of the assistants who accompanied them: they commemorate the relative results of both missions; and whilst the preaching of Palladius proved unsuccessful, that of Patrick gathered the whole nation into the fold of Christ: they register, in fine, how, even in the sixth and seventh centuries, it had become a proverbial saying in our island, that "not to Palladius, but to Patrick, was given by God the apostolate of the Irish."

CHAPTER V.

Dr. Todd's opinion, that St. Palladius was not a deacon of Rome.

The latest writer on the history of our apostle,* whilst illustrating many complicated questions connected with the early centuries of the Irish Church, has given his name to some theories which are repugnant to the traditions of Ireland, and are in direct contradiction to the explicit testimony of the earliest and most authentic of its records. We shall reduce to three heads the special theory connected with St. Patrick, thus put forward by the learned professor of Trinity College, Dr. James Henthorn Todd. He asserts:

1. That St. Palladius was not a deacon of the Roman Church, but only a deacon of the bishop of Auxerre, St. Germanus.

2. That St. Patrick did not enter on the apostolate of our island earlier than the year 440; and

3. That, consequently, St. Patrick's mission to our island had no connection with, or sanction from, the Roman pontiff, St. Celestine.

Let us make a few remarks on each of these heads:

Petrie had referred to St. Patrick all that was usually assigned to Palladius: Dr. Todd goes to the opposite extreme, and assigns to Palladius all that our writers have recorded regarding the mission of St. Patrick, and his connection with St. Germanus. To prepare the way for this singular theory, Dr. Todd† asserts that Palladius was not deacon of Rome, but merely deacon of Germanus. "It is nowhere said," he writes, "that Palladius was of Rome, or deacon of Rome, much less that he was deacon to pope Celestine. All this is unauthorized assumption and fancy. It seems much more natural to interpret the words

---

* St. Patrick, Apostle of Ireland, etc., by James H. Todd, D.D., Dublin, 1864.
† Todd, p. 276.

of Prosper's chronicle as signifying that Palladius was St. Germanus's deacon."

Now, without descending to examine the laws of Latin construction, the words of Prosper—"ad actionem Palladii diaconi, papa Celestinus Germanum Antissiodorensem Episcopum vice sua mittit,"—have been hitherto supposed, not only by the continental writers, but by Stillingfleet and Usher, and the other leaders of Anglican teaching, to imply that Palladius was deacon of Rome. The simple title *Palladii diaconi*, seems to suppose that his name and office were familiar to the Romans, for whom Prosper was writing. The phrase, "ad actionem *Palladii*," implies an influence in the deacon which, as we have seen, is quite consistent with his office in Rome, but which we have yet to learn would be allowed by the Roman pontiff to the deacons of other churches.

But is it true that *it is nowhere said that Palladius was of Rome, or a deacon of Rome, much less that he was deacon to pope Celestine?* Indeed, such an assertion might be justly characterized as *an unauthorized assumption and fancy*. Does not the famous Book of Armagh expressly style him *chief deacon* of pope Celestine—for it is thus Dr. Todd himself teaches us to translate *archidiaconus, archiepiscopus*, and similar words in the ancient monuments of our Church?* We have already given the long extract from the life of St. Patrick, by Muirchu-Maccu-Mactheni,† and Dr. Todd gives the same passage at page 288; it is given by Petrie in Transactions of the Royal Irish Academy, vol. xviii. part 2nd, p. 84; and it is found in the Liber Armacanus, fol. 2.‡ But it seems strange, indeed, that Dr. Todd, when translating that passage of our early writer, merely says: "Palladius was ordained and sent," etc.,§ and omits the phrase which would alone suffice to falsify his subsequent assertion: "*Palladius, chief deacon of pope*

---

* Page 14, seqq. † Chap. i. pag. 15.
‡ The following is the original passage from this monument of our early Church: "Certe enim erat quod Palladius archidiaconus papæ Cœlestini, urbis Romæ episcopi, qui tunc tenebat Sedem Apostolicam quadragesimus quintus a sancto Petro Apostolo, ille Palladius ordinatus et missus fuerat ad hanc insulam sub brumali rigore positam convertendam," etc.—Lib Armac. fol. 2.
§ Page 288.

Celestine, bishop of the city of Rome." Nor is the Book of Armagh the only monument that expressly describes Palladius as deacon of Rome. The Vita Secunda, in a passage which Dr. Todd himself judges " probably not later than the eighth century,"* but which, as we have remarked above,† might be well referred to the seventh century, not only speaks of *Palladius archidiaconus* being sent by pope Celestine,‡ but further expressly writes :§

"For pope Celestine ordained bishop the chief deacon of the Roman Church, named Palladius, and sent him into the island of Hibernia."‖

Again, does not the very ancient life referred to St. Aileran expressly state: " Palladius, chief deacon of pope Celestine was ordained by that pope, and sent to preach the faith in Ireland " ?¶ and, to omit other authorities, does not Probus, in express terms, style Palladius *the deacon of pope Celestine,*** and commemorate his ordination by that pontiff, and his mission to our island?

Dr. Todd,†† to render plausible his opinion in regard to Palladius being deacon of Germanus, refers to Bingham as illustrating how, according to the usages of that age, it is precisely his deacon that St. Germanus would send to negotiate with pope Celestine, and further adds, that the Palladian family had some members in France, and gave two archbishops to Bourges—one in the year 377, the other in 472.

Unfortunately, however, for Todd's theory, no historian records a negotiation of Germanus with St. Celestine; but they speak rather of a commission sent by pope Celestine to Germanus.‡‡

As regards the Palladian family, it was easy for Dr. Todd to find a few of them in Gaul. We find a Palladius, too, in Constan-

---

* Page 293. † Chap. i. pag. 7. ‡ Chap. xxiii. § Chap. xxiv.
‖ Ap. Colgan, Tr. Th. p. 13. ¶ Ibid, p. 38.
** "Necdum tamen vir Dei Patricius ad Pontificalem gradum fuerat promotus ; quod ideo nimirum distulerat quia sciebat quod Palladius archidiaconus Cœlestini qui quadragesimus quintus a S. Petro Apostolicæ Sedi præerat," etc.—Probus, cap. xxiv. loc. cit. p. 48.
†† Pages 277 and 279.
‡‡ Wishing to avoid all incidental questions, we make no remark on the statement of Dr. Todd that Germanus' deacon would be the proper officer to carry on this negotiation. Bingham has not one word that justifies this assertion.

tinople, and we have still preserved the letter addressed to him by St. Gregory Nazianzen; and we find a Palladius in Africa, whose relations with St. Austin are well known to the students of ecclesiastical history. Even were our Palladius born in Gaul, it would not affect his high dignity in the Roman Church. St. Laurence, though a Spaniard, became the deacon of pope Sixtus; and we find a Dalmatian signing the letter to Tomian, archbishop of Armagh, as "John, the deacon of the Roman Church."

Rome, however, was the centre from which all the Palladii went; and to mention merely a few coincidences with the *Palladius* of whom we speak, it is a singular fact, that in the very year 431, in which Palladius was sent by the pope as bishop to Ireland, another *Palladius*, holding high dignity in the imperial household, was sent by the emperors Theodosius the younger and Valentinian as bearer of their letters to the Council of Ephesus.* It is also a curious coincidence, that whilst *the deacon Palladius* was urging on pope Celestine to root out Pelagianism from Britain, there should be a Palladius commissioned by the emperors, then living at Ravenna, first to expel from Rome all infected with that heresy, and then to punish them with rigor in any other place wheresoever they might be found—" quibuscumque locis potuerint rursus reperiri.† The edict, promulgated in Rome by this Palladius, prefect of the Pretorium, and directed, "in Pelagium atque Cælestium Catholici dogmatis fidem sævis tractatibus destruentes," is still happily preserved.‡ Even in the ecclesiastical world of Rome, the name Palladius was not unknown; and in a fragmentary inscription from the Catacombs, of about the year 400, there is registered a *Palladius exorcista* as then belonging to the Roman Church.§

---

* "Corpus legum ab Imperatoribus Romanis ante Iustinianum latarum," by Gustavus Haenel, Leipsic, 1857. The original letter of the emperors with the title *Missæ per Palladium magisterianum*, is given, p. 246.
† Ibid, pag. 238.
‡ Haenel, loc. cit. pag. 239.
§ I am indebted for this interesting fact to the distinguished archæologist, Chevalier Giov. Batt. de Rossi, whose name is well known to the English visitors of Rome.

CHAPTER VI.

Dr. Todd's opinion, that St. Patrick did not commence his apostolate until 440, examined.

THE main point, however, of Dr. Todd's theory is, that St. Patrick did not begin his apostolate in Ireland till the year 440. We shall consider in order the arguments with which he seeks to establish this novel opinion.

First Argument.—In the epistle to Coroticus, which Dr. Todd ably proves to be a genuine production of our saint, and which must have been written between the years 480 and 490, St. Patrick states that he sends it to Coroticus " by a venerable priest whom he himself had instructed from infancy." From this passage Dr. Todd thus argues—" If he had brought up from infancy one who was then a priest, and fit to be put at the head of a delicate mission, we cannot assign less than 30 or 40 years to his previous episcopal labours. Therefore, taking some year between 480 and 490 as the approximate date of the epistle, we may assume 440 to 450, or, at latest, 460, as the limits within which must be found the year of the consecration of St. Patrick, and of his arrival as a missionary in Ireland."* Now, with Dr. Todd's kind leave, we must say that this argument is quite illogical. There is nothing in this passage or elsewhere to indicate that this " venerable priest" was baptized in the first year of St. Patrick's episcopate. Let us suppose, then, that our apostle administered to him the sacrament of regeneration in the year 450, why are we to assert that the year 450 was the first year of his apostolate? If St. Patrick came to Ireland in 432, might he not have baptized this holy man in the year 450, and hence is not the old chronology of St. Patrick's life quite consistent with this record of the letter to Coroticus? But we may say still more: this statement of our apostle, in his letter to Coroticus, is an additional proof to corroborate the long-cherished

---

* Dr. Todd, St. Patrick, pag. 392.

tradition of our island in regard to his missionary career. For if this letter was sent to Coroticus between the years 480 and 490, through one who was baptized by St. Patrick, and having, in after years, been ordained, had grown old in the sacred ministry, we must surely say that his baptism cannot be referred to a much later period than 433, and hence that so far from establishing Dr. Todd's theory, it corroborates more and more the unanimous attestations of our writers, that for sixty years St. Patrick preached the Gospel truths in our island. We have already cited many passages of the ancient writers, who expressly fix this period as the term of his apostolate. Thus Fiacc, in his hymn, relates:

> " He preached for three score years
> The crucifixion of Christ to the tribes of the Feni."*

And, as we have mentioned in a preceding chapter, (p. 26) the Leabhar Breac cites this verse of Fiacc as proving that "for sixty years he preached and baptized the men of Ireland." We have also cited the ancient annalists (p. 31), who, whilst recording the death of our apostle in 493, without a dissentient voice, register his mission to Ireland in the year 432.

Second Argument.—Dr. Todd next argues from the Irish version of Nennius, a work which, in the preface to the edition of the I. A. S., in 1848, is referred to the year 1050,—a rather late date, indeed, to upset the unanimous assertion of the ancient monuments of our country. This Irish Nennius, at page 107 (edition of I. A. S.), after mentioning the return of St. Germanus from Britain, adds:—

"At this time Patrick was in captivity in Erin, with Milchu, and it was at this time that Palladius was sent to Erin to preach to them. Patrick went to the south to study, and he read the canons with Germanus. Palladius was driven from Erin, and he went and served God in Fordun in Mairne. Patrick came to Erin after studying, and baptized the men of Erin."

Now Dr. Todd argues from this passage that "when Palladius was sent to Ireland, Patrick was a captive with Milchu in Dalaradia," whence it would necessarily follow, that as Palladius came

* Ap Colgan, pag. 1, and Petrie, Tara, pag. 75.

to Ireland in 431, St. Patrick could not have been sent as our apostle in the following year.*

Now if the learned doctor insists on the phrase *at this time* being taken in a strict sense, it would follow that his own theory is equally false with that of the other Irish writers; for as St. Patrick tells us, in his Confession, that he was forty-five years of age when he received episcopal consecration, and as he was only in his twenty-second year† when he was freed from captivity, it would follow from Dr. Todd's statement, that our apostle did not receive his mission till about the year 455, that is to say, fifteen years after the date assigned to it by Dr. Todd himself. However, the Irish phrase, *at this time*, is often used in a mere transition sense, and has its reference only to the chief subject of the subsequent narrative. For instance, in the Book of Lecan we read:—

"It was at this time of king Lughaidh that Patrick came to Ireland, and he went to Tara, where Lughaidh was, and offered him wheat without tillage, constant milk with kine during his life, and heaven at the end of his life, etc.; and because Lughaidh did not assent to that, Patrick cursed him," etc.‡

Now as Lughaidh did not ascend the throne till the year 479, we should, according to Dr. Todd's theory, conclude that St. Patrick did not arrive in our island till after that year. It is manifest, however, that the words, *at this time*, only refer to the main subject of the following context, that is, to the cursing of king Lughaidh by our apostle. Applying this rule to the passage above cited from the Irish Nennius, it results, that *at this time*, that is, when Germanus had returned from Britain, "St. Patrick was destined to Ireland,"—a statement which sufficiently refutes Dr. Todd's theory, and corroborates the ancient tradition of our island.

We are the more obliged to adopt this interpretation in the present instance, as this same Irish Nennius, in another passage, expressly mentions the year of St. Patrick's arrival in Ireland. When giving the chronology of the Pictish kings, it states that

---

* Todd, pag. 394.
† For both these statements, see Todd, pag. 392 and 394.
‡ See the original Irish text in Petrie's Tara, pag. 63.

"in the nineteenth year of king Drust, Patrick, the holy bishop, arrived in Ireland,"* which year, according to the Scotch writers, would coincide with 433 of our era. They place the commencement of his reign in A.D. 414.†

Third Argument.—There is a curious tract on the Synchronisms of the Irish Kings, which, "in an extract quoted by Usher and O'Flaherty, tells us that the battle of Ocha, in which king Oilioll Molt was slain, happened exactly xliii. years after the coming of Patrick to Ireland."‡ Resting on this principle, Dr. Todd thus argues: "The battle of Ocha, according to the Annals of Ulster, was fought A.D 482 or 483; and therefore counting 43 years back, A.D. 439 or 440, would be the date of Patrick's coming."§

The authority of this writer on the synchronisms of our kings is not well defined: Usher only styles him *non novitius* author; whilst O'Flaherty expressly accuses him of inaccuracy, even in the very passage to which Dr. Todd refers. We shall therefore be very brief in our remarks on this argument.

In the first place, the battle of Ocha is commonly placed in the year 478. Curry, in his Lectures, publishing some very ancient poems on this battle, always refers it to this year.‖ It is to the year 478 that it is also referred in the Annals of the Four Masters, in which we read " A.D. 478, Oilioll Molt, the son of Dathi, after having been twenty years on the throne of Ireland, was slain in the battle of Ocha."¶ The Chronicon Scotorum places the beginning of his successor's reign in 480.

But the numerals of the original text, which, as given by Dr. Todd, are written xliii., are a still weaker point in his argument. The learned writer, in the very next page, gives us an example of how easily the ancient *v* (which in the Irish MSS. is written like the modern *u*) is confounded with ii.** Another precisely similar case is given by Dr. Todd, in his translation of the Irish Nennius, for the I. A. S. pag., 160, in which the original iv. was mis-written iii.

Now, applying these simple data to the text of the above-cited

---

* Edition of I. A. S page 161. † Ibid. appendix, page xlvii.
‡ Todd, page 394.   § Ibid. 395.   ‖ Page 482, seqq.
¶ Edit. of O'Donovan, ad an. 478.   ** Page 395, note i.

Irish tract, we have the battle of Ocha fought in 478; and deducting the period of *xlvi years*, which intervened since the mission of St. Patrick, we have the date of this latter event once more accurately assigned to the year 432.

We must, however, make one further remark. Dr. Todd rests this argument on the date assigned to the battle of Ocha in the Annals of Ulster. And why then does he reject the clear statement which these same annals place as the starting point of all their chronology?

"Anno ccccxxxii. Patricius pervenit in Hiberniam, ix. anno Theodosii junioris, primo anno episcopatus Sixti."*

"In the year 432 St. Patrick arrived in Ireland, in the ninth year of Theodosius the younger, and the first of the popedom of St. Sixtus."

The *Fourth Argument* is taken from the following record of Tirechan, preserved in the Book of Armagh:—

"From the passion of Christ to the death of Patrick, are in all ccccxxxvi. years. But Leoghaire reigned two or five years after the death of Patrick, and the total duration of his reign was, in our opinion, thirty-six years."

From this passage, Dr. Todd argues that St. Patrick's death is recorded in the year 469 from the nativity of our Lord: whilst the beginning of king Leoghaire's reign is marked in 438. As, therefore, it was in the fourth year of this king's reign that St. Patrick came to evangelize our island, he surely cannot have come till many years after the death of St. Celestine.

It is certainly too bad for Dr. Todd to appeal to the authority of Tirechan, as supporting his novel theory in regard to the date of St. Patrick's mission to Ireland; for, Tirechan in a passage already quoted (p. 25) from the Book of Armagh, expressly records, that "In the thirteenth year of the emperor Theodosius, Patrick was sent by bishop Celestine, the pope of Rome, as bishop, to preach to the Irish:" and lest there should be any mistake as to the Patrick of whom he speaks, he adds, that this Patrick was sent by the angel of God, Victor, and by pope Celestine, and all Ireland received his

* Ap Petrie, Tara, pag. 82.

teaching," etc.* Here, St. Tirechan clearly states his opinion, and no vague calculations are required to conclude that St. Celestine commissioned our apostle to evangelize our island.

Let us, however, suppose Dr. Todd's calculations to be accurate. In the second argument, already produced, he asserts, that in 431 St. Patrick could not be more than twenty-two years of age. The Confession, however, of our apostle, clearly asserts that he was forty-five years old at the time of his consecration :† therefore, this consecration must be referred to the year 454. And, if St. Patrick died in the year 469, what then becomes of the *venerabilis senex* of Dr. Todd's first argument? And will Dr. Todd assign the year 454 as the fourth year of Leoghaire's reign? If so, since he reigned, according to the above passage, thirty-six years, he must have lived till 486 : and how then could his successor, Oilioll Molt, after reigning twenty years, be killed in 482, as Dr. Todd affirms in the third argument?

But, to seriously examine the meaning of the passage cited above from Tirechan, we must remark with Petrie, that it refers, not to the death of our apostle, but to Sen-Patrick, who, as we have seen (p. 4), died in 457, and our annals are at present found to vary as they did in Tirechan's time ; some assigning the death of Leoghaire to the year 458 or 459, some to the year 463.‡ Now, taking this last date as the one referred to by Tirechan, who precisely agrees with those annalists in marking thirty-six years for Leoghaire's reign, we should place the beginning of his reign in 428; and thus, in 432, St. Patrick might well be destined to our island by pope Celestine, as Tirechan expressly asserts, and both passages are found to proceed in harmony.

From this we should conclude that the date ccccxxxvi., in the passage above cited, was a mere error of the copyist for ccccxxvi. The Irish writers assigned the passion of our blessed Lord to the year thirty-one of our era, as a passage from the Leabhar Breac, given by Petrie,§ clearly proves : and hence, the year 426 from

---

* Book of Armagh, fol. 16 ; ap Petrie, Tara, pag. 85.
† Todd, pag. 392. ‡ Petrie, Tara, pag. 28.
Tara, pag 78-80.

the passion, would be the year 457 of our era, the precise date of the death of St. Sen-Patrick.

Fifth Argument.—The next argument of Dr. Todd is taken from an Irish bard of the eleventh century, named Gilla-Caemhain, whose testimony "supplies abundant evidence of the existence of a chronology inconsistent with the mission from Celestine."* This *abundant evidence*, however, is reduced to the simple fact, that having linked together several events between the arrival of St. Patrick and the death of St. Gregory, and marked out the respective number of years that intervened; it would appear from the sum of these intervals, that the " writer counts 162 years from the advent of St. Patrick to the death of pope Gregory the Great. Gregory the Great, as is well known, died March 12th, 604;† therefore, the advent of Patrick, according to Gilla-Caemhain, must be dated 442."‡

It is painful to be obliged to characterize so repeatedly this learned professor's arguments as illogical. In order that the present argument might be of any force, Dr. Todd should have informed his readers to what year *the Irish bard* referred the death of St. Gregory. It is certain that our Irish writers were often inexact in marking continental events. For instance, in the Leabhar Breac, there is a similar series of events linked together to mark the arrival of St. Patrick in Ireland. Its last link is:—

"Ten years from the death of Augustine until Palladius was sent by pope Celestine."§

At the same time the writer marks this latter year expressly as the 431st of our era, and the last of Celestine's pontificate. As, therefore, we are in this case obliged to assert, either that the copyists tampered with the dates, or that the writer erred in regard to St. Augustine's death (for its true date is 430), so we might, perhaps, without further investigation conclude, that some similar accident led to the defective chronology of our bard.

* Page 396.
† Dr. Todd himself, however, p. 302, had already referred this pontiff's death to A.D. 602.
‡ Page 396.   § Ap. Petrie, Tara, p. 79.

The reader will the more readily adopt this conclusion when he reflects that one, at least, of the links in this chronological series of our bard is plainly defective: "from the death (he says) of king Diarmait MacCarroll, to the death of pope Gregory, are thirty-three years." Now the death of king Diarmait, as registered in the Irish annals, must be referred to about the year 560. It is an important era, as it marks the abandonment of the royal abode of Tara. According to the Four Masters, Diarmait ascended the throne in 539; and all the ancient records, including the very poem we are speaking of, limit his reign to twenty-one years. The latest year assigned to his death is 465; and hence the interval of thirty-three years between his death and that of St. Gregory is manifestly erroneous.

We shall ask, however, why does not Dr. Todd admonish his readers, that in this very passage of the Irish bard which he refers to, an interval of 129 years is assigned from the arrival of St. Patrick to the death of king Diarmait? And as it is only a desire to discover truth that guides his inquiry, why does he not acknowledge, that such an interval is quite consistent with the arrival of St. Patrick in Ireland in the year 432? For if we place king Diarmait's accession to the throne in 539, as it is marked by the Annals of the Four Masters, whose date is adopted by Colgan* and many others, it will follow that 560 was the year of his death, with which date may easily be reconciled, without any special chronological acumen, the date 432, and the intervening period of 129 years.

We shall conclude by remarking, that Dr. Todd is rather unfortunate in the witnesses which he brings forward to show that St. Patrick's arrival in our island did not take place in 432: instead of rejecting, they are all found to corroborate, more and more, that precise date. Even the bard Gilla-Caemhain, in the passage produced by Dr. Todd, is far from impugning it; whilst, as we learn from the Transactions of the Iberno-Celtic Society for 1820, p. 80, this same poet and historian in another work, which commences "Noble Eriu, island of kings," and of which copies are extant in the Books of Ballymote and Lecan, "gives the names of the monarchs, and the

* Tr. Thaum. p. 6.

number of years that each reigned, until the coming of St. Patrick, in the reign of Leoghaire, A.D. 432."

Sixth Argument.—The last argument produced by Dr. Todd is taken from a chronological tract preserved in the book of Lecan, which says, that "Leoghaire reigned thirty years, and his successor, Oilioll Molt, twenty." This latter king was killed, according to the Annals of Ulster, in 482; therefore, 432 was only the first year of Leoghaire's reign.*

Here Dr. Todd's argument is once more based on the Ulster Annals, which refer the death of Oilioll Molt to 482. We have already remarked, in examining his third argument, that some of our annalists refer that event to 478, and that it is inconsistent in the learned writer to cull one incidental date from these Annals of Ulster, whilst he rejects their express statement regarding the year 432, which is the fundamental date of all their chronology, and in which they mark the arrival of St. Patrick in our island. The same Annals of Ulster thus register St. Patrick's death in 492: "Patricius Archipostolus Scotorum quievit, sexagesimo anno ex quo venit ad Hiberniam ad baptizandos Scotos."

As regards the passage from the chronological tract here referred to by Dr. Todd, its literal translation is as follows:—

"Now Leoghaire, son of Niall of the Nine Hostages, held the kingdom for thirty years after the arrival of Patrick did he retain the kingdom."

Dr. Todd arbitrarily puts a stop, and divides this passage after the word *years*, although even as the subsequent words, so is the corresponding preceding word *annis* written in Latin.

Petrie cites this very same passage from the same MS. Book of Lecan, and translates it as stating that "Leoghaire held the government thirty years after the arrival of Patrick."

O'Flaherty, in his Ogygia, p. 429, states that in his MS. of the Book of Lecan, the whole sentence was distinctly expressed in Latin—*triginta annis regnum Hiberniæ post adventum Patritii tenuit.*

What, however, removes all difficulty, and sets at rest for ever

* Pp. 396-7. † Tara, p. 63.

all doubt as to the meaning of this chronological tract, is the discovery made by Dr. Todd himself, that it is nothing more than "an enlarged copy of the older form of the same tract in the Book of Leinster."* Now, in the Book of Leinster this tract expressly states that Leoghaire, son of Niall, "*triginta annos regnum Hiberniæ post adventum Patricii tenuit.*"† Thus, then, so far from this chronological tract being an argument to reject the usually received date of St. Patrick's arrival in Ireland, it only serves to corroborate it more and more, and to explain the origin of the various dates assigned for the death of Leoghaire. The date of St. Patrick's arrival was the fixed point on which all were agreed; the beginning of Leoghaire's reign, in 428-9, was also a point which involved no controversy. The records, however, of the length of Leoghaire's reign were found to be ambiguous: some assigning thirty years for the whole duration of his reign, and hence placing his death in 458; others reckoning thirty years from the arrival of our apostle, and hence registering Leoghaire's death in 462. And thus, every record and tradition of our island combines in perfect harmony with the one great central point of all our civil and religious history—the arrival of St. Patrick in our island in the year 432.

Were we examining the opinions of another author, we should not have wasted so much time in refuting such trivial arguments. From the fact of so able a writer as Dr. Todd having been obliged to take hold of them, and rest on them his favourite theory, the reader may easily conclude what little solidity that theory possesses. It has not even the merit of novelty: for Tillemont already put forward the conjecture that St. Patrick did not come to Ireland till 440.‡ Tillemont, however, knew nothing of the ancient records of our island, and was, therefore, excusable.

This date (432) of our apostle's arrival is the one chief point on which all our annalists and writers are found to agree.

It is expressly assigned by the Chronicon Scotorum, the Annals of Ulster, of Innisfallen, of the Four Masters, of Marianus, etc.

---

* Ibid. p. 396, note 3. † Ap. Todd, ibid. p. 184.
‡ Memoires, etc., xvi. p. 784.

It is assigned by the most authentic of our records in the Book of Armagh; it is confirmed by all the writers of our apostle's life, who refer his mission to the last year of St. Celestine, or to the first year of his successor Sixtus; for Celestine died in 432, and Sixtus was chosen his successor in the summer of the same year. Indeed, so universal is the testimony of our writers on this head, that Colgan, when minutely discussing each particular of St. Patrick's history, deemed it unnecessary to cite any documents in proof of it: "hæc sententia videtur tam indubitata et tam recepta, ut pro ea non judicaverim operæ prætium esse producere testimonia."* Usher repeats the same: "There is no discrepancy," he says, "amongst Irish writers as to the year of St. Patrick's mission into Ireland;"† and Dr. Lanigan was able, even in his day, to conclude that "it would be a waste of time to adduce proofs of this being the true date."‡ And yet it was since Lanigan wrote that Tirechan's authority became known, confirming the same date—that the life in the Leabhar Breac was found to expressly record our apostle's mission in the year of the Christian era 432, "*the ninth year of Theodosius, king of the world, the first year of the episcopacy of Sixtus, coarb of Peter, and the fourth year of the reign of Leoghaire;*" and subsequently it adds, that Patrick came to Ireland in the year after Palladius: "*Ætius and Valerius were the two consuls of that year; it was in this year Xystus assumed the supremacy of Rome after Celestine. This was the fourth year of the reign of Leoghaire.*" Two ancient treatises on the Brehon laws were also brought to light, giving their testimony to confirm the same statement; one of them, alluding to the compilation of the Seanchus Mor, in 438, supposes that even then "the purity of the faith was acknowledged by the men of Ireland, and the Gospel of Christ was preached to them all." The other still more expressly cites an ancient proverbial quatrain:

> "Patrick baptized with glory,
> In the time of Theodosius;
> He preached the Gospel, without falsehood,
> To the worthy people of the sons of Milé;"

* Tr. Thaumat. p. 254.   † Primordia, p. 880.   ‡ Eccl. Hist. i. 209.

and a little lower down records "the coming of Patrick into Ireland to propagate baptism and faith, in the ninth year of the reign of Theodosius, and in the fourth year of Leoghaire, son of Niall, monarch of Ireland."* Hence, even Dr. Petrie, after all the progress made during late years in exploring our early monuments, was able to assert that the year 432 "is the year in which, according to all authorities, St. Patrick came to Ireland."†

CHAPTER VII.

Dr. Todd's opinion, that St. Patrick received no mission from Rome, examined and refuted.—It rests almost entirely on negative arguments; whilst the mission of our apostle from Rome is confirmed by positive evidence of the greatest weight.

THE third point of Dr. Todd's theory rested mainly for its support on the supposition that St. Patrick had not set out for our island till 440. From such a principle it would, indeed, be a very natural deduction, that his mission to Ireland had no connexion with the Roman pontiff, pope Celestine, who, in 432, had passed to a better life. This foundation, however, being removed, the assertion of Dr. Todd, that our apostle had no mission from St. Celestine, and had not prepared himself for his future apostolate under the guidance of St. Germanus, will be found to rest on very weak arguments for its support.

We have seen‡ the direct evidence which proves beyond all possibility of doubt the two-fold fact, of the mission of St. Patrick from Rome, and his preparation for the sacred ministry in the school of Germanus. Every monument of our early Church connected with the life of St. Patrick, serves to illustrate one or other of these main principles of his missionary career. Now, to all this positive evidence, Dr. Todd has merely to oppose the silence of four ancient documents, viz: the Confession of St. Patrick, the Hymn of St. Sechnall, the Hymn of Fiacc, and the Memoir of our

* See Petrie, Ibid. page 48 and 52-3. † Essay on Tara, page 75.
‡ Part. 1, c. iii. p. 12, and iv. p. 22.

Saint, by Muirchu-Maccu-Mactheni. We shall briefly examine whether these documents justify the conclusion which the learned author would fain deduce from them.

The Confession of St. Patrick was written towards the close of his apostolate, when the whole nation had been illumined with the light of faith, and many of its inhabitants were to be found aspiring to the highest degrees of religious perfection. His object in writing it was to proclaim to the world the mercies of God, shown to himself and the Irish people, that thus the faith of his spiritual children might be strengthened, and those who had upbraided him with rashly assuming such a spiritual charge, be persuaded that he was divinely guided to bend his shoulders to that spiritual burden: it thus begins:

"I, Patrick, a sinner, the rudest and least of all the faithful, and the most despicable amongst men, had for my father, Calphurnius, a deacon, son of the late presbyter Potitus; he was of the town Bonavem Taberniæ, and he had a farm in the neighbourhood where I was made captive, when I was nearly sixteen years old. I knew not the true God, and I was carried in captivity into Ireland with a multitude of men, according to our deserts; for we had withdrawn ourselves from God, and had not kept his commandments, and were not obedient to our priests, who used to admonish us for our salvation. And the Lord brought upon us the wrath of his displeasure, and scattered us among many nations, even unto this extremity of the world, where at present my unworthiness is seen to abide amidst strangers. And there the Lord opened the sense of my unbelief, that even late I should remember my sins and be converted with my whole heart unto the Lord my God, who had regard unto my lowliness, and had compassion on my youth and ignorance, and preserved me before I knew Him, and before I could distinguish between good and evil, and protected me, and comforted me as a father would a son. Wherefore, I am not able, neither would it be right, to be silent regarding such great benefits and such great grace, which hath been vouchsafed unto me, in this country of my captivity; for this is our return to Him, that on being corrected and brought to know God, we should exalt and confess His wondrous works, before every nation which is under the whole heaven."

He then makes a short profession of his faith in the most adorable Trinity, and adds:

"Wherefore, I thought of writing long ago, but hesitated until now for I was afraid of incurring the censure of men; because I have not read like others who have been well imbued with sacred learning, and have never abandoned their studies from infancy, but have ever added more and more to their perfection; but my speech and language have been exchanged for another tongue."

Thus he continues repeatedly acknowledging his own lowliness, and the debt of gratitude which he owed to God; and he concludes the first chapter:

"Be astounded all ye who are great, as well as ye who are small: ye learned ones who fear the Lord, and ye who are ignorant of the Lord, attend and examine who it was that selected me, a fool, from the midst of those who are wise and eloquent, and skilled in all things: and He indeed inspired me above others, though the most despicable of all others in this world. But it matters little that I be such, so as with humility and respect, and without reproach, I may faithfully benefit that people whom the charity of Christ bestowed upon me, even with my life, should I be found worthy to have that grace accorded me, and thus humbly and truly serve Him according to my ability."

Such are the sentiments which everywhere pervade this treatise of our apostle. In the subsequent chapters, only such facts are commemorated as reveal a special divine interposition in his favor: his being freed from captivity—the angelic visions which admonished him to undertake the Irish mission,—the divine fruitfulness which blessed his apostolate. In fine, he concludes the whole Confession with these words:—

"Behold, once again I briefly repeat the words of my confession, and I attest in truth and with joy, before God and His holy angels, that I never had any inducement except the Gospel and its promises, to return back to the nation from which I fled before. But I pray those who believe and seek and fear God, whosoever may condescend to look into, or receive this writing, which Patrick the sinner, although unlearned, wrote in Ireland, that what little soever I may have done or administered, may not be referred to me, but be ye persuaded, and verily believe, that it was the gift of God. This is my confession before I die."

The reader will probably ere this have asked, how can Dr. Todd have argued from the mere silence of such a spiritual treatise, that St. Patrick had no mission from Rome, and that his education by Germanus had no foundation as an historic truth? The following is the argument of the learned author:—

"One object of the writer of the Confession was to defend himself from the charge of presumption. . . . . Had he received a regular commission from the see of Rome, that fact alone would have been an unanswerable reply."—(p. 310.)

This argument, however, displays more ingenuity than solidity. Were St. Patrick accused of presuming to set out uncommissioned, and of his own accord, for the Irish mission, his appeal to Rome would have been unanswerable. But there is no indication, nor even hint, that any such accusation was made against him. The temerity of which he was accused, was merely that one so poor and lowly and ignorant, should have accepted such an onerous mission. His mission from Rome was a matter of course: and as St. Patrick does not commemorate his baptism, or his consecration as bishop, so neither does he deem it necessary to commemorate his mission from pope Celestine. His predecessor Palladius had received a similar mission, and though learned and high in position and authority, had failed. How was it that Patrick, without learning or any other temporal influence, could, without temerity, have accepted the same mission? Such, and such alone, was the accusation to which our apostle replies. His reply is one that would have been worthy of the apostle of nations: he acknowledges his earthly lowliness; the phrases by which he designates himself are *parvitas mea, pusillitas mea, ignorantia mea*. He dilates on his unworthiness, his ignorance, the sinfulness of his early life. But it pleased God, he adds, to magnify his power, by bestowing his mercies on the most despicable of all,—to make known to me his having chosen me for this apostolate,—and to sanction my mission, by giving fecundity to my ministry, and bestowing on me the whole Irish nation as the portion of my spiritual inheritance. The mention of a mission from Rome would have nothing to do with such an accusation. The special divine manifestations that were made to him, impelled him to accept the burden imposed on him by pope Celestine; and they are now commemorated as truly freeing him from the reproach of temerity, in accepting a task for which, humanly speaking, he was so unequal. We may further add, that the ancient biographers of our saint, whilst narrating his mission from pope Celestine, detail, at the same time, these supernatural manifestations of Heaven, summoning our apostle to Ireland, as the destined field where his missionary labours would bear abundant fruit.

The reasoning by which Dr. Todd endeavours to persuade his readers that St. Patrick had no connection with Germanus, is still more characteristic. St. Patrick, he says, had he studied in the schools of Germanus, could not write in such *rude Latinity*, nor style himself *ignorant* and *unlearned*.*

The school of St. Germanus, however, was not as Cambridge or Trinity College, or other such establishments of the British crown. It was a school of saints; and whilst each one, according to his condition, acquired the necessary secular learning, the main object of all was to mortify their passions, and acquire the practice of every virtue. St. Patrick's whole life, and the very work we are speaking of, proves what progress he had made in the school of sanctity. If he styles himself ignorant and contemptible, the apostle of nations had described himself in a like manner; for the saints of God did not preach the Gospel according to the Protestant rule of human wisdom, but resting on the power and wisdom of God. In the passage, however, above cited from the Confession, St. Patrick explains to us why his Latinity was not more elegant, and better impressed with the traces of the classic style of the Augustan age. His early life, he says, and especially his six years slavery, had rendered distasteful to him the higher pursuits of secular learning. Even the little literature he had acquired in the hallowed retreat of Lerins, must well nigh have been forgotten when the Confession was penned, and when, for almost sixty years, he had made himself all to all in our pagan island, and, as he himself expresses it, had exchanged his former style and language for the harsher accents of his spiritual children. However, with all the rudeness of his Latinity, St. Patrick, as Tillemont already observed, proves himself to be thoroughly acquainted with the sacred Scriptures, and shows that he had drunk in their spiritual meaning at no ordinary source.

* Todd, page 311.

Besides the Confession, there are a few other writings of our apostle, one of which, known as his Lorica Prayer, was ably vindicated to St. Patrick by Petrie, and has been presented to English readers in an elegant and accurate version by Dr. Todd. We may now ask this learned writer, why did he not appeal to the silence of this Lorica, as an additional proof of our apostle having had no mission from Rome? Simply, because no one in his senses would expect St. Patrick to thus commemorate in his form of prayer, his relations with Germanus and pope Celestine. And why, then, does Dr. Todd appeal to the silence of the Confession as a proof of his novel theory, since the Confession, too, is nothing more than a religious outpouring of our apostle's soul, and a record of the manifold supernatural mercies which had been vouchsafed to him by God. A few other fragments of our apostle are also preserved in the Book of Armagh; and as we have already seen (p. 14), one of his proverbial sayings there recorded, registers his having sought for spiritual wisdom in Gaul, and Italy, and the islands of the Tyrrhene Sea. Another (p. 25) linked the newly-converted Church of Ireland in the closest bonds of fellowship with Rome. By-and-by, too, we shall have occasion to refer to a canonical statute, by which he marked out Rome as the depository of apostolic truth, to whose tribunal all grave controversies should be referred. These express statements are a sufficient indication of the mission which our apostle bore with him to our shores.

The Hymn of St. Sechnall, better known by his Latin name, Secundinus, is nothing more than a commemoration of the virtues of our apostle. By recounting the many graces bestowed upon St. Patrick, that loving disciple wished to liken his master to the angels of God, and to the first apostles of our blessed Lord.* No special historic facts are mentioned in it; and Dr. Todd merely reveals the weakness of his cause, when he appeals to the silence of this document in regard to Germanus and Rome, as a proof that our apostle received no commission from the Holy See to evangelize our island. There is, however, one passage of the hymn which is certainly *mis-*

---

* Conf. verse i. in Liber Hymnorum, p. 11.

translated by Dr. Todd, as we shall see in the third part, and which, with as much precision as we could expect in such an eulogistic hymn, refers to this mission of St. Patrick from that central see of the Christian world. It occurs in the third verse, and eulogizes our saint as " being firm in the faith as Peter, upon whom the Church is built, and of whose apostolate he was made partaker by God, against whom the powers of hell cannot prevail."* This is a clear reference to the fact that St. Patrick received his mission from Rome, being thus made partaker of the apostolate and mission of St. Peter. We shall reserve to the next chapter (p. 80, seq.) a more minute examination of this interesting passage.

The Hymn of St. Fiacc is a very valuable fragment of our ancient Church; but, unfortunately, it commemorates merely a few facts connected with our apostle. All that St. Patrick possessed in common with others is passed over in silence; and hence, too, his mission from Rome, which was a matter of course in those ages, and which but a little while before had accompanied Palladius to our coasts. We may, however, be permitted to ask Dr. Todd why he deems the silence of St. Fiacc of such importance regarding one fact, whilst he rejects, without ceremony, another fact which is expressly attested by the same writer. We have cited above (page 18) the beautiful passage of this hymn which records the connection of St. Patrick with Germanus; and we have also seen how St. Fiacc assigns sixty years to the missionary labours of our apostle, who hence must have come to our island in the year 432. All this testimony, however, is declared to be valueless by Dr. Todd, whilst the silence of Fiacc regarding a fact which we nevertheless very naturally might expect to find omitted by him, is deemed of sufficient importance to reject that fact as groundless. This, indeed, is a novel theory in the philosophy of history.

There is one case illustrative of this matter, which we wish to recall to the mind of Dr. Todd. A few years after the death of St. Germanus, a lengthy and detailed life, commemorating his virtues, and especially his labours in rooting out Pelagianism from Britain, was written by a monk named Constantine: this life is

---

* Liber Hymnorum, p. 12.

justly regarded as one of the most precious monuments of the Church of France in the fifth century, and yet it makes no mention of the commission given to that saint by pope Celestine. Eric of Auxerre repeated in verse the life of the same saint Germanus, and he, too, is silent regarding that fact. Bede, too, sketches minutely that portion of Germanus's history, but makes no allusion to his mission from Rome. Nevertheless, other monuments commemorate it; and Dr. Todd, in his late work, devotes some pages to prove, that the mere silence of these writers is a matter of no consequence, when the fact which they omit is commemorated by other authentic monuments. Now, in regard to St. Patrick, how much less important must be deemed the silence of hymns composed more as a panegyric than a history, and which not only do not minutely detail the particular events of our apostle's life, but scarcely commemorate a single fact connected with his apostolate? Hence, though these documents were well known to Usher and other writers during the last two centuries, no one ever dreamed of deducing from their silence that St. Patrick had no mission from Rome, although many of the monuments which now illustrate this Roman mission of our apostle were then unknown, and have been brought to light only within the past few years.

Only one other document now remains, which, as Dr. Todd informs us, passes over in silence the mission given to St. Patrick by the then ruling pontiff St. Celestine, and whose silence is put forward as a sufficient counterbalance against all the explicit historic evidence which we have advanced in the preceding pages. This important document is the tract of *Muirchu-Maccu-Mactheni*, preserved in the Book of Armagh.

At the very outset, however, of our inquiry, we are struck by the singular contradiction which Dr. Todd's arguments present to us. One of the most explicit monuments that asserted the close relationship binding our apostle to St. Germanus, was this very tract of *Mactheni;* yet his express testimony is rejected by Dr. Todd as worthless, whilst his silence is, in the present case, put forward as of paramount importance.

What, however, is the fact regarding this document? It is an unfortunate and as yet unexplained circumstance, that within the last two hundred years, the first leaf of the tract of Mactheni has disappeared; and with it have been lost those chapters in which we would expect to find commemorated the close relations of St. Patrick and pope Celestine. I say within the past two hundred years, for in Usher's time the tract was complete; and yet Usher could record the mission of St. Patrick from Rome as attested, without a dissentient voice, by the historians of his life. Perhaps in future time another leaf may disappear, and then some disciple of Dr. Todd's historic school can appeal to the silence of Mactheni in regard to Germanus, as a resistless proof that the training of our apostle in that school of Catholic sanctity, was ignored by the ancient writers of his biography. Thus, then, the silence of *Muirchu-Maccu-Mactheni* is a rather mysterious silence, and one to which we hope Dr. Todd will not refer again.

Dr. Todd, however, further argues, that the account given in this tract of the ordination of St. Patrick by Germanus, and his subsequent departure for Ireland, is inconsistent with a mission from Rome; but we reply that this is all a mere gratuitous assertion of the learned writer. There are other monuments descriptive of St. Patrick's life, which commemorate in the very same terms as the present tract his ordination by Germanus; and, nevertheless, they too, in their preceding chapters, had referred his mission to the Apostolic See. It is thus in Probus, in the Vita Quarta, and other documents already cited.

In the text of *Muirchu-Maccu-Mactheni* regarding Germanus, there is not a word stating that St. Germanus had been authorized by pope Celestine to send St. Patrick to our island, but neither is there one word to exclude that hypothesis; and judging from the analogy of its record with the other ancient documents regarding our apostle, we should conclude that Germanus, on receiving intelligence of the death of Palladius, commissioned St. Patrick, with

---

* See Graves on the Date of the Book of Armagh; Reeves' Memoir of the Book of Armagh; Petrie, Tara, p. 86.

the blessing, and by the authority of pope Celestine, to evangelize our island.

But, adds Dr. Todd, when St. Patrick received the angelic summons to go forth and fish with evangelic net, he was apparently in France, and set out *immediately* to the work of the Gospel in Ireland (page 315). The word *immediately* is, no doubt, the basis of this argument; and unfortunately for the logic of him who constructs his argument on it, this word is altogether wanting in the original text of *Muirchu-Maccu-Mactheni*. Instead of it, the phrase *opportuno ergo tempore* is used by Mactheni: and in the corresponding words of Probus, we find *nactus ergo tempus opportunum*. This formula is carefully passed over unnoticed by Dr. Todd, and yet it is the key to the whole discourse of Mactheni. St. Patrick, though admonished by the angel Victor, that God had chosen him for the mission of Ireland, *did not set out immediately*, but waited till the opportune time should come, that is, he awaited the sanction of his mission by the divinely-constituted authority on earth, and having received this sanction, and the blessing of Christ's vicar, he joyfully set out to evangelize our people.*

But if there is no sufficient ground in the text of Mactheni for denying the mission of St. Patrick from pope Celestine, at least in the summary or heads of the lost chapters, sufficient data are presented to us for excluding this connection of our apostle with the Holy See. Thus argues Dr. Todd, page 315.

To understand this argument we may remark that in the Book of Armagh,† are preserved the titles of all the chapters of the preceding life of Mactheni, and amongst them are found those too of the chapters which have most unaccountably disappeared:—

1. "De ortu Patricii et ejus prima captivitate.
2. "De navigio ejus cum gentibus et vexatione deserti, cibo sibi et gentilibus divinitus delato.
3. "De secunda captura quam senis decies diebus ab inimicis pertulerat.
4. "De susceptione sua a parentibus ubi agnoverunt eum.

---

* See the original text of Mactheni, in Petrie, Tara, page 84.
† Fol. 20, *a*.

5. "De ætate ejus quando iens videre Sedem Apostolicam voluit discere sapientiam.
6. "De inventione Sancti Germani in Galliis et ideo non exivit ultra.
7. "De ætate ejus quando visitavit eum angelus ut veniret adhuc.
8. "De reversione ejus de Galliis et ordinatione Palladii et mox morte ejus.
9. "De ordinatione ejus ab Amathorege episcopo, defuncto Palladio."*

Here, then, argues Dr. Todd, it is stated that "St. Patrick desired to visit the Apostolic See, and there to learn wisdom; *but* that meeting with St. Germanus in Gaul, *he went no further.*"

In this argument of our learned theorist, we have an additional example of the means he has resorted to to prop up his cherished opinion: St. Patrick's going to the Apostolic See, and his meeting with St. Germanus, are two distinct sentences which are blended into one by Dr. Todd, in order to suit his own purpose. Now *Muirchu-Maccu-Mactheni* in his chapters does not follow the mere chronological order of events. For instance, the eighth chapter speaks of St. Patrick's leaving Gaul, etc.; whilst it is only in the ninth chapter that his ordination in Gaul by Amathorex is commemorated. There is no reason, therefore, why Dr. Todd should construct as one continuous sentence the two distinct summaries of the fifth and sixth chapters. As far as this testimony is concerned, St. Patrick's journey to Rome in search of heavenly truth forms a special epoch in his life: another distinct epoch being his sojourn with Germanus.

But what is the meaning of the latter formula in the summary of the sixth chapter? If we take it in its strict interpretation, it should imply that St. Patrick, having met with Germanus, "never more departed from him." No one, however, can suppose that this is more than a generic formula, expressive of our apostle's having placed himself under the spiritual guidance of Germanus, and adopted him as his master in the school of saints. St. Patrick may have journeyed to Lerins or Rome or elsewhere, and still have been as truly under the spiritual care of Germanus as if he were within the precincts of Auxerre. At all events, one interesting result is gained from the capitular summaries which we have quoted, that, forsooth, St. Patrick, *in search of sacred truth, directed*

* Ap Petrie, Tara, pag. 87.

his steps towards Rome; and that at another period of his life he chose for his guide and master one who was selected by pope Celestine to be special representative of the Apostolic See.

We shall, however, take one step further, and endeavour to reconstruct the last chapter of *Muirchu-Maccu-Mactheni*. It has often been remarked, that the life of St. Patrick which bears the name of Probus, is nothing more than an amended text of Mactheni. Many chapters have been published by Usher and Petrie.* Dr. Todd has given a further proof of this identity of the two lives in the very long translated extract from Mactheni, on the donation of Armagh made by the chieftain Dairé, to our apostle,† the original text of which had been already known from the essay of Reeves on the Churches of Armagh,‡ published in 1860. In fact it is now well known that when the summary of the chapter of Mactheni finds a corresponding subject in Probus, the narratives of the event in Mactheni and Probus are identical. Now as regard the seventh, eighth, and ninth chapters of Mactheni, with which the present text of the Book of Armagh begins, both narratives are completely identical; so do the titles of the fifth and sixth lost chapters find corresponding matter in the immediately preceding words of Probus. What, then, shall we conclude? Why we must conclude that the text of Probus still preserves to us these two chapters of Mactheni, which have mysteriously disappeared from the Book of Armagh, and that this portion of the lost work may thus, with all certainty, be reconstructed in the identical words of Probus:—

(5). "St. Patrick poured forth to the Lord the following prayer: Lord Jesus Christ, who hast guided my steps through Gaul and Italy to these islands, conduct me, I beseech Thee, to the seat of the Holy Roman Church, that thus receiving due authority to preach with confidence Thy truths, the people of Ireland may, through my ministry, be gathered to Thy fold.

"And not very long after the man of God, Patrick, proceeded as he had desired, from Ireland to Rome, the head of all churches, and there having asked for and received the apostolic blessing, he returned by the same road by which he had gone thither.

---

* Tara, page 53, 59, 84, etc. † Page 472-4. ‡ Page 45, seqq.

(6). "Having crossed, however, the British sea, and entered on his journey to Gaul, he came, according to his design, to Germanus, bishop of Auxerre, a most holy man, most revered for his faith and learning, (hominem sanctissimum ac probatissimum in fide ac doctrinâ) the illustrious head of all the Church of Gaul; and having remained with him in all submission for no little time in the practice of patience, obedience, charity, chastity, and perfect spotlessness in mind and soul, maintaining his virginity in the fear of the Lord, and persevering in goodness and simplicity of heart, during the whole time of his earthly pilgrimage."

Such were, undoubtedly, the fifth and sixth chapters of Mactheni, and such was a portion, at least, of the lost pages of the Book of Armagh. Surely they need no comment, that the reader may understand how St. Patrick affectionately revered the Apostolic See, and received from it the mission to evangelize our island.

We may now conclude our analysis of Dr. Todd's vain theory, as we hope to have made sufficiently manifest that Palladius was deacon of the Church of Rome; that St. Patrick's arrival in Ireland cannot be put back to the year 440; that in fine he received from pope Celestine his mission to preach the Gospel in Ireland.

Let us, however, before closing, for an instant suppose that the three contradictory assertions of Dr. Todd's theory are based on truth. It will result, that though there are many surprising incidents in the ancient lives of our apostle, the course adopted by their authors in regard to these three points would be the most surprising feature of all.

Though they were desirous, as Dr. Todd informs us, to consign to oblivion the acts of Palladius, they should have exalted him from being a mere deacon of Germanus to the high dignity of deacon of the Church of Rome.

Though they were most accurate in assigning the date of the mission of Palladius, as is confirmed by the record of Prosper and other continental writers, they should all have erred in registering the one all-important date of the arrival of our apostle in our island; and in the long array of monuments which mark the year of St. Patrick's mission, not even one should be found to disclose a ray of truth, and refer it to the close of Sixtus' pontificate, or to the twelfth year of king Leoghaire's reign.

In fine, if St. Patrick rested his preaching solely on a divine summons to evangelize our people, and rejected all ecclesiastical authorization derived from Rome. why is it that the ancient writers, all vieing with each other in extolling the special privileges of St. Patrick, and eulogizing his characteristic deeds, should have consigned to utter oblivion this the greatest of all his special privileges? and why would not some one of them, at least, have recorded that our apostle was not a missionary of the stamp of Palladius or Germanus, or other such who bore impressed on their preaching the seal of the pope of Rome, but that his mission was of a higher order, solely proceeding from the direct authority and inspiration of God?

We have seen, too, how often Dr. Todd appeals to the silence of records as a sufficient criterion for rejecting events: may not some student of history conclude, that in like manner the mysterious silence of all the ancient monuments of our Church, in regard to Dr. Todd's three principles, is an additional proof that such principles have no foundation in reality and historic truth?

ESSAY

ON

THE ORIGIN OF THE IRISH CHURCH,

And its Connexion with the Holy See.

PART THE THIRD.

SENTIMENTS OF THE EARLY IRISH CHURCH REGARDING ROME.

WE propose, in this third part, to inquire what were the sentiments entertained by our early fathers regarding the special prerogatives of St. Peter and the See of Rome. Did their hearts turn to Rome with filial reverence? did they acknowledge its divinely guaranteed authority? did they seek, in its decisions, for light, and guidance, and instruction, or rather, like the Protestants of now-a-days, did they delight in heaping obloquy on the successors of St. Peter? did they repudiate their claims of spiritual supremacy, and was insult to Rome a pass-word to pre-eminence and dignity in our sainted Church? To proceed with order in our inquiry—

We shall, in the first chapter, examine the few fragments that remain to us of our ancient writers;

We shall, in the second chapter, interrogate the canonical decrees which regulated the discipline of our Church;

And we shall also see, in the third chapter, that the deeds of our forefathers corresponded with their words, and displayed the fulness of affectionate devotion and filial piety for the vicars of Christ.

CHAPTER I.

EARLY IRISH WRITERS ON THE PREROGATIVES OF ROME.

Two Ancient Hymns of the Irish Church on St. Peter, published by Mone.— St. Cummian Fota's Hymn and Penitential.—St. Sechnall.—Dr. Todd refuted.—St. Mochla, of Louth.

WE are indebted to the eminent German antiquarian, Mone, for two very ancient hymns of the Irish Church, which he discovered amongst the papers of the old Irish monastery of Reichenau, and which he published, from Irish manuscripts of the 8th and 9th centuries, in his invaluable work entitled "Hymni Latini Medii Ævi."*

The first and most ancient poem is an alphabetical hymn on the apostle Peter, the initials of each strophe presenting successively the whole series of the letters of the alphabet. We now give it to the reader, as printed by Mone,† and we unite with it a literal translation, for which we are indebted to the kindness of the Rev. Mr. Potter, Professor of All-Hallows College, Dublin :—

1 "Audite fratres famâ
    Petri pastoris plurima
    Baptismatis libamina
    Fundit veluti flumina.
      Adsiut nobis sublimia
      Sancti Petri suffragia.

2 "Bis refulsit ut fulmina
    Sana sanctorum agmina

1 "List, Brothers, whilst our hymn of praise,
To Peter's name we humbly raise;
From whose blest hand the waters ran,
Which life restored to fallen man.
    May Peter's love our path attend,
    And guide us to our happy end.

2 "Bright as the lightning's glowing sheen,
He, twice, 'mid ranks of saints, was seen ;

* Friburg, 1855.

† Vol. iii. pag. 68.

Flentes duxit ex ordine	Whilst nations lost in fear and love,
Gentes divino carmine.	Hear chants divine from realms above.

3 " Celebravit egregia   3 "With fearless tongue he pleads the cause
    Evangelii præconia,   Of Christ's divine and holy laws;
    Factâ prostratâ legiâ   And all the baffled hosts of hell
    De Satana victoriâ.   His Master's glowing triumph tell.

4 " Dudum elegit dominus   4 "In years long past, in by-gone time,
    Petrum ut optimum oleum,   As highest prince, to post sublime
    Ut obitaret dominum   Was Peter chosen to succeed,
    Essetque pastor ovium.   And Christ's ne'er-failing flock to feed.

5 " Elaboravit ubique,   5 "Nor clime, nor space, might bound his zeal,
    Curæ datus historiæ,   And pages writ his deeds reveal;
    Fundamentum dominicæ   On him, the rock so strong, so sure,
    Ecclesiæ Catholicæ.   Christ's Church shall ever firm endure.

6 " Factâ crucis martyriâ   6 "Fixed to the cross, he closed his days,
    Fecit magna prodigia   And wonders dread proclaimed his praise :
    Sequutus per ætheria   To realms above, to die no more,
    Christiana vestigia.   He soar'd, as Christ had soar'd before.

7 " Gloriosum apostolum   7 "And, now, in deathless glory crowned,
    Deus ornavit gloria   The earth doth with his praise resound ;
    Romæ urbis quâ in   And thou, the first, sweet mother Rome,
    Vivit cum victoria.   His see, his battle-field, his home.

8 "Habundabat justitiâ,

   Plenus divinâ gratiâ

   Expandit retia sparsa

   Per mundi spatia.

9 "Judæorum malivolas

   Vitæ formavit animas

   Missusque capsit plurimas

   Evangelii per sagias.

10 "Kasta librorum legimus,

   Petri plenos virtutibus,
   Mœstas divinis fletibus,

   Pastoris summi nutibus.

11 "Luxit ut Phœbus sæcula,

   Christi secutus opera

   Binæ legis oracula

   (A line wanting).

12 "Mirum pastorem piissimum

   Flagitare non desino,

   Ne demergar cum pessima,
   Intercedas pro misero.

13 "Nunc dignare, apostole,

   Aperire cum clavibus

   Regnum quod olim quærimus
   Nos instantes præ foribus.

8 "Hence, in God's grace, in justice bright,
And led and guided by their light,
Through all the world, from end to end,
Did Peter's care his nets extend.

9 "E'en cruel Jews, from vice and strife,
Were led to walk the path of life;
And, soon, the Gospel's seine might tell
Of countless souls redeemed from hell.

10 "Historic lore proclaims his fame,
And all the glory of his name;
Whilst at his nod, from sinful eyes
Tears rise, as incense, to the skies.

11 "Like Phœbus shining o'er the world,
Christ's saving standard he unfurl'd,
And, walking in his Master's ways,
Proclaim'd God's laws through all his days.

12 "That I may be this pastor's care,
Shall surely be my constant prayer;
Oh, Peter, pray, lest I be tost
By angry waves, and, wretched, lost.

13 "Oh deign, apostle, pure and meek,
To guide us to the realm we seek;
We stand, we pray, we faint outside,
Oh, ope to us those portals wide.

14 "Opus delator sublimis,
　　Te rogamus assidue,
　　Recordare martyriæ
　　Et auxilium tribue.

14 "With never-failing lips we pray,
　　Thy aid and help, our hope, our stay;
　　And, mindful of thy own sad throes,
　　Grant help and comfort in our woes.

15 "Petri precamur veniam,
　　Si qua mala peregimus,
　　Resistentes dæmonibus
　　Nunc evalere legimus.

15 "Thy pardon, Peter, we implore,
　　With hearts resolved to sin no more;
　　With Satan's hosts fierce war to wage,
　　And, trusting, all our foes engage.

16 "Qui nostri spiritus ærias
　　Præsta salutis galeas,
　　Simon Johannis, audias
　　Nostras preces, ut audias.

16 "Then, Simon John, oh, list our cry,
　　And bear us succour from on high;
　　And on our brows bind helmets bright,
　　To keep us harmless in the fight.

17 "Regis regnum apostolorum,
　　Precor precamine,
　　Me morantem in limine
　　Mortis desolve valide.

17 "With humble cry, with humble prayer,
　　Apostles' Lord, I crave thy care;
　　That, trembling on death's awful shore,
　　Nor sin, nor hell, may claim me more.

18 "Salvat horis in munere,
　　Mundi ferebat famina,
　　Cui concessa numina,
　　Relaxare peccamina.

18 "As every hour the sinner's cry,
　　Doth rise in sadness to the sky;
　　His chains unbound—behold him free,
　　For God's right hand doth work with thee.

19 "Turbæ sanctorum magister,
　　Ovem errantem eruat,
　　Negligenter ne pereat,
　　Adjutorium tribuat.

19 "Oh, master of the sainted band,
　　O'er erring sinners keep thy hand;
　　And, lest our feet should sadly stray,
　　Oh, guide us in the narrow way.

20 " Uisitando cum trophæo,	20 "With faith's bright shield thy flock enshroud,
Fidei tectus clipeo,	And glad them with thy trophies proud ;
Cujus vires ut sapio	But mortal tongue may never tell
Fari omnino nequeo.	The saving strength we know so well.
21 " Xristi martyrum lucifer,	21 "Of martyrs bright the brightest name,
Legis lator altissimi,	God's people, all, thy praise proclaim ;
Cui dæmones pessimi	Whilst demons dread thy awful sway,
Obediebant impiissimi.	And trembling fiends thy power obey.
22 " Ymno dicto de laudibus	22 "As best we may, to Peter's praise
Petri, utcunque fecimus,	This humble song we humbly raise ;
Nostris virtutum opibus	May he our cry benign attend,
Propitiatur precibus.	And guide us to our happy end.
23 " Zona præcincti placidis	23 "With girded loins, with duty done,
Totis vivamus debitis,	With cheerful hearts, till all be won ;
Ut fruamur infinitis,	May we, when life's stern fight is o'er,
In angelorum editis "	Be crown'd with bliss for evermore. Amen."

We could not desire a fuller exposition of the prerogatives of St. Peter than is contained in this poem ; he is the apostle divinely chosen " to hold the place of Christ and feed his sacred fold ;" he is " the foundation of the Christian universal church" (*fundamentum Dominicæ Ecclesiæ Catholicæ*) ; he is " *the master of the choir of saints ;*" " the prince of the martyrs of Christ ;" the legislator of the Most High," and moreover, he is adorned " with the aureola of Rome, in which city he is destined to reign with a never-enduring triumph."

The second poem is equally explicit ; it styles the apostle the key-bearer of the heavenly kingdom, not for awhile only, but throughout all time; he is the pontiff of souls, the prince of apostles, the shepherd of all the fold of Christ. We now give it in full, with a literal translation:—

1. "Sanctus Petrus, apostolus,
   Quondam piscator optimus,
   Altum mare cum navibus,
   Temptabat remis, retibus.

2. "Qui de profundo gurgitum
   Magnam raptor fluctivagam
   Jactis nave reticulis
   Prædam captabat piscium.

3. "Christum vocantem sequitur
   Sponte relictis omnibus
   Dignus erat apostolus
   Factus piscator hominum.

4. "Sancto Petro pro merito
   Christus regni cœlestium
   Claves simul cum gratiâ
   Tradidit in perpetuum.

5. "Animarum pontificem,
   Apostolorum principem
   Petrum rogamus omnium
   Christi pastorem ovium.

1. "Great Peter, saint, apostle blest,
   In fisher's lowly garb once drest,
   With ship and oar did brave the deep,
   Whilst searching nets the billows sweep.

2. "Full oft where surges wildly play,
   Where, heedless, sport the finny prey;
   His fish he takes, in seine or weel
   Wide spread beneath his trusty keel.

3. "But, lo, he hears the Master's call,
   With joyful heart abandons all;
   And, office dread, unheard till then,
   Is fisher made of ransomed men.

4. "The keys which ope the portals blest,
   That lead the way to endless rest,
   To him Christ gives, with grace to tend
   And guide his flock safe to the end.

5. "Great Pontiff of Christ's chosen band,
   Apostles round thee humbly stand!
   O'er Christ's true flock strict watch still keep,
   Still guard His lambs, still guard His sheep.

6. "Ne mens gravata crimine
    Nostra torpescat pectore
    Reddamus Christo gloriæ
    Cantemus in perpetuum.
                  Amen.
	6. "Ne'er may our souls, with crime opprest,
	    Find rest or peace within our breast;
	    May we to Christ, glad songs of praise,
	    In realms of bliss, for ever raise. Amen.

St. Cummian Fota (*i. e.* the tall) was born about the year 590, and died in 661. He was bishop of Clonfert; and being remarkable for his skill in sacred literature, was styled by his contemporaries the *Gregory the Great* of our Irish Church. In the martyrology of Donegal, he is called (12th of November) "a vessel of learning—a learned preacher of the word of God." The scholiast on the Feliré of Ængus, states, that when he and other saints prayed to God for various graces, the gift of wisdom fell to the share of Cummian. So also in the old historical poems, cited by the Four Masters, when registering his death in 661, one verse declares:

> "If any one went across the sea,
> To sit in the chair of Gregory the Great.
> If from Ireland no one was fit for it,
> If we except Cummian Fota."*

A short hymn on the Apostles, written by this great ornament of our early Church, has fortunately been preserved to us; and though there is only one strophe commemorating each apostle, still, that which refers to St. Peter, sufficiently indicates his pre-eminence and special prerogatives. It is as follows:—

> " Celebra, Juda, festa Christi gaudia
> Apostolorum exultans memoria,
> Claviculari Petri, primi pastoris,
> Piscium, rete evangelii, captoris."†

---

* See Liber Hymnorum, I. A. S., pag. 85, seqq.
† Liber Hymnorum, I. A. S., pag. 73. The ancient gloss adds, that *Juda* indicates *the Church;* and that the word *Claviculari* is put for *claviculari*, which was a characteristic name for St. Peter in the early Church. Thus, St. Clement is styled by St. Althelm, " cœlestis claviculari primus successor."--De Laud. Virginit. §. 25.

"Rejoice, O New Jerusalem! solemnize the gladsome festivals of Christ, and exult in the commemoration of the apostles—of Peter the key-bearer—the first pastor—the mystic fisherman, who, with the Gospel-net, draws in the spiritual fish of Christ."

About two hundred years ago was first published, in the Collectanea Sacra of Fleming, from an ancient manuscript of Bobbio, the famous "Penitentiale S. Cummiani." This penitential code was the groundwork of many similar writings in the eighth, ninth, and tenth centuries. As there were many saints of the name of Cummian in our Irish Church, and as the manuscript from which Fleming published his text, added no special epithet to designate the author, many modern writers have referred it to St. Cummian Albus, who was abbot of Hy in the beginning of the sixth century; or again, to St. Cummian, who made a pilgrimage to Italy, and died at Bobbio during the reign of king Luitprand, about the year 720. A Vatican manuscript collection of canons of the beginning of the tenth century, fortunately removes all this uncertainty, for it expressly cites this Penitential as the work of St. Cummian the Tall.*

Now, in this Penitential, St. Cummian prescribes a fast of forty days for him who, through ignorance, should permit a heretic to celebrate Mass in a Catholic Church; this penance was to be extended to a whole year, if such permission was granted to any one whose heresy was publicly known:—

"But (adds the Penitential), should he thus permit any individual to celebrate through contempt for the Catholic Church, and for the customs of Rome, he himself shall be cast off as a heretic, unless he do penance; and his penance shall last for ten years."†

Thus, then, according to St. Cummian, a contemptuous bearing towards Rome, so far from being the forerunner of high ecclesiastical preferment, should be punished with the severest penalties, and be regarded as an indubious sign of irreligion and heresy.

---

* See some further remarks on this penitential in appendix No. 2.
† Fleming, Collectan. Sac.; Bibl. PP. Lugdunen. xii. 47; Wasserschleben, Die Bussordnungen der abendle. Kirch,—Halle, 1851, pag. 460.

St. Sechnall, generally called by his Latin name, Secundinus, was a disciple and relative of our apostle. Being advanced to the episcopal dignity, he assisted St. Patrick in the administration of the see of Armagh till his death, which is assigned by the Four Masters to the year 448. Ængus, in his Festology (27th of November) styles him :—

> "A stream of wisdom with nobility,
> Sechnall, the crown of our chief."

and another writer of the tenth century, whose quatrain is preserved in the Leabhar Breac, commemorates him as

> "Sechnall son of Ua Baird, the gifted,
> The most gifted of living men,
> Of the race of the pure, fierce, white-coloured
> Longobards of Letha."

His name is found in all our Irish martyrologies, and in that of Christ Church, published by the I. A. S. in 1844, he is thus mentioned :—

"Sancti Secundi episcopi et confessoris, qui Longobardorum nobili genere ortus, beatum Patricium ad Hiberniam secutus post eum primus episcopatum tenuit; ibique recto morum tramite exempla illius perfecte complens, quievit in pace."*

Such is the writer whom Usher† reckons as a clear assertor of the Protestant tenets regarding St. Peter and the see of Rome. His only work now preserved is an alphabetical hymn in praise of our apostle, and the Protestant primate appeals to one special passage of this hymn, which he thus translates :—

"Patrick is constant in the fear of God and immoveable in the faith; upon whom the Church is built as upon St. Peter, whose apostleship also he has obtained from God, and the gates of hell shall not prevail against him."

Dr. Todd, in his Memoir of St. Patrick, though cautious not

---

* Publications of Irish Arch. Soc. 1844, pag. 183.
† Religion of the Ancient Irish Church, p. 73.

to refer to the Protestantism of St. Sechnall, translates the passage in a somewhat similar manner:—St. Patrick, he says, is described as "constant in the fear of God, immoveable in faith, one upon whom, as a second Peter, the church is built, who obtained from God the apostleship of the Church, to the injury of which Church the gates of hell prevail not."*

Now even supposing the accuracy of this translation of the text of St. Secundinus, we would be far from admitting the justness of Usher's claim to number him among the witnesses of the Protestant teaching of our early Church. We should merely conclude from the passage thus translated, that St. Patrick was chosen to hold that post of honour and jurisdiction, and special privilege in the Irish Church, which belonged to St. Peter in regard to the universal Church.

We are indebted to the Irish Archæological Society for an elegant and accurate edition of the original text of this hymn of St. Sechnall.† Nothing, indeed, can be conceived more Catholic than the spirit which pervades the whole composition. St. Patrick is described as *keeping the blessed commands of Christ in all things: his good works shine illustrious before men, who, following his holy and wonderful example, thus magnify as their Lord the Father who is in heaven. He was sent by God to fish with the nets of faith, and thus draw the believers from the world unto grace; the chosen Gospel talents of Christ were dispensed by him with usury amongst the Irish people; he preached by works as well as by words, and stimulated to holiness by his example; he was humble in spirit and in body, and in his flesh bore the stigmata of Christ, in whose cross alone he gloried, being sustained by its saving power; he feeds the faithful with the heavenly banquet lest they should faint in the way of the commandments of Christ; his flesh he maintains in chastity through love of the Lord* (ob amorem Domini) *preparing it to be the temple of the Holy Ghost, and offering it as an agreeable sacrifice to God: he prays daily for the sins of his people, and offers in their behalf the*

---

* Page 312.
† Publications of I. A. S., 1855; Liber Hymnorum, p. 12, seqq.

sacrifice worthy of God; he is a faithful witness to the Lord by his Catholic teaching (in lege Catholica); *he chants the hymns, the Apocalypse, the Psalms, and expounds them for the instruction of the people.*

Surely, there is nothing in all this to justify a *prima facie* Protestant interpretation of our text; and equally un-Protestant is the beautiful versicle, which in the old manuscripts terminates the hymn, and which seems to have formed part of some ancient office of our saint:—

"Patricii laudes semper dicamus
Ut nos cum illo defendat Deus.

Hibernenses omnes clamant ad te pueri
Veni Sancte Patrici salvos nos facere."

"Let us unceasingly extol our apostle Patrick, that through him God may defend us.

"All the Irish youth cries out to thee: oh! come St. Patrick, hasten to protect us."

But to return to the passage to which Usher appeals, it forms the third strophe in the hymn, and runs thus in the original text:

"Constans in Dei timore et fide immobilis
Super quem edificatur, ut Petrus, ecclesia:
Cujusque apostolatum a Deo sortitus est
In cujus porta adversus inferni non prævalent."*

The word *porta* has been adopted from the Roman MS. of the Liber Hymnorum: the reading of the text, in the Dublin MS., is *portae*, which seems to have crept in, from the Gospel words of which this passage is a paraphrase, the literal translation of which must be as follows:—

"He is constant in the service of God, and immoveable in the faith as Peter, upon whom the Church is built, and whose apostolate he received from God, against whose bulwark the assaults of hell cannot prevail."

The translation which was given by Usher and Todd *upon whom* (Patrick) *as upon Peter*, or again, *upon whom as a second Peter*, is contrary to the grammatical construction, and would require the accusative form, *ut Petrum*, which was the reading, indeed, adopted by Usher, but is now no longer tenable, since the

* Lib. Hym., p. 12.

Leabhar Breac, and the Dublin MS. of the Book of Hymns, expressly read *ut Petrus;* and we may confirm their reading by the authority of the Roman MS., which retains precisely the same formula. Moreover, the phrase "*and* whose apostolate," etc., remains wholly devoid of sense in their interpretation. The ancient gloss on the text preserved in the Leabhar Breac expressly, too, excludes their translation; for it adds, in the beginning of the second line, to illustrate the subject to which reference is made:

"Super quem, id est, Petrum;"

and lest any one might, perhaps, suppose that it was referring to some other Peter, and not to the Prince of the Apostles, the same gloss adds:

"Petrus, ut dicitur: Tu es Petrus et super hanc petram edificabo ecclesiam meam."*

Thus, then, the relative does not refer, as Dr. Todd and Usher affirm, to St. Patrick, but to the apostle Peter; and hence, the translation must necessarily be as we laid down—" he is immoveable in the faith as Peter, upon whom the Church is built."

So far, therefore, from there being anything in the text of St. Secundinus to assail or depreciate the prerogatives of St. Peter, it serves to illustrate them more and more; as first, the firmness of St. Patrick's faith is eulogized by comparison with the immoveable solidity of the apostle Peter; second, the characteristic prerogative of this apostle is asserted, that forsooth " upon him Christ built his Church;" third, it is made a special eulogy of St. Patrick that he became partaker of St. Peter's apostolate; and fourth, hence is derived his spiritual solidity; for the powers of hell must ever rage in vain around the sacred citadel of Peter.†

St. Mochta of Louth, whose name was anciently written

---

* Lib. Hym. I.A.S., p. 12.

† To one unacquainted with the singular custom of transposing words which was followed by the Irish poets, it may seem strange to see the phrase, *ut Petrus*, placed so far down in the sentence. As a similar instance, we may quote the hymn to St. Martin, *Lib. Hym. Roman MS.* fol. xi., in which we read:

"Martine te deprecor pro me rogaris patrem,
Christum ac Spiritum Sanctum *habentem Mariam matrem.*"

Macteus,* was a disciple of St. Patrick, and his death is assigned to the year 534, by Tighernach, the Annals of the Four Masters, and the Annals of Ulster. His name is commemorated in our martyrologies on the 24th of March, and the 19th of August. Ængus adds to his name the epithets of faithful and devout—the great good leader; and Marianus O'Gorman styles him "the lamp of Louth—the father of an illustrious family." The gloss on Ængus adds, that he was bishop of Louth, and cites the following curious poem :—

> "Poverty abode not
> With the family of Mochta in his fort of Louth;
> Three hundred bishops and one hundred priests were there with him.
> Eighty psalm-singing noble youths
> Were his household : royal is the enumeration :
> Without ploughing—without reaping—without drying of corn,
> They laboured not, save at learning only."

Amongst our many ancient saints, he was remarkable for his longevity and abstinence, both which traits are thus alluded to by St. Cuimin of Connor, in his poem on the characteristic virtues of the Irish saints :—

> "Mochta of Lugh-magh (Louth), loved
> By law and by rule,
> That no dainty food should enter his body
> For the space of one hundred years."†

The life of this saint records that, guided by an angelic admonition, he proceeded to Rome, and there applied himself to the study of sacred literature; and it further commemorates the

---

* The Irish *a* being pronounced like the diphthong *au* or *o*, was one of the chief causes of the discrepancy in registering the name of this saint. In some manuscripts of Adamnan, he is styled *Mauctaneus*, *Maveteus*, and *Maucteus*. The Vita S. Dagei calls him *Moccheus*, and subsequently *Mochteus*. Jocelyn, in his life of St. Patrick, gives his name as *Moccheus*; and with continental writers, he is commonly known by the name *Macceus*. Tighernach thus records his death, in 534: "Dormitatio Moctai discipuli Patricii, xvi. kalend. Septembr. Sic ipse scripsit in epistola sua; *Mocteus peccator presbiter Sancti Patricii discipulus in Domino salutem.*" This same entry is given in the Annals of Ulster; but he is said to have signed his own name *Macutenus*.—See Reeves' Adamnan, page 6, seqq.; Colgan Acta SS. page 729, seqq.; Martyr. of Christ Church, I. A. S., 1844, page lxix.; Todd, St Patrick, page 39, seqq.; Ware, de Script. Hib. lib. ii. cap. 1.

† Martyrology of Tallaght, append. page 161.

offering of a *ceraculum*, or writing-tablet, which he made to the then ruling pontiff. When he visited Rome, the memory of the heretic Celestius was still familiar to the faithful of that city, and the well-known words of St. Jerome were fresh in their ears : " Satan, though silent himself, barks through a huge and corpulent mountain dog, who can do more damage with his claws, than even with his teeth ; for he is by descent of the Scotic nation, which is adjoining Britain, and like another Cerberus, according to the fables of the poets, must be struck down with a spiritual club, that thus he may be silent for ever with his master Pluto."* Some seem to have feared that Mochta might, perhaps, be infected with a similar contagion, and for this reason he was compelled to vindicate the sincerity of his faith, by presenting, about the year 460, to the great St. Leo, a profession of his belief, of which a copy, written about the year 700, was discovered by Muratori amongst the precious manuscripts of the once famous Irish monastery of Bobbio, and was published in his Anecdota Ambrosiana.†

St. Mochta, in this formula of faith, dwells almost exclusively on the doctrine of the blessed Trinity and on the Apostles' Creed ; indeed it presents a striking similarity with the creed recited by St. Patrick in his Confession, whilst scarcely a hint is given regarding any of those heresies which disturbed the Churches of Britain and the continent. Of his own Church, he says : " we are as yet only in the way to truth" *(nos adhuc in fenestra, id est, in via lucis);* and of himself he adds : " why do people interrogate me whence I come ? I am a pilgrim" (ut quid quaeritur patria mea? Peregrinus ego sum); and subsequently he thus briefly but beautifully tells us what was his opinion as to the special prerogative of Rome :

"If, for the fault of one individual, the inhabitants of the whole country are to be deemed accursed, let that most blessed disciple, too, be condemned, I mean Rome itself, from which hitherto not only one but two, or three, or even more heresies have gone forth ; and, nevertheless, none of them could get hold of, or contaminate the Chair of Peter, that is to say the see of faith."‡

* Comment. in Jerem. lib. iii. præfat. † Vol. ii. p. 1, seqq.
‡ "Si pro culpa unius, totius provinciæ anathematizanda generatio est, damnetur et illa beatissima discipula, hoc est, Roma, de qua non una sed

CHAPTER I.
(CONTINUED.)

EARLY IRISH WRITERS ON THE PREROGATIVES OF ROME.

Missal of St. Columbanus.—His letters to pope Boniface —Answer to the objections drawn from them by dean Murray of Ardagh.—St. Columbanus's letter to St. Gregory.

THERE is another monument which serves to illustrate more and more our present subject of inquiry, and for which we are also indebted to the archives of Bobbio. It is commonly known as the Missal of St. Columbanus, and was brought from Bobbio to the Ambrosian Library in Milan, by cardinal Frederick Borromeo. We are indebted for its publication to the learned Mabillon, who describes the manuscript as being in his day more than a thousand years old. Everything connected with it bespeaks its Irish origin; its material writing is that of the ancient Scotic school; its special forms of Latinity are those peculiar to the Irish writers; its multiplicity of prayers was a characteristic feature of the Irish liturgy, whilst its Penitential Canons strikingly and unmistakeably proclaim its origin in our island. In a word, the whole Missal attests its connexion with St. Columbanus, and probably it was used by him in his monasteries of Luxieu and Bobbio, to both of which, as is recorded by a writer of the seventh century, he bequeathed "*the Irish Liturgy.*"*

Now this ancient Irish Missal plainly attests the unbounded reverence entertained by the Church of our fathers for St. Peter and his successors. Amongst its Masses there is one specially assigned for the feast of the "Cathedra Sancti Petri," and in it

duæ vel tres aut eo amplius hæreses pullularunt et tamen nulla earum Cathedram Petri, hoc est, sed em fidei tenere potuit aut movere."—(Loc. cit. pag. 12). This *profession of faith* of St. Mochta being extremely rare, we will present it in full to the reader, with a translation, in the appendix No. 3.

* For further particulars regarding this important monument of our early Church, see the appendix No. 4.

that apostle is said to have received *omne jus gentium Judæorumque;* that is, "all authority over both Jews and gentiles," and his are declared to be* "*the keys of heaven, the dignity of the pontifical chair ; so great a power, that what he binds none can loosen, and what he loosens shall be loosed also in heaven; a throne of exalted dignity, where he will sit in judgment on all the nations of the earth.*" The first Collect of the same Mass thus begins :—†

"Oh God! who on this day didst give to St. Peter, after thyself, the headship of the whole Church, we humbly pray Thee, that as Thou didst constitute him pastor for the safety of the flock, and that Thy sheep might be preserved from error, so now Thou mayest save us through his intercession."

Similar expressions are elsewhere repeated in this ancient Missal. Thus, in the Mass for Sundays (Missa Dominicalis), it is said that the divine Redeemer, stretching forth His hand to St. Peter when sinking in the waves, was an emblem of how "the wavering faith of that apostle was consolidated, and he himself confirmed as Head of the Church."‡ And again on the feast-day of the apostles Peter and Paul (in Natali Petri et Pauli) it is declared that, "from the whole body of the apostles, the Redeemer chose St. Peter as the foundation of the Church, and confirmed his faith, to the great joy of all the disciples."§

The monastery of Bangor, eloquently described by St. Bernard as "multa millia monachorum generans, multorum monasteriorum caput," was the school of sanctity from which Columbanus went forth, towards the close of the sixth century, to renew the well-nigh spent civilization of Gaul, and Germany, and Italy. The memory of few of our saints has been better preserved on the con-

---

* Museum Italicum seu collectio veterum scriptorum ex Bibliothecis Italicis eruta a D. Johanne Mabillon et D. Michaele Germain ; Paris, 1724, vol. i. page 297-8.

† "Deus qui hodiernâ die beatum Petrum post te dedisti caput ecclesiæ . . . te supplices rogamus, ut qui dedisti pastorem ne quid de ovibus perderes ut grex effugiat errores ; ejus intercessione quem præfecisti salvifices."—Ibid. page 297.

‡ Pag. 381.

§ Ex quibus beatum Petrum in fundamentum ecclesiæ conlocasti cujus fidem omnium discipulorum tuorum gaudio conlocasti, etc."—Ib. 343.

tinent than that of Columbanus, and of none do so many written memorials still remain. It is owing to this circumstance that we are able to enter more fully into an examination of his teaching concerning the prerogatives of the Holy See, than we have done in regard to the other ancient writers of our Church. Indeed his letter to pope Boniface is so replete with expressions of reverential devotedness to Rome, that it is difficult to refrain from quoting the whole of that noble document. Our saint had just settled in North Italy, and on every side was encompassed by those who warmly defended the well-known schism of " the three chapters." King Agilulf, at whose request St. Columbanus wrote this letter to the pontiff, was himself the patron of the schismatics, and hence the holy man, fearing lest he might, perhaps, be betrayed into some error by the influence of those that surrounded him, at the very outset of his letter declares that whatever " he shall say useful or orthodox, was to be reputed to the pontiff's praise," but if any word, perchance, should bear the impress of intemperate zeal, it was to be referred " not to any insubordination, but to his own individual lack of wisdom and discretion."*

The letter is addressed "*to the most beautiful Head of all the Churches of the whole of Europe; to the beloved Pope; the exalted prelate; the most reverend overseer; the pastor of pastors,*" etc. Subsequently the popes are styled "*the masters, the steersmen, the mystic pilots of the ship spiritual, that is, the Church;*" whilst of his countrymen he says: " We are the scholars of St. Peter and Paul, and of all disciples subscribing by the Holy Ghost to the divine canon; all are Irish, inhabitants of the remotest part of the whole world, receiving nothing save what is the evangelic and apostolic doctrine. None of us has been a heretic, none a Jew, none a schismatic; but the faith just as it was at first delivered by you, the successors of the holy apostles, is held unshaken." And, at the close of his letter, he adds: " *We are, as I said before,*

---

* This letter, with the other writings of St. Columbanus, were collected by the Franciscan Fleming, and published by Sirinus, in Collectanea Sacra,—Louvain, 1667; it is also found in the Biblioth. Patt. of Gallandi, tom. xii. pag. 346, seqq.

bound to the Church of St. Peter. For although Rome is great and illustrious, yet it is only through this chair that she is great and renowned amongst us."

Surely these phrases should suffice to show, 1st, the close union that existed between Ireland and Rome in the sixth century; 2nd, The pre-eminence and special dignity of the see of Peter; and 3rd, The necessity of communion with the bishops of Rome, since none others can belong to the mystic ship of Christ, save those who are steered by the pilot Peter.

Nevertheless, it is precisely to this letter of St. Columbanus that some modern assailants of the Catholic tenets of our fathers appeal, in order to justify their attacks. Their various arguments are well condensed by the late Protestant dean of Ardagh, in his History of Ireland and her Church,* and we wish to examine them in detail, that thus the reader may more fully enter into the spirit of St. Columbanus, who was one of the greatest ornaments of our island in the sixth century, and see, at the same time, the flimsy reasonings, to which our adversaries are obliged to have recourse, to obscure in some way the bright lustre of the Catholic teaching of our sainted Church.

1. In the first place, then, they appeal to the general language of the letter, which they say is " too strong to allow us to suppose that the Irish monk who used it, considered pope Boniface, whom he was addressing, to be the head of the Church."

To this we reply, that the language of St. Columbanus is often strong indeed; the whole letter is written with frankness and liberty, and with all that energetic earnestness which we might expect from one who had grown old, not only in the practice of virtue, but also in the apostolate of Italy and Gaul. It is the saint himself, however, that reminds the pontiff that he writes "not as a stranger, but as *a friend, a disciple, a servant,*" and he adds, as if anticipating the difficulty which dean Murray would one day seek to deduce from the freedom of his words: " therefore, freely will I speak, for I address our spiritual masters, the steersmen and

---

* Pag. 79, seqq.

pilots of the mystic ship."—*Ut amicus ut discipulus, ut pedissequus vester not ut alienus loquar; ideo libere loquar nostris ut pote magistris ac spiritualis navis gubernatoribus ac mysticis proretis.*"*

2. The next difficulty they find is in the doctrine of Columbanus, by which he asserts that " it was possible for the see of Rome to forfeit apostolic honour by not preserving the apostolic faith."†

The original text of St. Columbanus to which this reasoning refers, is as follows:—" *Ut ergo honore Apostolico non careas, conserva fidem Apostolicam, confirma testimonio,*" etc. Thus, then, the arguments of our adversaries is a wilful corruption of the testimony of Columbanus. The successor of St. Peter might, perchance, be slow in stigmatizing the assailants of truth, and in cutting off from the unity of the Church the enemies that waged war against her: in the opinion of Columbanus, he would, for such negligence, merit reproach, not praise; but surely these demerits could not affect the dignity and preeminence of his see?

Our adversaries should have taken one step beyond the threshold of their inquiry: they should have asked, what did St. Columbanus mean when he summoned the pontiff *to preserve the Apostolic faith?* Did he look upon pope Boniface as a simple bishop, whom he exhorts not to be dilatory in defending the cause of truth? Oh! no; but he addresses him as the common father and pastor of the whole universe: " the Catholics of the whole world," he says, "*the sheep are affrighted by the approach of wolves; wherefore use, O Pope, the whistlings and the well-known voice of the true shepherd, and stand betwixt the sheep and the wolves, so that casting away their fear, the sheep may in everything find thee to be the first pastor.*" Again, he thus summons the holy pontiff:—" *Set, in a manner, higher than all mortals, and exalted near unto the celestial beings, lift up thy voice as a trumpet, that thou mayest show their wicked doings to the people of thy Lord, entrusted to thee by Him.*" Nor is even this sufficient: " I strive (he adds) to stir up thee as the prince of the leaders; for unto thee belongeth the peril of the whole of the Lord's army:" and then he again

---

* Biblioth. PP. xxii. 851. † Dean Murray, page 79

addresses him: "thou hast the power of setting all things in order,—of beginning the war,—of arousing the leaders,—of commanding arms to be taken up,—of drawing forth the ranks into battle array," etc. .... "fearing do I moan unto thee alone, who from among the princes, art the only hope, having authority through the privileges of the apostle Peter."

Truly, nothing can be more unprotestant than all this. St. Columbanus reminds the pope, that he is bound to be at his post; and he declares that that post is the office of first pastor who holds the care of the fold of Christ, the guardianship of the people of God. Surely few writers have more clearly than this asserted the privileges of St. Peter's see, and reading these passages, the mind recognizes instinctively the same spirit that dictated the words of the alarmed apostles, when the storm raged around them, and they cried out to the Redeemer, "Domine, non est tibi curæ quod perimus." It is with such sentiments, and such sentiments alone, that St. Columbanus summons the Roman pontiff to watch and preserve the flock of Christ from impending danger.

3. St. Columbanus, however, according to our adversaries, asserts "that *the sword of St. Peter* signifies, not temporal power or spiritual jurisdiction, but *a true confession of the faith in a synod.*" But how different are the original words of our great saint: "lest the old robber," he says, "bind men with this long cord of error, let the cause of schism, I pray, be immediately cut off by thee, with the sword of St. Peter, that is, by a true confession of the faith in a synod, and by the rejection and anathematizing of every heretic.* From this passage it results: 1. That the Roman pontiff wields "the sword of St. Peter." 2. That it belongs to him to cut off schism from the Church with that spiritual sword. 3. That the opportune means for cutting off the schism of which St. Columbanus speaks, was to synodically proclaim the faith of Peter, and then anathematize all who would not receive that faith. For which

---

* Ne igitur hoc fune erroris longissimo liget latro antiquus homines, causa schismatis incidatur, quæso, confestim a te, cultello quodammodo sancti Petri, id est verâ in synodo fidei confessione et hæreticorum omnium abominatione ac anathematizatione," etc.—Biblioth. Patt loc. cit.

reason he had already lamented that the Pope, who was endowed with full authority, (*ut pote qui potestatem legitimam habuistis*) had not, on the first appearance of the schism, solemnly proclaimed his faith, *and then condemned and excommunicated whosoever should even dare to slander the presiding see of the orthodox faith*" (qui vel infamare auderet fidei orthodoxæ sedem principalem).

These words of our great Irish saint are such as merit the attentive consideration of the learned Protestant dean and his associates; and were St. Columbanus writing at the present day, he would still cry out: Beware all you who heap calumny on the see of Rome!—repent, oh, you, who, alas! have been cut off by the sword of St. Peter from the sacred membership of the mystic body of Jesus Christ!

4. But, at all events, thus continues the good dean Murray, St. Columbanus explicitly lays down, " that the Chair of Peter is capable of being defiled by doctrinal error, and that it is possible for the Catholic faith not to be held in the Apostolic See."

To this we shall very briefly reply: There is no such explicit statement made by St. Columbanus; and neither can any such implicit teaching be found in his whole epistle. He speaks, indeed, of the mist of suspicion having gathered around the see of Peter, and of the popes being ranked among the patrons of heretics; but he takes good care to let the Holy Father and the readers of his letter know that such were not his own sentiments, but merely the sentiments of the schismatics, who, like many now-a-days, were maligners of Rome, and against whom St. Columbanus summons pope Boniface to unsheath his spiritual sword. Hence, in one place he says, that he had written this letter in order to arouse the pontiff " against those men who blaspheme such as are thine, and clamour against them as the receivers of heretics."

Subsequently he adds :—

" See that the mist of suspicion be drawn aside from the Chair of St. Peter ; for the reception of heretics is, as I hear, imputed to you : but, God forbid that I should believe it: it never has occurred, and never will occur till the end of time." (Quod absit credi verum fuisse, esse vel fore.)

Even all this did not suffice for St. Columbanus; and before concluding his letter, he again summons the pope to use courageously the spiritual sword,—

"That my glorying for you may not be in vain, and that your assailants may be confounded and not we ; for, as befits disciples in regard to their master, I declared in your name that the Roman Church admits to its communion none who impugns the Catholic faith."

Thus, then, the assailants of Rome in former times, and those who seek to obscure the glory of St. Columbanus in our own days, only serve to bring out in bolder relief the teaching of our early Church regarding Rome, and to present that great saint to us as an illustrious champion of the prerogatives of the Holy See. It would be easy to multiply other passages from his writings, in which he repeats the same sentiments of devotedness and affection for Rome. His soul glowed with the sacred fire of faith, and his great desire was to visit in person the Vicar of Christ, and drink in spiritual delights at the living source of truth:

"These questions," he thus writes in a letter to the great St. Gregory, would I have put to thee in person, were it not that my weak health and a solicitude for my pilgrim-companions kept me fast at home, although I was anxious to go to thee, that I might drink of that spiritual vein of the living water of knowledge flowing down from heaven, and springing up unto life eternal. And if the body would follow the mind, Rome should once again put up with a slight upon herself, just as we read in the narrative of the learned Jerome, how certain men, many years ago, went to Rome from the farthest limits of the Heuline shore, and, wonderful to relate, searched in Rome for something besides Rome itself. Just so would it be with me : I should eagerly seek out thee, not minding Rome, save in that reverence which is due to the ashes of the saints."*

* In Bib. Parum. Galland. xii. 346.

CHAPTER I.
(CONTINUED.)

EARLY IRISH WRITERS ON THE PREROGATIVES OF ROME.

Claudius.—Usher refuted.—Ancient Irish hymn.—St. Cummian.—Conference of Whitby and St. Colman.—Curry's MSS. in Catholic University.—Lives of St. Patrick, St. Furseus, Gillibert.

USHER, when inquiring into the doctrine of the ancient Irish Church, devotes his seventh chapter to "the great question which relates to the Head and the Foundation of the Church." On this important subject, however, he could only discover two Irish writers,* whose detached sentences seemed to insinuate something not unlike the Protestant tenets: one of these was St. Sechnall, whose testimony we examined in the preceding article: the other is Claudius, whose words we shall now cite; and who, as we shall prove, so far from attesting the Protestant feeling of our Irish Church in regard to Rome, repudiates in express terms every item of Protestant teaching, and, in perfect harmony with the other writers of our early centuries, asserts the privileges and prerogatives of the Vicar of Christ.

In the beginning of the ninth century, there were two distinguished writers in France, both known by the name *Claudius*. One was a Spaniard by birth, who, being advanced to the see of Turin, in Italy, fell into many errors. The other was an Irishman, better known as Claudius Clemens, who was appointed to the see of Auxerre, and was famed especially for his Gospel commentaries. The similarity of name has been a cause of great confusion regarding these writers—the more so, as Claudius of Turin was also

* Usher cites also some extracts from the Irish commentator, Sedulius; but as they merely commemorate the privileges of St. Paul, and have no bearing on the question now before us, I pass them over in silence. They convey beautiful Catholic sentiments, and express in the very words still used by Catholic writers, the singular privileges and dignity of the Apostle of Nations.

known to have written a commentary on many parts of the sacred Scripture.

As regards the commentary on the Gospels which bears the name of Claudius, and of which one copy was preserved in the university library of Cambridge, whilst two similar copies are found in Rome, there seems no doubt that its authorship must be referred to the Irish Claudius. In the first place, the style of its preface is quite different from that of the preface to the commentary on the Epistles of St. Paul, which was certainly the work of Claudius of Turin.* And secondly, in the Cambridge manuscript, the commentary on the Gospels, as Usher informs us, bears the indubious title, *Claudii Scoti commentarius*.†

For these reasons we, without hesitation, subscribe to the opinion of Usher, Harris, Ware, Colgan, and David Rothe—that the present commentary, of which we speak, was written by the Irish Claudius. Whether the commentary on the Epistles of St. Paul, which has been more than once reprinted, is to be attributed to our Claudius, or to the bishop of Turin, is a matter of uncertainty. A preface to a commentary on these epistles, published by Card. Maji (loc. cit.), is certainly the work of the Turin prelate; for his see is expressly described in that introduction as situated in the north-west of Italy, and as suffering from the Saracen invasions. Until, however, the full commentary connected with that introduction be published, we must remain in doubt as to whether the hitherto published commentaries are to be referred to him. The style of the commentaries themselves affords us no clue as to their author: for the commentary, as was usual in the ninth century, is nothing more than a series of testimonies of the ancient Fathers linked together, so as to form a continuous whole. The preface to the commentary on the Gospels, which is preserved in the Vallicellian manuscript, is the only criterion as to style which the ·published commentaries present to us. The style of Claudius of Turin, as is seen in the preface to the epistles, is

---

* See ap. Card. Maj., Scriptt. Vett. Vaticana Collect. 1838, vii. part 1, p. 274.
† Ap. Usher, Syllog. p. 37.

turgid and bombastic to an excessive degree; the style of the preface to the Gospel commentary is, on the contrary, plain, simple, and unaffected.

Usher deems the judgment of Claudius to be of great importance, as illustrating the Protestant teaching in regard to the see of St. Peter; and he devotes three pages of his work to extracts from Claudius's commentaries, in which, first, it is asserted that the foundation of the Church is Christ; second, St. Paul is made sharer in the apostolate and primacy of Peter; third, to all bishops are referred the words addressed by our Lord to Peter. We shall make a few remarks on each of these heads, in order to illustrate the Catholic teaching of Claudius regarding the prerogatives of Rome.

1. The first statement of Claudius is thus proposed by Usher: "The famous passage of Scripture* where the Romanists lay the main foundation of the papacy, Claudius expounds in this manner: *Upon this rock will I build my church; that is to say, upon the Lord and Saviour who granted to his faithful friend, lover, and confessor the participation of his own name, that from Petra* (the rock), *he should be called Peter.*"

We shall not readily pardon the worthy Protestant primate for asserting that these words of Claudius are in opposition with the the teaching and doctrine of the Catholic Church; for Catholics agree with Protestants in laying down, that Christ is the true rock on which the Church of God is built; Catholics, however, dissent from Protestants in this, that we assert that St. Peter was divinely made sharer and participator in our blessed Redeemer's privilege; and this precisely is what Claudius here asserts, when he declares that our Saviour granted to Peter "the participation of his own name."

There is another passage in Claudius's commentary† which is carefully passed over in silence by Usher, but which serves to render still clearer the words under consideration. He is commenting on the list of the Apostles, and he says:

---

* Matthew, xvi. 18. † Codex Vatic. p. 42 a.

"Primus Simon qui dicitur Petrus: idem ergo Græce sive Latine Petrus quod Syriace Cephas, et in utraque lingua nomen a petra derivatum est, haud dubium quin illa de qua 'Paulus dicit: Petra autem erat Christus.' Nam sicut lux vera Christus donavit apostolis ut lux mundi vocentur, sic et Simoni qui credebat in petra Christo, Petri largitus est nomen: cujus alias alludens ethimologiæ dixit: Tu es Petrus et super hanc petram ædificabo ecclesiam meam."

"The first was Simon, who is called Peter; the name, therefore, which in Latin is *Petrus*, and in Syriac *Cepha*, is derived from the rock—without doubt, from that rock of which St. Paul speaks; 'and the rock was Christ:' for, as Christ, the true light, granted to the Apostles that they might be called the light of the world, so too, to Simon, who believed in the rock Christ, was the name of Peter given: to the meaning of which name Christ alludes in another place, saying, 'Thou art Peter, and upon this rock I will build my church."

Thus does Claudius again repeat the Catholic doctrine, and employ, moreover, the very illustration of it used by Catholic theologians at the present day: Christ grants to Peter a participation of His own headship of the Church, precisely as he who was *the true light* of the universe, granted to all the apostles a participation of this prerogative, so that they too are styled "the light of the world."

2. Usher thus continues: "Yet does the same Claudius acknowledge that St. Peter received a kind of primacy for founding the Church, in reference to which he terms him the Prince of the Church, and the prince or chief of the apostles; but he adds, 'St. Paul also was chosen in the same manner to have the primacy in founding the churches of the Gentiles.'" This extract is from the commentary on the epistle to the Galatians; and Usher adds some other passages from the same commentary, in which St. Paul, in his apostolate and ministry, is compared with St. Peter.

We shall not dwell on these passages, as it is nowise certain that our Irish Claudius was the author of that commentary. Suffice it to remark, that we accept, without hesitation, all that is said in those passages in regard to the apostolate and prerogatives of St. Paul; and, moreover, we joyously hail the titles which he confers on St. Peter, "*Prince of the Church, Prince and Chief of the*

Apostles," together with the beautiful passage, of which only a portion is translated by Usher, but which runs as follows:—

"Petrum solum nominat et sibi comparat: quia primatum ipse accepit ad fundandam Ecclesiam; se quoque pari modo electum ut primatum habeat in fundandis Gentium ecclesiis."*	"He only names Peter, and compares him with himself: because on Peter was conferred the primacy for the foundation of the Church; and, in like manner, he himself was chosen to hold the primacy in founding the churches of the Gentiles."

From this we must conclude that to St. Peter was granted an universal primacy, comprising *the whole Christian Church,* whilst to St. Paul a primacy, too, was granted, which, however, was limited to *the churches of the Gentiles.* Surely we could not wish for a clearer statement of the Catholic doctrine of St. Peter's exalted prerogative.

3. In the next passage Usher returns to the genuine commentary of our Claudius on St. Matthew; and it is difficult not to accuse him of "bad faith" in his manner of citing it: "it is also observed by Claudius," he says, "that as when our Saviour propounded the question generally to all the apostles, Peter answered as one for all; so what our Lord answered to Peter, in Peter he answered all; and, therefore, 'however the power of loosing and binding might seem to be given by the Lord to Peter, yet without doubt it is to be known that it was given to the rest of the apostles also, as Himself witnesses, who, appearing to them after the triumph of His passion and resurrection, breathed on them and said to them all, receive the Holy Ghost, whose sins ye remit,'" etc.

We may well understand that it was but little to Usher's purpose to add the words which immediately follow the passage just cited, and in which Claudius declares that by the Redeemer's words was granted not only to Peter and the other apostles, but also to all bishops and priests till the end of time, *the power of remitting sins.* But what excuse can the learned archbishop plead for omitting two other passages, one of which immediately precedes,

* Ad Galat. cap. ii.

the other follows in the same page the text now cited, and which alone afford the key to understand the commentary given by Claudius in regard to the dignity of St. Peter?

The first passage, then, which Usher omits is as follows:—

"Tibi dato claves regni cœlorum. Non est ergo clavis ista mortalis artificis aptata manu, sed data a Christo est potestas judicandi. Qui regem cœlorum majori præ cæteris devotione confessus est, merito præ cæteris ipse conlatis clavibus regni cœlestis donatus est."*

"To thee will I give the keys of the kingdom of heaven. The word *key*, then, does not here refer to anything material formed by the hand of man, but it indicates the judiciary power. He who with a zeal greater than the rest, acknowledged Christ, was deservedly in a special manner endowed with the keys of the kingdom of heaven."

Thus, according to Claudius, all the apostles, indeed, received the judicatory power from Christ; but in a special manner, and *præ cæteris*, the power of the keys was granted unto Peter.

The second passage which is omitted by Usher is still more important; for after stating that to all the apostles, nay, and to all bishops and priests, was given the power *ligandi atque solvendi*, Claudius adds:—

"Sed ideo beatus Petrus qui Christum vera fide confessus, vero est amore secutus, specialiter claves regni cœlorum et principatum judiciariæ potestatis accepit, ut omnes per orbem credentes intelligant, quia quicumque ab unitate fidei vel societatis illius quolibet modo semetipsos segregant, tales nec vinculis peccatorum absolvi nec januam possint regni cœlestis ingredi."

"But blessed Peter, who had acknowledged Christ in the fulness of faith, and loved Him with a true love, received, in a special manner, the keys of the kingdom of heaven and the princedom of judiciary authority, that thus all the faithful throughout the universe might understand, that whosoever in any manner separates himself from the unity of his faith and communion, such a one can neither be absolved from the *bonds of sin, nor enter the portals of the kingdom of heaven.*"

Now why did Usher omit these beautiful words? If he was desirous of illustrating the opinion of Claudius, surely this passage, in the clearest manner, presents his opinion to us; but probably the Protestant primate feared to let his readers see how explicitly our Irish commentator, as far back as the year 800, asserted the dignity and prerogatives of St. Peter, and how he expressly declared, that the power and privileges granted to the Church by the divine Redeemer, were all centred in that chosen apostle; and perhaps, too, he feared that some of his readers might meditate on the concluding words of Claudius, that whosoever, throughout the whole world, is not united with St. Peter in the bonds of communion and faith, can neither obtain the remission of his sins, nor enter into the enjoyment of the heavenly kingdom.

Claudius was, indeed, a curious witness to bring forward in favour of Irish Protestantism. As the prophet of old, when brought to curse, pronounced blessings on the people of Israel, so do all the Irish writers who are cited by our adversaries, invariably proclaim the Catholic teaching of our Church.

We have already, more than once, referred to the fragments of our ancient writers preserved in the Liber Hymnorum, or ancient collection of hymns used in the Irish Church. Only a portion of this valuable repository has been as yet published by the Irish Archæological Society; and in the unpublished portion is a short rhythm on the apostles Peter and Paul, which we cite in full, as illustrative of our present subject; it occurs in fol. 13 of the Roman manuscript:—

> "Deus dele facinora,
> Nostra peccata plurima,
> Tua magna clementia,
> Et pietate nimia.
> Per sanctorum suffragia
> Apostolorum fortia
> Petri clavicularia
> Cui data potentia,
> Pauli et tali gloria
> In divina scientia
> Et per Christum in sæcula
> Dominantem infinita."

Thus is invoked the aid of God through "*the powerful intercession of St. Peter, to whom was given the key-bearing authority, and of St. Paul eminent for his divine knowledge, and through Christ who rules unto eternal ages.*"

Amongst the letters of our early sainted writers, published by

Usher in his valuable *Sylloges Epistolarum*, there is one on the Paschal Question, addressed to Segienus, abbot of Hy, and to Beccan, who is styled "a solitary, and a brother both in spirit and blood" (Beccanoque solitario, caro carne et spiritu fratri). The writer of this letter was St. Cummian, who himself led the penitential life of a solitary; the abode of such hermits was known by the name *disert** amongst the Irish, and hence St. Cummian's monastery was called *Disert-comin*, and subsequently *Kil-comin* by our ancient annalists. It was situated not far from Roscrea; and it was from this *hermitage* that he wrote his famous letter in 634; for in one passage he states : "These things, I say, not in order to impugn your teaching, but to defend myself who, as the solitary sparrow, am lying hid in my resting-place." At another period of his life, he seems to have ruled as abbot the famous monastery of Durrow,† and, perhaps, also that of Hy; one other fact can also, with certainty, be mentioned connected with his life, that forsooth, he enriched his monastery of Disert-Comin with relics of St. Peter and Paul, which were venerated there for many years, till they were for greater security translated to Roscrea.‡

In his letter St. Cummian speaks with all reverence of Saint Columbkille, and the other saints who had followed the Irish computation; but he declares himself compelled, by the practice of the universal Church, to abandon that ancient system and conform to the new computation. He says, that he consumed a whole year in studying the subject in dispute, searching the holy Scriptures,

---

* See Reeves' Adamnan, p. 366.   † See Lanigan, ii. 397.

‡ Some have confounded this writer with St. Cummian Fota; but the Irish scholiasts, though diffuse in detailing the leading features of Cummian Fota's life, are silent as to his connection with Durrow. (Conf. Todd, Book of Hymns, p. 81-93.) Other writers have identified our author with St. Cummian the Fair (Albus), who was abbot of Hy, and died in 669. This was Colgan's opinion (Acta SS. p. 411); and it certainly has the ancient tradition of Ireland in its favour. Modern writers generally reject it, though on very slight grounds. It seems, at first sight, hard to reconcile his being abbot of Hy, with the fact that the monks of Hy continued even till 716, to warmly defend the old paschal computation. However, this difficulty disappears when we call to mind that Adamnan, who was an equally ardent upholder of the Roman computation, was abbot from 679 to 704; and. nevertheless, was unsuccessful in his efforts to bring around the monks of his monastery to adopt that paschal observance.

exploring the records of ecclesiastical history, and inquiring into the various cycles that had acquired celebrity in the Oriental or Western Church. To illustrate his subject he quotes passages from Origen, St. Cyprian, St. Jerome, St. Augustine, St. Cyril of Alexandria, and St Gregory the Great. Especially important was the testimony of St. Jerome. His opponents appealed to the practice of their Fathers; he therefore adopts St. Jerome's words:—

"*An old authority,*" says Jerome, "*rises up against me. In the meanwhile, I shout out, whosoever is joined to the Chair of St. Peter, with him shall I be.*"— (Usher, Syllog. Epp. page 20.)

A chief point of St. Cummian's argument is the necessity of maintaining inviolable the unity of the Church:—

"*I turn me,*" he says, "*to the words of the bishop of Rome, pope Gregory, whose authority is acknowledged in common by us, and who is gifted with the appellation of the golden mouth, and who, though writing last of all the Fathers, is deservedly preferred to all; and I find him writing on the passage of Job: Gold hath a place wherein it is melted: that the gold is the great body of the saints: the place of melting is the unity of the church: the fire is the suffering of martyrdom: and he who is tried by fire out of the unity of the Church, may be melted, indeed, but cannot be cleansed.*"

Subsequently he more than once returns to this argument from the unity of the Church, and beautifully exclaims:—

"*Can anything more pernicious and injurious to Mother Church be conceived, than to say Rome errs, Jerusalem errs, Alexandria errs, Antioch errs, the whole world errs, the Irish and Britons alone are right!*"

Whilst to St. John he gives the peculiarly Irish title *pectalicus*, that is to say, "St. John *of the bosom,*" from his having reclined on the bosom of our blessed Redeemer; he assigns the characteristic designation *clavicularius* to St. Peter, that is, having the key-bearing authority, which, as we have seen, was so commonly given to that apostle by our Irish writers. He curiously, too, adds, of "the Britons and Scots," that they were merely "the extremity, and, so to say, the lowest of the whole world."*

* Qui sunt pene extremi, et, ut ita dicam, mentagræ orbis terrarum.— Usher, Syllog. Epp., No. xi, p. 19, and Conf. Irish Glosses, by Whitley Stokes, 1860, p. 145.

After studying for a whole year the various matters connected with the paschal controversy, he resolved, he says, to "interrogate his fathers, that they might declare to him—and his elders that they might narrate to him." Those whom he interrogated were the neighbouring bishops of Emly, Clonmacnois, Birr, Mungret, and Clonfertmolva; and these bishops " having met together in Magh-lene, " some being personally present, others sending their legates to re- " present them, they decreed and said : *our predecessors, as we* " *know from meet witnesses, of whom some are still living, others now* " *sleep in peace, enacted that we should humbly and without scruple* " *receive whatever things were better and more to be esteemed when* " *they were sanctioned by the source of our baptism and faith, and* " *brought to us from the successors of the Lord's apostles.* After- " wards they in common set forth to us, as the custom is, a man- " date upon this matter, to keep Easter the coming year along with " the whole church." . . . .

"After this, in accordance with the commandment: 'if a difference arise between cause and cause, and if judgment shall vary between leprosy and leprosy, they shall go up to the place which the Lord hath chosen;'* and with the synodical decree, that *when causes were of great moment, they should be referred to the head of cities* (si causæ fuerint majores, juxta decretum synodicum ad caput urbium sint referendæ), our seniors judged it proper to send wise and humble men as children to their mother (velut natos ad matrem), and by God's will some of them, having had a prosperous journey, reached Rome in safety, and returned to us the third year, and saw that all things were done precisely as had been told to us: and they were the more convinced of these things, seeing them, than if they merely heard of them; for, abiding together with Greek and Oriental, and Scythian and Egyptian, they found all celebrating together in St. Peter's Church at Easter, and before the Holy of Holies, they attested to us, saying : *throughout the whole earth, Easter is, as we know, thus kept.* And in the relics and the Scriptures which they brought with them, we found that there was the blessing of God; for with our own eyes, we saw a young girl who was blind restored to her sight at these relics ; and we saw a paralytic walk, and many wicked spirits cast out."

This testimony gives us a clear insight into the theological teaching of Ireland at this early period. The unity of the Church

* Deut. xvii. 8.

was the great central point of the whole theological system: this unity was preserved by clinging to Rome, and remaining inseparably attached to her doctrines and practices; and if controversy arose, its last all-ruling tribunal, was the Chair of Peter; for Rome possessed the key-bearing authority; it was the source of our faith and regeneration; the spiritual mother to whose bosom we should recur with filial reverence, as to a secure refuge in all difficulties and dangers.

The Irish monasteries of Hy and Lindisfarne were, during the sixth and seventh centuries, the great centres whence religion and literature were diffused throughout the distracted kingdoms of the Picts, Britons, and Saxons. The founder of Lindisfarne, St. Aidan, won for himself the title of "the Apostle of Northumbria," and for seventeen years ruled the whole ecclesiastical province of York. His second successor was St. Colman. He too, as we learn from Bede, was a monk of Hy, and was sent from that sacred retreat to evangelize the English nation.* For three years St. Colman had given proof of zeal and piety as abbot of Lindisfarne, and bishop of North England, when in 664, Oswin, king of Northumberland, invited the defenders of the Roman and Irish pascha computation to defend their respective opinions in his presence at Whitby.

St. Wilfrid, who had been educated by St. Aidan at Lindisfarne, and subsequently learned at Rome the corrected paschal computation, was, at this time, abbot of Ripon. That monastery was an off-shoot of the Columbian Order, but the Irish monks were expelled from it by Alchfrid, through the exertions of Wilfrid, and it was given to his charge to establish in it the Roman observances. He appeared at Whitby as the chief opponent of the Irish computation. His associate was Agilbert, a native of France, but who had been instructed in sacred literature in Ireland,† and who was at this time bishop of the West Saxons.‡

---

* "Unde erat ad prædicandum verbum Dei, Anglorum genti destinatus"—Bede, Eccles. Hist. lib. iv. cap. 4.
† "Natione quidem gallus sed tunc legendarum gratia Scripturarum non parvo tempore in Hibernia demoratus."—Bede, loc. cit. lib. iii. cap. 7.
‡ He subsequently returned to France, and was made bishop of Paris.

St. Colman appeared at Whitby in the name of the monks of Hy and Lindisfarne, to defend the Irish computation. His argument was a simple one: "The Easter computation which I follow, I received from my elders, by whom I was consecrated bishop, for this country: and all our fathers, men beloved by God, as their virtues and miracles attest, are known to have celebrated Easter in the same manner." He did not censure those who adopted the Roman cycle; neither should they disturb him and his companions whilst following the usage of their fathers.

His opponents replied almost in the very words of St. Cummian's letter:—

"The Easter computation which we follow we have seen adopted by every one at Rome, where the blessed apostles Peter and Paul lived, taught, suffered, and were buried. We have seen it also in every part of Italy and France that we have traversed. It is observed at one and the same time in Africa, Asia, Egypt, and Greece, and, in short, throughout the whole Christian world, except by the Irish monks and their associates, the Picts and Britons."

To Colman's argument from the sanctity of St. Columba and other saints who had followed the Irish computation, Wilfrid well replied that they were, indeed, holy men, and "I believe had they been rightly informed on the subject, they, too, would have conformed to the universal usage." And, addressing Colman, he added that the defenders of the Irish usage could plead that ignorance no longer:—

"You and your associates certainly commit sin if, after hearing the decrees of the Apostolic See, nay, of the Universal Church, and these confirmed by the holy Scriptures, you disdain to follow them. For although your fathers were saints, yet in their small number in the very extremity of the world, they must not be preferred to the whole Church. And however holy and illustrious performer of miracles your Columba was, is he to be preferred to the most blessed prince of the apostles to whom the Lord has said, 'Thou art Peter, and upon this rock I will build my church, and the gates of hell shall not prevail against it, and I will give unto thee the keys of the kingdom of heaven'?"

This argument was one that made a great impression on the English king, and turning to St. Colman, Oswin said—"Is it true that the Lord has thus spoken to Peter?" St. Colman replied in the affirmative. The king then asked—" Can you show that so great a power was granted to your Columba?" The saint answered " that he could not." Whereupon king Oswin continued :—" Do you on both sides agree in this, that the cited words of the divine Redeemer were specially addressed to St. Peter, and that to him the keys of heaven were given by our Lord?" The disputants on both sides replied—" We are all agreed in this." " Well, then," concluded the king, " I will not oppose the heavenly gate-keeper ;" and he decided in favor of Wilfrid's opinion.*

One happy result, at least, followed from the conference at Whitby, that, forsooth, it preserved an indubious record of how the Irish and Roman clergy, even in the warmth of their controversy, were found of one accord asserting the prerogatives and supreme authority of St. Peter. St. Wilfrid and Agilbert were themselves, indeed, witnesses as to the teaching of the Irish schools, whilst Colman combined in himself the doctrine of Lindisfarne and Iona, nay more, of the whole Irish Church; for, on being expelled from his monastery by king Oswin, he retired to Ireland and founded there the monasteries of Inisbofin and Mayo, being venerated by all for his learning and sanctity.†

The learned Protestant dean of Ardagh, to whose singular opinions we have more than once referred in the preceding pages, thus comments on the Whitby conference:—Colman, when he found his opinions rejected, resigned his see of Lindisfarne, rather than submit to this decision of the king, *thus furnishing us with a remarkable proof that the Irish bishops in the seventh century rejected the authority of the pope.*‡ This, indeed, is singularly strange reasoning. His

---

* Bede, Hist. Ec. iii. 25 ; Roger de Wendor, vol. i. page 157. See also Dr. Lanigan, Ec. Hist. iii. 66-7, for some very just remarks on the false reasoning of Wilfrid, who, though defending a good cause, erroneously appealed to the law of Scripture and the enactments of the universal Church and Rome regarding the then approved cycle. No such law or enactments existed on the subject.

† The Annals of Four Masters, ad. an. 667, record his coming to Inisbofin : "S. Colmannus episcopus cum aliis sanctis venit ad insulam Inisbofin, et ibi extruxit monasterium quod ab ipso nominatur." The same Annals mark his death on 8th August, 674.

‡ Loc. cit. page 65.

logical conclusions should rather have been—1. That as there was no exercise of the pope's authority, St. Colman could not have resisted it. 2. That he even openly and expressly acknowledged the authority of Rome. 3. That he moreover furnishes us with a most striking proof of the opinion of the Irish Church in the seventh century, that the judgment of the court or crown was very far from being decisive on matters of ecclesiastical discipline; and hence— 4. That St. Colman would deem it strange, indeed, to be classed by the worthy dean amongst the members or abettors of the Anglican Church.

A very ancient tract, in the Irish language, entitled, "On Injury and Assault to Ecclesiastics," is preserved in the Leabhar Breac, and also forms part of the Brehon Laws. It proceeds by question and answer, and lays down the ancient legislation of the civil government of Ireland in regard to the honor due to ecclesiastics, and to the fine or punishment to be inflicted on those who insult or injure them. We are indebted for its translation to the late Eugene Curry, Esq., who also, in his Lectures, more than once refers to it.* In this curious tract we read:—

"Which is the highest dignity on earth? Answer—The dignity of the Church. Which is the highest dignity in the Church? Answer—The dignity of a bishop, and the highest of bishops is the bishop of Peter's Church, to whom the Roman kings are subject."

After assigning the respective *eric* or fine for inflicting injury on the various grades of the ecclesiastical order, the tract thus continues :—

"Where is this doctrine found? Answer—It is found in the treatise which Augustine wrote upon the Degrees of the Church, and upon the dirês (that is, the fine paid for injury in person or property to each degree), and the reparation to be made; *and it is thus, according to the rule of the Church of Peter, empress of the whole world.*"†

In the first part of this essay,‡ we had frequent occasion to refer to

---

* See Lectures, etc., page 352, seqq.
† Curry MSS. in the Catholic University of Ireland.
‡ Chapters iii. and iv.

the various lives of our glorious apostle St. Patrick, as registering facts connected with his mission to our island. We may now view them under another aspect, as conveying to us, forsooth, the sentiments and feelings of the Irish Church in regard to Rome at the period when they were composed. Thus the scholiast on St. Fiacc's hymn introduces St. Germanus as saying to St. Patrick—"Do you, therefore, proceed to the successor of St. Peter, who is pope Celestine, that he may ordain you (for the Irish mission); for this office belongs to him."* *Muirchu-Maccu-Mactheni*, and the author of Vita Secunda describe St. Celestine as "*bishop of Rome, holding the Apostolic See.*" The Vita Tertia says that "Patrick wished to visit Rome, the head of all churches, whither flocked the faithful from all parts of the whole world."† The Vita Quarta, referred by Dr. Todd to the eighth century, not only styles Rome *the Apostolic See*, and speaks of the *apostolic permission* given to St. Patrick by pope Celestine, but further adds: "Germanus sent blessed Patrick to Rome, that he might go forth to preach with the sanction of the bishop of the Apostolic See: for due order so requireth."‡ The Vita Septima, referred to St. Evin, relates that when St. Patrick was divinely inspired to prepare for the Irish mission, "*he resolved first to visit Rome, the citadel and teacher of Christian faith.*"—*Statuit prius Romam ad doctrinæ et fidei Christianæ arcem et magistram proficisci.*§ And subsequently it adds, that guided by the counsels of the angel Victor, "*St. Patrick determined to visit the See of Peter, the teacher of our faith, and the fountain-source of every apostolate: that by its apostolic authority, his mission might be sanctioned and confirmed.*"|| Coennechaire, who is better known by his Latinized name, Probus, is judged by Lanigan and other competent authorities to be the most accurate historian of our apostle St. Patrick. The age in which Probus lived is uncertain. Usher referred his work to the

---

* Pergas ergo tu ad successorem S. Petri nempe Cœlestinum, ut te ordinet: quia hoc munus ipsi incumbit."—Tr. Thaum. p. 5. See ante, p. 27.

† *Romam caput videlicet omnium ecclesiarum ad quam Christiani ex omnibus mundi partibus conveniebant.*

‡ Ut cum Apostolicæ Sedis episcopi licentiâ ad prædicationem exiret; sic enim ordo exigebat.—Tr. Thaum. p. 39.

§ Tr. Th. p. 121. || Ibid. p. 122.

eighth century; Ware, Harris, and Colgan are generally cited as authorities who assign the year 920 as the date of its composition. Yet these writers only put forward this opinion as a matter of conjecture, whilst the reasons which they advance in support of it, do not bring with them even the slightest shade of probability.* The only Irish writer of the name that acquired a continental fame was Probus, who, after devoting himself for many years to the study of sacred and classical literature in Ireland, retired to Mentz, where he died on the 26th of May, 859.† Usher's opinion, however, seems to approach far nearer to the truth, as he grounded it on the manuscripts which he consulted. At all events, this, to say the least, ancient and accurate writer, having recorded the prayer breathed by St. Patrick, that Heaven might conduct him to the Apostolic See, adds: "Not long after, the man of God *came, as he had desired, to Rome, the head of all churches,* and having asked and received there the apostolic blessing, returned to Ireland."‡

Thus, then, Rome is the See of Peter, the Apostolic See, the source of Catholic apostolate, the centre of Christian faith: her's it is to dispense the blessings of heaven, and the treasures of grace; her's, too, to strengthen the Christian missionary, to

---

* The only plausible argument for this opinion is, that Probus inscribes his work to a Paulinus. Now, in the tenth century there was a Mael-Paulinus, bishop and abbot of Indenen, who died in 920; whilst there was a contemporary, Coencachair, lecturer in the school of Slane, who was burned to death in the tower of that monastery by the Danes, in the year 950.—(See Petrie's Round Towers, p. 368.) However, though the Irish on the continent often Latinized their names, this was a rare occurrence when their writings were addressed to their friends in Ireland. Moreover, the writer thus addresses Paulinus in conclusion: "Ecce habes *frater Pauline,*" etc.—(Tr. Th. p. 61.) This is certainly not the style in which the religious of Slane would address the bishop and abbot of Indenen. It is also probable that Paulinus held that abbacy for many years; the abbot and bishop Ferghil, who seems to have been his immediate predecessor, died in 902. The following quatrain was composed on the death of Paulinus:—

"Mælpoil, who was in great dignity,
 A bishop who took the road of a king;
 A sage who enforced the law upon all—
 A man who dispensed peace all around."
—(See O'Donov. Four Masters, ad an. 920)

† See Histoire Litteraire, etc, tom v. p. 209, seqq.   ‡ Tr. Th. p. 48.

give vitality to his teaching, and to impart a heavenly fecundity to his spiritual labours.

With such sentiments in the minds of our forefathers, it will not surprise us to find the ancient writer of the life of St. Furseus registering the following words, as' addressed by that great saint to the central see of the Catholic world—

"O Rome! exalted above all cities by the triumphs of the apostles, decked with the roses of martyrdom, decorated with the lilies of confessors, adorned with the palms of virgins, strengthened by all their merits, enriched with the remains of so many and so renowned saints; we hail thee! May thy sacred authority never cease, which has been illustrated by the dignity and wisdom of the holy Fathers : that authority by which the body of Christ, that is to say, our blessed mother the Church, maintains its undying consistency and vigour."*

We shall conclude this article with an extract from the famous letter of Gillibert, *de usu et statu Ecclesiastico*. It was well nigh seventy years before the English landed on the Irish shores, that Gillibert was appointed bishop of Limerick. His Irish name was Gille-Esperic : he visited Rome and France, and at Rouen formed the friendship of St. Anselm. On his return to Ireland he ruled as abbot the famous monastery of Bangor, and was thence in 1090, as Usher thinks, but according to others, some years later advanced to the see of Lumneach, now known by its English name of Limerick. One of the first acts of the new bishop was to write a letter of congratulation to St. Anselm, expressing the joy with which he learned that at length he had succeeded " in inducing the untameable minds of the Normans to submit to the canonical decrees of the holy Fathers ;" and this letter was accompanied with a gift of twenty-five Irish pearls. The letter on the ecclesiastical orders was drawn up at the request of the Irish clergy, and is addressed: " To the bishops and priests of all Ireland, the last of bishops Gille of Lumneach wishes health in Christ." He lays down in detail the relative duties of each order, and in conclusion thus faithfully sketches the position of the successor of St. Peter in regard to the Christian Church :—

---

* Ap. Bolland. Januarii, tom. ii., p. 50.—" Quâ corpus Christi videlicet beata mater Ecclesia viget solidata."

"The picture I have drawn showeth that all the Church's members are to be brought under one chief bishop, to wit, Christ and His vicar, blessed Peter the apostle, and the pope presiding in his see, to be governed by them ...... As Noah was placed to rule the ark amidst the waves of the flood, just so does the Roman pontiff rule the Church amid the billows of this world ..... The position held in the Eastern Church by the patriarchs is that which belongs to archbishops in the West; and both patriarchs and archbishops are subject in the first degree to the Roman pontiff. As the patriarchs, however, govern the apostolic sees, Jerusalem, Antioch, Alexandria, it is their privilege to ordain archbishops, and, in a manner, are likened to the bishop of Rome. To Peter alone, however, was it said: 'Thou art Peter, and upon this rock I will build my Church.' Therefore the pope alone is exalted in dignity above the whole Church, and he alone has the privilege of ordaining and judging all."*

CHAPTER II.

CANONICAL ENACTMENTS OF THE IRISH CHURCH REGARDING ROME.

Canon of St. Patrick, that difficult cases are to be referred to Rome—Usher admits it to be genuine—Found in Book of Armagh—Quoted by synod of Magh-lene in 630—Contained in an Irish collection of canons, of the year 700—Dr. Todd refuted—Ancient Irish canons regarding appeals to Rome—Dean Murray's objections.

IT is a characteristic feature, and hence, too, a special glory of our Irish Church, that her apostle, by an express decree, marked out for her and sanctioned the hallowed course she should pursue in reference to Rome. The statute of St. Patrick is preserved in the ancient Book of Armagh,† and, moreover, in *"that part of the same old MS. which was copied from the book written by St. Patrick's own hand."*‡

After indicating some cases of special importance reserved for the decision of the bishop of Armagh, to whom, as it is decreed, "perveniet caussa totius negotionis cæteris aliorum judicibus præ-

---

* Ap. Usher, Syllog. Epistt. No. xxx. p. 54, seqq.   † Fol. 21, b. b.
‡ Curry's Lectures, p. 372; Petrie, Essay on the History and Antiquities of Tara Hill: Dublin, 1839, pag. 81.

termissis,"—" the examination of the whole matter will be reserved, all other inferior judges being passed over," it is further enacted:—

"Item quæcumque causa valde difficilis exorta fuerit atque ignota cunctis Scotorum gentium judicibus ad cathedram archiepiscopi Hibernensium (id est Patricii) atque hujus antistitis examinationem recte referenda.

"Si vero in illa cum suis sapientibus facile sanari non poterit talis caussa prædictæ negotionis, ad Sedem Apostolicam decrevimus esse mittendam, id est ad Petri apostoli cathedram auctoritatem Romæ urbis habentem.

"Hi sunt qui de hoc decreverunt id est, Auxilius, Patricius, Secundinus, Benignus."*

"Moreover, if any case of extreme difficulty shall arise, and one which the various judges of the Irish nation cannot decide, let it be referred to the see of the chief bishop of the Irish (that is of Patrick), and submitted to his episcopal examination.

"But if such a case of the aforesaid importance cannot easily be decided in that see with the assistance of its wise counsellors, we have decreed that it be sent to the Apostolic See, that is to say, to the chair of the apostle Peter, which holds the authority of the city of Rome.

"These are the persons who decreed as above, viz., Auxilius, Patrick, Secundinus, and Benignus."

We may add the translation of this passage that is given by Usher in his dissertation on the Religion of the Ancient Irish :‡

"Whenever any cause that is very difficult and unknown unto all the judges of the Scottish nations shall arise, it is rightly to be referred to the see of the archbishop of the Irish (that is to say, of Patrick), and to the examination of the prelate thereof. But if *there*, by him and his wise men, a cause of this nature cannot easily be made up, we have decreed it shall be sent to the See Apostolic—that is to say, to the chair of the apostle Peter, which hath the authority of the city of Rome."

The reader will be anxious to learn what were the remarks of Usher on this important text:

"It is most likely," he says, "that St. Patrick had a special regard for the Church of Rome, from whence he was sent for the conversion of this island: so as, if I myself had lived in his days, for the resolution of a doubtful question, I should as willingly have listened to the judgment of the Church of Rome, as to the determination of any church in the whole world: so reverent an estimation have I of the integrity of that Church as it stood in those days."

* See the whole passage with a fac-simile of the original in Curry, loc. cit. pag. 611, append. (p.)
† Page 84.

Now, we willingly accept many of the principles here laid down by Usher. It is indeed manifest, first, that St. Patrick, in enacting that canon, "*had a special regard for the Church of Rome;*" second, as that canon was enacted for the guidance of the Irish hurch in after-ages, it is also manifest that St. Patrick wished his spiritual children to cherish *a reverent estimation of the integrity of the Church of Rome.* We shall, however, further add, thirdly, that it is not a mere wish that is here expressed, but it is a canonical enactment that is made by our apostle, commanding the clergy and faithful of Erin, whom he had enlightened with the doctrines of our saving faith, to recur in their doubts and difficulties to the successors of St. Peter.

It should, moreover, be remarked, that it is not merely on account of some peculiar and individual opinion, as to the integrity of the Church of Rome, that St. Patrick commands all cases of doubtful controversy to be referred to its decision; he himself expressly assigns the principle which guided him in this enactment; such controversies, he says, shall be referred *to the Apostolic See*—that see which is held by the successors of St. Peter, and rules the Church by the authority of Christ. Thus was the golden rule enacted by our apostle for the guidance of the Irish Church: Rome was to be reverenced; its judgment was to be revered; its decisions were to be unimpeachable, because it was characteristically *the Apostolic See.* Such, too, is the rule which Ireland has invariably followed for fourteen hundred years; inherited from her glorious apostle, she loves and cherishes it at the present day in the period of her comparative prosperity, even as she did in the period of her suffering and trials; and ever shall the decisions of Rome be revered and loved by us, as proceeding from the central source of all ecclesiastical authority—*from the Apostolic See.*

The genuineness of this canon cannot be impugned. Its being found in the Book of Armagh brings us back well nigh to the time of St. Patrick himself. We have already seen how that ancient manuscript was transcribed in the year 807; and even then the original which was copied was believed to have been written by our apostle. In the synod of Magh-lene, in 630, the assembled prelates acted on this decree; and St. Cummian, who himself was present at the synod, thus in 634, in his letter on the paschal computation, attests the fact: "in accordance with the canonical decree, that if questions of grave moment arise, they shall be referred to the head of cities, we sent such as we knew were wise and humble men to Rome."* There is even a third ancient witness to confirm the same truth. It was about the year 700 that a collection of canons was made for the use of the Irish Church, and amongst the canonical enactments which it registers, is precisely the decree of St. Patrick, that should any questions arise in our island, they were to be referred to Rome:—

"Patritius ait: si quæ difficiles quæstiones in hac insula oriantur ad Sedem Apostolicam referantur."†

"St. Patrick defines: should any grave controversies arise in this island, they shall be referred to the Apostolic See."

We shall just now make some remarks on this ancient collection of canons, the importance of which is not sufficiently known; but we must first warn the reader against some difficulties which might, perchance, betray him into an erroneous conclusion regarding the canon now before us.

It has been generally spoken of as forming part of the enactments of the synod held by SS. Patrick, Auxilius, etc., whose Acts are published in Ware, Wilkins, Villanueva, etc.; and Dr. Todd, in his late work on St. Patrick, passes over this canon in utter silence, being content with some general arguments to prove that the acts of that synod must be referred to a later date. Now we must remark:

1. That the canon preserved in the Book of Armagh does not form part of the acts of the published synods of our apostle. The synod which bears the name of SS. Patrick, Auxilius, and Iserninus, was discovered by Spelman amongst the papers of Corpus Christi, Cambridge, in a very ancient but very incorrect manuscript.

* Usher, Syllog. Epp. No. 30.
† Collect. Hib. Canonum, lib. xx. cap. 5.

Neither in that MS. nor in any of the editions made from it, has the decree regarding Rome been published; and hence, even should we admit that the published acts of that synod are interpolated or belong to a later date, the canon regarding Rome preserved in the Book of Armagh, and corroborated by such ancient authority, must retain its full weight and importance.

2. Dr. Todd remarks, that in the acts of the published synod, no mention is made of St. Secundinus,* "whose history being purely Irish," he thinks, was unknown to the continental compiler. Now, in regard to the canon of which we speak, it is immediately added, after the other canon in the Book of Armagh, that SS. Auxilius, Patrick, Secundinus, and Benignus, were those who enacted it: "Hi sunt qui de hoc decreverunt, id est, *Auxilius, Patricius, Secundinus, Benignus.*"† Thus, then, not only the Irish St. Secundinus, but also the Irish St. Benignus is expressly commemorated, and there is no trace of an ignorant continental compiler.‡

3. Dr. Todd's reasoning on the date of St. Patrick's printed synod is based on uncertain and erroneous grounds. At page 483 he assigns it "to the ninth or tenth century;" but page 4, he was still more modern in his views, and limiting his praise, asserts that it was "probably not later than the tenth or eleventh century." To justify his assertion, he, at page 486, seqq., mistranslates its decrees, and falsifies their meaning, and then rests his theory solely upon these false grounds. Thus, he particularly dwells on the sacred ecclesiastical tonsure, though the decrees of the synod have no reference at all to it; he appeals to the marriage of the clergy as asserted in the sixth canon, though the sixth canon contains no such assertion; and he triumphantly refers to the "*ancient custom in Ireland of presenting offerings,*" mentioned in this synod,

---

* Page 486. † Lib. Armac. loc. cit.

‡ As St. Secundinus died in 448, according to our ancient annalists, the published synod might have been held subsequent to that year, since the Annals of Ulster record the death of Auxilius in 459 (or 460), and of Iserninus in 468. There was surely a sufficient interval between 448 and 460 to celebrate that synod after Secundinus' death; and thus the absence of his name from the printed Acts, is nowise an indication of their having been penned by a continental interpolator.

whilst the synod makes mention, indeed, of a *mos antiquus* of presenting offerings, but makes no mention of such being *an ancient custom in Ireland.* To enter fully into these erroneous statements of the learned writer, would bring us too far from our present subject, and we refer the reader for a more detailed exposition of them to the appendix (No. 5); the more so, as the whole theory of Dr. Todd, though calculated to deceive the inattentive observer, can in no way interfere with the canonical decree regarding Rome, which we are discussing; for though we should grant that the printed synod of St. Patrick belongs to the twelfth century, surely that cannot affect the present decree, which was transcribed as early as 807, from another copy which, even then, was considered ancient—so ancient as to be ascribed to and venerated as written by St. Patrick himself, and which, moreover, was expressly registered in the Irish collection of canons, compiled about the year 700, as a decree which emanated from our own apostle St. Patrick.

We may now return to this Collection of Canons made at so early a period for the guidance of our Irish Church, and we propose to present in full to the reader, the course of reverential submissive obedience which, as it enacts, should be ever followed by the Irish faithful in regard to Rome. More than one manuscript of this collection has fortunately been preserved to us. The Imperial Library of Paris possesses two copies—one of the twelfth century, the other of the eighth century; Darmstad is enriched with a copy of the ninth century; St. Gall, in Switzerland, has another ancient copy of it; a beautiful minuscule manuscript of the Vallicellian Archives of Rome of the tenth century, also presents it to us; the Cottonian Codex of the eighth century, which contains this collection, has become celebrated on account of its being used by Usher, Spelman, Wilkins, and others; a Cambray MS., also of the eighth century, contains a copy of it, transcribed by order of Albericus, bishop of Cambray, who died in 790.*

Whilst thus the manuscript copies extant bring us back to the

---

* See Wasserschleben, Die Bussordnungen, etc.; Halle, 1851, introduction; Zeuss, Gram. Celt., xxxiii. ; Proceedings of R. I. Acad., v. 223, Dec. 8th, 1851.

eighth century, the intrinsic characteristic features of the collection refer its origin to at least the very commencement of that century.* Notwithstanding the high antiquity of this ecclesiastical repertory of our Irish laws and observances, and the many copies of it which are known to exist, it has hitherto remained a sealed book to the generality of our ecclesiastical writers; and even Dr. Todd, in his late work, laments that only a few fragmentary extracts from it have been presented to the public.†

It will not, therefore, be uninteresting to present an analysis of its decrees, which point to Rome as the great centre of spiritual authority, and the tribunal by whose decision all doubtful controversies must be judged. The twentieth book or division of the collection is entitled De Provincia, and after some preliminary definitions, it enacts that each district should decide its own controversies. Then it repeats the decree of the synod of Rome:—

"Quicumque causam habuerit apud suos judices judicetur et ne ad alienos causa vagandi et proterve despiciens patriam suam transeat sed apud metropolitanum episcopum suae provinciae judicetur."

"Whosoever has a cause to be judged, let him present it to his own judges, and let him not refer it to strangers through a desire of rambling, and through a contempt for his own country; but let him be judged by the metropolitan bishop of his province."

Lest justice might be impaired by thus limiting the decision of controversies to the local tribunals, it is enacted in the fourth chapter, that a province, in order to enjoy its privileges, should always have in readiness wise counsellors, capable of deciding all

---

* See appendix No. 6.
† Page 145 seqq. In the Proceedings of the R.I.A., vol. v. p. 224, Dr. Graves, after pointing out "the importance of having the antiquity of these Irish canons established" in so conclusive a manner, adduced instances to show that they illustrated the early civil history of Ireland. "Though professedly (he said) a collection of ecclesiastical canons, they contain amongst them several laws that are purely of a civil character, and many allusions to the existing state of society. In the ancient Brehon Laws still extant in the Irish language, the very same institutions are to be found, forming parts of a system which is altogether similar and coherent. Thus the independent testimony of the Canons, whose age is now fully ascertained, demonstrates the genuineness and antiquity of our Brehon Laws."—Dec. 8th, 1851.

controversies that might ordinarily arise; and on this subject the words of an ancient Irish synod are adopted:

"Synodus Hibernensis: sedes patriarcharum et cathedra legis et ordo sacerdotalis contempta et deordinata fuit; cum, reges et judices et personas dignas non habuerit nisi ab alienis eos evocasset."*

"The Irish synod declares that the patriarchal see and the chair of the law, and the priestly order, were slighted and despised when they had not kings and judges, and fit persons, without summoning them from other districts."

Thus far, however, provision was only made for the ordinary and every-day cases of controversy and litigation. Should *more difficult and intricate questions arise* (*maximæ et incertæ causæ*), then another tribunal might be appealed to. But even on this head, the first care of our fathers was to admonish the faithful that instruction was nowise, and under no circumstances, to be sought for amongst the heretics, or amongst those *who rejected the observances of Rome:*

"Cavendum est ne ad alias provincias aut ecclesias referantur causæ, quæ alio more et alia religione utuntur; aut Brittones qui omnibus contrarii sunt et a Romano more et ab unitate ecclesiæ abscedunt: aut hæreticos quamvis sint in ecclesiæ causis periti, et studiosi fuerunt."†

"Care must be taken, that no controversies be referred to other provinces or churches which follow different customs and profess a different religion; or to the Britons, who are contrary to all, and separate themselves from the Roman usages, and from the unity of the church; or to heretics, even when they are affable and skilled in the ecclesiastical causes."

Whilst thus, all heretics were to be carefully shunned, and in general all those whose teaching or discipline might generate some suspicion of heterodoxy, was there no peculiar tribunal to which the prelates of Ireland might turn their eyes with confident security, and on whose judgment they might implicitly rely? It is precisely to point out such a secure tribunal, that the decree of St Patrick is compendiously produced:

* Col. Hib. Can. xx. 4.   † Ibid. xx. cap. 6.

"Patricius ait.: Si quæ difficiles quæstiones in hac insula oriantur ad Sedem Apostolicam referantur."*

"St. Patrick enacts: If any grave controversies arise in this island, they shall be referred to the Apostolic See."

Even these words of our apostle were not deemed sufficient, and the decree of Rome itself is repeated, to guide the inquirer to the secure tribunal in all controversy :—

"Canones Romani : si majores caussæ fuerunt exortæ ad caput urbium sunt referendæ."†

"The Roman canons decree, that when the more difficult questions arise, they are to be referred to the head city."

And subsequently another canon of the Roman Church is adopted :

"Synodus Romana : si in qualibet provincia ortæ fuerint quæstiones et inter clericos dissidentes non conveniat, ad majorem sedem referantur."‡

"The Roman synod enacts, if in any province controversies arise which cannot be arranged amongst the contending parties, let the matter be referred to the chief see."

Thus, then, is clearly traced for the Irish Church the canonical course it should pursue whensoever momentous questions and matters of grave controversy should arise. Even the canons which Rome itself enacted, are adopted as the rule and law of Ireland; and whilst other churches might inspire diffidence and distrust, the Apostolic See was the guiding star that would not mislead,—the central and supreme tribunal of the whole Church, in whose decision all confidence might be securely placed.

Elsewhere in this Collection of Canons reference is more than once made to the See of St. Peter, so as to render still more clear and indubious its teaching in regard to the supremacy and prerogatives of the Vicar of Christ. Thus, in the 38th book (Codex Vallicellianus, sæc. x. No. xviii.), which is entitled De Principatu, the 18th chapter lays down, that in some cases a bishop might appoint his own successor before his death, and for this purpose quotes the decrees of an Irish synod sanctioning such a usage. It then continues as follows :—

* Col. Hib. Can. xx. cap. 5.   † Ibid.   ‡ Ibid. xx. cap. 5.

"It was thus that the divine Redeemer before his death appointed St. Peter his successor, saying: Thou art Peter, etc.; and it was thus, too, that Peter before his death, in the assembly of the brethren, said: The day of my death approaches; I therefore appoint Clement my successor; to him I leave the chair of preaching and teaching, because he was my companion in all things."*

Thus, then, St. Peter was appointed to hold the place of Christ on earth (according to this ancient monument of the faith of our fathers); and in the Roman pontiffs is perpetuated the central source of unerring teaching and doctrine, whose decisions should be reverenced as proceeding from the vicars of Christ and holders of the Apostolic See.

Elsewhere, in the 21st Book, which is entitled, *De Ordine Inquisitionis Cousarum*, the course is prescribed which was to be followed when inquiring into any matter of uncertainty or doubt. It is by adopting the words of pope Innocent, that this canonical course is laid down. Should the inspired writings, says that great pontiff, not be sufficiently clear, the inquirer shall have recourse to the tradition of the Church, recorded in the writings of her doctors and fathers; should he not even here find that which he desires, "*let him interrogate the canons of the Apostolic See*"—*canones Apostolicæ Sedis intuere.*†

Thus, that *reverent affection* for the See of St. Peter, of which Usher speaks, was not confined to St. Patrick, but lived in his children, and in the eighth century found an indubious expression, whilst it bequeathed to us an incontrovertible monument in the beautiful collection of canons, which we have just now been examining. The reverence for Rome, taught by St. Patrick, was handed down uninterruptedly from sire to son: what St. Patrick enacted, was repeated and confirmed in the collection of canons, in 700; and we may say it was sanctioned anew when, a hundred years later, was compiled for the see of Armagh, the now famous Liber Armacanus, in which, dictated by Torbach,‡ archbishop of that see, is found fully registered, the often-quoted canon of our

---

* Col. Hib. Can. xviii.   † Ib. xxi. 1.
‡ See Paper by Rev. Charles Graves, A.M., in Proceedings of the Royal Irish Academy, vol iii.

apostle: "Should any difficult questions arise in this island, let them be referred to the Apostolic See."

The learned Protestant dean of Ardagh, in the work more than once referred to, entitled "Ireland and her Church," could find no argument for impugning the authority of these decrees of our early Church: however, even thus his courage did not fail him, and full of confidence, he writes: "Now, supposing for one moment, that this canon and decree were genuine, were they ever acted upon before the twelfth century? The ancient Irish Church on no occasion ever appealed to the bishop of Rome."*

We shall just now see whether this positive statement of the learned writer is consistent with truth. Let us, however, to use his own expression, *for one moment suppose* that the Irish Church before the twelfth century never appealed to Rome; is it not, at least, a fact worthy of remark, and deserving the good dean's attention, that during the whole of the eventful period from the fifth to the twelfth century, it was the solemn canonical rule of the Irish Church, that should any questions of grave controversy arise, they were to be referred to the decision of the Apostolic See, and that this decree of our apostle was no secret or hidden enactment, but was repeated from age to age, and formed the living guiding rule of our faithful people? It should, moreover, strike the unbiassed reader, with what simplicity the worthy dean identifies his teaching with that of the Irish Church from the fifth to the twelfth century; and, nevertheless, he describes Rome at that period, as *the great centre of corrupted Christianity*,† whilst the Irish Church proclaimed it to be the depository of truth, the great centre of the orthodox faith: he asserts that no appeals should be made to its tribunal, whilst our apostle, and our sainted fathers, declared that precisely to its tribunal, all questions of moment and grave controversy should be referred: he exultingly dwells *on the corruptions of the Romish Church*;‡ and yet Ireland, whilst interdicting appeals to any see infected with heresy, or even differing on points of discipline from the Holy See, pointed to Rome as the safe guide

---

* Page 29.   † Page 59.   ‡ Loc cit.

and guardian, at whose maternal bosom our faithful people would find repose, and consolation, and instruction.

If we have referred nominally to the work of dean Murray, we wish it to be understood, that his production is merely mentioned as a sample of the Protestant literature of our days, and of the false reasonings with which the enemies of the Holy See seek to deceive their deluded readers, and imbue their minds with the prejudices and fatal errors of heresy. The press of England incessantly pours tracts and books upon our island, not only ignoring its traditions, but falsifying its monuments; misinterpreting its records, and leaving no means untried to give a colouring of Protestantism to the tenets and faith of our sainted forefathers. On the other hand, each new fragment of our ancient writers that comes to light, as well as the whole series of the records that remain to us, attests that Ireland clung to Rome as the source of its spiritual strength, and venerated the successors of St. Peter as the chief pastors of the Catholic Church, holding on earth the place of Jesus Christ, teaching by His authority, and ruling by His power.

CHAPTER III.

IRISH PILGRIMAGES TO ROME.

Commenced in the days of St. Patrick.—Pilgrimage of Germanus, son of an Irish chieftain.—St. Enna, St. Ailbe.—St. Conlaedh brings vestments from Rome.—St. Nennidh.—St. Finnian's pilgrimage, probably the same as St. Frigidian of Lucca.—Gildas, St. Molua, St. Flannan, St Laserian, St. Wiro, etc.—Irish Bishops at Roman Synod in 720, and Third Synod of Lateran.

It seems to be a matter agreed on by all our historians, that during the sixth and succeeding centuries, crowds of pilgrims set out from our Irish shores, and, travelling through Germany or France, hastened to visit the shrines of the Apostles. Strangers, however, may well be supposed to visit that city of wonders, as the sons of Albion at the present day, without sentiments of devotion, and devoid of filial reverence for St. Peter's successors. We shall, therefore, now enter on the inquiry, and cite some examples to enable the reader to decide, whether it was in the spirit of modern sight-seers that the Irish pilgrims flocked to that city of God, or whether it was not rather in the spirit of the holy writer who exclaimed: "Oh, happy Rome! depository of truth! centre of faith! enriched with the relics of the Apostles, empurpled with the blood of countless martyrs, sanctified by the virtues of so many holy children of Christ, we hail thee! we love thee!"

Contemporary with St. Patrick was the son of an Irish chieftain, who being baptized by St. Germanus of Auxerre, assumed in after-times the name of that great saint. Precisely as our own apostle, so was the younger Germanus sent in after-years by the bishop of Auxerre to visit the shrines of Rome; and his life records that, prostrate before the tombs of the Apostles, he remained for a length of time in prayer, shedding tears of consolation and spiritual joy.* It further adds, that the interval of his stay in Rome was devoted by him to visiting the churches and sanctuaries by day, whilst at night he ever hastened to the church of St. Peter, and it seemed he could never satiate his reverential ardour by kissing, again and again, its hallowed threshold.†

St. Enna, or Enda, was a disciple of St. Patrick, and is famed amongst our hagiologists as the great St. Anthony of the Irish Church. Having obtained a grant of the isles of Arran, he founded there a monastery, which for centuries was the most celebrated in the land: so numerous were the religious who flocked thither to pursue the practice of perfection, that it was commonly known by the epithet *Arann of the Saints*, and the Life of St. Ailbe thus describes it: "Great is that island, a land of saints, because God alone knows the number of saints that

---

* "Prostrato toto corpore, incumbens orationi diutissime oravit cum lachrymis," etc.—Acta SS. Maji, i. 266.

† "Romæ ergo aliquandiu immoratus Ecclesiarum Dei loca circuibat diebus, nocte vero ad S. Petri basilicam revertebatur et prædulcia figens oscula in ecclesiæ liminibus, sic sancto desiderio vix satiabatur."—Ibid.

repose there."* Marianus O'Gorman styles Enda "the virginal saint from Arann island;" and St. Cuimin of Connor thus commemorates his virtues:—

> "Enda loved glorious mortification
> In Arann—triumphant virtue!
> A narrow dungeon of flinty stone,
> To bring the people to heaven."

This saint was companion of St. Ailbe in Rome, where he passed his time, as his life records, "imitating the example of the saints, and preparing himself for the holy sacerdotal order."† Being at length ordained, he founded a monastery in the vicinity of Rome, which he styled *Laetium*, that is, *monastery of heavenly joy*; and it is added that this name well became his monastery, "for in it was rigorously observed the precept of the love of God and of our neighbour."

This is not the only fact which illustrates the history of St. Enda's journey to Rome. It is also mentioned by an ancient writer, that whilst he was in Rome, the holy pontiff died. It was the custom for the clergy and people to assemble in St. Peter's Church to elect a successor; thither, too, went our saint, with Ailbe and another companion, named Benedict. Whilst all were prostrated in prayer around the altar, a dove, after flying around the church, alighted on the shoulder of our Benedict: clergy and people at once pronounced this to be a heavenly omen of his being chosen for the Papal See, and hailed him as their pontiff. No argument, however, could induce him to accept the proffered dignity; still the name *Papa*, or *Papeus*, remained his characteristic designation in our ancient writers.‡ It is added that St. Enda, on departing from Rome, received the blessing of the newly-elected pope, and also a gift of the four gospels, and a chasuble richly wrought in silver and gold. St. Enda died about the year 540.§

St. Condlaed was appointed bishop of Kildare about the year 490, and he died before the great patroness of Ireland, on 3rd May, 519. He was a skilful artificer in gold, silver, and other metals;

---

* Acta SS. p. 712.   † Acta SS. p. 705.
‡ See Acta SS. pp. 708 and 711.   § See O'Donovan; Todd, p. 442.

and in the metrical life of St. Brigid, attributed to St. Brogan, it is specially mentioned of him, that returning from Rome, he brought with him a set of rich vestments:—

> "How many miracles she wrought
> No man can fully tell.
> She blessed the vestments of Condlaed,
> Which he brought with him from Leatha."*

These vestments were subsequently famous in the Irish Church, and Cogitosus, in his life of St. Brigid, relates that "she followed the example of the most blessed Job, and never suffered the needy to pass her without a gift; for she gave to the poor the transmarine and rare vestments of bishop Condlaed of glorious light, which he was accustomed to use when offering the sacred mysteries at the altars, on the festivals of our Lord, and the vigils of the Apostles."†

St. Nennidh "of the pure hand," so called from having administered the holy Viaticum to our great patroness, St. Brigid, is also recorded to have made a pilgrimage to Rome.‡

Fortunately, too, the sentiments of the same great foundress of Kildare, in regard to the successors of St. Peter, have been registered in her metrical life by St. Coelan,§ of Inis Keltra, who lived before the close of the seventh century: "She was desirous," he thus writes, "to proceed to the city of Rome, but as this journey was impossible for her, she was blessed by God with a heavenly vision, in which she was present in spirit at the Apostles' shrines, and assisted at the Holy Sacrifice which was offered up over their hallowed remains. She subsequently sent a priest to Rome (perhaps the Nennidh of whom we have just spoken), who would visit

---

* Confer Todd, page 23, seqq., who justly remarks, that in the text just cited, there can be no doubt of the name Leatha being referred to Rome. See the original text in Colgan, Tr. Th. pag. 517.

† Trias Thaumat. page 522. This same ancient writer further informs us, that the tomb of St. Condlaed, placed at the right of the altar of Kildare, "was adorned with gold and silver, and gems and precious stones, with crowns of gold and silver suspended from above."

‡ Acta SS., page 114.

§ This metrical life has been published, but from very imperfect manuscripts, by Colgan, Tr. Thaumat. page 582, seqq., and by the Bollandists. A far more accurate and ancient copy of it is preserved in the Barberini Archives, Rome.

the pontiff in her name, and be instructed, at the same time, in the rites and ceremonies of the holy city: and this delegate of our saint, having tarried some time in Rome, brought back to St. Brigid, and her holy nuns of Kildare, many gifts from the vicar of Christ, and with them the liturgical books and sacred chaunt.

St. Finnian of Cluain-Iraird (now Clonard, Co. Meath), is called, by the Martyrology of Donegal, and the Four Masters, *the tutor of the saints of Ireland*. Aengus thus commemorates him on the 23rd of December:—

> "A tower of gold over the sea,
> May he be the friend of my soul,
> Is Finnian the fair, the beloved founder
> Of the great Cluain-Iraird."*

Three thousand scholars are said to have flocked to his monastery, to be instructed in science and piety: and his ancient hymn records, that, whilst *his teaching was sweeter than the honey-comb*,

> "Trium virorum millium
> Sorte fit doctor humilis
> Verbi his fudit fluvium
> Ut fons emanans rivulis."†

Twelve of his disciples attained special eminence in this school of perfection, and they are known as the twelve apostles of the Irish Church.‡ A fragment of an old life of this saint, quoted by Ware, says that, "like the sun in the firmament, he enlightened the world with the rays of his virtues, wholesome doctrine and miracles: and the fame of his good works attracted many illustrious men from divers parts of the world, to his school, as to a holy repository of wisdom, partly to study the sacred Scriptures, and partly to be instructed in ecclesiastical discipline."§ O'Clery, too, in his Calender of Irish Saints, describes his monastery of Clonard, as "a holy city, full of wisdom and virtue, so that its founder obtained the name of Finnian *the wise*." In his office he is commemorated as "Doctor Hiberniæ, lictor infidelium, thesaurus Clonardiæ."‖

---

* See original in Martyr. of Christ Church, I.A.S. pref. p. lxxxvi.
† Acta SS. p. 401.   ‡ Ibid. page 405; Todd, St. Patrick. page 99.
§ Ware's Antiquities of Ireland, page 241.
‖ Ap. Colgan, loc. cit. page 401.

This saint was the special friend of the two ornaments of the Welsh Church, David and Cathmael or Cadoc. It was with the latter, and also accompanied by his own great disciple Mobius, that Finnian undertook a pilgrimage to Rome. An angel, however, appeared to them on the way, and admonished them to return to their own spiritual charge; for, God had accepted the will for the deed. St. Finnian then asked, what would be the blessing granted to him for this his pilgrimage, and the angel said to him: "Erect an altar to God, and whosoever with devotion visits that altar, will receive the same graces that he would receive at Rome."*

This is the narrative of the ancient Latin life of St. Finnian. There is also extant an Irish manuscript sketching our saint's career; it, too, refers to *his desire to visit Rome*, and mentions that an angel came to him and said—"What would be given to thee at Rome shall be given to thee here."†

This assuredly proves that it was to gain the special blessings of heaven that our greatest saints proposed to themselves the pilgrimage to the shrines of the holy Apostles.

St. Finnian of Maghbile (now Moville) flourished in the same century; his death is commemorated by the Annals of Ulster and Tighernach, in 589.‡ In former times he was revered as the special protector of the counties of Down and Antrim. Thus in the Psaltar-na-Rann, a poem of the ninth century, we read:—

> "The judge of Erin is Patrick,
> Of the great city of Armagh;
> Blessed for ever is the holy man,
> The royal gem of grace.
> The Hy-Neill are under the patronage of Columbkille:
> It is not under the shelter of a brake.
> Under the protection of Finnian of Maghbile
> Are all the Ulidians."§

---

* Vita S. Finniani Acta SS page 394. Dr. Todd, page 100, remarks that this life of St. Finnian consists of two parts, of which the first is much older, and more authentic than the latter. The narrative given above, is taken from the first part, cap. ix. Dr. Todd says that St. Finnian took his departure from his Welsh friends, when about to visit Rome: the life, however, to which he refers, expressly states the contrary.

† Ap Todd, loc. cit. page 101. ‡ See Todd, St. Patrick, page 102-3.
§ See the original in append. to Cambr. Evers. vol. ii. Celtic Society 1850, page 775.

St. Finnian was placed under the instruction of St. Colman, first bishop and founder of Dromore, who flourished in that see about the year 510, and subsequently he lived in the monastery of Neudrum, under the guidance of the holy abbot Coelan.* Being of a princely house of Ulster, many sought to connect him with their families by marriage ; but guided by a divine light (superno lumine radiatus), he resolved to devote himself wholly to God, and set out on a pilgrimage to Rome, to visit the tombs of the Apostles. His fame for virtue and learning had preceded him thither, and hence he was honorably received by the reigning pontiff, Pelagius. For three months he remained in the holy city, "learning the apostolical customs and the ecclesiastical laws," and then having received the apostolic blessing, he returned to his native land, bearing with him the corrected text of the Hieronymian Vulgate, relics of the saints, and those penitential decrees which, says the author of his ancient life, "are still called the canons of St. Finnian."† These penitential decrees of Finnian still happily exist ; they are cited in the Collectio Hibernensis Canonum, and they were published from St. Gall, Vienna, and Parisian manuscripts of the eighth and ninth centuries, by Wasserschleben, at Halle, in 1851. St. Finnian's copy of the Gospels is famous in the ecclesiastical history of the sixth century, and is commemorated in the lives of St. Fintan, Comgall, and Columba.‡ Many authorities have supposed that St. Finnian was the same as the Irish patron of Lucca, who is known in Italy by the name *Frigidiano*. The arguments of O'Connor § and Colgan ‖ have rendered this opinion almost evident ; and the additional facts brought to light by Dr. Todd, when illustrating the hymn of St. Mugint,¶ place this opinion in still clearer light. The date commonly assigned to St. Finnian's death was the chief stumbling-block which induced Lanigan and Reeves to judge him to be a distinct personage from the Frigidian of Lucca. It was only in his just-

---

* See Reeves' Eccl. Antiq. of Down and Connor, page 187, seqq.; Todd, Lib. Hymn., page 98, seqq. where many questions connected with the history of this saint are ably illustrated.
† Acta SS page 638.   ‡ See Todd, St. Patrick, page 105-7.
§ Rerum Hib. Script.   ‖ Loc. cit. page 642.
¶ In Liber Hym page 98-108.

published work on St. Patrick, that Dr. Todd succeeded in identifying the date of 588 or 589, in the Ulster Annals, as the year of the death of St. Finnian of Maghbile, and thus was gained a new and unlooked-for confirmation of the identity of both saints; for the the Italian Annals, as cited by Ughelli in his Italia Sacra, expressly assign the death of Frigidian to 588.*

If our St. Finnian was thus the patron and bishop of Lucca, he would have St. Gregory the Great himself as his panegyrist.† Certain it is, at least, that the holy patron of Lucca was an Irishman, and that by his virtues and miracles in the sixth century, he won for himself not only a heavenly crown, but also an undying fame and veneration throughout all Italy.

The fame, however, of St. Finnian is not less illustrious in our own island. The old life of St. Comgall calls him, "Vir vitæ venerabilis S. Finnianus Epus. qui jacet in miraculis multis in sua civitate Maghbile."‡ Marianus O'Gorman styles him "Finnianus corde devotus;" whilst an ancient Irish poem thus extols his memory: "O blessed school, the resting-place of Finnian: how blessed that one saint should be the tutor of a fellow-saint!" The martyrology, too, of Aengus on the 10th of September, gives a curious quatrain which commemorates, at the same time, the richness of the sacred gift of the corrected text of the Scriptures which St. Finnian had borne to our island from Rome, and the grief of our Church for its brightest ornament, the holy bishop of Maghbile:

> "The body of red gold with purity
> Comes hither across the sea:
> Erin laments its choicest son,
> Finnian of Maghbile."§

---

* See ap. Lanigan, ii. 25.   † In lib. iii. Dialog.
‡ Ap. Fleming Collectan, p. 303, col. 2.
§ See many of the old Irish scholiasts on this verse, cited by Colgan, p. 643, col. i. and Todd, p. 104. All our Irish scholars agree that the quatrain is obscure in its meaning. Colgan was content to paraphrase it as follows:—

> "Roma aureus et præfulgidus,
> Qui contulit libros legis ultra mare,
> Quemque selectissimum Hiberni deflent
> Findbarruss de Maghbile."

The celebrated Gildas was born in Britain, about the year 490. He may, nevertheless, be ranked amongst our Irish saints, on account of his missionary labours in our island. It is expressly recorded of him, that he came to Ireland to drink from its pure streams of sacred learning. Subsequently, he was himself invited to teach the sacred sciences in Armagh; at the same time, he became illustrious throughout our island for his sanctity, and he is reckoned amongst the great masters of the second class of our Irish saints. Towards the close of his life, he was again invited to visit Ireland, by the monarch Ainmire (A.D. 568-571), who was a cousin of St. Columbkille.* St. Gildas, in compliance with the king's request, made a circuit of Ireland, and laboured everywhere to restore the fervour of religion, and bring back the straying sheep to repentance. His death is recorded by our annalists in 570.† During the pontificate of Agapitus, he visited Rome, and offered to the holy father, as a token of his homage, an exquisitely adorned bell, which he had brought with him from Ireland. It is mentioned in the life of St. Cadoc, that seeing, on one occasion, this beautiful bell of Gildas, he was charmed with its ornamentation, and colour, and tone,‡ and wished to purchase it; but Gildas replied that it was intended as *an offering on the altar of St. Peter in Rome*, and hence he would not part with it for any price, till he presented it in person to the then pontiff, St. Agapitus.§

St. Molua, of Clonfert-Mulloe (Queen's County), is thus eulogized by St. Cuimin:

> "Molua of Cluain-ferta, loved
> Humility glorious and pure,
> Submission to tutor, submission to parents,
> Submission to all men."‖

---

* See Reeves' Adamnan, p. 342. † See Todd, St. Patrick, p. 112.

‡ Invenit Gildam cum pulcherrima quadam campanula de Hibernia illuc advenisse cumque decor et color sonusque placuisset Gildam sibi Nolam vendere imploravit, in notis.—Ap Colgan, Acta SS. page 178.

§ See Colgan, loc. cit.; Lanigan i. 476, seqq., who proves very clearly that *Gildas Badonicus* was not a distinct person from *Albanius*, as Colgan, Usher, and others had imagined. It is a curious fact, that St. Gildas is said to have sent another small bell as a gift to St. Brigid, about the year 520.

‖ Calendar of Irish Saints, page 167.

A legend connected with this saint records his desire to visit Rome in pilgrimage, in order "to pray before the relics of the Apostles, and to pay his vows at their hallowed shrines."* St. Molua died in the year 609.

St. Flannan, styled by Aenghus "the king of meekness," (Dec. 18) is the patron saint of Killaloe. He was educated in the school of St. Molua, and subsequently spent many years in silent retreat in the far-famed monastery of Lismore. He thence proceeded to Rome, on a pilgrimage to the tombs of the Apostles, and was there consecrated by the pope, first bishop of Killaloe.† The life of the bishop adds, that after his death, an assembly of Irish princes and prelates was held at Killaloe, to prepare a befitting shrine for his sacred remains. They were accordingly deposited in a rich urn of silver and gold, and solemnly placed over the high-altar of the church.

St. Flannan was not the only Irish saint that received the episcopal consecration at the hands of the successors of St. Peter, in the city of Rome. Some years earlier, St. Carthage (the elder) was consecrated there, and from that fact derived his characteristic designation, as we find thus marked by Aenghus, on the 5th of March :—

> "The silent man went with renown
> Eastwards over the sea,
> Carthage, the royal one of Rome."

The chief monastery of this saint was on the banks of the Maug he flourished before the year 580.

To this class of our saints belongs Laserian, bishop, and now patron, of Leighlin. His festival is marked in the Irish calendars on April the 18th, on which day Aenghus remarks:

> "We count the festival of the seven
> Noble protecting deacons,
> With Laserian of burning virtues,
> Abbot of bright-shining Leithglinn."

---

* Colgan, Acta SS., page 213. It is partly given by Todd, page 115.
† See Ware, Bishops of Killaloe, who, however, in his narrative, confounds pope John IV. with John VI.

He pursued his studies in Rome, and received the holy orders of deacon and priest at the hands of St. Gregory the Great. On returning to our island, the same great pontiff gave to him a copy of the gospels, and commanded him to preach the doctrines of faith. At this time a holy abbot named Gobhan, whilst preaching on the banks of the Barrow, saw in vision a host of angels hovering over Leighlin, and announced to his disciples that one day a fervent stranger would gather together in that spot as many servants of God as there were angels in that heavenly host. St. Laserian soon realized this vision, and before the year 680 the fame of his sanctity had already gathered 1,500 monks to his hallowed monastery.* He defended with energy and success the Roman computation of Easter in the synod of Maghlene, and was destined by the assembled fathers to proceed, as their delegate, to the holy city (*ad sanctam civitatem*). Whilst there, in 633, he was elevated to the episcopal dignity, and received the imposition of hands from pope Honorius the First. Thus were our Irish pilgrims, even in the earliest ages, bound by the closest bonds with the successors of St. Peter.

SS. Wiro and Plechelm, two bright ornaments of our Irish Church towards the close of the seventh century, were also elevated to the episcopate in Rome. Their ancient hymn at vespers sings:—

> " Invitos Scotia destinat infulis,
> Sacram confugiunt ad cathedram Petri,
> Sed mandante papa tandem hierarchicis
> Sublimantur honoribus."

Their life, written about the tenth century, describes our island as " uber sanctorum patrum insula, stellarum numeris sanctorum coæquans patrocinia;"† and subsequently narrates how, when having been chosen bishop of his district, Wiro, before receiving

---

* "Happy college!" exclaims his biographer, "whose virtues were heralded by the army of heaven."

† Ap. Acta SS. Maij, tom. ii. p. 309, et seq. Many interesting details regarding these Irish saints may be seen in "Antiquitates Monasterii S. Martini," by Kessel (Coloniæ, 1863), p. ii. iii. and 129, and Lanigan, iii. 113.

consecration, set out on a pilgrimage for Rome, with the secret design to be relieved by the pope from that threatened burden: he was accompanied thither by his cherished associate in deeds of piety, St. Plechelm. In Rome "they reverently kissed the threshold of the apostles Peter and Paul; they watered with their tears its hallowed pavement; they visited without ceasing the shrines of the saints of God, and through their intercession solicited aid from on high."* Being presented to the Holy Father, St. Wiro detailed his mission and his own desires: "The pope, however, was not moved by his petition, and anxious to consult for the interests of that distant see, he confirmed his election, and, with his own hands, conferred on him and on St. Plechelm the episcopal consecration."†

In the life of St. Sylas it is mentioned that his sister set out from Ireland, desirous, as was "customary with the Irish"‡ to pray before the relics of the Apostles. This favour, however, was not granted her by God, and in Lucca she closed her earthly pilgrimage: St. Sylas soon after visited Rome. The dynast of his district had sought to subject to burdensome exactions the churches and monasteries of his diocese: these were resisted by St. Sylas, who wished, moreover, to have his decision sanctioned by the apostolic authority of Rome. On returning from the Holy See he, too, tarried in Lucca, and received there his eternal crown. His body was interred in the church of St. Justina: and such was the fame of his virtues and miracles, that he was soon associated with the other Irish patron, St. Frigidian, and numbered amongst the saints of Lucca.§

It was in 721 that pope Gregory II. convened a council, in Rome, to anathematize the Iconoclast emperor, Leo the Isaurian.

---

* "Limina SS. app. Petri et Pauli, labris premunt impressis, marmor pavimenti irrigant lachrymis," etc.—Acta SS. p. 316.
† Ibid. 316.
‡ "Almorum Petri apostolorum principis ejusque coapostoli Pauli gloriosa limina sicut moris est gentis illius, orationis causa corporaliter visitare disponens," etc.—Vita, p. 101.
§ There was formerly a MS. life of St. Sylas preserved in the Monastery of St. Justina, in Lucca, and, by Wadding, it was judged *pervetusta*. It was published by Fiorentini, in 1662, in the appendix to his Italian life of St. Sylas, and occupies pp. 99-104.

An Irish bishop assisted at this synod, and amongst the names subscribed to the synodical decrees, we find that of "Sedulius, an Irishman, bishop in Britain."* A few centuries later the third council of Lateran was also held in Rome. In it the Albigensian heretics were condemned, and many disciplinary laws were enacted for the Church. More than one Irish bishop took part in this council, but of one in particular it is narrated, that when the bishops were interrogated as to their means of support, he replied that " his whole sustenance depended on three milch cows, and according as any one of these became dry, another was substituted by his parishioners."† Thus did the Irish bishops take a part even in the synods held in the city of Rome.

Disciple and companion of St. Columbanus was Dichuill, better known on the continent as Deicola. His life, written before the year 900, is published by Colgan‡ and the Bollandists. Having founded a monastery in the diocese of Besançon, he dedicated its church in honor of the apostles Peter and Paul. He subsequently set out for Rome,§ to visit the capital of the Christian world, and obtain for his monastery the blessing and protection of the Vicar of Christ. "I am a native of the island of Erin, and a pilgrim for Christ's sake," he thus addressed the pontiff; "the oratories which I erected bear the names of the noble apostles Peter and Paul, to whom belongs this Roman citadel.|| They have been enriched with many gifts and possessions by the surrounding princes; and I have now come to thee, the chief bishop,¶ to commit them to thy apostolic care." All that the holy abbot desired was readily accorded to him; the charter of his monastery was confirmed by the *seal of apostolical*

---

* " Ego Sedulius epus. Britanniæ de genere Scotorum huic constituto a nobis promulgato subscripsi."—Labbé, Collect. Concil.

† Erat ibi etiam Hybernicus epus. qui retulit se non habere alios redditus præter tres vaccas lactantes, quas in defectu lactis, parochiani sui per alias innovabant.—Hist. Æp. Bremen, pag. 64. Two Scotch bishops were also present, one of whom made the journey, through France and Italy, on foot; the other made it on horseback.

‡ Acta SS. Hib. page 115; Bolland. tom. ii. ad diem 18 Januarii.

§ " Romanam petiit celsitudinem."—Loc. cit. page 120.

|| " Qui hanc Romanam possident arcem."—Ibid.

¶ " Præsul capitalis."—Ib.

authority;[*] and he himself returned to his spiritual children, laden with the rich treasure of relics of the holy martyrs, and with many ornaments for his sacred edifices.[†]

It was about the year 686 that St. Kilian and his companions set out from Ireland, to win for themselves the crown of apostles, together with the martyrs' palm, in Germany. The life of these glorious saints, written with all the simplicity of the ninth century, thus records their visit to the city of the seven hills :—

"There was in Ireland a holy man of princely birth, by name Kilian. Assembling some of his disciples, he exhorted them to despise the transitory goods of the world, and in the spirit of the Gospel, to forsake country and kindred, and to follow Christ. They yielded to his persuasions, ... and having landed in Germany, their holy leader, Kilian, thus again addressed them: Brethren, how beautiful is this country, how cheerful are its people; and still they are in the darkness of error. If it seem good to you, let us do as we said when we were in our own country; let us go to Rome, to visit the threshold of the prince of the Apostles, and present ourselves before the blessed pope John; and if it be the will of God, when we shall have received the sanction of the Apostolic See, we shall, under its guidance, return again to this people, and preach to them the name of our Lord Jesus. Without delay, their deeds corresponded with these words, and they set out for the threshold of St. Peter, the prince of the Apostles. On arriving there, the holy pope John had already passed to his eternal rest; but they were lovingly and honorably welcomed by his successor, pope Conon. And this holy pontiff, having heard whence and for what motive they had come, and to what country they were desirous to devote themselves with such zealous ardour, received their profession of our holy faith, and then commissioned them in the name of God and St. Peter to teach and preach the Gospel of Christ."[‡]

This, surely, was in accordance with Catholic teaching; and soon St. Kilian and his companions sealed with their blood the Gospel of truth and the devotion of our island to the successors of St. Peter.

---

[*] " Apostolicâ auctoritate sigillatam."—Colgan.

[†] " Cœlestibus oneratus muneribus, id est, prætiosis martyrum pignoribus et ornamentis ecclesiasticis, simul cum privilegio suo apostolico firmato sigillo."—Ibid. 121.

[‡] " Audita illius fide, pariter et doctrina, dedit illi a Deo et sancto Petro principe apostolorum, licentiam et potestatem prædicandi et docendi."— Ap. Acta SS. Julii die 8vo tom. ii. page 613. The editors of the life prove it to have been written about the year 800. See also Canisius, Antiq. Lect. tom. iv.; Messingham, Florilegium, page 318; Mabillon, Acta Benedict. tom. ii. page 991.

CHAPTER III.
(CONTINUED)

IRISH PILGRIMAGES TO ROME.

Pilgrimage of St. Canice to Rome—Of St. Foillan—St. Senanus—St. Dagan—St. Caidoc—St. Marianus—St. Willibrord—St. Boniface, a native of Ireland—His journeys to Rome—Appointment of Albuin to See of Buraburg by Pope Zachary.

St. Canice was another great ornament of our Church in the sixth century. Born in 516, he was, during his whole life, the friend and companion of SS. Columba, Comgall, Brendan of Birr, and Fintan of Clonenagh. St. Cuimin writes of him:—

> "Cainnech of the mortifications loved
> To be in a bleak woody desert
> Where there was none to attend on him
> But only the wild deer."

From his life, accurately edited by the marquis of Ormond in 1853, we learn that before entering upon his apostolic ministry, he determined to visit Rome and venerate the Apostolic See.* Carrying out this holy design, he passed through many towns of Italy, which long cherished a fond remembrance of his virtues and miracles; in one city especially the local prince presented to him a grant of land, and St. Canice built a monastery there, wishing to spend in it the remaining years of his life. It was only when an angel admonished him that Ireland was "the place of his resurrection," that he abandoned the sunny south and returned to our island.†

St. Foillan or Foelan is venerated as one of the chief patrons of Brabant. His feast is kept on the 31st of October, and Aengus commemorates his martyrdom on the same day. "*Foillan, with his many labourers,*" he says, and the gloss adds, "he was the brother of Fursa, and a martyr." From his life we learn that he laboured for some time in England, till his monastery was destroyed

---
* Page 4 and 47. † Ibid. cap. v. seqq.

by a party of marauders; he then set out for Rome, where pope Martin the First (649-654) governed the Church, and being kindly received by the common father of the faithful, he was authorized by him to preach the Gospel in Gaul, where, adds his biographer, "he brought forth many spiritual children to Christ."*

St. Senanus was bishop of Inniscattery, an island in the lower Shannon, and patron of the Hy-Connail; he was born before the death of our apostle, in 488. His acts relate that "he set out for Rome to visit the sacred shrines of the Apostles, and having performed his devotions in Rome, he returned through France, and visited the great monastery of St. Martin, at Tours."† After his return he founded a church at Inniscarra, five miles from Cork, on the banks of the Lee. We mention this particular fact on account of a special circumstance which the life of our saint records: "Soon

---

* Colgan, ad diem 16 Jan., has given some extracts from the corrected office of St. Foillan. We give the hymns, as used in the Church of Liege, before these corrections were made, in Appendix No. 8, from a MS. of the Vallicellian Archives. We here insert the beautiful lessons read in the same ancient church, on the saint's feast day, from the same MS.:—

1. Foillanus patre Phillano principe Hiberniæ, matre vero Gergegha Scotorum regis filia natus. Sacris et humanioribus litteris a Brandano epo. est eruditus: fama vero ejus sanctitatis late circumfusa Hybernorum epus. accersitur, quo munere ut fungebatur et jam omnium plausum conscivisset timens vitam fumosa nominis gloria maculare cessit et ignotus maluit apud Anglos apostolicum munus ac doctorem agere; sed postea vastatâ Anglia et monasterio quod ibidem struxerat diruto ad urbem Romam peregrinatus est, quem Martinus papa benigne suscipiens prædicationis gratia ad Gallias destinavit in quibus multos Jesu Christo filios peperit.

2. Cumque apud Gertrudem virginem aliquamdiu moratus esset, liberalis virgo de patrimonio terræ Fossensis spatia viro ssmo. donavit: ubi idem vir Dei monasterio ædificato aliquamdiu resedit tandemque illius optimis disciplinis fulgentis curam (ut verbi Dei dispensationi liberius instaret) fratri suo Ultano reliquit: quadam vero die dum vir Dei a labore et prædicatione indefessus per quamdam silvam cum paucis fratribus iter haberet, applicuerunt se illis nefarii homines qui simulato pacis et hospitii nomine ut lupi ovina contecti pelle sanctos erronee ducunt. convitiis afficiunt telisque confossos gladio tandem peremerunt, utque scelus lateat corpora inhoneste projicientes in silva absconderunt.

3. Inhumata corpora cum diu jacuissent sancta Gertrudis virgo monita ab angelo, necnon beatus Ultanus, visâ dum orationi vacaret, sanguine perfusâ columbâ per signum igneæ columnæ a tellure qua sanctorum reposita erant corpora ad cœlum usque porrectæ, nihil grave sed redolentia suave repererunt, et honesto loco sepelierunt ac subinde volente Deo corpus beati martyris Foillani Fossas translatum fuit, qua in translatione illud memoriæ proditum est fluvium Sumbrim aquis tunc solito magis tumidum stetisse atque sacro corpori dum plaustro ferretur hinc inde stantibus aquis solidum iter præbuisse.

† Acta SS. p. 532.

after the foundation of this church," it says, " a vessel arrived there with many religious pilgrims; amongst these were fifty religious Romans, whom the desire of a penitential life, and of the study of the Scriptures, then flourishing amongst us, had attracted to our island: they desired to be placed under the guidance of the holy men who were famed for their sanctity of life and their observance of religious discipline."* Thus were reciprocally bound together the churches of Ireland and Rome: Rome was famed in Ireland, as being the Apostolic See, and hence, our saints went on pilgrimage to venerate the Vicar of Christ, and pay their vows at the shrines of the Apostles; Ireland, too, was famed in Rome,—her religious perfection, and sanctity, and skill in sacred science, won the admiration of the faithful of the holy city; and when their own monasteries were laid waste, and their sanctuaries pillaged by ruthless invaders, we find them seeking a sacred asylum in Ireland, in whose hallowed retreat they might pursue undisturbed the highest paths of spiritual perfection. Dr. Petrie, when treating of the Round Towers, makes mention of "the crowds of foreign ecclesiastics, Egyptian, Roman, Italian, French, British, and Saxon, who flocked to Ireland as a place of refuge, in the fifth and sixth centuries. Of such immigration," he adds, " there cannot possibly exist a doubt; for, not to speak of the great number of foreigners, who were disciples of St. Patrick, and of whom the names are preserved in the most ancient lives of that saint, nor of the evidences of the same nature so abundantly supplied in the lives of many other saints of the primitive Irish Church, it will be sufficient to refer to that most curious ancient document, written in the year 799, the Litany of St. Aengus, the Culdee, in which are invoked such a vast number of foreign saints buried in Ireland. Copies of this ancient litany are found in the Book of Leinster, a MS. undoubtedly of the twelfth century, preserved in the Library of Trinity College, Dublin; and in the Leabhar Breac, preserved in the Royal Irish Academy."† He then gives a long extract from this litany of Aengus, as cited by Colgan.‡ We shall have occasion to return

* Acta SS. p. 533.   † Page 134.   ‡ Page 535.

again to this litany, when we shall give it more in full from the translation of Eugene Curry.

St. Dagan is designated in our martyrologies by the various epithets of the *warlike*, the *pilgrim*, the *meek*, and the *noble*. He was one of the most ardent defenders of the old Scotic computation of Easter, and as such is commemorated by Bede, in his Ecclesiastical History.* About the year 600 he visited Rome, and sought the approbation of the great pontiff St. Gregory, for the rule of his own master, St. Molua, in whose life we thus read— "The abbot, Dagan, going to Rome, brought with him the rule which St. Molua had drawn up and delivered to his disciples; and pope Gregory having read this rule, said in the presence of all: 'the saint who composed this rule has truly guarded his disciples even to the very thresholds of heaven.' Wherefore St. Gregory sent his approbation and benediction to Molua."† St. Dagan, however, was not the only one of our sainted forefathers that sought the sanction of the Holy See for the religious rule which they adopted. In the Leabhar-nah-Uidhre,‡ it is incidentally mentioned that "St. Comgall, of Bangor, sent Beoan, son of Innli, of *Teach-Dabeog*, to Rome, on a message to pope Gregory (the Great), *to receive from him order and rule.*"§

It would, however, be tedious to mention in detail the innumerable cases commemorated in the records of our early Church, of pilgrimage from our island to the Apostolic See.

Of St. Caidoc, apostle of the Morini, in Gaul, such a pilgrimage is mentioned in the seventh century. A little later, St. Albert bishop of Emly, with nineteen companions, "set out on pilgrimage, and paused not till, according to the custom of his countrymen, he reached Rome, the mother and guardian of faith, and venerated the exalted dignity of the Apostolic See."‖ In 854 the Irish Annals mention the death of Indrechtach, successor of St. Columbkille,

---

* Lib. ii. cap. 4.   † Acta SS. p. 585.   ‡ Fol. 36.
§ See app. Reeves' Eccles. Antiq. of Down and Connor, p. 376.
‖ Donec Romam, religionis nostræ matrem et matricem pervenerunt, apostolicæque dignitatis apicem more suæ gentis venerabundi salutaverunt.—Acta SS. p. 39, col. a.

who was martyred by Saxon plunderers on his way to Rome.* Two years later, another pilgrim, Diarmaid, "the wisest of the Irish," or, as he is styled in the Annals of Ulster, "sapientissimus omnium doctorum Europæ," met with a like fate.

It was "through the merits and fasting and prayers of the holy man, Cele-Dabhall," abbot of Bangor, that the northern plunderers were driven from Ireland in the beginning of the tenth century. The annalist adds, "he was a holy and pious man, and had great zeal for the Christians; and besides strengthening the heroes of Erin against the pagans, he laboured himself by fasting and prayer, and he sought freedom for the churches of Erin."† This venerable abbot, "bishop, scribe, preacher, and wise doctor, died on his pilgrimage, in Rome, on the 14th day of September, in 927." The death of another holy man, "Ferghil, abbot of Tyrdaglass," is recorded in the following year. In 1024 is marked the death of "Fachtua, lector and priest of Clonmacnoise, airchinneach of Fennor, and the most distinguished abbot of Ireland; he died in Rome on his pilgrimage." It was in 1064 that Donogh O'Brien, son of the famous Brian Boroimhe, went to Rome to expiate his misdeeds by pilgrimage and penance: he offered a collection of Irish canons to the pope, and many other presents; and, embracing the monastic state, closed his days in Rome, in the monastery of St. Stephen. Less than a century later, Imhar O'Hegan, by whom the church of SS. Peter and Paul, at Armagh, was built, and who was tutor of St. Malachy, and styled by St. Bernard "vir sanctissimæ vitæ," set out to venerate the shrines of the Apostles, and in Rome finished his earthly pilgrimage. We may take another example from the Acts of our Saints at this same period.

It was in the year 1067 that Muiredhach Mac Robartaigh, known in Germany as St. Marianus, a native of Donegal, taking two companions, John and Candidus, set out on a pilgrimage for Rome. Having arrived in Germany, they stopped for some time at Bamberg, in the Benedictine monastery, and at the suggestion of Otho, the bishop of the place, they became members of

* Fragments of Irish Annals, published by I. A. S. in 1860, p. 120, seq.
† Ibid. p. 227, and Annals of Ulster, ad. an. 927.

that order. No sooner, however, had that bishop passed to a better life than, mindful of the object for which they had at first quitted the shores of Tirconnell, forsooth to visit the shrines of the apostles SS. Peter and Paul, "as Irishmen were wont to do," they solicited the permission of their superior to continue their journey to Rome. Arriving in Ratisbon, they met with an Irish recluse named Muircertach, who made known to them the will of Heaven that that city should be their permanent abode. They bowed to the divine decree, and founded there the monastery of Weich-St.-Peter, which soon acquired a wide-spread fame, and filled Germany with filiate foundations for Irish monks.*

So frequent indeed were these Irish pilgrimages, that they became proverbial on the continent, and Ricemarch, in his life of St. David of Wales, characterises their pilgrim ardour as insatiable, "cum inextinguibile Hibernensium desiderium ad sanctorum Petri et Pauli apostolorum reliquias visitandas arderet." Another foreign chronicler, Ethelwerd, after mentioning the journey by sea of three Irishmen to England (one of whom is styled "artibus frondens, litterâ doctus, magister insignis Scottorum," ad an. 892), adds that, though graciously received by king Alfred, they, *ut soliti*, pursued their pilgrimage to Rome. In 845 was held the synod of Meaux, in which complaints were made to the French king, of the state of ruin into which the houses for the reception of the Irish pilgrims were allowed to fall, in many parts of France; these *hospitalia* were founded at a much earlier period by pious persons of the Irish nation, as Fleury tells us, to serve as a temporary resting-place for their many countrymen who flocked in pilgrimage towards the tombs of the Apostles and Jerusalem.†

---

* Acta Sanctorum, Febr. tom. ii. p. 365, seq. ; also a paper of Dr. Reeves, R.I.A., April 9, 1860.

† Harduin, Conc. t. iv. p. 1490, gives the decree of the council of Meaux: "Hospitalia Scotorum, quæ sancti homines gentis illius in hoc regno construxerunt et rebus pro sanctitate sua acquisitis ampliaverunt, ab eodem hospitalitatis officio funditus sunt alienata. Et non solum super venientes in eadem hospitalia non recipiuntur, verum etiam ipsi, qui ab infantia in eisdem locis sub religione Domino militaverunt, et exinde ejiciuntur, et ostiatim mendicare eoguntur." In the same way as in France, the Irish were afterwards expelled from their monasteries in Germany, which passed into the hands of Scotch or English.

There are, moreover, very many examples of such pilgrimages being undertaken by foreigners, who had been trained to spiritual wisdom in the Irish schools, as also by those who, though born in Ireland, are commonly reckoned amongst the ornaments of other churches, on account of their lives having been devoted to missionary enterprise at a distance from our shores. We shall take merely one example from each of these classes.

Amongst the many Saxons who studied in Ireland in the seventh and eighth centuries, none bore a more illustrious name than Willibrord. From his infancy he was educated by the Irish monks of Ripon; and, subsequently, he spent twelve years in the study of the sacred Scriptures in Ireland.* His first step was " to hasten to Rome, the apostolical chair of which was then filled by pope Sergius (A.D. 687–701), that by his sanction and blessing he might begin the wished-for work of announcing the Gospel to the heathen." This blessing was gladly accorded to him, and being enriched with relics of the holy martyrs, he fearlessly announced the doctrines of faith to the inhabitants of Friesland; and after a few years we find him again journeying to Rome, where, at the request of Pepin, he was consecrated by the same pope first bishop of that territory.

St. Boniface, the illustrious martyr and apostle of Germany, was a native of Ireland :† passing in his youth to England, he received in its monasteries the name of Winfrid; subsequently, as archbishop of Mentz and founder of the great monastery of Fulda, he bore the name of Bonifacius. It was from pope Gregory II. that he received his mission to labour in preaching the Gospel of Christ among the pagans; and the Holy Father in giving that commission, speaks‡ " in the name of the indivisible Trinity, and

---

* Alcuini, Vita S. Willibr. Opp. tom. ii. p. 183 seqq. Bede, Hist. Ecc. lib. v. cap. 11. seq. Alcuin, in his metrical life of this saint, says : " Doctaque nutrivit studiis sed Hibernia sacris." And again : " Patria Scottorum clara magistra fuit."— Opp. ii. pp. 197, 200.

† See the monuments which prove this in Pertz's Monumenta Germ. Historica, vol. vii. in Chronic. Mariani, passim ad an. 737, 745, 762, 765. Also in Tentamen Vitæ, S. Galli published by Pertz, Ibid. Trithemius in his Script in like manner refers St. Boniface to Ireland. Marianus, who must be supposed well acquainted with the history of this great apostle, expressly styles him " tum matre tum patre Scottus."

‡ See Inter Opp. S. Bonifacii, epist. Greg II.; edit. Giles, p 26.

by the authority of the blessed Peter, the prince of the Apostles, whose office of teaching he held, and whose holy see he administered." When the labours of the missionary were seen to be blessed by God, we find him again summoned to Rome to receive episcopal consecration, which sacred ceremony was performed by the pope, on the feast of St. Andrew, in 723. More than once during his subsequent apostolate he visited Rome to consult the Holy See on the spiritual interests of his flock; more than once, too, we find him disputing with Irish missionaries; but both they and he are ever found to agree on the one main principle of controversy, to refer, forsooth, their disputes to the one common supreme tribunal of Rome.

It was in 742, towards the close of his missionary toils, that St. Boniface solicited from Rome the appointment of an Irishman named Albuin (known in Germany by the name *Witta*,) to the see of Buraburg, near Fritzlar, in Hesse. The letter of pope Zachary in reply is still happily preserved.* It begins as follows:

"Dilectissimo nobis, Wittæ sanctæ ecclesiæ Barbaranæ Zacharias papa.

"Domino co-operante et sermonem confirmante ad dilatandam Christianitatis legem et orthodoxæ fidei tramitem ad prædicandum juxta quod prædicat sancta hæc Romana, cui Deo auctore præsidemus, ecclesia, innotuit nobis sanctissimum et Revmum. fratrem Bonifacium nuper decrevisse et ordinasse in Germaniæ partibus episcopales sedes, ubi præest vestra dilectio et provinciam in tres divisisse parochias. Quo cognito cum magna exultatione extensis ad sidera palmis, illuminatori et datori omnium bonorum Domino Deo et Salvatori nostro Jesu Christo gratias egimus 'qui facit utraque unum.' Flagitavit autem a nobis per suas syllabas jam dictus sanctissimus

"To our most beloved Witta, of the church of Buraburg, pope Zachary,

"We have lately heard that our most holy and most rev. brother Boniface, God having been pleased by His blessing and power to propagate the Christian law, and the teaching of the orthodox faith, and the doctrine as preached in this holy Roman Church, in which, through God's will, we preside, decreed and directed that the territory in which you preach amongst the Germans should be divided into three dioceses. Having heard this we raised our hands to God with ineffable joy, returning thanks to the author and giver of all good gifts, our Lord and Saviour Jesus Christ, who gathers all to His saving fold. The aforesaid most holy man solicited by his letters

---

* Opp. S. Bonifacii edit. Giles, vol. i. page 112.

vir per apostolicam auctoritatem vestras confirmari sedes. Propter quod et nos ardenti animo et divino juvamine auctoritate beati Petri principis apostolorum, cui data est a Deo et Saluatore nostro Jesu Christo ligandi solvendique potestas peccata hominum, in cœlo et in terra, confirmanus atque solidas permanere vestras sedes sancimus episcopales," etc.

that, by our apostolic authority, we should confirm your sees. Wherefore, with sincere solicitude and with the divine aid, by the authority of the blessed Peter, prince of the Apostles, to whom was given, by our Saviour Jesus Christ, the power of loosing and binding in heaven and on earth the sins of men, we confirm and decree, that your episcopal sees shall remain unchanged," etc.

CHAPTER III.
(CONTINUED.)
APPEALS OF IRISH SAINTS TO ROME.

St. Columbanus —St. Virgil.—Paschal Question.—St. Cummian.—Synod of Magh-lene.—Bishops who were present.—Words of Dr. Lynch.

It was before the close of the sixth century that St. Columbanus and his companions set out from the peaceful sanctuary of Bangor, to rekindle the fire of charity on the continent. His monasteries of Luxieu and Fontaines soon attracted the attention of the French Church; but whilst none failed to admire the extraordinary piety of the Irish pilgrims, and the lustre of their virtues, some of the French clergy were alarmed at the new rite of celebrating Easter which the strangers introduced, and at some other peculiar usages of the Irish Church, which, if allowed to continue, might, they feared, be an occasion of dissension and discord among the Christians of Gaul. For this reason, having assembled in synod, the French bishops deemed it expedient to prohibit these peculiar usages of St. Columban and his disciples. The saint acknowledged the authority of the prelates; but, he had received these usages from his fathers in the faith, and hence he appealed to the superior authority of the Roman pontiff, that thus the decision of the Gaulish bishops might be revoked, and he and his disciples be allowed to pursue the observances of their country.

St. Gregory, justly honoured with the epithet of *the Great*, then filled the papal chair. To him our saint addressed his letter of appeal; and whilst he invoked his supreme sanction for the Irish paschal computation, took occasion to interrogate him on some other dubious matters, requesting the pontiff to prescribe the course which he should pursue.

This letter of Columbanus seems never to have reached its destination. The French bishops having again assembled in synod, resolved no longer to tolerate the innovations of the Irish pilgrims; and whilst St. Columban wrote a letter to them, explaining his reasons for not complying with their wishes, and referring to the document he had addressed to Rome, he at the same time appealed again to the judgment of the Roman pontiff, Boniface IV., who had succeeded St. Gregory in the chair of St. Peter. This appeal is addressed, "To the holy Lord and Apostolic Father in Christ, the Pope;" and St. Columbanus having declared that though for a long time he had determined to visit "those who held the Apostolic See—the prelates most dear to all the faithful—the fathers most to be revered for the privilege of their apostolic dignity," he adds, that hitherto he had been impeded by the seditions and tumults of the nations that intervened; and thus solemnly invokes the decisive judgment of Rome:

"To thee alone do we pour out our supplications, through our Lord Jesus Christ and the Holy Ghost, and through the unity of faith which is common to us, that thou mayest bestow upon us, labouring pilgrims, the solace of thy holy decision, with which thou willst strengthen the tradition of our elders, if it be not contrary to faith; that thus we may, during our pilgrimage, be enabled, through thy adjudication, to keep the rite of Easter as it was handed down to us by our fathers."*

This is a clear case of appeal from an inferior authority to the highest tribunal on earth; but before his letter could be replied to, St. Columban was obliged to fly from the persecution of Brunechild, and abandon the shores of France.

In the eighth century another Irish pilgrim, Virgilius, shed lustre

* Biblioth. PP. Galland. xii. 349.

on our island by his virtues and learning. He was for some years abbot of Achadhbo in Ireland, but desirous to devote himself to the conversion of unbelievers, he set out for the continent. Bavaria was the first theatre of his zealous labours; he soon became associated with St. Boniface, bishop of Mentz; subsequently he was appointed bishop of Saltzburg by pope Stephen the Second, and he is now venerated as the patron and apostle of Carinthia. He is designated by his German biographers as "*the most learned amongst the learned.*" Alcuin composed a poem in his honour, in which he thus extols him:—

> "Egregius præsul meritis et moribus altus,
> Protulit in lucem quem mater Hibernia,
> Instituit, docuit, nutrivit,
> Vir pius et prudens, nulli pietate secundus."*

It was whilst sharing the missionary toils of St. Boniface that a controversy arose which, for a while, interrupted their mutual harmony. Some of the clergy were supposed to vitiate the pronunciation of the Latin words in the sacred form of Baptism, and St. Boniface judged that the sacrament thus administered was invalid. St. Virgil, however, though as yet a simple priest, had learned, in the Irish schools, to distinguish with more precision between the accidental and essential parts of the sacrament, and in the case at issue, pronounced it to be his opinion that the baptism was valid; hence he appealed from the decision of the bishop Boniface to the authority of the Holy See. The result of this appeal is well known to all students of divinity, and the holy pontiff soon gave the seal of his approbation to the opinion of St. Virgil.

In the domestic annals of our Church we meet with few matters of controversy that demanded the intervention of a distant see.

---

* His Irish name was *Ferghil*, and he is one of the few Irishmen who became illustrious on the continent, and nevertheless have their names registered in our domestic annals. The Four Masters thus record his death—"A.D. 784, *Ferghil* the geometer, abbot of Achadhbo, died in Germany in the thirteenth year of his episcopate" He is also commemorated in the Annals of Ulster, in A.D. 788. His life is published by Mezger in his Bishops of Saltzburg.

The paschal controversy alone threatened for a while to disturb the religious concord of the island, and to require the decision of the supreme ecclesiastical tribunal to restore union among the conflicting prelates of our Church. It is not necessary here to enter into the details of this controversy; the synod of Magh-lene alone, in which the bishops of Leinster and Munster assembled, now claims our attention. We shall describe its proceedings in the words of St. Cummian, who assisted at it, and was one of its most distinguished members :—

" 'An old authority,' says Jerome, 'rises up against me. In the meanwhile I cry out, whosoever is joined to the chair of St. Peter, that man is mine.' What more ? I turn to the words of the bishop of Rome, pope Gregory, gifted with the appellation of the Golden Mouth, who, though he wrote after all, is deservedly preferred before all; and I find him thus writing on this passage of Job—Gold hath a place wherein it is melted, etc. 'The gold is the great body of the saints; the place of melting is the unity of the Church; the fire the sufferings of martyrdom : he, therefore, who is tried by fire out of the unity of the Church, may be melted, but cannot be cleansed.' "

Having laid down this principle, he adds :—

"What can be deemed more injurious to mother Church than to say Rome errs, Jerusalem errs, Alexandria errs, Antioch errs, the whole world is in error; only the Scots and Britons know what is right? . . . . . Having, therefore, studied the matter for a year, I asked my fathers to declare to me, my elders to tell me (the successors, forsooth, of our first holy fathers, bishop Ailbe, Kieran of Clonmacnoise, Brendan, Nessan, Lugid), what they thought of our being separated from the above-mentioned apostolic sees. And having all met together in the plain of Magh-lene, some in person, some by legates sent in their stead, they decreed that 'our predecessors, through meet witnesses, of whom some are still living, whilst others sleep in peace, commanded us to humbly receive, without hesitation, whatever things were better and more estimable, whensoever they were approved of by the source of our baptism and wisdom, and brought to us from the successors of the Apostles of the Lord.' Afterwards they, of one accord, set forth to us, according to custom, a mandate upon this matter, to keep Easter, the coming year, in unison with the whole Church. But after a while there arose up a certain white-washed wall, feigning to hold fast by the traditions of the elders, and he, instead of healing dissension, promoted division, and in part rendered null what had been promised: whom God, I hope, will punish according as He deems fit."

It was when matters had arrived at this point that the assembled bishops adopted the course already described in the words of Cummian, in a former page (110-112). Recalling the synodical statute, that when such questions of moment arise they should be referred to the head of cities, they destined humble and prudent men to visit the apostolic city, and learn what was the course pursued in that centre of the blessing of God. Thus, their case is not precisely an appeal to the judgment of the Roman See; it is even something more; for they resolve to be guided by what they would find practised in that Apostolic See. The deputies soon returned from Rome, bearing with them the tidings that their Irish usage was not in accordance with what they found practised in that head of cities; and thus was set at rest for ever in the southern division of Ireland, the question of the paschal solemnity. Of this happy result Bede informs us; and, speaking of a fact that occurred in 635, he adds, that whilst the northern Irish clung to their own ancient usage, "the southern Irish had long since, at the admonition of the bishop of the Apostolic See, adopted the observance of the canonical rite."*

We shall conclude this narrative of the assembled bishops of Magh-lene† with the words of Dr. Rock, who thus recapitulates the letter of Cummian:

"In going over these extracts from the writings of Cummian, we catch a near insight into the way things were done at home by the early Irish Christians; and whither it was they looked when they cast their eyes abroad and sought advice beyond the shores of their own island, and where they deemed their spiritual mother to dwell. We find then, 1st, when a doubt arose in the mind of any individual, he addressed himself to his ecclesiastical superiors for its solution. 2nd, In their uncertainties the latter met in a provincial synod, and comparing the tradition handed down to them, decided the matter by that Catholic standard. 3rd, But if a question of any magnitude was mooted, keeping in sight the universal

* Hist. Ec. ii. 19. "Gentes Scottorum quæ in australibus Hiberniæ partibus morabantur jamdudum ad admonitionem Apostolicæ Sedis antistitis pascha canonico ritu observare didicerunt."
† The synod of Magh-lene was held in 630; the messengers from Rome returned in 633; and Cummian wrote the same year his letter to Segienus. Hence he is silent about the letter of Honorius, written in 634, which was brought to Ireland by Laserian, and was solemnly read in the synod of Lethglin, or Leighlin, in 635.—See Lanigan, ii 392. (coll. 397, note 43.)

ecclesiastical rule, they referred it to the head of the Church—to the pope, and went to Rome for judgment 'as children going up to their mother.' 4th, That it was not every tradition which was good with the Irish, but such only as were liked and approved of by the source of their baptism and their wisdom, that is, Rome; and had been brought to Ireland from the popes, the successors of the Lord's Apostles, Peter and Paul."*

A few years after the Easter Question had been thus happily settled in the south, the archbishop of Armagh and the chief clergy of the north endeavoured to establish a like harmony in Ulster. The course which they adopted confirms the conclusions just now recorded. They resolved on seeking the decision of Rome, and a letter to that effect was addressed to pope Severinus, in 640. Unfortunately the Roman See was vacant ere that letter reached its destination. The Roman clergy, indeed, replied; but as their sentence was directed against the Quartodecimans, the defenders of the old Irish rite deemed themselves free from all censure. The Roman Church was subsequently too much distracted by other cares, and we find no decision on record regarding the paschal controversy which was agitated in our island: for our present purpose, however, it must suffice, that the archbishop of Armagh, and the other prelates, when seeking for a supreme tribunal to decide on this angry matter of dispute, precisely as the southern bishops, turned their eyes and addressed their letters to Rome.

The reply of the Roman clergy makes known to us the names of those who thus solicited the decision of Rome: they are such as fully represent the northern portion of our island. It is addressed "to the most beloved and holy Thomian, Columban, Cronan, Dimma, and Baithan, bishops; to Cronan, Ernian, Laistran, Scallan, and Segienus, priests; to Saran, and the other Irish doctors and abbots," etc.†

Thomian was archbishop of Armagh. His life is given by Colgan.‡ He was appointed to the see in 624, and died in 660.

---

* Letter to Lord J. Manners by Dr. Rock, p. 66.
† See Usher, Syllog. Epp. No. 9; Lanigan, Hist. Ec. ii. 409, seqq.; Reeves' Eccles. Antiq. p. 149.
‡ Acta SS. p. 53.

Columban was bishop of Clonard, who died on the 6th of February, 652.

Cronan was bishop and and abbot of Nendrum (which name in our annalists was mistaken by Dr. Lanigan and many others for Antrim), and, according to the Ulster Annals and Tighernach, died on the 7th January, 642.

Dimma was bishop of Connor. He belonged to the princely Dalcassian line, and studied under St. Colman-Elo. He is known in our ancient records by the name Dimma *Dubh* (*i. e.*, the black). He died on the 6th January, 658.

Baithan was of the race of Niall, and seems to have been bishop of a place which was called from him, Tegh-Baithan; he, too, is mentioned by our annalists as flourishing at this time.

Cronan, the first in the list of priests, was abbot of Maghbile (*i. e*, Moville), in Down. He died on 7th August, 650.

Ernian, abbot of Torcy Island, flourished also about 650.

Laistran was abbot of Ard-mac-nasca, on the banks of the present Belfast Lough.

Scallan was abbot of Bangor, and died in 662.

Segienus presided as abbot over the great monastery of Hy, from 623 to 652.*

The last named was St. Saran O'Critain, who died in 661. He seems to have been a *scriba*, which class was highly honoured in the ancient Church of Ireland.†

These names are of great importance, as proving that the petition to Rome to have some decision delivered regarding the controverted paschal computation, was not the petition of one alone, but was addressed to the Vicar of Christ by all the great monasteries, as well as the chief bishops who adhered to the northern or Columbian tradition. As a matter of discipline, they clung to the practice of their fathers, and when that peculiar discipline gave scandal to their brethren, and was looked on with suspicion by neighbouring churches, they turned their eyes to the common Father of all, to seek from him instruction and guidance.

* Reeves' Adamnan, p. 373. † Reeves' Antiq. p. 149.

We may conclude this chapter with the words of Dr. Lynch, the learned archdeacon of Killala, who, refuting the calumnies of Giraldus Cambrensis, wrote :

"If I allowed myself to detail at length the intercourse of the Irish with Rome in former ages, my page would swell to unreasonable limits, and exhaust my power of language, though not the subject itself. To sum up, then, in a few words: No dissension on religious matters ever arose in Ireland, which was not referred to Rome for adjudication. From Rome Ireland had her precepts of morality, and her oracles of faith. Rome was the mother, Ireland the daughter; Rome the head, Ireland the member. From Rome, the fountain-source of religion, Ireland undoubtedly derived, and with her whole soul imbibed, her faith. In doubtful matters the pope was the arbiter of the Irish ; in things certain, their master; in ecclesiastical matters, their head; in temporals, their defender; in all things their judge; in everything their adviser; their oracle in doubt, their bulwark in the hour of danger. Some hastened to Rome to indulge their fervour at the tomb of the Apostles; others to lay their homage at the feet of the pope, and others to obtain the necessary sanction of his authority for the discharge of their functions."*

* Edit. of Celtic Society, 1850, vol. ii. p. 635.

ESSAY

ON

THE TEACHING OF THE ANCIENT CHURCH OF IRELAND, REGARDING THE BLESSED EUCHARIST.

THE real presence of the divine Redeemer in the blessed Sacrament, and the offering of His sacred body and blood upon our altars in the sacrifice of the Mass, are principal doctrines of our holy faith, which draw a clear line of separation between the Catholic Church and all the various sects of Protestantism. We therefore propose to inquire whether the teaching of the early Irish Church, regarding this holy sacrament and sacrifice, coincided with the Protestant tenets of our times, or whether it was not rather identical with the Catholic doctrine which the children of Ireland now, in unison with the Catholics of the whole world, proclaim from the rising to the setting of the sun.

To proceed with order in this historical inquiry, we shall arrange the documents which illustrate this point of doctrine of our early Church under the following heads :—

1. Liturgical treatises.
2. Penitentials and other records of our ages of faith.
3. The teaching and practice of our early saints.
4. The ancient Irish writers to whom our adversaries appeal as favourable to Protestantism.

CHAPTER I.

ANCIENT LITURGICAL TREATISES.

The Stowe Missal.—Its evidence on the blessed Eucharist.—The Bobbio Missal.—The Antiphonarium Benchorense.—Hymn regarding Bangor; (note.)—Hymn, Sancti Venite.—Testimonies from the Leabhar Breac, and from Treatise on Vestments, from Curry's MSS. in Catholic University.—Different Orders of Irish Saints.

In the wholesale destruction of the ancient monuments of our island in the sixteenth and seventeenth centuries, most of the documents connected with our early liturgy were destroyed; sufficient fragments, however, still remain to prove that in all its essential parts it was identical with the Catholic liturgy of the present day.

The manuscript now generally known as the Stowe Missal, is one of the most valuable of the Irish fragments that have been happily handed down to us. Its silver *cumdhach* and ornaments have formed the subject of an elaborate dissertation in Dr. O'Conor's Rerum Hibernicarum Scriptores, and are also most fully described in the appendix to the catalogue of the Stowe Manuscripts.* In 1856, another interesting paper on this Ancient Irish Missal was read by Dr. Todd before the Royal Irish Academy, and was printed in its Transactions.† From the inscriptions which yet remain on the cover of the Missal, it is certain that it originally belonged to some church of Munster, and, in all probability, to the monastery of Lothra or Lorha, in Lower Ormond, which was founded by St. Ruadhan in the sixth century. Dr. Todd informs us that "the original manuscript was written in an ancient Lombardic character, which may well be deemed older than the sixth century."‡ And he also states—"It is by no means impossible that the MS. may have been the original missal of St. Ruadhan himself, the founder of the monastery of Lothra, who died A.D., 584. . . . .

---

* Vol. i. Appendix No. 1. † Vol. xxiii.
‡ The Ancient Irish Missal, etc., by James Henthorn Todd, read before R.I.A., June 23rd, 1856, and printed from the Transactions of R.I.A. in 1857, page 16.

He belonged to the second class of saints, who had different missals and different monastic rules, ... that is to say, they did not confine themselves to one form of celebration, but adopted freely the forms or missals which they found elsewhere on the continent of Europe; and it is probable that the MS. we are now to speak of was one of these different missals."*

The Mass begins with the litanies of the saints, which are preceded by the antiphon *peccavimus*. Then follows the *gloria in excelsis Deo*, with the collect or prayer, and the lesson from the first Epistle to the Corinthians, chapter xi., relating to the blessed Eucharist. In the versicle which follows, the blessing of salvation is asked for " those who are present at the sacrifice." The Gospel is that of St. John, in the sixth chapter. The Creed, too, forms part of the Mass, which is a remarkable peculiarity of this missal at so early a period; for the use of the Creed did not become general in the Church until many years later. What, however, is most important for our present purpose, not only are the words of consecration given as used at the present day, but also the subsequent prayers " agreeing literally with the Roman canon down to the memento for the dead;"† and thus, as in the nineteenth century, so in the Church of our sainted fathers of the sixth century, was used that beautiful prayer—" Humbly, we beseech thee, O Almighty God, command this offering to be carried by the hands of thy holy angel unto thy heavenly altar in the presence of thy divine Majesty, that all of us who receive through the participation of this altar the most holy body and blood of thy Son, may be filled with every heavenly blessing and grace, through the same Christ our Lord." Such is the language of this venerable monument, whose writing, to use the words of Dr. Todd, is of itself a sufficient guarantee that "it is certainly not later than the sixth century."‡

In addition to the every-day Mass, the *Missa Cotidiana*, this missal presents to us a " Missa Apostolorum," a " Missa Martyrum," a " Missa Sanctorum et Sanctarum Virginum," also a

---

* Ancient Irish Missal, page 15.   † Ib. p. 32.   ‡ Ib. p. 18.

Mass "pro pœnitentibus vivis;" and, in fine, a "Missa pro mortuis."* Surely this must be confessed to be a very un-Protestant-looking record of the faith of our fathers in the sixth century.

We have already spoken of the Bobbio Missal, which was bequeathed by St. Columbanus to his Irish disciples in Italy: it, too, contains the prayer just now referred to, and with it the whole Canon of the Mass, from the commencement to the Agnus Dei, substantially the same as found in the Roman liturgy. This missal, moreover, has many peculiar prayers which illustrate the doctrine of our ancient church regarding the blessed Eucharist. Thus, in its daily Mass we find the prayer:—

"Gratias tibi agimus Dne. sancte, Pater omnipotens æterne Deus, qui nos corporis et sanguinis Christi filii tui communione satiasti."†

"We give thee thanks, O holy Lord, omnipotent Father, eternal God, who hast satiated us by the communion of the body and blood of Christ thy Son."

Again, in the Mass for Lent, "Missa Quadragesimalis," after the commemoration of many blessings imparted to us by Christ, it is added:—

"Cujus carne a te ipso sanctificata, dum pascimur, roboramur; et sanguine dum potamur, abluimur."‡

"By participating of whose flesh, blessed by thee, we are strengthened, and by drinking of whose blood we are cleansed."

Another invaluable liturgical fragment has been preserved in the Antiphonarium Benchorense. It is a communion hymn beginning with the words *Sancti venite*, which, in the ancient choralbook of the great Irish monastery of Bangor, is entitled "a hymn whilst the priests communicate." The venerable antiquity of the manuscript in which this hymn is preserved, brings us back to the seventh century, the golden period of our Irish Church.§ The remarks, however, of Dr. Todd, in his edition of the Liber Hymno-

---

* Dr. O'Conor's Stowe Catalogue, page 45; Todd, loc. cit. page 34.
† See ap. Mabillon, Museum Italicum, i. 281.
‡ Ib. page 303, similar phrases occur also page 344 and elsewhere.
§ It was written about the year 691, as Drs. O'Conor and Lanigan have sufficiently proved.

rum for the Irish Arch. Society, have established the claim of the hymn itself to a still higher antiquity. In the ancient Irish preface to the hymn of St. Sechnall on St. Patrick, preserved in the Leabhar Breac, it is said that, on a certain occasion, whilst Sechnall was offering the holy sacrifice, our apostle went to visit him; and *it was when Sechnall had finished the Mass, except taking the body of Christ, that he heard that Patrick had arrived at the place:*" leaving the altar, he prostrated himself at the feet of St. Patrick, and when both subsequently approached the church, "*they heard a choir of angels chanting a hymn at the Offertory in the church, and what they chanted was the hymn whose beginning is* ' *Sancti venite, Christi corpus,*' *etc., so that from that time to the present, that hymn is chanted in Erin when the body of Christ is received.*"* Now, the preface from which we have taken this extract " has been supposed by the best Irish scholars (as Dr. Todd informs us), judging from its language and style, to be a composition of about the seventh or eighth century;"† and yet, it describes the beautiful communion hymn, *Sancti venite,* as not only then in use, but, moreover, as having been from time immemorial chanted in the churches of Erin.

The connection of this hymn with the monastery of Bangor redoubles its importance. We may soon expect from the learned pen of Dr. Reeves a full account of that monastery. In the meantime, we shall be content with the eulogy passed on this ancient asylum of piety and literature, by the holy abbot of Clairvaux, in his life of St. Malachy:—

"A most noble monastery had been founded in Bangor by St. Comgall, which brought forth many thousand monks, and was the head of many monasteries. It was a place truly holy, pregnant with saints, and bringing forth most copious fruit to God: so much so, that one of the members of that holy congregation, Molua by name, is said to have been the founder of one hundred monasteries. Its branches overspread both Ireland and Scotland. Nor were these the only countries blessed by its religious: as bees from the parent hive, they flocked to foreign shores, and one of them, named Columbanus, proceeding to Luxieu, founded there a monastery which soon grew into a great people."‡

---

* Lib. Hymnor. pp. 30 and 31. † Ib. p. 44.
‡ Vita S Malachiæ, cap. v. There is a hymn in praise of this monas-

We now give in full, from the old MS. of Bobbio, this golden fragment of our ancient Irish liturgy, with a literal translation :*

1. "Sancti venite, Christi corpus sumite; Sanctum bibentes, Quo redempti sanguinem.	1. "Approach, you who are holy, Receive the body of Christ, Drinking the sacred blood By which you were redeemed.

tery inserted in the old Antiphonarium Benchorense; and hence, dating back at least to the seventh century, which we here insert in full, as being inaccessible to many of our readers :

"Benchuir, bona regula,
    Recta atque divina,
    Stricta, sancta, sedula,
    Summa, justa ac mira.

"*Muinther** Benchuir beata,
    Fide fundata certa,
    Spe salutis ornata,
    Caritate perfecta.

"Navis numquam turbata,
    Quamvis fluctibus torsa,
    Nuptiis quoque parata,
    Regi Domino sponsa.

"Domus deliciis plena,
    Super petram constructa,
    Necnon vinea vera,
    Ex Ægypto transducta.

"Certe civitas firma,
    Fortis atque munita,
    Gloriosa ac digna,
    Supra montem posita.

"Arca cherubim tecta,
    Omni parte aurata,
    Sacrosanctis referta,
    Viris quatuor portata.

"Christo regina apta
    Solis luce amicta,
    Simplex simulque docta,
    Undecumque invicta.

"Vere regalis aula,
    Variis gemmis ornata,
    Gregisque Christi caula,
    Patre summo servata."

* The Irish word for *familia*.

---

* See a beautiful metrical translation of this hymn from the pen of Denis Florence M'Carthy, Esq., in the Ancient Irish Church, by Rev. James Gaffney; Dublin, 1863, p. 23, seqq.

2. "Salvati Christi
　　Corpore et sanguine,
　　A quo refecti,
　　Laudes dicamus Deo.

3. "Hoc sacramento,
　　Corporis et sanguinis,
　　Omnes exuti
　　Ab inferni faucibus.

4. "Dator salutis,
　　Christus filius Dei,
　　Mundum salvavit,
　　Per crucem et sanguinem.

5 "Pro universis
　　Immolatus Dominus,
　　Ipse sacerdos
　　Existit et hostia.

6. "Lege præceptum
　　Immolari hostias:
　　Qua adumbrantur
　　Divina mysteria.

7. "Lucis indultor
　　Et salvator omnium,
　　Præclaram sanctis
　　Largitus est gratiam.

8. "Accedant omnes,
　　Pura mente creduli;
　　Sumant æternam
　　Salutis custodiam:

9. "Sanctorum custos,
　　Rector quoque Dominus,
　　Vitæ perennis,
　　Largitor credentibus

10. "Cœlestem panem
　　Dat esurientibus;
　　De fonte vivo
　　Præbet sitientibus.

11. "Alpha et omega
　　Ipse Christus Dominus
　　Venit, venturus

　　Judicare homines."

2. "Saved by the body
　　And blood of Christ,
　　Now nourished by it
　　Let us sing praises unto God.

3. "By this sacrament
　　Of the body and blood,
　　All are rescued
　　From the power of hell.

4 "The giver of salvation,
　　Christ, the Son of God,
　　Redeemed the world
　　By his cross and blood.

5. "For the whole world
　　The Lord is offered up;
　　He is at the same time
　　High-priest and victim.

6. "In the law it is commanded
　　To immolate victims:
　　By it were foreshadowed
　　These sacred mysteries.

7. "The giver of all light,
　　And the Saviour of all,
　　Now bestows upon the holy
　　An exceeding great grace.

8. "Let all approach,
　　In the pure simplicity of faith;
　　Let them receive the eternal
　　Preserver of their souls:

9. "The guardian of the saints,
　　The supreme Ruler and Lord,
　　The Bestower of eternal life,
　　On those who believe in Him.

10. "To the hungry he gives to eat
　　Of the heavenly food;
　　To the thirsty he gives to drink
　　From the living fountain.

11. "The alpha and omega,
　　Our Lord Christ Himself
　　Now comes: He who shall one day come
　　To judge all mankind."

This beautiful little hymn speaks for itself, and needs no comment: suffice it to say, that its author might well defy any polemical writer of the present day to express with greater clearness and precision the teaching of the Catholic Church.

The Protestant German hymnologist, Daniel, inserted this hymn in his "Thesaurus,"* but, strangely enough, omitted the third verse. The suppression, however, of this strophe must not be imputed to him; for on discovering his error, he honourably apologized to his readers, and declared that he was led into error by copying this hymn from the "Anthologia" of Mr. Rambach, another Protestant writer, who in reality "suppressed the third verse, as it seemed to speak too emphatically regarding the sacrament of the Eucharist."†

We may now proceed to consider some other monuments illustrative of the liturgy of our early church.

The perfect acquaintance of the late Eugene Curry with the ancient Gaelic dialects, has placed within the reach of modern inquirers many records of the religious tenets and practices of the early church of Ireland, which were "scaled books" even to the most pains-taking and enthusiastic Irish antiquaries of the last two centuries. Amongst the religious treatises which he translated, one of the most important is an "Exposition of the Ceremonies of the Mass," of which the original is preserved in the Leabhar Breac, R. I. Acad. fol. 125. This interesting little tract explains

---

* Vol. i. page 193.

† "Suppressit stropham tertiam quippe grandius quid de sacramento sentire videbatur.—Daniel, Thes. Hym. vol. iv. page 109, Lipsiæ, 1855. Dr. Todd, when editing the Liber Hymnorum, fasciculus 1mus, in 1855, page 43, note c., was not acquainted with the fourth volume of Mr. Daniel's work, and hence accused him of rejecting the title prefixed to our hymn: however, Daniel, in the fourth vol. (loc. cit.), states that when publishing the first volume, he was not acquainted with the Bobbio manuscript; and that he now retracted his former opinion, having learned that the title was found in that venerable old monument. Dr. Todd does not seem to have adverted to the omission of the third verse by his Protestant contemporary. Mr. Daniel justly remarks, that there exists a great affinity between the hymn "Sancti venite" and an antiphon used in the early church of Gaul during the time of the Paschal Communion, from which he gives this extract: "Venite populi ad sacrum et immortale mysterium. . . . . quoniam propter nos agnus Dei Patri sacrificium propositum est."—See St. Gregory of Tours, in his Treatise "de Miracul. S. Martini," ii, 13.

in detail the peculiar ceremonies which were used by the old Irish Church in the sacred liturgy ; but for our own purpose, one extract already published by Mr. Curry in his "Lectures on the MS. Materials of Irish History"* will suffice, to show what was the doctrine which was held by our fathers in regard to the real presence of our divine Redeemer in the holy Sacrament of the altar. We shall merely premise that Mr. Curry judged the language of this treatise to be in the purest dialect of the Brehon Laws, and to belong to the earliest centuries of the Christian era in our island :—

"This is the foundation of the faith which every Christian is bound to hold, and it is upon this foundation that every virtue which he practises, and every good work which he performs, is erected.

"For it is through this perfection of the faith, with tranquil charity and with steadfast hope, that all the faithful are saved. For it is this faith, that is, the Catholic faith, that conducts the righteous to the vision, that is, to see God in the glory and in the dignity in which He abides. It is this vision which is offered as a golden reward to the righteous after the resurrection.

" The pledge for this vision which has been left to the Church here for the present, is the Holy Spirit, which resides in, which comforts, and which strengthens her with all virtues. It is this Spirit that distributes his own peculiar gifts to every faithful member in the Church, as He pleases and as they require to receive it from Him. For, it is by the Holy Spirit these noble gifts following are bestowed upon the Church, among men, viz., Baptism and Penitence, and the expectation of (enduring of) persecutions and afflictions.

" One of the noble gifts of the Holy Spirit is the Holy Scripture, by which all ignorance is enlightened, and all worldly affliction comforted ; by which all spiritual light is kindled, and all debility is made strong. For it is through the Holy Scripture that heresy and schism are banished from the Church, and all contentions and divisions reconciled. It is in it well-tried counsel and appropriate instruction will be found for every degree in the Church. It is through it the snares of demons and vices are banished from every faithful member of the Church. For, the divine Scripture is the mother and the benign nurse of all the faithful who meditate and contemplate it, and who are nurtured by it until they are chosen children of God by its advice. For, the Wisdom, that is the Church, bountifully distributes to her children the variety of her sweetest drink and the choicest of her spiritual food, by which they are perpetually inebriated and cheered.

* Page 376-7.

"Another division of that pledge which has been left with the Church to comfort her, is the Body of Christ and His Blood, which are offered upon the altars of the Christians: the Body, even, which was born of Mary the Immaculate Virgin, without destruction of her virginity, without opening of the womb, without presence of man; and which was crucified by the unbelieving Jews out of spite and envy; and which arose after three days from death, and sits upon the right-hand of God the Father in heaven, in glory, and in dignity, before the angels of heaven. It is that body, the same as it is in this great glory, which the righteous consume off God's table, that is, the holy altar. For, this body is the rich viaticum of the faithful who journey through the paths of pilgrimage and penitence of this world to the heavenly fatherland. This is the seed of the resurrection in the life eternal to the righteous. It is, however, the origin and cause of falling to the impenitent who believe not; and to the sensual who distinguish it not though they believe Woe then to the Christian who distinguishes not this holy body of the Lord by pure morals, by charity, and by mercy. For, it is in this body that will be found the example of the charity which excels all charity, viz., to sacrifice Himself without guilt, in satisfaction for the guilt of the whole race of Adam.

"This, then, is the perfection and the fulness of the Catholic faith as it is taught in the Holy Scriptures."

The whole of this passage is so striking and so illustrative of the teaching of the Catholic Church, that it would almost seem to be borrowed from the fourth book of the "Imitation of Christ," by Thomas à Kempis. It is not necessary to call the reader's attention to any particular portion of it; but, surely, he will be struck with the emphatic words by which the Eucharist is declared to be "the very body that was born of the Immaculate Virgin, and was crucified by the unbelieving Jews." No Catholic doctor of the present day could use more emphatic words to distinguish between the teaching of the Church and the Protestant tenets.

To this golden exposition of the Catholic faith of the early Irish Church in regard to the blessed Eucharist, we add, on account of the peculiar beauty of its sentiments, a treatise on "the Mass-Vestments,"* which clearly propounds the same doctrine, whilst it, at the same time, reveals to us the reverential awe with which the holy sacrifice of the Mass was regarded by our fathers more than one thousand years ago:—

---

* The original is preserved in the Leabhar Breac, the most valuable repository of the ancient ecclesiastical treatises of our Irish Church.

"It is asked by whom were various colours introduced into the chasuble of the sacrifice? I answer—it was Moses, the son of Amram, that first placed them in the sacrifice-chasuble of Aaron, his brother, who was the first priest of the Mosaic law.

"It is asked how many colours were set by Moses in Aaron's chasuble? I answer—eight: viz., gold, (or yellow,) blue, white, green, brown, red, black, and purple. This, therefore, is the number of colours which every sacrifice-chasuble ought to have in it from that time to the present.

"It is asked why these various colours were introduced into the sacrifice-chasuble, instead of having it of one colour? I answer—through mystery and figure.

"It is not lawful, therefore, for any priest *to approach the body of Christ for the purpose of sacrifice* without having a chasuble of satin (*i.e.* shining cloth) upon him with these eight colours in it. The priest's mind should agree with the variety and meaning of each distinct colour, and he should be filled with vigilance and awe, and be withdrawn from ambition and pride when he reflects on what these various colours typify.

"What the yellow now typifies, when the priest looks at it, is, that the clay and dust of this earth are the materials of his body, and that it is into the same dust he shall go again. Therefore, no sentiment of pride should ever arise within his breast.

"What the blue typifies, when he looks at it, is, that he shall separate his mind from the ambitious designs and vices of the world, and turn his face towards heaven in humility and lowliness, to God the Father who is in heaven.

"What the white typifies when he looks at it, is, that he should be filled with confusion and shame if his heart be not chaste and shining, and his mind like the foam of the wave, or like chalk on the gable of an oratory, or like the colour of the swan in the sunshine; that is, without any particle of sin, great or small, resting in his heart.

"What the green typifies when he looks at it, is, that he be filled with great faintness and distress of heart and mind; for, what is understood by it is, his interment at the end of his life under the mould of the earth; for green is the original colour of all the earth; and it is therefore that green is represented among the colours of the Mass-chasuble.

"What the brown typifies when it is gazed upon, is, that the priest should call to mind the separation of his soul and body in death, and that his dwelling after death shall be the grave, till the end of the world, and that hell shall be the lot of both body and soul after the judgment, unless his deeds be faithful here upon earth.

"What the red typifies when he looks upon it, is, that his heart should start and tremble in his breast through terror and fear of the Son of God; for the scars and wounds of the Son of God were red upon the cross when he was crucified by the unbelieving Jews.

"What the black denotes when he looks upon it, is, that he should shed bitter tears for his sins, lest he be condemned to the society of the devil, and dwell perpetually in endless pain.

"What the purple denotes when the priest looks on it, is, that he call to his mind Jesus who is in heaven, in the plenitude of glory and majesty, and with the nine orders of angels, who praise the Creator throughout all eternity.

"What becomes the priest on this occasion, is, that he withdraw his mind from the wickedness of the world, and fix his thoughts on the enjoyments and delights which our Father hath prepared in heaven.

"These are the eight degrees that are designated by the eight colours which are in the Mass-chasuble, according to the figure and mystery of the heavenly Father. Thus, the Mass-chasuble is the focus in which are concentred eight different colours, which defeat and overthrow the temptations of the devil in many battles, and destroy the vices of the world, and which increase and magnify the virtues and the good deeds.

"It is not lawful, therefore, for any one to introduce the satin into his garments, or into his vesture, on account of its lustre and nobleness, *excepting the priest alone, when he goes to sacrifice the body of Christ and His blood, upon the holy altar; for it is a satin chasuble that he has a right to wear at that time.*"*

These documents, surely, allow no doubt to be entertained as to what was meant by the Irish writers of the early centuries, when they speak of offering up the sacrifice of the Mass. There may have been various rituals and various liturgies; the missal of Bobbio is distinct from that of Stowe; but all are found to agree in the great doctrinal truth, that in the holy sacrifice is offered to God the victim of our salvation, the body and blood of Jesus Christ. With this principle before our minds, the ancient catalogue of saints published for the first time by Usher becomes an interesting record of the identity of faith as professed by St. Patrick, and transmitted through successive orders of saints to posterity; whilst it indicates, at the same time, the liberty that existed in regard to ceremonial and ritual, and marks the period to which our varying liturgies must be referred.

According to this catalogue, then, the Irish saints may be divided into three classes, of which the first was most holy; the second, very holy; the third, holy. The sanctity of the first order was like the sun in its meridian splendour, the second like the moon, the third like the stars.

The first class begins with St. Patrick, and numbers 350 saints, all bishops, and founders of churches: men eminently holy, and

---

* From the Curry MSS. in Catholic University.

full of the spirit of God; "they had one head, our divine Redeemer; one leader, St. Patrick; one Mass; one mode of celebration; one tonsure, from ear to ear."

The second order consists of 300 saints, the greater number being simple priests; they, too, had one spiritual head, but introduced changes into the liturgy, and followed " various Masses and various rules."

The third order, too, comprised many priests and few bishops, and reckons 100 saints. They inhabited desert places, and lived on herbs and water, and had no property of their own; they continued to sanction by their usage a difference " of liturgy and rule."

The first order extends from 432 to 534; the second from 534 to 600; whilst the third terminates in 664. Their rules and ceremonies may have varied at intervals, but all these bishops and priests are found linked together in the Christian bonds of sanctity and faith; all are gathered around the same altar, and with every variety of ceremonial, all offer to God the same holy sacrifice of the Mass, from St. Patrick in the beginning of the fifth, to St. Cronan, who closes the catalogue, in the middle of the seventh century.*

---

* This ancient catalogue is generally supposed to have been written about the close of the seventh century; it is given in full by Usher in his Primordia, and is translated by Todd in his Memoir of St. Patrick, p. 88. We shall have occasion to speak of it again hereafter, when we shall present it, with some remarks, to the reader.

CHAPTER II.

IRISH PENITENTIALS, AND OTHER RECORDS.

Penitential of St. Cummian and St. Finnian.—Penitential of Bobbio.—Pœnitentiale Bigotianum.—St. Columbanus's Canons.—Ancient Irish Canons cited by Usher.—Canons regarding the Viaticum.—Brehon Laws on the Orders of the Church.—Irish Synod of 807, celebrated under pope Leo III.

THE ancient Irish Penitentials generally suppose the reader to be fully instructed in the doctrines of the Church; and hence, when laying down rules regarding the holy Sacrament of the altar, generally designate it by the common titles of "the Sacrifice," "the Mass," "the Communion," "the Eucharist." It is only incidentally that they present some details which reveal to us the fulness of the faith of our early Church in reference to this great sacrament.

The Penitential of St. Cummian dates from the beginning of the seventh century; it prescribes various penances for those who should be guilty of negligence when preserving *the sacrifice* entrusted to their care;* and subsequently enacts that, should any one, without due reverence, receive the sacred blood, he should do penance for seven days. "*Qui communicaverit sanguinem inconscius, septem dies pœniteat.*"†

St. Finnian of Maghbile, towards the close of his Penitential, lays down many rules for the guidance of married people, and concludes, that by the observance of these rules, they will be worthy to receive the body of Christ: "*Digni erunt corpore Christi.*"‡

The Bobbio Penitential enacts, in its seventeenth canon, that

---

* Ap. Wasserschleben. Die Bussordnungen, etc.; Halle, 1851; Pœnitent. Cummian, xiii. 5, seqq. These canons clearly prove that the blessed Sacrament was preserved for the devotion of the faithful, as in the Catholic Church at the present day. See this same disciplinary practice illustrated in the same Penitential, xiv. 12.
† Chap. xiii. 24. ‡ Ibid. Pœnit. Finniani, can. 46.

whosoever should show neglect "in regard to the Eucharist, which is the body of the Lord," should do penance for a whole year: "Si quis Eucharistiam, corpus Domini, neglexerit, aut perdiderit, unum annum pœniteat."* Again, in its forty-sixth canon it commands, that the spot on which the blessed Eucharist might happen to fall, "should be covered for forty days, lest any one should trample on the blood of Christ:" *ut non conculcetur sanguis Christi.*

The Irish Penitential which, from the library where it was discovered, is designated by the name "Pœnitentiale Bigotianum," has a special chapter entitled, "That no one should receive the sacrifice, unless he be pure and perfect, and free from every mortal stain;"† and it adds the following beautiful illustration:

"When Christ commanded the girl that was dead to arise, He directed that food should be brought to her; that is, when she was perfectly restored to health, and no longer detained in her infirmities, for she was healed by the Redeemer in the presence of Peter, James, and John, and also of her father and mother; so, too, each one of us having confessed his sins, and eradicated them from his soul, and being enriched with the grace of God, in the presence of his heavenly Father and of the Church, may, when strengthened by good works, receive the sacrifice."

Equally explicit and emphatic is the teaching of the Penitential of St. Columbanus, which, in its concluding canon,‡ enacts as follows:

"Confessiones autem dari diligentius præcipitur, maxime de commotionibus animi, antequam ad missam eatur, ne forte quis accedat indignus ad altare, id est, si cor mundum non habuerit. Melius est enim exspectare, donec cor sanum fuerit et alienum a scandalo ac invidia, quam accedere audacter	"Special diligence must be used in confessing our sins and imperfections, before the celebration of Mass, lest with an unclean heart we should approach the holy altar. It is better to delay a little, and wait till our heart be free from scandal and envy, than audaciously to approach to the judgment-seat:

---

* Ibid.; also Mabillon, Mus. Ital. vol. i. can. 17.
† De eo quod nemo debet accipere sacrificium nisi sit mundus et perfectus et nihil mortale in eo inventum."—Ibid. cap. vii. On this and the other penitentials see appendix.
‡ Canon xi. 11.

ad judicium tribunalis; *tribunal enim Christi altare est, et corpus suum inibi cum sanguine judicat indignos accedentes.* Sicuti ergo a peccatis capitalibus cavendum est antequam communicandum sit, ita etiam ab incertioribus vitiis et morbis languentis animæ abstinendum est ac abstergendum ante veræ pacis conjunctionem et æternæ salutis compaginem."

for *the altar is the tribunal of Christ, and His body, present there with His blood, judges those who unworthily approach.* It is, therefore, not only from heinous crimes that we must be free, before approaching to communicate, but also from the lesser faults, and the infirmities of our sinful soul, that thus we may be possessors of true peace, and sharers of eternal blessedness."

The importance of this explicit teaching of St. Columbanus must surely strike even the superficial observer. His teaching links together Bangor, Luxieu, and Bobbio; that is to say, Ireland, France, and Italy, and attests to us the common doctrine of all, that forsooth, in the holy Sacrament of the altar are really present the body and blood of the divine Redeemer.

Besides the distinct teaching of his Penitential, there are many incidental facts connected with his life which illustrate more and more his belief regarding the blessed Eucharist. For instance, in one of the nunneries founded by him on the continent, we find that the virgins "received the body of the Lord and drank His blood."* In the life of his illustrious disciple, St. Gallus, it is further mentioned, that on receiving some valuable presents, amongst which was an exquisitely-wrought silver cup, that saint ordered Magnoald to distribute all these gifts among the poor. Magnoald wished to reserve the cup for the use of the altar, but St. Gallus replied: "My master, Columbanus, *is wont to offer unto the Lord the sacrifice of salvation*, in brazen vessels, since our Saviour was affixed to the cross with brazen nails," and hence ordered the cup, too, to be given to the poor.† When, again, at a later period, the same Gallus and Magnoald performed the last obsequies for St. Columbanus, we find it recorded that they celebrated the divine mysteries, and offered to God the "sacrifice of salvation" for his repose.‡

---

* Ap. Usher. loc. cit. p. 38, from Jones, in Vit. Burgundoforæ.
† Usher, ibid, p 35; Vit. St. Galli, vol. i. p. 18.
‡ Loc. cit. i. p. 26.

To illustrate the belief of the early Irish Church in regard to the blessed Eucharist, Usher cites the ancient Irish Collection of Canons, made about the year 700; but he is content with producing one only canon, which enacts, forsooth, that a bishop may bequeath a certain portion of his goods* as a legacy to the priest who administers to him the sacrifice or viaticum. Now, there are many other canons in this collection much more to the purpose, as illustrative of the true and hidden nature of the holy Sacrament: thus, in ii. 4, it is said, that to priests was given the charge of the Sacraments of God: " præsunt enim ecclesiæ Christi *et in compositione corporis et sanguinis* consortes cum episcopis sunt:" that is, " they share with the bishops the sacred power and privilege of changing the bread and wine into the body and blood of Christ." In iv. 2, the office of the subdeacons is described :—

" Isti oblationes in templo Dni. suscipiunt a populis; isti vasa corporis et sanguinis Christi diaconis ad altarium offerunt."	" They receive the offerings of the faithful in the churches; they present to the deacons at the altar the vessels of the body and blood of Christ."

Again, in ix. 1, it is said that the acolythe, at his ordination, should receive—

" Urceolum vacuum ad suggerendum vinum in Eucharistiam corporis Christi."	" An empty cruet, for preserving wine for the Eucharist of the body of Christ."

A most beautiful contrast is made in xlix. 3, between him who becomes heir of God by baptism, and him who attains his crown by martyrdom :—

" Baptizatus fidem suam confitetur coram sacerdote et interrogatus respondit: et hoc martyr facit coram persecutore. Ille post confessionem	" He who is baptized professes his faith, and being interrogated responds: so is it with the martyr before the persecutor. The for-

---

* " Decem Scripulos :" Collect. Hib. Canon. xlii. 4. The Latin word is used for the Irish *Schrepall*. One thing clearly results from this canon, that, viz., the blessed Eucharist was preserved after Mass, and brought to the faithful as a sacred viaticum.

spargitur oleo et aqua: hic aspergitur sanguine vel intinguitur igni. Ille manus impositione pontificis accipit Spiritum Sanctum: hic locutorium Spiritus Sancti efficitur, dum non ipse est qui loquitur sed spiritus Patris per illum loquitur. Ille communicat Eucharistiam in communione corporis Christi: hic ipse Christo commoritur," etc.	mer having professed his belief, is sprinkled with oil and water; the latter is sprinkled with his blood, or plunged into fire. The one by the imposition of the bishop's hands receives the Holy Ghost; the other becomes the mouth-piece of the Holy Ghost, for, it is not he who speaks, but the Spirit of the Father that speaks through him. The former receives the Eucharist, participating of the body of Christ; the latter himself is by death associated with Christ."

From this last passage it may be concluded, that in the Irish Church, as in many other churches of the age of St. Augustine, the blessed Eucharist was administered immediately after baptism. It is, perhaps, for this reason that the Brehon Laws declare "*the holy communion*" to be one of "*the fundamental ordinances from which neither law, nor judgment, nor reason, nor philosophy can absolve.*" It was especially at the moment of death, however, that this participation of the holy communion was deemed necessary for the faithful; hence, in the Collection of Canons just referred to (xvii. 8) the words of St. Jerome are adopted as a rule:—

"Quicumque viaticum vitæ in vita sua non acceperit, post mortem non potest adjuvari."	"Whosoever does not receive the vivifying viaticum during life, cannot be assisted by it after death."

That is, the sacrifice of the altar was only offered up for those who, before death, had received the holy sacraments of Baptism and the Eucharist. And, elsewhere, when treating of those who, after expressing a desire of repentance, should become unconscious, it enacts:—

"Testimonium dent qui eum audierunt, et si continuo moriturus (sit), reconcilietur per manus impositionem, et infundatur ori ejus Eucharistia."—(xlviii. 22.)	"Let those who heard him express such a desire give their attestation to that effect; and then, if his death seems to be approaching, let him be reconciled by the imposition of hands, and let the Eucharist be poured into his mouth."

Hence, too, a still more ancient Irish synod declared, that the holy communion was so called—

"Eo quod omnium fidelium in exitu vitæ communis est victus. Ergo quidam viaticum nominant, id est vitæ* custodiam, custodit enim animam usquedum steterit ante tribunal Christi, nec bonus angelus ad vitam, nec malus angelus ad pœnam perducere talem animam valent nisi prius divino judicio censeatur."†

"Because it is the common food of all the faithful at the end of their lives. Hence, some call it the *viaticum*, because it guards our life and journey; for it protects the soul until it comes before the tribunal of Christ, and neither the good angel can conduct the soul to heaven, nor the evil one to torments until sentence has been passed on it by Christ."

In a tract of the Brehon Laws, called "Seanchus Beagh," on the duties of the seven ecclesiastical orders, it is prescribed as the duty of the subdeacon "to take charge of the altar-cloths, and to spread the linens upon the altar, and to provide water and wine for the sacrifice." To the deacon it is assigned "to hold the chalice and to put wine into it, and to treasure up all the sacraments till they are required;" but to the priest belongs "to offer the body of Christ, and to sing requiem for the souls of the faithful."‡

Another old Irish treatise on "the Consecration of a Church," the language of which is so ancient that it is beyond the reach of all published Irish dictionaries, as Mr. Curry remarks, after describing the consecration of the table of the altar, etc., adds, "The fourth division is the consecration of the *impertor*, that is to say, *the dish or little cloth off which the body of Christ is received.*"§

A treatise "on the Rights and Duties of the Church and Churchmen," which also forms part of the Brehon Laws, contains many beautiful ordinances regarding the reverence due to bishops and other ecclesiastics. One extract will suffice for our present purpose:—

---

* A Vatican MS. reads: "Id est *viæ vel vitæ custodiam*."—Codex Vatic. 1339, sæc. decimi, fol. 167.
† Collect. Hib. Canonum, ii. 18.
‡ From the MSS. of Eugene Curry, in Cath. Univ.; see also for som account of the above tract, Petrie, Round Towers, p. 377.
§ Curry, MSS.; also his Lectures, 357.

"Every one who does not respect the rule of the spiritual director who is placed over him, is not obedient to God or man; he is not entitled to have communion administered to him, neither should his requiem be chanted, nor his burial be allowed in the Church of God; because it was he that refused to be obedient to God in the churches of the land of Erin. For, the manner in which those who are in holy orders ought to be respected, and their directions followed, is the same as if they were the angels of God among men; because it is through them the kingdom of heaven is gained, *by baptism and communion, and chanting of prayers, and the sacrifice of the body of Christ and of His blood,* and the preaching of the Gospel, and the building of the churches of God."*

A fragment of an ancient Irish synod is fortunately preserved in the archives of the Vallicellian Library, Rome. This synod is described as held in 807 or 808, during the pontificate of pope Leo III. (795–816), and the episcopate of Torbach,† successor of St. Patrick. We shall translate a portion of it which illustrates the subject of which we now treat:

"IRISH SYNOD UNDER POPE LEO THE THIRD.

"Amongst other things decreed regarding the church discipline, the holy synod of Ireland, in which Leo, bishop of the see of Rome presided,‡ during the reign of Karl, king of the Francs, together with Torbach, archbishop§ of the English and the Irish, and many other bishops of

---

* Curry MSS. in Catholic University.

† *Torbach* is named as "Coarb of St. Patrick," and immediate successor of *Condmach*, in the see of Armagh, in Colgan's list (republished by Todd from the Bodleian MS. p. 174), as also in the Leabhar Breac, and Yellow Book of Lecan—(Ap. Todd, pp. 177 and 179). Lanigan calls him Forbach, which reading is also once (probably by typographical error) found in Colgan. Ware gives him his true name, and the lists published by Todd (loc. cit.) place the matter beyond all controversy. As Condmach's death is registered by the Four Masters in 806-7, and as all the lists cited above mark only one year for the primacy of Torbach, it follows that this synod must have been held in 807-8. All the dates marked in the MS. agree very well, as pope Leo III. was chosen pontiff in 795, and died in 816. Charlemagne reigned alone in France from 771 to 814.

‡ From these words we should conclude that pope Leo was present, either in person or by his deputy, at this synod. Perhaps this may explain the words of the Four Masters, which have hitherto seemed an enigma. They thus write in 807: "In this year the *Ceilé Dé* (servus Dei) came over the sea with dry feet, without a vessel; and a written roll was given him from heaven, out of which he preached to the Irish, and it was carried up again when the sermon was finished." It was about this time that pope Leo visited, at the desire of Charlemagne, the north of Italy, France, and Germany. Could it be that he also visited Ireland? —See Sandini, Vitæ Pontiff, pp. 242-3.

§ Ireland was at this time so celebrated on the continent and in the court of Charlemagne, that we can scarcely be surprised at the archbishop

these parts, thus enacted: Should a priest fall into sin, although according to the apostolic canons he should be deposed, yet according to the teaching of the blessed pope Sylvester, if he has not been hardened in vice, but of his own accord confesses his guilt, and seeks to arise from it, he shall do penance for ten years in the following manner : For three months he shall live retired, separated from all others, taking for food each evening only bread and water; on Sundays, however, and on festival days, he may take a little wine and some fish or herbs, but no meat or fine herbs,* or eggs, or cheese; clothed with sackcloth, he will lie on the ground, and by day and night constantly implore the mercy of the all-powerful God. The three months being completed, he can leave his retreat; let him not, however, appear in public, lest the faithful should be scandalized : for the priest's penance should not be public, as that of the laity. After a little while, having resumed sufficient strength, he will fast for a year and a half on bread and water, excepting the Sundays and principal festivals, on which he may take the canonical measure of wine, and herbs (sagmina), and eggs, and cheese. The first year and a half being finished, *he will partake of the body and blood of Christ, the Lord, and be restored to communion, lest he should become hardened in his course*; he may sing the psalms with the brethren, holding the last place in choir," etc.†

Two canons of the Irish synod, published by Spelman, Wilkins, and Ware, as a "Synodus secunda S. Patricii," also regard the blessed Eucharist. This synod, indeed, has been referred to a much later period than the time of St. Patrick by Dr. Todd,‡ following Tillemont, Lanigan, and others. Their arguments, however, are all based on slight grounds, and are for the most part little more than conjectural. Several of its canons are cited in an Irish penitential (edited by Wasserschleben, loc. cit.) drawn up during the pontificate of Gregory II., that is, about the year 731; and more than one of them is also introduced in the Collectio Hibernensis Canonum, which was made about the year 700. Thus, then, this synod may safely be appealed to as evidence, at least, of the teaching of

---

of Armagh being styled "archbishop of England and Ireland." In the life of St. Patrick, by Probus, the divine promise is recorded as announced by an angel to our apostle, that his spiritual kingdom would embrace "Ireland and Brittany, England and Normandy."—Trias Thaumat. p. 51.

* The original word is *sagmen*, which strictly means *a sacred herb;* as it is here placed in opposition with *legumina*,—*pulse*, it must be taken in its strict meaning. Perhaps it designates the *shamrock*, which in early times was often used for food.

† See the original text of the whole fragment in appendix.

‡ Pages 488-9.

our early Church. In its thirteenth canon it treats of *the sacrifice of the altar*, " de sacrificio," and says that it was typified by the paschal lamb; the paschal lamb was consumed in each family, and could not be given to externs: so is it only in the bosom of the Church " that Christ is believed and participated of in the communion."* The twenty-second canon, which is entitled, " de sumendâ Eucharistiâ post lapsum," enacts, that the repentant sinner, " after mortifying his body, should approach the Eucharist, especially on Easter day, when whosoever does not communicate, should not be reckoned amongst the faithful. Therefore, the period of penance with us is short and limited, lest the faithful soul should perish, if long deprived of its spiritual food; the Lord having said: *Unless you eat the flesh of the Son of man, you will not have life in you.*"

CHAPTER II.

(CONTINUED.)

IRISH PENITENTIALS, AND OTHER RECORDS.

Rules, Monastic or Cenobitical, regarding the blessed Eucharist.—Rule of St. Mochuda of Rahan.—He assigns Duties of Abbot and Priest.—Asks for the Viaticum.—St. Maelruain of Tallaght, county Dublin.—His words regarding the Mass.—Aengus.—His Feliré.

THERE is another class of documents which may be said to participate of the nature of the ecclesiastical ordinances already cited in this article, viz., the *monastic* or *cenobitical rules*. Many of these were drawn up at a very early period, by the great founders of the religious establishments in our island; and though they are generally devoted to the every-day actions of the monastic life, yet they occasionally illustrate the doctrines which were held by

---

* Cap. xiii. "Quid aliud significat quod in una domo sumitur agnus, quam quod sub uno fidei culmine creditur et communicatur Christus."

the religious, and which formed as if the centre of their spiritual activity, the source of all their vitality and energy whilst journeying on towards their heavenly country. We shall at present confine our remarks to the rules drawn up by two great saints, St. Carthage and St. Maelruain, whose monasteries were remarkable for their sanctity, and at their respective periods exercised a widespread influence throughout the whole island.

St. Mochuda (or Carthage), junior, patron of Lismore, died in 636. "He received that name in baptism," says his biographer, "on account of being beloved by God and man on earth and in heaven."[*] He is thus commemorated by St. Cuimin of Connor:

> "The beloved Mochuda, of mortification,
> Admirable every page of his history;
> Before his time, there was no one that shed
> Half as many tears as he shed."

Aengus, too, on the 14th of May, thus marks his festival:

> "SS. Corona and Victor,
> With their company without deduction,
> And with them the bright perpetual solemnity,
> The noble feast of *Carthage* of Raithin."

One antiphon of his office, as used in the old Church of our fathers, has been preserved to us; it is the antiphon sung at the *Magnificat*, and we give it in the simplicity and sweetness of the original text:

> "Gloriose Præsul Christi, venerande Carthace,
> Apud Deum tuo sancto nos juva precamine,
> Ut detersa omni sorde, et abluti crimine
> In cœlesti sempiternum collætemur culmine."

This great saint was trained in his early years by St. Carthage, senior, in his famous monastery on the banks of the Mang. He subsequently took part in the schools of St. Comgall and St. Molua, and founded his own monastery of Raithin (now Rahan, King's County), in the year 590. It was after governing this monastery

---

[*] Acta SS. Maij. iii. 378.

for forty years that he travelled southwards, and having received from the chieftain of the Decies " a wild tract, extensive and secluded, rich in forests and in fish," he erected there the famous school of Lismore, which soon became " a great and renowned city, a lamp of science to Ireland and to Europe."

Usher makes mention of the *rule* drawn up by this saint for his monastery;* we are, however, indebted for its translation to the indefatigable and lamented O'Curry.

In this rule, under the rubric for the abbot, it is said that "*to him belongs the offering of the sacrifice of the body of the great Lord upon the holy altar.*" Subsequently, on " the duties of a priest," it is said :—

> " If you be a priest you will be laborious—
> You must not speak but truth :
> Noble is the order which you have taken,
> *To offer up the body of the King.*"

And it is added :—

> "Noble is thy co-operative, man,
> The Holy Spirit from Heaven."

Again, the rule declares :—

> "To sing the requiems
> Is thine by special right . . . . . .
> Mass upon lawful days,
> Sunday along with Thursday,
> If not upon every day . . . . . .
> Masses for all the Christians,
> And for all those in orders ;
> Masses for the multitudes,
> From the lowest to the greatest . . . .
> When you come unto the Mass,
> It is a noble office :
> Let there be penitence of heart, shedding of tears,
> And throwing up of the hands . . . .
> For, *pure is the body which thou receivest,*
> Purely must thou go to receive it."†

---

* Primord. p. 919. † Curry, MSS. in Cath. Univ.

St. Mochuda, in his own life, exemplified the reverence which he had commanded to be shown to the holy Sacrament of the altar. On finding that his death approached, he gave many exhortations to his brethren, and being favoured with an angelic vision, asked to receive " the body and blood of the Lord" (corpus et sanguinem Domini) : and his biographer adds, that " having partaken of the sacrament of the body and blood of Christ," he embraced each of his disciples, and slept in the Lord.

St. Maelruain, in the year 769, founded the church and monastery of Tallaght (about five miles from Dublin), on a site which had been offered " to God, to St. Michael the Archangel, and to Maelruain," by Donnchadh, king of Leinster. This monastery was soon eminently distinguished for the number of its learned men, and it has acquired an undying fame in our history by the hagiology tracts which it handed down to us.

St. Maelruain drew up a rule of life for the Ceilé Dé, or servants of God, by which name his own monks were probably designated. "It contains," says Curry, "a minute series of rules for the regulation of their lives, their prayers, their preachings, their confessions, their communions, their ablutions, their fastings, their abstinences, their relaxations, their sleep, their celebrations of the Mass, and soforth."*

There is one passage in this rule which beautifully illustrates the belief of our sainted fathers in regard to the holy Sacrament ; we give it according to the translation of the learned Celtic scholar just referred to, whose invaluable manuscripts, through the exertions of the worthy ecclesiastic now so ably presiding over the Catholic University, have been secured for that institute, which promises to restore, at no distant day, the ancient pre-eminence of our island in learning and sanctity.

"What gives freedom to the Church of God," thus writes St. Maelruain, "is baptism and communion, and the chanting of prayers, and the instruction of children in learning, and the offering of the body of Christ upon every altar. A church is not entitled to tithes, unless it contain

---

* Lectures, etc., 375.

the lawful ministrations of a church, in baptism, and communion, and in the chanting of prayers for its supporters, both living and dead; and unless there be sacrifice offered on its altar on Sundays and days of solemnity."

Contemporary with St. Maelruain, and one who followed the Ceilé Dé rule of that great saint, was Aengus. Descended from the royal race of Dalaradia, he, for many years, led an heremitical life not far from the monastery of Clonenagh, at a spot which was in after years known by the name of *Disert-Aengus*. A writer of the ninth century describes him as "illustrious for his virtues, often favoured with angelic visions, renowned for learning, the sun of western Europe;" and Colgan thus compendiates the many eulogies which have been handed down to us regarding him: "Tantum sibi sanctimoniæ et doctrinæ comparavit nomen ut neminem suo ævo in patrio solo habuerit omnigenæ eruditionis laude parem, neminem sanctitatis opinione superiorem."[*]

His most famous work is the "Feliré," or Festology, to which we have more than once referred in the preceding pages. On each day he marks the chief recurring festivals, and commemorates in a few expressive words the distinctive virtues especially of our Irish saints. In the invocation with which he concludes this great work, he takes occasion to express his own faith, and the unvarying belief of our Church, regarding the holy Eucharist. After beseeching the mercy of the Redeemer for himself and for all mankind through the merits and sufferings of the saints, he continues his supplication "through all the sacrifices offered of the Saviour's own body and blood, as it is in heaven, upon our holy altars."[†]

---

[*] Acta SS. p. 579.
[†] See an elaborate description of this Festology, with many beautiful extracts from it, in Curry's Lectures, p. 365 seqq.

CHAPTER III.

THE TEACHING AND PRACTICES OF THE IRISH SAINTS.

The Daughters of king Leoghaire—St. Patrick receives Viaticum from St. Tassach.—St. Benignus.—St. Brigid; extract from her life, by Coellan; she receives Viaticum from St. Nennidh.—St. Columbkille. St. Canice.—St. Fursa—St. Colgu—St. Kieran.—Catholic expressions regarding the Eucharist in Irish writers.—St. Munnu of Taghmon.— St. Comgall—St. Cuthbert.—St. Fechan.—St. Ita.—St. Brendan of Clonfert—St. Malachy punishes a monk for doubts regarding the real presence.

THE life of St. Patrick is so identified with the faith and teaching of the whole Catholic Church in the fifth century, that it may seem idle to inquire what was his doctrine regarding the blessed Sacrament of the altar. Still, that our historical inquiry may be more complete, we shall gather together some few incidents from the fragmentary memorials of his life, to illustrate his belief and teaching regarding the holy Eucharist.

Amongst those illumined with the rays of faith through the preaching of our apostle, were the virgins Ethne, the fair, and Fedhelmia, the ruddy, daughters of king Leoghaire. St. Patrick having announced to them the power and majesty of God, as also the doctrine of the blessed Trinity, the virgins said, as if with one mouth and one heart:—

"Teach us, without delay, how we may attain the knowledge of his name and serve the true God, or how we ought to believe in him; and whatsoever thou shalt say to us, we will do. St. Patrick said: Believe ye in baptism after the sin of the first parents? They answered him: We believe.

"Believe ye in life after death? They answered : We believe.

"Believe ye in the resurrection at the day of Judgment? They answered : We believe.

"Believe ye in the unity of holy church? They answered : We believe.

"Then St. Patrick baptised them, and put upon them a white and spotless garment. Being baptised, they asked to see the face of Christ; and the bishop, St. Patrick, said to them : except *ye taste of the body and blood of Christ*, and except ye experience corporal death, ye cannot see Christ in his glory.

"They answered: *give us the sacrifice of the body and blood of Christ*, that we may be freed from the corruption of the flesh, and may see our spouse who is in heaven.

"*Then St. Patrick celebrated mass, and both the daughters of the king approached the communion* with great hope and perfect faith; and when they had communicated, they immediately rested in peace."

We have given this narrative in the words of Probus,[*] who who is reckoned the most accurate of the biographers of our saint. It agrees in substance with the text of the Vita Tripartita, and with the translation of Tirechan, given by Dr. Todd. We must await the publication of the original text of the latter which Dr. Reeves has now in hands, before deducing any argument from the formulas which it uses. The Vita Tripartita, which, as we have already seen, certainly belongs to a very early period of our Church, makes use of some peculiar expressions, which, whilst identical in meaning, still more distinctly formulize the Catholic doctrine. For instance, the last cited words of our apostle are expressed as follows: "whilst you are clothed with mortal flesh you cannot see the Son of God; but to behold him in the brightness of His majesty, it is necessary to lay aside this corruptible flesh, and *first to receive His body and blood, concealed in an invisible manner, beneath the visible form and species of bread and wine.*" Such is the paraphrase of our apostle's words recorded in the ancient life which Curry, judging from its original Irish text, pronounced to be written in the dialect of the sixth or seventh century.[†]

Another fact connected with our saint's visit to Tirerrill, in the county Sligo, serves to illustrate the liturgical usages of our island in those early ages; it is thus recorded in the Tripartite Life. "After crossing the Shannon, Patrick and his companions came to a place called *Dumhagraidh*, and there he ordained the worthy priest Ailbe; he it is who is venerated in the church of *Senchua*, in the country of the Ui-Oiliolla. But when the requisites for the divine service, and the sacred vessels were wanting, the holy prelate, divinely instructed, pointed out to the priest an altar

---

[*] Tr. Th. p. 58.   [†] See Lectures, p. 345 seqq.

under ground in a stone crypt; this altar was of exquisite workmanship (*mirandi operis*), and on its four corners were four glass chalices; and he admonished them to dig very cautiously lest the glass should be broken."*

When St. Patrick was admonished by the angel Victor, that the end of his pilgrimage was at hand, he received the viaticum of life to prepare himself for his eternal home. St. Fiacc records, that it was the bishop Tassach who thus administered the last communion to him:—

> "Remansit Tassach post eum
> Quando ministravit communionem ipsi,
> Dixit quod communicaturus esset Patricium,
> Nec prophetia Tassachi falsa erit."†

The Tripartite Life registers the same fact in the following words: "When the hour of his death approached, he received the sacrifice from the bishop Tassach; it was at the admonition of the angel Victor that he received the Viaticum of eternal life."‡ Indeed, in the tradition of the Irish Church, this was the characteristic glory of St. Tassach; and our great hagiologist, St. Aengus, thus, on the 14th of April, commemorates his privilege:—

> "The royal bishop Tassach,
> Who gave, on his arrival,
> The body of Christ, the King truly powerful,
> As communion, to Patrick."§

With St. Patrick we may associate his own loved disciple, Benean, or Benignus, whom he had enriched with the blessings of faith, and consecrated for the see of Armagh. St. Benignus died on the 9th of November, and his immediate preparation for his passage to eternity is thus recorded in his life:—

"The man of God, seeing that the time of his dissolution was at hand,

---

* Tr. Thaumat. p. 134. This fact is also commemorated in the Liber Armacanus, fol. 11, where the altar is styled "*altare mirabile lapideum*."
† Tr. Th. page 3.   ‡ Ibid. p. 128.
§ This quatrain is cited in the original Irish in the Ecclesiastical Antiq. of Dr. Reeves, p. 142; and Curry's Lectures, p. 368.

sent for St. Jarlath, and received most devoutly from his hand, *the earnest and pledge of eternal happiness, the body of the Lord;* and thus prepared himself for death, and for his entrance to his heavenly country."*

After the glorious apostle of our island, no other national saint is so endeared to the Irish heart as the "Mary of Erin," our great patroness, St. Brigid.

Cogitosus has given a very detailed description of the church of Kildare, which adjoined the convent of this virgin saint. It was built of wood, but its decorations and ornaments of silver and brass were worked in a most exquisite manner. Its paintings, too, are especially commemorated. To the sanctuary of this church there were two entrances; "The one," says Cogitosus, "through which the bishop, with his clergy and the assistants at the altar, entered, when about to offer up the sacred sacrifice of our Lord (sacra et Dominica immolare sacrificia): the second door was at the left side of the altar, and through it the abbess alone, with her virgins and faithful widows, entered, to partake of the banquet of the body and blood of Jesus Christ (ut convivio corporis et sanguinis fruantur Jesu Christi)."†

There is another invaluable metrical life of our great saint, composed by Coellan of Inniskeltra, in the seventh century. Amongst other things bearing on our present subject, it records a vision of St. Brigid, which, in a special manner, illustrates her belief in the holy Sacrament of the altar. One night, whilst the

---

* "Ex ejus manu arrham et pignus æternæ beatitudinis corpus Domini devotissime sumit."—Vita S. Ben. chap. xviii.

† Vita, by Cogitosus, cap. 35. Petrie has clearly proved that Cogitosus wrote before the year 835; he also thinks, that this life was not written before 800; but his arguments for this assertion are not so conclusive.— (Round Towers, p. 202.) Dr. Todd also assigns Cogitosus to the beginning of the ninth century, on the grounds that no Cogitosus is mentioned in the Martyrology of Aengus, written about the year 800.—(Memoir of St. Patrick, p. 11.) It was probably after the printing of this portion of Dr. Todd's work that Dr. Graves made the discovery referred to by Dr. Todd, at page 402, that Cogitosus is the latinized form of the Irish name Mactheni. It is, moreover, certain, from the Book of Armagh, that an Irish writer of the name Cogitosus flourished about the middle of the seventh century: if the silence of Aengus does not affect the existence of this Cogitosus, why does it in the case of our author? As, however, Aengus more than once gives us the name Mactheni, we may easily pardon the absence of Cogitosus.

sisters were engaged in prayer, she was wrapt in ecstasy, and saw the earth and heavens filled with youths, who were dressed in garments of angelic whiteness; Christ, the King of kings, was enthroned on high, whilst the assembled multitude gathered around his throne, and intoned the sacred canticle, "Holy, holy, holy is the Lord of hosts;" heavenly music accompanied this hymn of praise, and the angelic choirs re-echoed the responsive allelujahs. This vision filled our saint with spiritual joy, and at the dawn of day its meaning was unfolded to her, when the holy bishop Ibar came to her cell to offer up the holy sacrifice of the Mass.*

Another ancient biographer of St. Brigid,† commemorates the prophetical announcement made by her to St. Nennidh, that on her death-bed she would receive from his hand "the communion of the body and blood of our Lord Jesus Christ (communionem corporis et sanguinis Domini nostri Jesu Christi.)" In the same text this, her last communion, is called the *divine viaticum;* and

---

* Colgan has published this life in his Trias Thaumaturga, p. 584 seqq., but, as he himself laments, from a very imperfect manuscript. The passage referred to in the text is quite unintelligible in Colgan's edition, wherefore we give it complete, from the beautiful Barberini Codex:

"Quadam nocte suis præcepit sancta puellis
Fortiter in precibus, devota sistere mente,
Ipsa repleta Deo, magnis intenta secretis:
Cumque diu tacitis oculos ad sidera verbis
Auribus attonitis in templo sancta levabat;
Illa, tacete modo, dixit; magnalia Christi
Cernere quis poterit? Numquid vos cernitis ipsæ?
Nunc video cœli, terræ, maris, aeris alti,
Concava lata, spatium penetrabile sursum
Est plenum pueris indutis vestibus albis,
In medio Christus, Rex Regum, summa potestas,
Et palmam manibus retinentes, cantica dicunt
Nunc Sanctus Dominus, nunc Sanctus, Sanctus Zapaot,
Sedibus excelsis, Genitori, gloria Nato,
Organa dulcisono resonant cœlestia cantu:
Hoc pueri pariter cantantes, hoc seniores,
Angelici populi respondent Alle-que-luja.
Intima valde meam demulcet visio mentem
Gaudet quid populus cœlestis, nescio tantum.
Cum sol mane novo croceam de pectore pallam
Sustulit, et rutilum noctis de limine vultum
Viderat atque oculis terrarum concava claris,
Manserat in terris nec nigræ tunica noctis,
Clara dies fuerat; Præsul venerabilis illam
Ibarus ad cellam vir sanctus venerat ipse
Dicere missarum populis solemnia cunctis."

† Vita, by Animchad, *i. e.*, Animosus, in Trias Thaum. p. 559.

it is added, that immediately before her death, "she received the body and blood of our Lord Jesus Christ, the Son of the living God, from the most pure hand of St. Nennidh, as she herself had predicted" (corpus et sanguinem Domini nostri Jesu Christi, filii Dei vivi de mundissima S. Nennidii manu, etc.).*

Another bright ornament of our ancient Church was St. Columbkille. His life, written by Adamnan, his successor in the far-famed monastery of Iona, before the close of the seventh century, is a monument not only of the individual belief of these great saints, but further unfolds to us how fully the Catholic doctrine was maintained in that monastery, which for many years was a main centre of Irish missionary enterprise, and the favourite resort of all who were famed for learning and sanctity in our island. It is whilst describing the early life of St. Columba that the following miracle is commemorated:

"Whilst the holy youth was in Ireland, acquiring the wisdom of the holy Scriptures under the guidance of the bishop, St. Finnian (of Maghbile), it happened on a certain festival that wine was wanting for the mysterious sacrifice *(ad sacrificale mysterium)*. Columba hearing the ministers of the altar lamenting this deficiency, took the cruet to the fountain, that as deacon he might prepare the water for the celebration of the sacred Eucharist (ad sacræ Eucharistiæ ministeria); and then the holy man blessed the watery element that he had taken from the spring, invoking the name of the Lord Jesus Christ, who had changed water into wine in Cana, Galilee; and the same miracle being now renewed, the watery substance passed into the more pleasing one of wine. Returning to the church, he placed near the altar the cruet having this wine, and said to the ministers: You now have wine which the Lord Jesus sends, that his mysteries may be celebrated (ad sua peragenda mysteria)."†

Whilst St. Columba, at another time, was stopping at the monastery of Trefoit (now Trevet, in the county Meath, near Skreen), another circumstance occurred which illustrates this point of doctrine. The monks had invited a certain priest, noted for his virtuous deeds, to perform the solemn rite of the Mass (*ad Missarum peragenda solemnia*); our saint seeing him consecrate the sacred Eucharistic mysteries, (sacra Eucharistiæ mysteria),

---

* Trias Thaum. p. 559. † Reeves' Adamnan, p. 104.

pronounced the terrible sentence, "the clean and the unclean are now united: that is, the pure mysteries of the sacred oblation are ministered by this sinful man."*

Especially beautiful is the narrative of the visit of St. Cronan to Columba in his monastery of Iona. St. Cronan was a bishop from the province of Munster, but when visiting our saint, wished to conceal his episcopal character. The following is the narrative of Adamnan:

"Through humility, he sought as much as possible to conceal himself, so that no one might know that he was a bishop; this, however, could not be kept a secret from Columba: for, when on a Sunday he was ordered by St. Columba *to consecrate, according to custom, the body of Christ* (Christi corpus ex more conficere), he called our saint, as a brother priest, to unite with him in breaking the bread of the Lord. Columba, approaching the altar, intuitively looking into his face, said to him: May Christ bless thee, brother; do thou follow the episcopal rule, and distribute it alone."†

Here we have an altar, and a priest, and a consecration; Sunday was the day on which the sacrifice was offered, and that sacrifice is called the body of Christ. In the early Irish Church it was oftentimes customary for several priests to offer together the holy sacrifice; they were of equal rank, and, as Reeves expresses it, "acted as concelebrants, *simul verbis et manu conficientes.*" Reeves, however, adds, that in the present instance it is not clear whether the phrase *dominicum panem frangere* is to be referred to the celebration or to the distribution of the blessed Eucharist. Innes refers it to the former, and hence concludes: "it appears that in Yeolmkill a priest, even the abbot St. Columba himself, looked upon a bishop as so far superior to him, that he would not presume, even though invited, to concelebrate or celebrate the holy mysteries jointly with him."‡ For us it is sufficient to remark that the phrase *Christi corpus conficere* is one that has ever been considered characteristic of the Catholic doctrine, and which is consequently of frequent recurrence in the liturgical treatises of Rome.§

---

* Reeves' Adamnan, pp. 76-7. † Ibid. pp. 85-6.
‡ Civil and Ecclesiast. Hist. p. 175.
§ The same phrase occurs in the life of St. David, who was a disciple

Elsewhere incidental mention is frequently made of the holy sacrament, and the formulas then used to designate it, reveal more and more the sacred reverence with which the blessed Eucharist was regarded in those early ages, and their unity of faith with our belief at the present day: thus we find it called by the various epithets of 'Missa,' 'sacra Missarum solemnia,' 'sacra oblatio,' 'Eucharistia,' 'sacra Eucharistiæ mysteria,' etc.*

Another memoir of St. Columbkille was composed by Cumineus Albus, who was for many years contemporary with that great saint, and was his successor in the monastery of Iona. In it the same characteristic phrases occur at every page to designate the blessed Eucharist. We shall take one which regards a holy bishop of the province of Leinster, by name Columbanus. Our saint had seen in vision this bishop summoned to his eternal rest; therefore he summoned his religious brethren, and ordered everything to be prepared for the "sacred oblation," saying, "it is my duty to celebrate *the sacred mysteries of the Eucharist* for the holy soul which, during the night, passed to the angelic choirs;" and the historian adds: " whilst he was offering up *the sacred mysteries of the holy sacrifice* (inter sacra sancti sacrificii mysteria), he said to the brethren: to-day we are to pray for the holy bishop Columbanus."†

Few of our ancient saints have been so fortunate in their biographers as the great saint of whom we have just spoken. Still their scattered and fragmentary memoirs present one unvarying testimony, that the present doctrine of the Catholic Church, in regard to the blessed Eucharist, was that which was universally believed in the Church of our fathers.

St. Canice.—The life of St. Canice, edited by the Marquis of Ormond, records‡ how, when death approached, "he was unwilling to receive the sacrifice from any of the members of his own monastery, saying: The Lord will send another one to minister to

---

of the Irish schools: "Dominici corporis hostiam puris conficiebat manibus."—Act. SS. p. 427.

* Loc. cit. pages 158, 229, 233, 221, 282, etc.
† Vita S. Columbæ auctore *Cumineo* ap. Mabillon, Acta SS. ord. Bened. i. 343.
‡ Chap. 56.

me the body of Christ. Then St. Fintan, divinely directed, came to him, and the holy man having received the Eucharist at his hands, departed to the Lord." Another ancient MS. life, in the British Museum, describes the same scene, almost in the same words: "The man of God was unwilling to receive the saving viaticum from the hands of his brethren, saying: The Lord will send to me a holy man to minister the sacred body to me. Then St. Fintan Maeldub, sent by God, came to him, and from his hands he received the body of the Lord."

St. Fursa, patron of Peronne, in France, died in 650. Amongst our Irish saints he is celebrated as:—

> "Furse, the truly pious, loved
> Nothing more admirable are we told of,
> In a well as cold as the snow
> Accurately to sing his psalms."*

Whilst on the continent he is invoked as:—

> "Fursace, lampas sideris,
> Tui memor sis generis,
> In nos cum mors jam pendulum
> Suum fuderit jaculum."†

An ancient life of this saint is extant, judged by Usher‡ to have been written before the time of Venerable Bede, and in it we read that when some supernatural manifestations were promised to him by an angel, he prepared himself to receive them "*by asking for and partaking of the communion of the sacred body and blood.*"§ This holy man was, moreover, favoured with the instructions of his relatives SS. Beoan and Mellan, both of whom are named in our Irish martyrologies. In one of the instructions recorded in St. Fursa's life, we find the following remarkable words: "Let the bishops and priests of the Church of Christ stimulate the faithful to tears of repentance for their crimes, and strengthen them with

---

* Hymn by St. Cuimin of Connor. † Hym. in Vet. Officio.
‡ Discourse on the Religion, etc., p. 37.
§ Sacri corporis et sanguinis communionem.—Ap. Usher, loc. cit.; and Acta SS. Bolland. Jan. i. 37.

the spiritual food of faith, and *by the participation of the sacred body and blood.*"* When death approached, St. Fursa hastened to participate of this food of life, and "having received the enlivenment of the sacred body and blood," rested in the Lord.†

St. Colgu, surnamed *the Wise*, flourished in the eighth century. From his youth he was attached to the school and monastery of Clonmacnoise, and such was his fame, especially for sacred learning, that he was commonly styled " the Scribe and Doctor of all the Irish." He was superior of Clonmacnoise when Alcuin addressed to him the beautiful letter published by Usher in his Sylloge (No. 18). Alcuin styles him "his blessed master and pious father," and sent with the letter some presents for the Irish bishops and the religious of Clonmacnoise. St. Colgu was the author of many devotional treatises breathing the most ardent love and elevation of the soul to God. The most celebrated, however, of these treatises is a prayer entitled, in Irish, "Scuar Chrabhaigh," of which the following extract will give some idea:—

"O holy Jesus! O beautiful Friend! O Star of the Morning! O full noon-day Sun! . . . . For the sake of the merciful Father, from whom thou didst come unto us upon earth; for the sake of thy divinity, which that Father modified so as to receive Thy humanity; for the sake of the immaculate body from which Thou didst come, in the womb of the Virgin; for the sake of the Spirit with the seven forms which descended upon that body, in unity with Thyself and with Thy Father; for the sake of the holy womb from which Thou didst receive that body without destruction of virginity; . . . for the sake of the holy tree upon which Thy side was torn; for the sake of the innocent blood which trickled upon us from that tree; *for the sake of Thine own body and blood which are offered upon all the holy altars which are in all the Christian churches of the world;* . . . . dispense, and give, and bestow, Thy holy grace and Thy holy Spirit to defend and shelter me from all my present and future sins, and to light up in me all truth, and to retain me in that truth to the end of my life."‡

---

* Et participatione sacri corporis et sanguinis. See the Vita cit. ap. Bolland. p. 39. This passage from St. Fursa's life is quoted in the Vatican MS. Collection of Canons, No. 1,339, sæc. x. fol. 69.

† "Post sumptam sacri corporis et sanguinis vivificationem."—Loc. cit. p. 49.

‡ Curry's MS. See also his Lectures, p. 379 seq. Colgan, in Act. SS. p. 378, gives his life, and speaks of his writings; he had in his possession a copy of the prayer just cited from a MS. of Clonmacnoise : "Et ex aliis vetustis membranis."

St. Kieran, or Ciaran, who founded the great monastery of Saigir (now Seir-Kieran, in King's County), is styled by our ancient writers *primicerius sanctorum Hiberniæ*, which means not first-born, as some curiously enough translate it, but "first in dignity of the choir of Irish saints." A prophecy regarding him is attributed to our apostle St. Patrick :—

> "Saigir the cold, Saigir the cold,
> Raise a city on its brink.
> At the end of thirty fair years
> We shall meet there, I and thou."

Which words seem to be intended to declare, that thirty years after the death of our apostle, the future glory of Saigir would be born. He is described by Aengus as *Kieranus populosus*, which epithet is interpreted by the scholiast as indicating the great number of those who pursued the paths of perfection under his guidance. The sketch of his life, given by Cathal Maguire from the old narrative of Carnech (who, according to Colgan, was almost contemporary with our saint), represents him as rich in flocks and herds, "yet he himself partook not of their fruit, but divided all amongst the poor of Christ. His only food was a little barley bread, which he partook of, in the evening, together with some uncooked herbs; his only drink was water: his garments were made of skins, and when he lay down to rest, the hard ground was his only couch."*

Amongst his other deeds of virtue it is recorded, that on every Christmas night, when his own religious community had "*received the sacrifice from his hand,*" he proceeded to the distant nunnery of Ross-Benchor "*to offer up the body of Christ*" (ut Christi corpus offerret), and when the consecrated virgins received the holy communion at his hands (communionem Dominicam), he again returned to his monastery.†

St. Munnu, founder of Taghmon (*i. e.*, Teach-munnu), in the county Wexford, flourished at the close of the sixth century. He

---

* Ap. Colgan, Acta SS., p. 471, col. a.
† Acta SS. p. 461.

studied under the guidance of St. Comgall, at Bangor, and subsequently lived for eighteen years in the monastery of Cluain-inis. He was one of the most ardent supporters of the old Irish Easter computation, but in the synod of Magh-lene consented to adopt the practice of Rome. At his death, on the 21st October, 635, his biographer records that "he summoned his religious brethren around him, and imparted to them his blessing; and having participated of the body and blood of Christ, he rested in the Lord."*

St. Comgall, to whom Ireland is indebted for the great monastery of Bangor, was one of the most illustrious ornaments of our Church in the sixth century. He was born about the year 510, and died, according to the Four Masters, in 601, after governing his great monastery for well nigh fifty years.† His great disciple, Columbanus speaks of his "most copious and polished teaching" (luculentissimam elegantissimamque doctrinam); and an alphabetical hymn in his praise is preserved in the ancient MS. of the Antiphonarium Benchorense.‡ His life, published by Sirinus (in Fleming's Collectanea Sacra), and the Bollandists (at 10th May), is judged very ancient and authentic by Usher. It states that for some days before his demise, his religious urged him to receive the sacred viaticum. He, however, replied that God would send a holy abbot from Leinster to administer the holy sacrament to him; and so, in reality, it came to pass: for St. Fiachra, abbot in Idrone, near the river Barrow, came to his monastery "to administer to him the body and the blood of Christ" (ut accipiat de manibus ejus corpus et sanguinem Christi), and soon after his arrival, St. Comgall received at his hands "the communion of our Lord" (communionem Dominicam).§

Similar expressions are to be found in all the ancient lives of the Irish saints that have come down to us. Thus, we learn from Bede, that St. Cuthbert, whom recent investigations justly rank

---

* Acta SS. Bolland. 21st Oct., p. 340.
† The Martyrology of Tallaght, at x. Maij, expressly states that he presided over Bangor for fifty years.
‡ We give this hymn in the appendix.
§ Vita S. Comgalli, cap. liii.

amongst our Irish saints, on his death-bed "received the communion of the Lord's body and blood, as Herefrid, abbot of the monastery of Lindisfarne (who was the priest that then administered the holy sacrament to him), made report unto the same Bede."* In his metrical work on the life of Cuthbert, the same Venerable Bede adds :†

> "*Pocula degustat vitæ, Christique supinum*
> *Sanguine munit iter.*"

"He tastes the cup of life, and protects his upward journey with the blood of Christ." Amongst the facts recorded in St. Cuthbert's life, there is one which bears on our present subject: An officer, forsooth, of Egfrid's household, entreated him "to send a priest that might minister to his wife, who was dying, the sacraments of the Lord's body and blood."‡

St. Fechin of Fore, is one of those commemorated in the poem of Cuimin, on the characteristic virtues of the Irish saints:

> "The hospitable Fechin of Fore, loved,
> It was not a false mortification,
> To lay his fleshless ribs
> Upon the hard rocks, without clothes."

In his life we read that "having been strengthened by the sacrament of the most holy body and blood of the Lord, he resigned his soul to his Creator."§

Of the holy virgin St. Ita, it is also recorded that on a festival day, being anxious to receive from a venerable priest "*the body and blood of Christ*," she proceeded to the monastery of Clonmacnois, and there at his hands "secretly received the body and blood of the Lord." The religious, after a little while, discovering that the blessed Sacrament had disappeared, were filled with alarm, not knowing, says the historian, "what had been done with the body and blood of the Lord." They, therefore, observed a rigorous

---

* Ap. Usher, loc. cit. p. 39.
† De vit. Cuthberti, carm. cap. xxxvi.
‡ Dominica corporis sacramenta.—Cap. xv.
§ Vita, cap xlviii.

fast, in which the faithful joined, until it was discovered that the holy Eucharist had been administered to Ita.* After St. Bridget, this saint was one of the most venerated of the virgin-saints of our island. "Mida (thus she was commonly called) loved to foster saints; firm was her humility, without dejection:" such is her eulogy in St. Cuimin's hymn. She was the patroness of Hy-Conaill, in the county Limerick, and is described in her life as "rivalling the great St. Brigid in her merits and virtues."† Aengus, too, celebrates her as "the glowing lamp of the females of Munster; the virgin that suffered continual pain, and subjected herself to many mortifications."

The learned Reeves, in his notes to the edition of Adamnan, records another example bearing on our present subject:

"We read in the life of St. Brendan of Clonfert," he says, "that this saint was ordered to celebrate Mass by St. Gildas, the abbot of the monastery. The *custos templi* (*i. e.*, the sacristan) said to him: *Præcepit tibi Sanctus Senex noster, ut offeras corpus Christi. Ecce altare, hunc librum Græcis litteris Scriptum, et canta in eo sicut abbas noster.* That is, our holy superior commands you *to offer the body of Christ*. Here is the altar, and the missal written in Greek characters; chant in it 'as our abbot is wont to do.' "‡

Many similar illustrations might be taken from other lives of our Irish saints; but those already produced sufficiently evince what was the belief of our sainted fathers in regard to the Eucharistic mystery. We shall, therefore, conclude this article with the example registered by St. Bernard, in his life of the great archbishop of Armagh, St. Malachy. A monk of the monastery of our saint being tempted with doubts regarding the holy Sacrament, fell into error, and asserted that "it contained neither the grace nor the reality of the body of Jesus Christ, but was merely a sign of both." What was the course pursued by St. Malachy? Surely we may learn from the course adopted by him in reference to this religious, what would be his judgment regarding the heretical tenets of modern times! He not only reproved, but

---

* Vita, cap. xvii. † Acta SS. 15 Jan. cap. xxxiii.
‡ Reeves' Adamnan, p. 354.

moreover excommunicated the erring brother; and it was only when he abjured his erroneous novelty, and performed a long series of penitential deeds, that the prodigal son was re-embraced in his father's bosom, and re-admitted to a participation of the holy Sacrament of the altar. Surely, this one fact should suffice to convince every impartial inquirer what doctrine was revered as truth, and what was regarded as erroneous in the untainted Church of the Island of Saints.

CHAPTER IV.

TESTIMONY ON THE BLESSED EUCHARIST OF THE IRISH WRITERS APPEALED TO BY OUR ADVERSARIES.

The Poet Sedulius.—Usher's opinions regarding him examined.—The Commentator Sedulius.—Claudius's teaching regarding the Eucharist.

FROM the time of Usher to the present day, it has been fashionable with a certain class of Protestant writers to contend that the early Church of Ireland recognised nought save bread and wine in the blessed Eucharist; and they invariably repeat some detached sentences of the poet Sedulius, the commentator Claudius, and a few other Irish writers, as affording sufficient evidence of the Protestantism of our fathers. To meet such pretensions, we have examined in detail the evidence of each witness cited by our adversaries, and the result of our inquiry is, that so far from any one of them asserting the Protestant tenets, each and all of them inculcate the teaching of the Catholic Church, and place in still bolder relief the doctrine of the real presence, as taught from the very earliest ages of faith in Ireland.*

---

* In this chapter we are to keep in mind that the Irish Church, in the ages in which the writers now about to be treated of lived, was in the strictest bonds of union with the churches of the continent, as appears from the continual visits of pilgrims and missionaries from Ireland to those churches, and *vice versa*. Now everyone versed in theology knows that the researches of Catholic writers have placed the fact beyond all

THE POET SEDULIUS.

In the first place, let us examine what is the nature of the testimony given by the greatest of our ancient poets, Sedulius, who bore to the continent the fame of our island in the fifth century, and won for himself a high post among Christian writers, by his Carmen Paschale, and its corresponding paschal prose.* So esteemed were these writings in Rome and other Catholic countries, that pope Gelasius styled their author "the venerable Sedulius," and commended them to the use of the faithful. Venantius Fortunatus also made them the subject of the highest eulogy; and St. Hildephonsus described Sedulius as "an evangelical poet, an eloquent orator, and a Catholic writer."

Since Sedulius did not propose to himself to compose a dogmatic treatise, it would, perhaps, be vain to seek for theological precision in his writings; but at the same time, as he undertook to sketch the life of our divine Redeemer, we must naturally expect to meet with frequent reference to the gospel narratives, adorned though they may be with all the ornaments and figures that a poetical imagination might suggest.

Now, this celebrated writer, says Usher, explicitly affirms that bread and wine alone are offered to God in the Christian sacrifice. To establish this assertion, the learned Protestant primate brings forward two passages from the writings of Sedulius, viz., one from the paschal poem, and the other from the paschal prose. The testimony cited by Usher from the paschal poem is as follows:

> "Denique Pontificum princeps, summusque sacerdos,
> Quis nisi Christus adest, gemini libaminis auctor
> Ordine Melchisedech, cui dantur munera semper
> Quæ sua sunt, fructus segetis et gaudia vitis."

controversy, that the doctrines of the Church in those ages regarding the blessed Eucharist were precisely what they are at present.—(See the great work La Perpetuité de la Foi, etc.) If Ireland held a different doctrine from the continent, the bonds of union could not have been maintained.

* Usher refers Sedulius to about the year 490. The best edition of his Carmen Paschale is that of Arevalo, published in 4to, Rome, 1794

That is to say:—" Who else presides as chief pontiff and high-priest but Christ, institutor of the two-fold libation, of the order of Melchisedech, to whom his own gifts, the fruit of the corn and the joy of the vine, are always offered."*

The meaning of this passage, adds Usher, is rendered still more clear by the corresponding words of the paschal prose, in which the Eucharist is styled:

"The sweet meat of the seed of wheat, and the lovely drink of the pleasant vine."

Such are the passages which, in Usher's opinion, should suffice to establish the Protestantism of Sedulius, regarding the holy Sacrament of the altar.

Now, first of all, we must remark that it was a somewhat hazardous undertaking in Usher to claim as a clear assertor of Protestantism one whose writings are commended by the Holy See, and extolled by the saints of the Catholic Church. Secondly, it was, to say the least, uncandid in the Protestant primate to cull a few detached words from the paschal prose, and seek to persuade his readers that they conveyed the full meaning of the author; whilst, had the whole text been given, the figurative language of the poet would have been made apparent, and the Catholic doctrine regarding the Eucharistic mystery would be seen most plainly proposed. The text thus unfairly cited by Usher is as follows:

" Quis enim nisi Dominus Christus pontifex Pontificum, sacerdos sacerdotum, gemini libaminis auctor et conditor, cujus secundum ordinem Melchisedech munera, quæ pro nobis obtulit crucifixus, *sui corporis consanguinitate offeruntur*, triticeæ sementis cibus suavis, et amœnæ vitis potus amabilis."

Which words we may thus translate: 'For who but the Lord is present, the Pontiff of pontiffs, the Priest of priests, the Author and founder of the two-fold libation, whose gifts, according to the order of Melchisedech, which he offered for us upon the cross,

* Carmen Pasch. lib. iv. versic. 206, edid. Arevalo, p. 297.

changed into his own flesh, are the sweet food of the wheaten seed, and the lovely drink of the pleasant vine.'

Thus, then, the gifts which, by the institution of Christ, are offered to God, though beautifully and poetically styled "the sweet fruit of the corn, and the joy of the vine;" and again, "the sweet food of the wheaten seed, and the lovely drink of the pleasant vine;" yet they are not to be regarded as *mere bread and wine*, unless we wish to assert that only such gifts were offered for us on the cross. For the poet expressly says, in the passage omitted by Usher, that those Eucharistic gifts are the very same which were offered by the Redeemer crucified, "quæ pro nobis obtulit crucifixus." Surely, no Catholic could desire a more beautiful exposition of the Catholic belief; whilst in the passage from the paschal poem, we recognise a long-cherished description, in all the vividness of poetic imagery, of the holy Sacrament, which, under *the species of bread and wine*, presents to us the true body and blood of Christ. It is under a like imagery that the Catholic Church every day presents the holy mystery to her children, when she applies to it the words of the prophet Zachary, "frumentum electorum, et vinum germinans virgines."*

But as Usher was investigating the true belief of our ancient poet in regard to the blessed Eucharist, it is, to say the least, surprising that he omitted all reference to the many other clear and indubious passages in which Sedulius declares the body and blood of the Redeemer to be truly present in the Sacrament of the altar. Thus, the passage in which the poet describes the paschal supper of the divine Redeemer—one, indeed, to which the historical inquirer on such a subject should naturally turn, as a primary source of the information which he seeks—clearly lays down the Catholic doctrine.

> . . . . . . "Nam corporis atque
> Sanguinis ille sui postquam duo munera sanxit
> Atque cibum potumque dedit, quo perpete nunquam
> Esuriant, sitiantque animæ sine labe fideles."†

---

* Chap. ix. 17.   † Carm. Pasch. lib. v. line 34-37.

That is to say :—He instituted the two gifts of his body and blood, thus giving a sacred food and drink, by participating of which the faithful spotless souls might ever be inebriated with spiritual delight; which idea is expressed in like manner, and almost in the same words, in the corresponding passage of the paschal prose.

"Posteaquam corporis sui Dominus Jesus Christus et sanguinis duo vitæ numera consecravit propriisque discipulis spiritalem cibum potumque porrexit, quo cœlestibus epulis saginatæ famem sitimquæ sentire nequeant animæ jam fideles."

Thus, in the Eucharist are contained the two vivifying gifts of the body and blood of Christ, which, as a heavenly food, satiate the souls of the faithful, and preserve them from spiritual death. In another place, speaking of the blood and water which issued from our Saviour's side, the poet again takes occasion to commend this sacred banquet :—

"Hæc sunt quippe sacræ pro religionis honore
Corpus, sanguis, aqua, tria vitæ munera nostræ—
Fonte renascentes membris et sanguine Christi
Vescimur, atque ideo templum deitatis habemus:
Quod servare Deus nos annuat immaculatum
Et faciat tenues tanto mansore capaces."*

The prose text is, if possible, still more explicit :—

"O quam Catholico dogmati sociatur hæc causa? O quantum Trinitatis fides conveniunt hæc sacrata? Corpus namque sanguis et aqua, tria vitæ nostræ sunt munera. Omnes enim, qui, Christo duce nostro, in aquarum fonte renascimur, ejus corpus et sanguinem sumentes edimus ac potamus, ut sancti Spiritus templum esse mereamur."

The latter words of which passage, which alone regard our present subject, may be thus translated :—

"All of us, who, under Christ our leader, are regenerated in the fountain of waters, taking His body and blood, do eat and drink thereof that we may deserve to enjoy the Holy Ghost."

---

* Carm. Pasch. lib. v. line 289, seqq.

That is to say :—Baptism is the first entrance to the spiritual life; but its sanctifying waters being poured upon our heads, we become capable of receiving the body and blood of Christ; which holy sacrament perfects in us the life of grace, and makes us the living temples of the Holy Ghost.

Elsewhere, when describing the feast prepared by the Redeemer on the shore, for His disciples, he adds, that the fish was emblematic of the sacrament of baptism; the loaf was an emblem of Christ, whose very body is our Eucharistic food; whilst the fire indicated the Holy Ghost, who sanctifies our soul.

> . . . . . . "Quippe est aqua piscis
> Christus adest panis, sanctusque Spiritus ignis
> Hinc etenim abluimur, hoc pascimur, inde sacramur."*

And in the corresponding prose text :—

"Nam piscis aqua videtur intelligi, qua nos ablui certum est, ac renasci : panis Christum significat salvatorem, *cujus eodem corpore vescimur ad salutem*: ignis Spiritus sancti gerit imaginem, quo devoti consecramur ad fidem."

THE COMMENTATOR SEDULIUS.

Another witness to the Protestantism of our Irish Church in the ninth century, cited by Usher, is the abbot Sedulius, who is chiefly known by his Commentaries on the New Testament. It is sufficient, however, to read the very passages produced by Usher himself to understand that no sentiment is uttered by this writer not fully consonant to the Catholic teaching of the present day.

The following are the extracts quoted by the Protestant primate. In the Commentary on the Epistle to the Hebrews, Sedulius writes :—

"Melchisedech offered bread and wine to Abraham, for a figure of Christ, offering His body and blood unto the Father upon the cross."

And again :—

"But we offer daily for a commemoration of the Lord's passion, once endured, and for our own salvation."

---

* Carm. Pasch. lib. v. line 402, seqq.

One of these passages is taken from the Commentary on the fifth chapter to the Hebrews, the other from the Commentary on the tenth chapter; nevertheless, they are united together so as to form one continuous sentence by primate Usher.* Whether taken united, however, or separate, they contain nothing repugnant to the teaching of our holy Church; for, all Catholics recognize in the holy sacrifice of the altar a divine commemoration of the Redeemer's passion, whilst Catholics too, and Catholics alone, still rejoice with Sedulius, that from the rising to the setting sun it is offered on our altars to give glory to God, and obtain from Him the blessings of *salvation*.

Usher adds that "elsewhere, expounding the words of our Saviour, *do this in remembrance of me*, he brings in the similitude used before him and after him by others, 'He left us a memorial of Himself even as if one that was going on a far journey, should leave some token of affection with a loved companion; that as often as he beholds it, he may call to mind his benefits and friendship.'"

The learned historian well remarked that this was a phrase often made use of by other writers: he might have added, that it occurs repeatedly in the sacred liturgy and office which Catholics still use even on the feast-day of the blessed Sacrament. His good faith, however, is not apparent whilst he separates the above passage from its context, and omits the preceding words, which clearly and emphatically present the Catholic teaching: it is thus Sedulius writes:—"*Take and eat, this is my body. As if St. Paul said: beware not to eat that body unworthily, whereas it is the body of Christ.*"†

Thus again, this Irish abbot of the ninth century, so far from broaching the Protestant tenets, is found to inculcate the doctrine of the Catholic Church.

CLAUDIUS.

The chief witness, however, to whose testimony Usher‡ appeals

---

* Loc. cit. p. 42. † Comment. in 1 ep. Corinth. xi. 24.
‡ Loc. cit. p. 42-3.

with special confidence, is the Irish commentator Claudius. It must have been that Usher hoped that no Catholic would have access to the original text of that writer's commentary; for, certainly it is difficult in any other hypothesis to explain how he could have ventured to so utterly misrepresent and corrupt the doctrinal teaching which that commentary presents to us.

Before we come to the many passages in which Claudius clearly and repeatedly lays down the Catholic doctrine, let us see what extracts Usher has been able to cull from this ancient author to justify his assertion, that he must be ranked amongst Protestant writers. The first passage is as follows:—

"Our Saviour wished first to deliver to His disciples the Sacrament of His body and blood, which He presented in the breaking of the body and the effusion of the chalice; and afterwards to immolate the body itself upon the altar of the cross."

These words, so far from conveying the Protestant tenets, are a clear statement of the Catholic faith: the Eucharist is styled "the Sacrament of Christ's body and blood;" and the subsequent words still more clearly repeat, that the very body* of Christ, which was immolated upon the cross, is there distributed to the faithful.

Usher's argument from this text is amusing. "Claudius," he says, "expressly distinguishes the sacrament of the body, which was delivered unto the disciples, from the body itself, which was afterwards offered upon the cross." But what has this remark to do with the Protestant tenets? All Catholics at the present day draw the same distinction between the Sacrament of the altar and the sacrifice of the cross. Usher should rather have remarked, that whilst, according to Protestant teaching, the Eucharist is *mere*

---

* Usher himself remarks on the phrase, "*the breaking of the body,*" as follows: "At first sight I did verily think that in these words an error had been committed in my transcript, *body* being miswritten for *bread*; but, afterwards, comparing it with the original, I found that the author retained that manner of speaking."—(Loc. cit. p. 42.) We are happy to be able to confirm Mr. Usher's remark, and to corroborate his reading by the Vatican text, which is as follows:—" Voluit ante discipulis suis tradere sacramentum corporis et sanguinis sui quod significavit in fractione corporis et effusione calicis et postea ipsum corpus immolari in ara crucis." — Codex Vatican, 3828, fol. 119.

bread and wine, Claudius attests his belief that it is *the body and blood of Jesus Christ.*

The second passage which, according to Usher, bears the seal of Protestantism, is one which the reader will find repeated by all Catholic theologians, from the council of Trent to the present day. The question is often proposed: Since both the body and blood of Christ are really present under either species, why is it that the species of bread is referred to the body, and the species of wine to the blood of our Redeemer? Claudius answers: " Because bread strengthens the body, and wine produces blood in the flesh; therefore, the one is mystically referred to the body of Christ, the other to His blood."*

Thus, then, the whole Protestantism of Claudius is reduced to this mystical reference of the sacred species,—a reference quite in accordance with the teaching of the Catholic Church.†

Let us now see a few passages which Usher was careful to pass over unnoticed, and which clearly convey the Catholic doctrine.

After commemorating the fact of the healing of the leper by the divine Redeemer, and the words addressed to him, " Go and present yourself to the high-priest," Claudius thus continues:—

---

* We give from the Vatican Codex, the complete text of Claudius, as it serves to illustrate not only the difficulty proposed by Usher, but also the custom of mixing a little water with the wine to be used in the holy Sacrifice :—" Quia panis corpus confirmat, vinum vero sanguinem operatur in carne, hic ad corpus Christi mystice, illud refertur ad sanguinem. Verum quia et nos in Christo et in nobis Christum manere oportet, vinum dominicæ calicis aqua miscetur, attestante enim Johanne, aquæ populi sunt; et neque aquam solum neque solum vinum sicut nec granum frumenti solum sine aquæ admixtione et confectione in panem, cuiquam licet offerre, ne talis videlicet oblatio quasi caput a membris, secernendum esse significet, et vel Christum sine (fructu) nostræ redemptionis a morte pati potuisse, vel nos sine illius passione salvari ac Patri offerri posse confingat. Quod autem dicit : Hic est sanguis meus Novi Testamenti ad distinctionem respicit veteris Testamenti quod hircorum et vitulorum est sanguine dedicatum, dicente inter aspergendum legislatore, hic sanguis Testamenti quod mandavit ad vos Deus. Necesse est enim exemplaria quidem verorum bis mundari, ipsa autem ecclesia melioribus hostiis quam istis."—Vatican Codex, 3828, fol. 110.

† Dr. Lanigan, who was only acquainted with the commentary of Claudius by these extracts of Usher, nevertheless most justly remarked, that " these extracts were quite opposite to Usher's theory"; and "if ever there was an author who clearly announced the doctrine of the real presence and the sacrifice of the Mass, Claudius was one."— Eccles. Hist. iii. 319.

"Should any one be surprised that our Saviour thus seems to sanction the Mosaic sacrifice, which is not received by the Christian Church, let him call to mind that as yet that sacrifice had not been instituted, which is the Holy of Holies, the very body of Christ."*

Elsewhere, he calls the blessed Eucharist *the Sacrament of Christ's body*, distinguishing it at the same time from the spiritual food of faith;† and, again, he designates it as the mystery of His flesh and blood—" suæ carnis et sanguinis mysterium."‡

What is most unpardonable, however, in primate Usher is, that he passes over in silence the beautiful words with which our commentator describes the actions of our divine Lord, in preparation for and during the celebration of the last supper. It is, indeed, a rather novel mode of conducting an historical inquiry into the opinion of an ancient writer on any subject, to pass unnoticed those chapters in which that subject is expressly treated of. In the present instance, however, Usher's object seems to have been different from that which the title of his work indicates; and instead of instituting *an historical inquiry* into the doctrines of our early Church, he seems merely to have proposed to himself to gather from early writings, not easily accessible to the public, some stray and ambiguous sentences, which might serve as a plea or an excuse for those who are unwilling to embrace the faith of their fathers.

Claudius, therefore, when illustrating the history of the last supper, begins with the interrogation of the disciples: "Ubi vis paremus tibi comedere Pascha?" Upon which he remarks:—

"The fourteenth day of the first month is called the first day of the azyms; for in it the Jews were accustomed to lay aside the leaven, and immolate the paschal lamb; wherefore, the apostle writes: Christ, our pasch, is immolated. For though it was on the following day, that is, the fifteenth moon, that He was crucified, yet it was on the night of the sacrifice of the lamb that He both *instituted for His disciples the Sacrament*

---

* Codex Vatican. fol. 33: "Meminerit nondum esse coepisse sacrificium, sanctum sanctorum, quod corpus ejus est."
† Ibid. fol. 26.
‡ "Discipulis suæ carnis et sanguinis mysterium credit."—In Cod. Vallicell. fol. 133, verso.

of His flesh and blood, and Himself was arrested by the Jews; thus commencing the sacrifice of Himself, in His sacred passion."*

Subsequently, after expounding the words of our divine Lord to Judas, he thus continues:—

"Also at the present day, and throughout all time, woe to that man who sinfully approaches the altar of God, and with wickedness in his mind and treachery in his heart, fears not to become partaker of the most holy oblations of the Sacrament of Christ; for thus he, too, after the manner of Judas, betrays the Son of man: not, indeed, to the sinful Jews, but still to sinners, forsooth to his own sinful members, with which he dares to contaminate that inestimable and inviolable Sacrament of the Lord's body and blood."†

Surely this was a passage that might have thrown some light on the historical subject that Usher was investigating: the unworthy communicant renews the scene of Judas, for "he receives into his sinful members the body and blood of Christ." Claudius again repeats this exposition of the Eucharistic doctrine, when he commemorates the words of institution:

"Whilst they were at supper, Jesus took bread, and blessed, and broke, and gave to His disciples, saying, 'Take and eat: This is my body.' The ceremonies of the ancient Passover being at an end, He passes to the New Pasch, which He wished the Church to observe as a memorial of its redemption; thus, forsooth, instead of the flesh and blood of the lamb, *substituting the Sacrament of His own flesh and blood,* and showing Himself to be Him of whom was written: The Lord hath sworn, nor shall He repent: Thou art a priest for ever, according to the order of Melchisedech."‡

---

* Codex Vatican. fol. 109, b. "Hac tamen nocte qua agnus immolabatur et carnis sanguinisque suis discipulis tradidit mysteria celebranda et a Judæis tentus," etc. The word *suis* should probably be *sui:* in the translation, however, we deemed it better to follow the text as extant in the Vatican MS. This portion of the Vallicellian MS. is wanting.

† Sed et hodie quoque et in sempiternum væ illi homini qui ad mensam Domini malignus accedit; qui insidiis mente conditis, qui præcordiis aliquo scelere pollutis, mysteriorum Christi oblationibus sacrosanctis participare non metuit: et ille enim in exemplum Judæ filium hominis tradit, non quidem Judæis peccatoribus, sed tamen peccatoribus, membris videlicet suis, quibus illud inæstimabile et inviolabile dominici corporis et sanguinis Sacramentum temerare præsumit.—Ibid. fol. 110.

‡ "Transiit ad novum Pascha quod in suæ redemptionis memoriam ecclesiam frequentare volebat: ut videlicet pro carne agni et sanguine, sui corporis sanguinisque Sacramentum substitueret, ipsumque esse monstraret cui juravit Dominus et non pœnitebit eum: tu es sacerdos in æternum secundum ordinem Mechisedech."—Ibid. fol. 110.

Thus, in the last supper Christ was truly high-priest, according to the order of Melchisedech, offering to God that sacrifice which was typified of old, and substituting to the flesh and blood of the paschal lamb, the heavenly banquet of His own most precious body and blood.

Even in his subsequent commentary, Claudius returns again and again to commemorate the Eucharistic mystery. Thus, on the passage " et hymno dicto," etc., he writes:

"This hymn may be understood of the thanksgiving-hymn of our Lord, in which, with eyes uplifted to heaven, He prayed for Himself and the disciples, and those who through their ministry would believe in Him. And strikingly, indeed, does He lead out the disciples to the Mount of Olives, when he had strengthened them *with the Sacrament of His body and blood*, and commended them to His Father by the intercessory hymn: thus typically instructing us, that through the efficacy of His sacraments and intercession, we must tend to the highest virtues and graces of the Holy Ghost."*

When our Saviour's body was laid in the tomb, he again takes occasion to remark:

"We may, in a spiritual sense, learn from these words, that the body of the Lord is not to be placed upon gold or gems or silk, but upon plain linen: . . . Hence is derived the custom of the Church, to offer the sacrifice of the altar not upon cloths of silk or of rich dye, but only upon simple linen cloths, according to the decree of the blessed pope Sylvester."†

These testimonies should certainly suffice to rank our illustrious Irish commentator amongst the most explicit assertors of the Catholic doctrine of the blessed Eucharist. Still, before we take our leave of him, we wish to cite one other passage from his writings—a passage, indeed, which has been preserved to us by Usher himself, but which he takes care to make no mention of

---

* "Pulchre discipulos Sacramentis sui corporis ac sanguinis imbutos et hymno piæ intercessionis Patri commendatos in montem educit olivarum," etc.—Ibid. fol. 111.

† "Possumus juxta intelligentiam spiritalem hoc sentire quod corpus Domini non auro non gemmis et serico sed linteamine puro obvolvendum sit. . . . Hinc ecclesiæ mos obtinuit ut Sacrificium altaris non in serico neque in panno tincto sed in lino terreno celebretur," etc.—Ibid. fol. 118, b.

when discussing the doctrinal teaching of our ancient Church. This beautiful passage is extracted from Claudius's commentary on Leviticus, a work which seems, alas! to be now irretrievably lost:

"Christus (he thus writes) in cruce carnem suam fecit nobis esibilem. Nisi enim fuisset crucifixus, sacrificium corporis ejus minime comederetur. Comeditur autem nunc in memoria Dominicæ passionis. Crucem tamen præveniens in cœna Apostolorum seipsum immolavit, qui post resurrectionem in cœli tabernaculum, suum sanguinem introduxit, portans cicatrices passionum."*

Thus, then, the sacred flesh of Christ is indeed our food: the Redeemer, in the last supper, offered a true sacrifice to the Father, anticipating, in a certain sense, the sacrifice of the cross; and further, Claudius declares that this mysterious sacrifice must be referred to the self-same mystery and the self-same power, by which the divine Redeemer bore with Him His sacred wounds, when entering into His eternal glory.

CHAPTER IV.

(CONTINUED.)

TESTIMONY ON THE BLESSED EUCHARIST OF THE IRISH WRITERS APPEALED TO BY OUR ADVERSARIES.

Manuscript of the Gospels, by Maelbrighte.—Toland refuted.—Dr. Reeves and Dr. O'Conor determine the age of this MS.—St. Manchan.—Objections from Scotus Erigena examined.

It was after the time of Usher that another document came to light, which was eagerly laid hold of, as corroborating the Protestantism of our ancient Church. This was the Codex Maelbrighte, or Transcript of the Four Gospels, with an interlinear commentary made by an Irish scribe named Maelbrighte.

* Ap. Usher, Syllog. Epp. No. 20.

The first to bring forward this beautiful manuscript, to support the tottering cause of the Protestant tenets, was the well-known John Toland, in his letters published in London under the name Nazarenus, in 1718. Toland was an apostate from the Catholic Church. Having laid aside his ancient faith, he deemed it also advantageous to renounce his family name, which was that of O'Toolan, and to calumniate his country,—for he was a native of Ireland, being born at Eskaheen, in Inishowen, near Derry. According to this writer, the Codex Maelbrighte was written before the year 900; and in its marginal commentary it is expressly stated, if we can believe Mr. Toland, that "the Eucharist is a figure of the body of Christ—the first figure of the New Testament—a figure daily reiterated and received in faith;" and lest any one should hesitate to receive his translation, he adds the original text: "mysterium et figura corporis Christi—prima novi testamenti figura—hæc vero figura quotidie iteratur, accipitur in fide," etc. "Nor is this all," writes Toland, "for the commentator on the words 'This is my body,' further added the remark, that 'these words were used by Christ, lest any one might erroneously believe that the daily sacrifice was the body of Christ'— hoc dixit ne nostra dubitaret fides de sacrificio quotidiano in Ecclesia quasi corpus Christi esset."

Dr. Lanigan, when making some remarks on the theory of Toland, was obliged to add: "I must take his word for the genuineness of his extracts, for I have not access to the said manuscript." This shelter, however, no longer remains for the unfortunate Toland, as the Codex Maelbrighte is preserved in the British Museum, and many extracts have been published from it in full by Dr. Reeves, in his paper read before the Royal Irish Academy, January 13th, 1851.

1. As regards the age of the manuscript, Toland lived long enough to find it proved by Wanley, in his Catalogue of the Oxford Manuscripts, that it was written about the middle of the twelfth century. Dr. O'Conor, in his "Rerum Hibernicarum Scriptores," rendered still more evident the date assigned to it by Wanley, and Reeves repeats the argument of O'Conor. In the colophon to the

whole manuscript it is expressly stated, that it was written "in the year of the assassination of king Cormac MacCarthy by Turlough O'Brien," which event is recorded by the Four Masters in the year 1138. At the end of the Gospel of St. Luke the writer also added: "A prayer for Maelbrigid, who wrote this book, in the twenty-eighth year of his age. This is the second year after the great storm."* This great storm is precisely recorded by the Four Masters in the year 1137: "A great storm throughout Ireland, which prostrated many trees, houses, churches, and other buildings, and swept men and cattle into the sea in Moy-Conaille."† Thus, then, the date assigned to it by Toland at once falls to the ground.

2. The corruption of the text, however, must bear with it a far more severe reproach than the ignorance of the true date of the manuscript. Indeed, the date of the work itself being fixed, we might refrain from any further remarks,—for no one questions the Catholicity of the teaching of the Irish Church at the time when SS. Celsus and Gelasius and Malachy rendered it illustrious on the continent by their learning, as well as by their sanctity and miracles. We will, therefore, merely remark, that Toland omits all reference to the repeated formulas by which the blessed Eucharist is styled the body of Christ, as he also omits the beautiful sentiment by which it is declared that there is now offered to God a true sacrifice, not the mere figures of the old law—"corpus meum; id est, ut sit hæc vera hostia, non agnus, non vitulus, non hircus, non taurus."‡ Toland affirms that the Eucharist is styled "figura corporis Christi," yet these words are his own, and nowhere occur in the text of Maelbrighte. He also cites the Latin phrase "hæc figura accipitur in fide," and yet this Latin is his own composition, and instead of it we read in the original text, "corpus Christi accipitur in fide, benedicitur in abundantia, frangitur in tormentis, datur in exemplis." The other phrases regarding the figurative reference of the ceremonies of the Holy Sacrifice, need no explananation; they are repeated by all Catholics to the present day.

* Ap. Reeves, loc. cit. † Ap. O'Donovan, ad h. a.
‡ Ap. Reeves, loc. cit. pag. 23.

The concluding passage, cited by Toland, merits more attention, as it is not the commentary of the scribe Maelbrighte, but is given by him from the writings of an early Irish saint, named Manchan. There were many of that name who flourished in our Irish Church. There was one who was surnamed *the Wise*, and *the Master*, whose death is recorded by the Annals of Ulster, in 652, and who, under the name of St. Munchin, is venerated as founder and patron of Limerick. Another St. Manchan was abbot of Leighlin, in 718; a third is commemorated as abbot of Tomgrany, in the county Clare, who died in 735. Though the scribe, Maelbrighte, does not mention to which of these he refers, there can be but little doubt that the cited extracts are from the writings of the first-mentioned, who alone is known to have been famous for his Scriptural learning. We shall give in full the two extracts from St. Manchan, in regard to the Eucharist, preserved in the Codex Maelbrighte, that thus the reader may have a new testimony to the Catholic teaching of our Irish Church in the middle of the seventh century, and, at the same time, a new instance of the arts to which the traducers of our sainted fathers are obliged to have recourse, in order to assimilate their teaching to that of the Protestant Church. The first extract from Manchan is given at fol. 54 of the Codex Maelbrighte, as a commentary on the words *accepit panem*. It is as follows:—

"Primo quæritur si hæc assumptio panis et calicis figura an historia, an sensus figura sit. Fractio autem panis figurat corpus confractum a militibus in cruce; et in omnibus sanctis iterata passio est dum patiuntur a Christo usque ad finem mundi. Sed tamen non ut fiebant figuræ legis quæ cessaverunt, hæc vero figura quotidie iteratur."

The second extract from the same saint is preserved in fol. 55, and regards the Redeemer's words, *hoc est corpus meum*; it is as follows:—

"Et hoc dixit (Jesus) ne nostra dubitaret fides de sacrificio quotidiano in ecclesiis quod corpus Christi est, quoniam Christus in dextra Dei sedet."[*]

---

[*] Ap. Reeves, loc. cit. p. 23.

And thus, so far from the words cited by Toland being found in the text, the very contrary is expressly laid down, viz. :—

"Our Saviour used these sacred word, 'This is my body,' lest any one in future times should, on account of Christ being enthroned in glory at the right-hand of the Father, doubt of His being truly present in the daily sacrifice offered on our altars."

Thus, then, to the many clear assertors of the Catholic doctrine, regarding the blessed Eucharist in our early Church, must be added the founder of the church of Limerick, in the seventh century, St. Manchan, *the Wise*. This testimony needs no comment, and to admit of any Protestant meaning, had to be corrupted as given above in the words of the miserable Toland.

In conclusion, we wish to offer a few remarks on some incidental statements of the learned Protestant primate Usher, regarding the question now before us.

1. In the first place, he states that the author of the work "De Mirabilibus Sacræ Scripturæ" passes over the Eucharist in silence, whilst were he imbued with the Catholic doctrine, he should, like Catholics at the present day, regard it as the "miracle of miracles." To this we reply, that the author of that work was undoubtedly an Irishman, and an ornament of our Church in the seventh century. He himself assigns us the date of his work, the year 655, and informs us that three years before *Muinchin* (which name he latinizes Manicheus) *the Wise* had died—an event which is recorded by the annals of Ulster and by Tighernach, under the year 652. In the conclusion of his *Prologus*, he speaks of this Manchan as his venerated instructor; and as we already know from the extract given in the preceding page what was the doctrine of this holy man, we may conclude what would have been the belief of his disciples regarding the blessed Eucharist, did an occasion present itself of expressing such a belief in the tract now before us. Such a profession of faith, however, would be wholly out of place in this treatise. At the very outset the writer, *Augustinus*, declares that he undertook this task by command of his

spiritual father, *Eusebius*, and that he intended to embrace the *Mirabilia*, or the wonderful things narrated in the Law, the Prophets, and the New Testament. He moreover defines the class of events which it was his intention to explain, and says that they were such facts as were seen to present a deviation from the everyday order of nature, "in quibus extra quotidianam administrationem aliquid factum videtur." Hence, the many wonders of the supernatural order fall not within his sphere. He is silent as to the Mystery of the Incarnation—the miracle of miracles, in which our earthly nature was assumed by the second person of the blessed Trinity; he is silent, too, as to the miracle of Calvary, in which the world was redeemed by the blood of the God-man; in fine, not to mention all the supernatural miracles of the order of grace, he is silent as to the institution of the sacrament of baptism, though surely it is no small miracle and mystery that by the invocation of the blessed Trinity, and the pouring of water on the infant's head, its soul is cleansed from original sin, and robed with grace and innocence even as the angels of God. Thus, the blessed Eucharist was not a matter that fell within his sphere. He speaks of the plague of blood in Egypt, and again, of Lot's wife being changed into a pillar of salt; of the sun standing still at the command of Josue, and of the iron axe-head swimming in water, as mentioned in the Book of Kings. Even his incidental questions are of the same nature; as, for instance, when he inquires whence came the waters of the deluge—why terrestrial animals suffered more than aquatic—how wild animals were brought to the islands of the sea. And on this question he gives us the earliest information as to the wild animals known in Ireland in the seventh century: "Quis," he says, "lupos, cervos, et sylvaticos porcos, et vulpes, taxones, et lepusculos, et sesquivolos in Hiberniam deveheret?" "Who could have brought wolves, deer, wild boars, foxes, badgers, hares, and squirrels into Ireland?"

Whilst, then, the facts which he scrutinizes are such as fall under the observation of our senses, it was natural that the blessed Eucharist should not come within his sphere, since to our senses it remains unchanged, though in reality it becomes the body and blood of Jesus Christ.*

2. *John Scotus Erigena* is supposed by Usher to have been the author of a treatise, "De Corpore et Sanguine Domini," which was condemned in the synod of Vercelli in 1049; and though this work has long since been lost to the literary world, its condemnation affords a *prima facie* proof that its author inculcated the Protestant tenets.

As we shall have occasion to speak hereafter of this subtle but rationalistic writer of the ninth century, we shall, for the present, make merely a few remarks regarding his teaching on the question of the blessed Eucharist. The able editor of Erigena's works, *Henricus Josephus Floss*, in 1853, having searched the various archives of Europe, corroborated by his testimony what had been already asserted by many other writers, viz., that the treatise mentioned above, and interdicted in 1049, was not the work of Scotus, but of Ratramn, although Berengare and his followers attributed it to our countryman, that they might the better insinuate their errors under the cloak of his great name. All that can be said for certain is, that when Paschasius Radbertus broached his errors in France regarding the blessed Eucharist, Scotus was invited by the French bishops to defend the Catholic doctrine. In the tract which he

* This treatise is printed in the third volume of the works of St. Augustine. Were it not for the identity of name of the author with the great ornament of the African Church, it is probable this fragment of our ancient ecclesiastical school would have been long since lost to us. An interesting paper on our Augustine and his treatise was read by Dr. William Reeves before the Royal Irish Academy, June 10, 1861; and the learned writer (page 9) remarks that "in a theological point of view, it is the most interesting relique of Irish learning." The prologue is addressed, " Venerandissimis urbium et monasteriorum Episcopis et Presbyteris, maxime *Carthaginensium*, Augustinus per omnia subjectus optabilem in Christo salutem." The word *Carthaginensium* is a manifest corruption of the text, made by the scribe who referred the treatise to the great African doctor. The Benedictine editors suggest, as a correction, *Cantuariensium*, or *Cambrensium*. The writer, however, himself affords a key to the true reading; for he says he was exhorted to undertake his task "ab uno vestrum, id est, Bathano." Now, the Annals of the Four Masters precisely record the death of a Bathan in 663, " bishop of *Clonmacnoise*." Thus, the Irish Augustinus was probably a subject of that bishop, and his work was addressed to bishops and priests, and especially to those of his own monastery of *Clonmacnoise*.

then wrote, there were many errors and extravagancies, "errores et ineptiæ;" but these seem to have regarded the mode of Christ's presence in the Eucharist, which was the question discussed by Paschasius, and not the reality of the presence itself, on which subject no controversy was raised. The continued favour enjoyed by Erigena in the French court, and the eulogistic letter of Anastasius (known by the appellation of *Bibliothecarius*) of Rome, sufficiently prove that whatever may have been his extravagant subtleties, he did not reject the teaching of the Catholic Church. The chief errors imputed to him by his contemporaries were those of Semipelagianism and Pantheism; and now that his writings have been carefully edited by Floss, it must be confessed that many obscure passages would seem to insinuate these errors. The works of Scotus Erigena that still remain are characterized by great originality of sentiment, subtlety of distinctions, and obscurity of expression, which gave occasion of imputing many errors to him of which certainly he should not be accused. We must also add that Berengare's disciples were accused of corrupting the text in many passages of Scotus's writings, that thus they might defend their novelties by the authority of so distinguished a writer. At all events, until further evidence be produced, we must not add to the rationalistic errors of our too subtle countryman, the Protestant unbelief in regard to the blessed Eucharist.

Usher concludes by devoting three pages of his *Historical Inquiry* to prove that it would be absurd to assign to the words of our Redeemer, "this is my body," any meaning save that of the Protestant Church. This, however, is virtually to abandon the field which he had chosen for discussion. The historian does not inquire what the Irish Church ought to have believed, but merely interrogates her monuments and records, to learn what may have been her actual doctrine and teaching. We would willingly follow the Protestant primate into the new ground on which he thus enters, but it would lead us too far away from our present purpose. We shall, therefore, merely remark, that our apostle St. Patrick, and his spiritual children who won for our country the proud epithet of *Island of Saints*, knew nothing of these absurdities which Usher deemed inherent in the Eucharistic doctrine; they received, in the fulness of faith and with simplicity of heart, the words of life which fell from the Redeemer's lips, and unhesitatingly embraced the blissful truth inculcated by the Catholic Church, that in the holy Sacrament of the altar is truly present the heavenly vivifying food of the body and blood of Jesus Christ.

ESSAY

ON

DEVOTION TO THE BLESSED VIRGIN,

IN THE

ANCIENT CHURCH OF IRELAND.

CHAPTER I.

Ancient Litany taken from Curry's MSS. in Catholic University.—Hymn of St. Cuchumneus.—Prayers in Bobbio Missal.—Festivals of Blessed Virgin observed in Ireland.—Hymns regarding St. Brigid, in which she is praised as like the Blessed Virgin.—Extract from Leabhar Breac.

DEVOTION to the Mother of God has always been regarded as a characteristic feature of the Catholic Church, distinguishing her from all the varying and conflicting sects of heterodoxy. Now, from the earliest period of Christianity in our island, we find a most tender devotion, a most reverential affection cherished by our fathers for this Virgin of virgins. The question which we propose to treat is one of fact, and, as a matter of historic truth, must be proved by the monuments of our early Church.

The first old Irish document we shall cite is in the form of a litany, which presents, with all the vividness of oriental imagery, the many exalted titles and peerless privileges of the blessed Mary. It is preserved in the Leabhar Breac, that invaluable repository of our earliest ecclesiastical records, which is justly styled by Petrie "the oldest and best MS. relating to church history now preserved (in Ireland), or which, perhaps, the Irish ever possessed."* A few

---

* The Hist. and Antiq. of Tara, by George Petrie, published from the Transactions of the R.I.A., Dublin, 1839, pag. 74.

extracts from this litany have been already published by Mr. Curry, by whom it is pronounced to be "as old, at least, as the middle of the eighth century."*

THE LITANY OF THE BLESSED VIRGIN MARY.

"O Great Mary.
O Mary, Greatest of Marys.
O Greatest of Women.
O Queen of the Angels.
O Mistress of the Heavens.
O Woman full and replete with the Grace of the Holy Spirit.
O Blessed and Most Blessed.
O Mother of Eternal Glory.
O Mother of the Heavenly and Earthly Church.
O Mother of Love and Indulgence.
O Mother of the Golden Heights.
O Honour of the Sky.
O Sign of Tranquillity.
O Gate of Heaven.
O Golden Casket.
O Couch of Love and Mercy.
O Temple of the Divinity.
O Beauty of Virgins.
O Mistress of the Tribes.
O Fountain of the Parterres.
O Cleansing of the Sins.
O Washing of the Souls.
O Mother of the Orphans.
O Breast of the Infants.
O Solace of the Wretched.
O Star of the Sea.
O Handmaid of God.
O Mother of Christ.
O Resort of the Lord.

"O Graceful like the Dove.
O Serene like the Moon.
O Resplendent like the Sun.
O Destruction of Eve's Disgrace.
O Regeneration of Life.
O Beauty of Women.
O Chief of the Virgins.
O Enclosed Garden.
O Closely-locked Fountain.
O Mother of God.
O Perpetual Virgin.
O Prudent Virgin.
O Serene Virgin.
O Chaste Virgin.
O Temple of the Living God.
O Royal Throne of the Eternal King.
O Sanctuary of the Holy Spirit.
O Virgin of the Root of Jesse.
O Cedar of Mount Lebanon.
O Cypress of Mount Sion.
O Crimson Rose of the Land of Jacob.
O Blooming like the Olive Tree.
O Glorious Son-bearer.
O Light of Nazareth.
O Glory of Jerusalem.
O Beauty of the World.
O Noblest-born of the Christian Flock.
O Queen of Life.

"O Ladder of Heaven, hear the petition of the poor, spurn not the wounds and the groans of the miserable.

"Let our devotion and our sighs be carried through thee to the presence of the Creator, for we are not ourselves worthy of being heard, because of our evil deserts.

"O Powerful Mistress of Heaven and Earth, dissolve our trespasses and our sins; destroy our wickedness and our corruptions; raise the fallen, the debilitated, and the fettered; loose the condemned; repair through thyself the transgressions of our immoralities and our vices; bestow upon

* Lectures on the MS. Materials, p. 380.

us through thyself the blossoms and ornaments of good actions and virtues; appease for us the Judge by thy voice and thy supplications; allow us not to be carried off from thee among the spoils of our enemies; allow not our souls to be condemned, but take us to thyself for ever, under thy protection.

"We beseech and pray thee further, O Holy Mary, through thy great supplication, from thy only Son, that is, Jesus Christ, the Son of the living God, that God may defend us from all straits and temptations; and obtain for us, from the God of Creation, that we all obtain from Him the forgiveness and remission of all our sins and trespasses, and that we may obtain from Him farther, through thy supplication, the perpetual occupation of the heavenly kingdom, through the eternity of life, in the presence of the Saints and the saintly Virgins of the world; which may we deserve, may we occupy, in secula seculorum. Amen."

This litany speaks for itself. It is a glory of our early Church to have produced such a sweet invocation of the Mother of God; and the reigning pontiff, pope Pius IX., to attest how dear to him was this fine old Irish prayer, granted an indulgence of one hundred days to all who shall duly recite it.

St. Cuchumneus,* a contemporary of Adamnan, towards the close of the sixth century, composed a Latin hymn in honour of the Mother of God, which soon became celebrated, and had a place assigned to it amongst the liturgical hymns of our Church. The German hymnologist, Mone, discovered three MSS. of this hymn, one belonging to the ninth, the others to the eighth century.† Colgan,‡ too, had an ancient copy of it in his possession, and it is also contained in the celebrated Liber Hymnorum, from which we now present it to the reader:—§

1. "Cantemus in omni die concinentes varie,
   Conclamantes Deo dignum hymnum sanctæ Mariæ.

2. "Bis per chorum hinc et inde collaudamus Mariam,
   Ut vox pulset omnem aurem per laudem vicariam.

3. "Maria de tribu Juda, summi mater Domini,
   Opportunam dedit curam ægrotanti homini.

---

* Colgan after commemorating this hymn, adds: "Ut colligitur ex argumento eidem hymno præfixo, author floruit tempore Adamnani Abbatis et Longseci Hiberniæ Regis qui cœpit regnare anno 694."—Tr. Th. 218.
† Hymni Med. Ævv. vol. ii. p. 384.
‡ Trias Thaum. p. 218.
§ Archiv. S. Isid. in urbe, No. xi. fol. 14.

4. "Gabriel advexit verbum sinu Patris paterno,
   Quod conceptum et susceptum in utero materno.

5. "Hæc est summa, hæc est sancta virgo venerabilis,
   Quæ ex fide non recessit sed extitit stabilis.

6. "Huic matri nec inventa ante nec post similis
   Nec de prole fuit plane humanæ originis.

7. "Per mulierem et lignum mundus prius periit,
   Per mulieris virtutem, ad salutem rediit.

8. "Maria mater miranda patrem suum edidit,
   Per quem aquâ late lotus totus mundus credidit.

9. "Hæc concepit margaritam, non sunt vana somnia,
   Pro qua sane Christiani vendunt sua omnia.

10. "Tunicam per totum textam Christo mater fecerat,
    Quæ peracta Christi morte, sorte statim steterat.

11. "Induamus arma lucis loricam et galeam,
    Ut simus Deo perfecti, suscepti per Mariam.

12. "Amen, amen, adjuramus merita puerperæ,
    Ut non possit flamma pyræ nos diræ decerpere.

13. "Christi nomen invocemus angelis sub testibus,
    Ut fruamur et scribamur litteris cœlestibus,
                        "Cantemus in omni," etc.

TRANSLATION.*

1. "In alternate measure chanting, daily sing we Mary's praise,
   And, in strains of glad rejoicing, to the Lord our voices raise.

2. "With a two-fold choir repeating Mary's never-dying fame,
   Let each ear the praises gather, which our grateful tongues proclaim.

3. "Judah's ever-glorious daughter—chosen mother of the Lord—
   Who, to weak and fallen manhood, all its ancient worth restor'd.

4. "From the everlasting Father, Gabriel brought the glad decree,
   That, the Word divine conceiving, she should set poor sinners free.

5. "Of all virgins pure, the purest—ever stainless, ever bright—
   Still from grace to grace advancing, fairest daughter of the light.

6. "Wondrous title—who shall tell it—whilst the Word divine she bore,
   Though in mother's name rejoicing, virgin purer than before!

* We are indebted for this translation to the kindness of Rev. Mr. Potter, All Hallows' College.

7. "By a woman's disobedience, eating the forbidden tree,
   Was the world betray'd and ruin'd—was by woman's aid set free.

8. "In mysterious mode a mother, Mary did her God conceive,
   By whose grace, through saving waters, man did heav'nly truth receive.

9. "By no empty dreams deluded, for the pearl which Mary bore,
   Men, all earthly wealth resigning, still are rich for evermore.

10. "For her Son a seamless tunic Mary's careful hand did weave;
    O'er that tunic fiercely gambling, sinners Mary's heart did grieve.

11. "Clad in helmet of salvation—clad in breast-plate shining bright—
    May the hand of Mary guide us to the realms of endless light.

12. "Amen, amen, loudly cry we—may she, when the fight is won,
    O'er avenging fires triumphing, lead us safely to her Son.

13. "Holy angels gathering round us, lo, His saving name we greet,
    Writ in books of life eternal, may we still that name repeat!
        "In alternate measure chanting," etc.

To this beautiful hymn is added, in the Liber Hymnorum, the versicle, "Sanctæ Mariæ meritum imploramus dignissimum; ut mereamur solium habitare altissimum."

In the Irish MS. of Bale* containing this hymn, there is further added a prayer to the Blessed Virgin, beginning, "singularis meriti sola sine exemplo, mater et Virgo Maria."† We have to lament that Dr. Todd did not publish the remainder of this prayer, for it must be a beautiful one, indeed, if we may judge from the sweet invocation which its first line presents to us. Even after the hymn to St. Brigid, in the same MS., there follows another fervent invocation of the Mother of God—"Sancta virgo, beatissima Virginum Maria, intercede pro nobis."‡

Each strophe of the above hymn of St. Cuchumneus proclaims some prerogative of the holy Virgin. She is "the Mother of the

---

* This MS. was one of those used by Mone in his edition. It is preserved in the library of Bale, and is marked A. vii. 3. It is an Irish copy of the Greek Psalter, and in its first leaves has the hymn just cited; then follows a hymn to St. Brigid, with some other fragments of our ancient liturgy.—See Todd, Lib. Hym. fas. i. page 55.
† Todd, loc. cit.
‡ Dr. Todd (loc. cit. page 56) remarks that over the words *sancta virgo* is written, in the original hand, *beatissima*.

great Lord," "the greatest, the holy venerable Virgin;" "none, throughout all time, is found like unto her," and even in her birth she is uninfected with the stain common to all other mortals.* She it is that gives a healing remedy for the wounds of man; and as the world was once ruined by Eve and the forbidden tree, so through the virtue of this new Eve is it restored to the blessings of Heaven. Hers it was to weave the seamless garment of Christ,—emblem of the Church's unity; and hers is it now to present us to God, and protect us from all the attacks of the evil one.

That the chief festivals of the Blessed Virgin were celebrated in the early Irish Church admits of no controversy. In the Martyrology of Tallaght, on the 18th of December, is marked the "*salutatio Mariæ ab Elizabeth*," a festival which at that period is scarcely known to have been celebrated in the continental churches.† Aenghus Ceile De, in his Metrical Calendar, composed before the year 800, at the 3rd of May thus notices the Feast of the Immaculate Conception which, in other countries, was celebrated on the 8th of December:—

> "3rd May.—The chief finding of the tree of the cross
> Of Christ with manyvirtues;
> The death of *Condlaedh*, noble chief;
> The great festival of the Virgin Mary."‡

The chief monument of our ancient liturgy that has come down to us, the Bobbio Missal, contains two masses in honor of the Blessed Virgin, one for her general feasts, the other for the Assumption. In the former we find the prayer—" Hear us, O Lord, holy Father, all-powerful God, who by the overshadowing of the womb of blessed Mary, didst deign to illumine the whole world; we suppliantly pray Thy Majesty that what we cannot acquire by our merits, we may obtain through her protection. We beseech thee, too, O Lord, that the joys of blessed Mary may accompany us, and

---

* Verse 11, strophe 6.
† Conf. Martyr. of Tallaght. Dublin, 1857. Preface viii. and page 27.
‡ Ibid, page 157. The translation is from the pen of Eugene Curry. On this peculiarity of the Irish Church see Bollandists' Acta SS. ad tertium Maij.

by her merits may our chirographa of sin be cancelled." In the latter Mass she is declared to be "charitate decens, pace gaudens, pietate præcellens; ab Angelo gratiâ plena, ab Elizabeth benedicta, a gentibus prædicatur beata: cujus nobis fides mysterium, partus gaudium, pacem quam in assumptione matris tunc præbuisti discipulis, nobis miserere supplicibus." And again she is styled "speciosus thalamus de quo decorus procedit sponsus; lux gentium, spes fidelium, prædo dæmonum, confusio Judæorum, vasculum gloriæ, templum cœleste." She is then compared with Eve: "ista mundo vitam protulit, illa legem mortis invexit: illa prævaricando nos perdidit, ista generando servavit." And in conclusion, it is said "her soul is wreathed with various crowns; the apostles render sacred homage to her, the angels intone their canticles, Christ embraces her, the clouds are her chariot, paradise her dwelling, where, decked with glory, she reigns amidst the virgin-choirs."*

Moreover, the Canon of the Mass gives the usual commemoration, "memoriam venerantes inprimis gloriosæ semper virginis Mariæ, genitricis Dei et Domini nostri Jesu Christi."†

In the foregoing passages we find that the early Irish Church took occasion to commend the privileges of Mary, by contrasting the blessings we receive through her with the miseries which we inherit from our first parent Eve. There is, however, another comparison which the old Irish documents continually repeat, and which supposes in our fathers the same exalted idea of the blessedness and privileges of the Mother of God: I refer to the frequent passages of our ancient writers in which our great patron St. Brigid is compared with the Mother of God. In all the vividness of Irish poetry, St. Brigid is styled the wonder of womankind, the most holy and exalted of mortals; but always their highest point of praise, the climax of their eulogy, is, that she is *like unto the Mother of God.* The real privileges and dignity of Mary are supposed to have been in a manner shared by Brigid; and what Mary is for the whole Church, that, Brigid is for Ireland—whence

---

* The Bobbio Missal, apud Mabillon Museum Italicum, tom. i. part ii. page 298, seqq.
† Ibid, page 279.

her usual title, "the Mary of the Irish." We shall give a few instances of this peculiar language of our fathers.

In the hymn "Alta audite τα εργα," on the privileges of St. Brigid, the last strophe declares that in glory " consedit in cathedra cum matre Maria."* Also, in the hymn " Christus in nostra insula," it is said that no tongue could suffice to relate all the wondrous deeds of virtue performed by Brigid, neither are they found recorded of any one except our Saint, "*who was like unto holy Mary.*"

> " Quæ nostris numquam auribus si sint facta audivimus,
> Nisi per istam virginem Mariæ Sanctæ similem."†

And the Irish gloss adds an explanation of this last word, " for Brigid is the Mary of the Irish."

In the Leabhar Breac there is a sketch of St. Brigid's life, which thus extols her innumerable virtues:

"She was abstinent, unblemished, prayerful, patient, joying in the commandments of God, benevolent, humble, forgiving. charitable. She was a consecrated shrine for preserving the body of Christ. She was a temple of God. Her heart and her mind were a resting-throne for the Holy Spirit. She was meek before God. She was distressed with the wretched. She was bright in miracles. And hence it is that her type among created things is the dove among birds, the vine among trees, and the sun above the stars. The father of this holy virgin was the Heavenly Father; her son was Jesus Christ;‡ her tutor was the Holy Spirit. And it was, therefore, this holy virgin performed those great innumerable miracles. It is she that relieves every one that is in difficulty and in danger. It is she that restrains the roaring billows and the anger of the great sea. She is the prophesied woman of Christ. She is the Queen of the South. She is the Mary of the Irish"§

In the hymn of St. Brogan Cloen to St. Brigid, the same comparison is introduced:

---

* Mone, loc. cit. iii. 241.
† Liber Hymn. St. Isidori, fol. 7. Dr. Todd, loc. cit. pag. 57.
‡ Dr. Todd objects to the words in which it is said that the Eternal Father is the father of St. Brigid, and Jesus Christ her son. But do we not all daily invoke "Our Father, who art in heaven;" and did not our Lord say, "Whosoever shall do the will of my Father, ... he is my brother and sister and *mother*"?—Matt. xii. 50.
§ Todd, loc. cit. pag. 65.

> "There are two Virgins in heaven,
> Who will not give me a forgetful protection,
> *Mary and Saint Brigid.*
> Under the protection of both may we remain."

And in the same poem he had already said:

> "The veiled Virgin that drives over the Curragh,
> Is a shield against sharp weapons;
> *None was found her equal except Mary;*
> Let us put our trust in my *strength.*"*

Thus the sanctity, and power, and privileges of Mary were deemed the highest type with which the virtues of our great national patron could be compared; and whilst St. Brigid was supposed by our countrymen to surpass all others, one alone was the exception which was invariably made—forsooth, "the holy Virgin-Mother of God."†

CHAPTER II.

DEVOTION TO THE BLESSED VIRGIN.

Felire of Aengus.—Prayer of St. Colgu.—St. Columbanus.—Irish recluse in Austria.—Sedulius's Poems.—Sedulius, abbot of Kildare.—Claudius Scotus.—St. Mochta.—St. Laurence O'Toole.

In the famous Felire, or Festology of Aengus, written in the eighth century, we find a further illustration of the reverence of our early Church for the blessed Mother of God. When recapitulating his work, and commemorating the saints under certain heads, he invokes "the saintly virgins of Erin, under the holy St.

---

* The last word is a play on the Irish word *brigi*, which means strength, and is almost identical with the name of Brigid. See Todd. loc. cit. 67, who gives the original of these verses from the Liber Hym. Colgan published the whole hymn, with a Latin translation, Tr. Th. pag. 515.

† Hector Boetius, Hist. Scot. lib. ix. records that, in the Gælic tradition, St. Brigid was supposed to hold *the second place* amongst the virgin-saints in heaven.

Brigid of Kildare," but "the virgins of the whole world, under the blessed Virgin Mary." When showing how the names of the persecutors are forgotten, whilst those of their victims are held in veneration, he gives as an instance that " Pilate's wife is forgotten, whilst the Blessed Virgin is remembered and honoured from the uttermost bounds of the earth to its centre ;" and, in conclusion, he beseeches the Redeemer, "*through the intercession of His Mother*, to save him, as Jacob was saved from the hands of Esau, and as Paul was saved from the venom of the viper."*

The beautiful prayer of St. Colgu (who died about A.D. 790), presents several invocations of the various classes of saints. Amongst the others we meet: " I beseech the intercession with thee of all the perfect virgins of the world, with the Virgin Mary, Thine own holy mother ;" and subsequently he thus addresses the Redeemer :—

" For the sake of the merciful Father from whom Thou didst come unto us upon earth ; for the sake of Thy divinity which that Father modified so as to receive Thy humanity; for the sake of the immaculate body from which Thou didst come in the womb of the Virgin ; for the sake of the Spirit with the seven forms which descended upon that body in unity with Thyself and with Thy Father ; *for the sake of the holy womb from which Thou didst receive that body without destruction of virginity* . . . dispense, and give, and bestow Thy holy grace and Thy holy Spirit to defend and shelter me from all my present and future sins, and to light up in me all truth, and to retain in me all truth to the end of my life."†

This devotion to the Mother of God, so cherished in our island, accompanied our missionary saints to the various nations of the continent, and even in Italy we find that the great St. Columbanus, in the beginning of the seventh century, founded an oratory dedicated under the invocation of the holy Mother of God : " Ubi (in Bobbio) etiam ecclesiam in honorem almæ Dei genitricis, semperque Virginis Mariæ ex lignis construxit ad magnitudinem sanctissimi corporis sui."‡

---

* Eugene Curry's Lectures on the MS. Materials, etc. p. 367, seqq.

† Curry, MSS. For some notice of the saint see Curry's Lectures, p. 379 ; Dr. Kelly, Calendar of Irish Saints, p. 76 ; Colgan, Acta SS. Hib. ad diem 20th Feb.

‡ Vita S. Columb. in Florilegio, edited by Messingham, p. 240 ; confer Petrie on the Round Towers, etc., p. 347.

This same saint was author of a commentary on the Psalms, which was long attributed to St. Jerome. It is preserved in the famous Ambrosian Codex (c. 801), and published by Vallarsi in the appendix to the works of St. Jerome. Vallarsi, however, justly suspected that this commentary had Columbanus, not St. Jerome, for its author;* and this opinion has been placed beyond all doubt by the investigations of Peyron† and Zeuss,‡ who published in the appendix to his invaluable Grammar the first pages of this commentary, together with the Irish glosses which accompany it.§ St. Columbanus, in this commentary, when explaining the words of the 77th Psalm, verse 14, " Et deduxit eos in nube diei," thus writes : " Behold the Lord comes into Egypt in a light cloud. By the light cloud we ought to understand the body of our Saviour, for it was light and laden with no sin; or, certainly, we should interpret it of the Blessed Virgin; and beautifully is she called a cloud of day, for that cloud was never in darkness, but was always in light;" that is, was never involved in the shades of sin, but was ever arrayed in the beauteous light of heavenly grace.∥

Long after St. Columbanus, we find another Irish pilgrim embracing the penitential life of a recluse, near the town of Krems, in Lower Austria, being, for his devotion, immured by St. Altmann in a cell adjoining the church of the Mother of God. " In this venerable bishop's time (we thus read in the life of St. Altmann), there came a priest to Mount Gottweich, an Irishman, in profession a monk, in conversation a religious. The name he bore, which was John, signifying 'God's grace,' was in accordance with his disposition. Bishop Altmann loved this grace which was in him; and that he might the more readily abide with him, a narrow cell was assigned him beside the church of the blessed Mary, in which, agreeably to his wish and solicitation, he was immured." ¶ This holy recluse was a companion of the famous Marianus, who, departing

---

* Præf. ad Appendix, tom. vii. pp. 20, 21.
† Fragm. Ined., p. 189.   ‡ Gram. Celtic, vol i. præf. xxx.
§ See Gram. Celtic, vol. ii. append. f. p. 1063.
∥ Opp. S. Hieron. Vallarsi, tom. vii.
¶ Acta SS., August 8, tom. ii. p. 387.

from Ireland in 1067, soon became celebrated in Germany by his beautiful transcripts as well as commentaries on the sacred Scriptures.*

The poet Sedulius, however, was the chief writer of Ireland that acquired a wide-spread fame throughout the continent. In the "Carmen Paschale," which is his most celebrated composition, he more than once takes occasion to dwell on the special dignity and privileges of the holy Mother of God. Thus, in the second book, after treating of original sin, he adds :—

> " Et velut e spinis, mollis rosa surgit acutis
> Nil quod lædat habens, matremque obscurat honore ;
> Sic Evæ de stirpe sacra veniente Maria
> Virginis antiquæ facinus nova virgo piaret,
> Ut quoniam natura prior vitiata jacebat,
> Sub ditione necis, Christo nascente renasci
> Posset homo et veteris maculam deponere carnis."†

The first lines of which passage have been well translated thus—

> " Safe from the rugged thorn springs up the tender rose,
> In honor hides the parent stem, in beauty's softness grows ;
> So from the sinful stem of Eve all-sinless Mary came,
> To cover and to expiate her mother's deed of shame."‡

The Prosa Paschalis of Sedulius perhaps still more clearly expresses the same spotless immunity of Mary, as it declares that she came forth from the sinful race of Eve, "arrayed in sacred light" :—

> "Et velut rosa suavis atque molissima de spinoso cespite nascitur, nil læsura matrem quam gratia jucunditatis obscurat : ita de stirpe nocentis Evæ Mariâ sacro veniente cum lumine, primæ virginis lucem sequens virgo dilueret," &c.

---

* Conf. The Irish Monasteries in Germany, by Dr. Wattenbach, 1856, translated by W. Reeves, p. 16.

† Edition of Arevalus, lib. ii. lin. 28-34, page 200.

‡ Essay on the Im. Conception, by the Rev. M. Tormey. Dublin, 1855 ; page 93.

A few lines after our poet, having commemorated the birth of the divine Redeemer, bursts forth into the following sweet address to the Virgin-Mother:—

> "Salve sancta parens, enixa puerpera regem
> Qui cœlum terramque tenet per sæcula, cujus
> Numen et æterno complectens omnia gyro,
> Imperium sine fine manet, quæ ventre beato
> Gaudia matris habens cum virginitatis honore
> Nec primam similem visa es nec habere sequentem
> Sola sine exemplo placuisti femina Christo."*

These words have been hallowed by their universal use throughout the Church, and to the present day they are recited in the office of the Blessed Virgin:—

"Hail, holy Mother, who hast given birth to the Almighty King who rules the heavens and the earth .... in thy blessed womb thou didst unite the joys of motherhood with the honour of virginity; none has hitherto been like to thee, nor shall hereafter any such be found; thou alone, above all others, hast been beloved by Christ."

The same idea is repeated in the Paschal Prose:—

"Salve parens optima tanti regis puerperio consecrata .... cui nulla penitus æqualis femina reperitur, quæ tuum decus similiter præcesserit aut sequatur, sola placens singulariter Christo nulli compararis exemplo."

Again, in the fifth book, he commemorates the honour ever rendered to Mary in the Catholic Church:—

> "Discedat synagoga suo fuscata colore'
> Ecclesiam Christus pulchro sibi junxit amore
> Hæc est conspicuo radians in honore Mariæ
> Quæ quum clarifico semper sit nomine mater
> Semper virgo manet."

Or, as it is expressed in the prose work—

"Christus sibi pulchram niveo decore sociavit ecclesiam. Hæc honorem

---

* Edit. Areval, lin. 63-69, page 203.

Mariæ præstat ad gloriam quæ quum charitate conspicua semper mater esse cernatur, semper tamen virgo conspicitur."*

We shall close these extracts from our sacred poet with the beautiful distich which occurs in his elegiac poem:—

> "Sola fuit mulier, patuit qua janua letho;
> Et qua vita redit, sola fuit mulier."†

There was another Sedulius, abbot of Kildare,‡ in the eighth century, who won a distinguished fame by his commentaries on the Gospels and on the Pauline Epistles. Two fragments of his work on the Gospels were published by the late eminent palæographer, Cardinal Maj.§ Another fragment is contained in the Codex Palatinus, No. 242, amongst the Vatican manuscripts, being an exposition of the genealogy of our Saviour, as given in St. Matthew. On arriving at the last formula, *Joseph virum Mariæ*, he thus explains the name of Mary, and with it concludes his treatise:—

"*Maria*, illuminatrix vel stella maris interpretatur; syro sermone Domina dicitur, *Illuminatrix*: quia per ipsam lux totius mundi natus est Christus. *Stella maris*: quia sicut nautæ in aliquam terram remigantes aliquod sydus eligunt, cujus signo luceque radiante, sine errore possint adduci; ita Sancta Maria in mari hujus mundi navigantibus stella maris data est par quam ad portum perpetuæ quietis valeant perduci. *Domina dignissima* nominatur quæ Dominum peperit salvatorem, decentissime namque mater regis Christi, regum regina, mater Domini, Dominorum Domina nuncupanda est per quam lumen fidei accepimus, qua ad visionem Dei perpetuo cum matre simul et filio gavisuri perducamur."‖

Reading this passage, the mind at once goes back to the eloquent discourses of St. Bernard on the Mother of God; and one

---

* Edit. Arevali, lib. v. lin. 357-361, page 350.
† Areval, page 361.
‡ Conf. Lanigan Eccles. Hist. iii. 256-7.
§ Scriptt. Vett. Vaticana Collect. tom. ix.; and Spicilegium Roman. tom. ix.
‖ Cod. 242, p. 8 (sæc. xmi). The MS. is entitled "Explanatio Sedulii Scotti in quattuor Evangelistas," and originally belonged to the monastery of Canons Regular of S. Maria Magdalene de Franchentall, "inter Spiram et Wormatiam."

might almost conclude that this great doctor had the treatise of our Irish abbot before him, when writing on the peerless dignity of Mary, so similar is the language and imagery which he employs.

Almost contemporary with this illustrious ornament of the Church of Kildare was the commentator Claudius Scotus, to whose work Usher so frequently appeals, in his treatise on the religion of the early Irish. To illustrate the doctrine of Claudius regarding the Blessed Virgin, one passage from his commentary on St. Matthew will suffice. He is speaking of the virginity of the Mother of God; and whilst he rejects the errors of Helvidius, he by anticipation stigmatizes as blasphemous and heretical, the teaching of so many of the modern sectaries in regard to this holiest of creatures. St. Joseph, he says, being aware of the prophecy of Isaias, had no doubt but that this prophecy would be verified in his virgin-spouse:

"Non diffidebat in ea prophetiam esse complendam. Sed si eam occulte dimitteret neque acciperet conjugem, et illa sponsa pareret, pauci essent qui eam virginem et non potius autumarent esse meretricem. Unde consilium Joseph repente consilio meliore mutatur ut videlicet ad conservandam Mariae famam, ipse eam celebrato nuptiarum connubio comitem acciperet sed castam perpetuo custodiret." And he adds: "Maluit namque Dominus aliquos modum suae generationis ignorare quam castitatem infamare suae genitricis."

After a few sentences, he thus again dwells on the perpetual virginity of the Mother of God:

"*Hoc totum factum est.* Quid totum? hoc per Unigeniti descensionem: hoc de ista Christi incarnatione: hoc de angeli ad virginem destinatione: hoc de ipsius virginis desponsatione, vel castitate: hoc autem totum factum est ad totius mundi salutem: hoc totum factum est ut unum compleretur et unum consummaretur. Quid illud est? quod virgo genuit, quod virgo permansit: quod mater fuit et intacta virgo perseveravit."

And soon after he concludes:

"Sciendum est quod fuerint haeretici qui propter hoc quod dictum est 'non cognoscebat eam donec peperit filium suum' crederent Mariam post natum Dominum cognitam esse a Joseph et inde ortos eos quos fratres Domini Scriptura appellat, adsumentes et hoc in adjutorium sui erroris quod primogenitus nuncupatur Dominus. Avertat Deus hanc blasphemiam a fide omnium nostrum, donetque nobis Catholica pietate intelligere, parentes nostri Salvatoris intemerata semper fuisse virginitate præclaros," etc.*

Even when addressing our divine Redeemer, the ancient writers of our island loved to commemorate the virginal maternity of Mary. Thus, in the beautiful matins' hymn, which, from the very first ages of faith, was used in the Irish Church, we meet with the following address:

> " Ante sæcla tu fuisti factor primi sæculi,
> Factor cœli, terræ factor, congregator tu maris,
> Omniumque tu creator quæ pater nasci jubet,
> Virginis receptus membris Gabrielis nuntio
> Crescit alvus prole sancta, nos monemur credere
> Rem novam nec ante visam virginem puerperam."†

Again, in the hymn to St. Martin, which is preserved in the Liber Hymnorum, the very second strophe commemorates this privilege of the Virgin-Mother:

> " Martine te deprecor, pro me rogaris Patrem,
> Christum, ac Spiritum Sanctum, habentem Mariam matrem."

With our saints, in like manner, it was not unusual to introduce in their solemn asseverations this dignity of Mary; as, for instance, in the formula " the Son of the Virgin knows,"‡ which was so frequently employed by St. Canice and other chief saints of our Church.§

---

* Codex Vatican. Palatin. 3828; Claud. in Matth. lib. i. fol. 3.

† This hymn begins: " Hymnum dicat turba fratrum," etc. It is preserved in the Liber Hymnorum, from which the above text is printed; also, in the Antiphon. Benchoren. It is, moreover, commemorated by Ven. Bede and Hincmar. It is inserted with notes by Daniel, in his Thesaur. Hymnolog. vol. i. pag. 191.

‡ There is a church near Bray dedicated to the Virgin's Son. It still retains the Irish name, Kilmacanogue.

§ Conf. Vit. S. Kannechi, edited by the Marquis of Ormond, 1853, pag. 10, 12, etc.

Even as early as the fifth century, we find this, her sacred privilege, commemorated in a profession of faith which a native of our island, and a disciple of St. Patrick, presented in Rome to the great St. Leo:

"Filium credimus," he says, "in novissimis diebus natum esse, de Virgine et Spiritu Sancto carnem naturæ humanæ et animam suscepisse. .... Virginem quoque de qua natum scimus, et Virginem ante partum et Virginem post partum, ne consortes Helvidiani erroris habeamur."*

In conclusion, we may remark that it was not merely in theory that this high dignity of the Mother of God was commended by our forefathers. It entered as a vital element into their spiritual life; and even the fine old domestic salutation, still preserved by many of the Irish-speaking of our countrymen, was couched in the sweet words, "God and Mary be with you!" and the reply, "God and Mary and Patrick."

St. Laurence O'Toole was the last saint of our Church before our island became a prey to every disorder, and well nigh barbarism, in consequence of the English invasion. In his life we read of his having "built a new church in Dublin, to the honour of God and of the blessed Virgin-Mother."† Another church was dedicated by him in Wales to the same holy Virgin; but the most striking proof of his devotion to the Mother of God was evinced in restoring to life a priest of the diocese, named Gallwed. The first act of this priest on awakening from his slumber of death, was to return thanks to God and the Blessed Virgin; and he declared to the bystanders, "I saw the Archbishop Laurence on bended knees before God and the glorious Virgin Mary, His Mother, humbly entreating for my restoration to life."‡

---

* Apologia presented by Bachiarius Macceus to pope Leo, about 460, edited by Muratori, from a Bobbio MS. of the seventh century. Anecdota, tom. ii. Milan, 1698, pag. 18. Miræus, in Auctuario ad An. Eccl. says he was a native of Ireland. Bale further informs us that he was "Divi Patritii discipulus." The intrinsic arguments which Muratori and others refer to, are all in favour of his claims to Irish birth. We have already referred to this writer at pag. 93, where the various names he bore are explained in note.

† Ap. Messingham, pag. 382.

‡ Ap. Messingham, pag. 385.

Oh! may this great St. Laurence, and all the other saints of Erin, continue to pray unceasingly to God and the Immaculate Queen in behalf of our poor island; and may they obtain the grace of conversion and spiritual life for those misguided individuals who insult our Catholic people, and outrage the holy name of " the Son of the Virgin" !

APPENDIX.

No. I.

ADDITIONS TO PAGE 94 AND PAGE 166.

Additional testimony of St. Mochta regarding the Pope's authority.—Further Illustration of the Real Presence from the Bangor Antiphonary.

At page 94 of the Essay on the Origin of the Irish Church, we quoted some words of St. Mochta on the Pope's authority. In the subsequent chapters of his work, St. Mochta declares that to his holiness belonged "to judge what was heresy and what was truth;" and again, that he hesitated not to present his treatise to the pontiff, since his office it was to build up the spiritual edifice of faith; "non moramur fidei nostræ Regulam Beatitudini Tuæ, qui artifex es ipsius ædificii demonstrare."*

ADDITION REGARDING THE EUCHARIST TO THE HYMN "SANCTI VENITE."†

In the other anthems of the *Bangor Antiphonary*, the same doctrine of the real presence of our blessed Redeemer in the holy Eucharist is expressly laid down; thus, in the communion antiphon we read:

"Corpus Domini accepimus et sanguine ejus potati sumus, ab omni malo non timebimus, quia Dominus nobiscum est."	"We have received the body of the Lord, and we have drunk his blood: we will fear no evil, for the Lord is with us."

* In Muratori's text, instead of *ædificii* is printed *artificii*. The present correction, and several others in the text of the fourth appendix, are taken from the original manuscript. † Page 166.

Again, we find the sweet versicle:

"Hoc sacrum corpus Domini et Salvatoris sanguinem sumite in vitam æternam, Alleluja."

"Receive this sacred body of the Lord, and the blood of the Redeemer, unto eternal life, Alleluja."

And immediately afterwards is added:

"Refecti Christi corpore et sanguine tibi semper Domine dicamus, Alleluja."

"Nourished with the body and blood of Christ, may we ever cry out to thee, O Lord, Alleluja."

APPENDIX No. II.

IRISH TRACT ON THE VARIOUS LITURGIES.

Translation and conjectures as to the sense of this tract.—The Pater Noster according to the ancient liturgy.—The Gloria in Excelsis.—The Apostles' Creed from St. Columbanus's Missal and the Antiphonary of Bangor.—The hymn Benedicite.

WE give this curious tract in its original form, as published by Spelman, from a very ancient manuscript, corrected in some parts by Usher and others. However, the text is in many places manifestly inaccurate, and quite unintelligible. It seems to have been written by an Irish monk in some monastery of France; and whilst it traces the origin of the various liturgies, generally limits its view to the use of these liturgies in the French Church. It first assigns the origin of the Roman liturgy as used in France; then speaks of the Gallic liturgy (Cursus Gallorum), the Irish liturgy (Cursus Scottorum), on which it dwells at considerable length; the oriental liturgy, the liturgy of St. Ambrose, and, in fine, the liturgy of St. Benedict, approved by St. Gregory for the Benedictine Order. Spelman refers the tract to about the year 680:*

---

* The translation is, in some passages, little more than conjectural, as the text, in its present form, not making any sense, obliged us to adopt the meaning which seemed to be required by the context.

CANTUUM ET CURSUUM ECCLESIASTICORUM ORIGO.

1. Si sedulo inspiciamus cursus auctores in exordio reperimus decantatum fuisse, non sicut aliqui imperiti fuisse, vel varia objectione pertulerunt, adhuc multi conantur fore.*

2. Beatus Trofimus episcopus Arelatensis, et Sanctus Photinus, martyr et episcopus Lugdunensis, discipulus S. Petri, Apostoli, sicut et refert Josephus et Eusebius Cæsariensis episcopus, cursum Romanum in Galliis tradiderunt.

Inde postea relatione beati Photini, martyris, cum quadraginta et octo martyribus retrusi in ergastulum, ad beatum Clementem quarto loco successorem beati Petri Apostoli deportaverunt: et beatum Irenæum episcopum, beatus Clemens ordinavit. Hoc in libro sancti ipsius Irenæi, episcopi et martyris reperies, edocti a beato Polycarpo Smyrnæorum episcopo et martyre, qui fuit discipulus Joannis Apostoli, sicut refert historiographus Josephus et Irenæus episcopus in libro suo.

3. Johannes Evangelista primum cursum Gallorum decantavit. Inde postea beatus Polycarpus, discipulus Sancti Joannis; inde postea Irenæus qui fuit episcopus Lugdunensis in Galliis. Tertius ipse, istum cursum decantavit in Galliis.

4. Inde et modulationibus, series Scripturarum novi ac Veteris Testamenti, diversorum prudentium virorum paginis non de propriis sed de sacris Scripturis receperunt antiphonas et responsoria, seu sonus et alleluias composuerunt, et per universum orbem terrarum, ordo cursus est. Non sicut multi opi-

ON THE ORIGIN OF THE SACRED CHANT AND LITURGY.

1. If we diligently inquire into the authors of the liturgy, we shall find its origin far different from what many unlearned persons have asserted, and still continue to object to us in a manifold manner.

2. Blessed Trophimus, bishop of Arles, and Saint Photinus, martyr, bishop of Lyons and disciple of Saint Peter the Apostle, as Josephus (?) and Eusebius of Cæsarea relate, brought the Roman liturgy to Gaul.

Subsequently, blessed Clement, the fourth successor of St. Peter, was again referred to by desire of Photinus, when, with forty-eight martyrs, he was thrown into prison: and blessed Clement consecrated the blessed Irenæus bishop of that see. This we find recorded in the book of the same blessed Irenæus, bishop and martyr, who was instructed by blessed Polycarp, bishop of Smyrna and martyr, and disciple of the Apostle John, as the historian Josephus (?) and Irenæus the bishop relate.

3. St. John the Evangelist was the first who chanted the Gallican liturgy; then St. Polycarp, disciple of St. John; then Irenæus, who was bishop of Lyons, in Gaul. He was the third who chanted that liturgy in Gaul.

4. Then, with various modifications, extracts from the sacred Scripture of the Old and New Testaments were introduced, and antiphons, and responsories, and allelujas, which were drawn up by holy men, and composed not according to their own fancy, but in the words of the sacred

---

* Perhaps *fari*.

nantur ut Gallicanus quidam clericus Britto modulatione deditus quod ipsum edidisset, quod non facit, quod beatus Hieronymus presbyter, Germanus et Lupus, episcopi, Pelagianam hæresim vel Gallianam (quæ nomine ipsius titulatur) ex Britanniis et Scotiis proviuciis expulerunt, unde alium cursum qui dicitur præsente tempore Scottorum, que.....sa opinione jactatur.

Sed beatus Marcus Evangelista, sicut refert Josephus et Eusebius in quarto libro totam Ægyptum vel Italiam taliter prædicaverunt, sicut unam ecclesiam, ut omnes *Sanctus* vel *Gloria in excelsis Deo*, vel *Oratione Dominica*, et Amen, universi tam viri quam feminæ decantarent. Tanta fuit sua prædicatio uuita, et postea evangelium ex ore Petri Apostoli edidit.

Beatus Hieronymus affirmat, ipsum cursum qui dicitur præsente tempore Scottorum, beatus Marcus decantavit, et post ipsum Gregorius Nauzanzenus, quem Hieronymus suum magistrum esse affirmat. Et beatus Basilius frater ipsius Sancti Gregorii, Antonius, Paulus, Macharius, vel Joannes, et Malchus secundum ordinem Patrum decantaverunt.

Inde postea beatissimus Cassianus, qui in Lerinense monasterio beatum Honoratum habuit comparem. Et post ipsum beatus Honoratus primus Abbas, et Sanctus Cæsarius episcopus qui fuit in Arelata et beatus Porcarius

Scripture; and such is now this liturgy throughout the whole world. It was not, as many imagine, some Gallican cleric or Briton who was fond of chant that thus transformed it; this cannot be true, for the liturgy was thus used by blessed Jerome the priest, and by Germanus and Lupus, bishops who expelled the Gallican heresy, or (as it was called from its author) Pelagianism, from Britain and Ireland. Thus had its origin the liturgy, now called the Irish liturgy, *Cursus Scottorum,* which is impugned with much acrimony.

But blessed Mark the Evangelist, as Josephus and Eusebius in the fourth book tell us, preached throughout all Egypt and Italy, that as all were members of one Church, so all the faithful, both male and female, should join in chanting the *Sanctus* and the *Gloria in excelsis,* and the *Lord's Prayer*, and Amen. This formed part of all his preaching, and afterwards he wrote the Gospel from the lips of the Apostle Peter.

Blessed Jerome writes that the liturgy which is now called *the Irish liturgy,* was that chanted by Saint Mark, and used subsequently by Gregory Nazianzen, whom Jerome styles his master. Also, blessed Basil, brother of the same St. Gregory, with Anthony, Paul, Macarius or John, and Malchus, used it according to the rule of the fathers.

Subsequently, too, the most blessed Cassian, who had the blessed Honoratus as his associate in the monastery of Lerins; and after him the first abbot, who was blessed Honoratus, and St. Cesarius, who was bishop of Arles, and

(Eucherius?) abbas qui in ipso monasterio fuit, ipsum cursum decantaverunt, qui beatum Lupum et beatum Germanum monachos in eorum monasterio habuerunt. Et ipsi sub norma regulæ ipsum cursum ibidem¶ decantaverunt et postea in episcopatus cathedra summum honorem pro⁺ reverentia sanctitatis eorum sunt adepti.

Et postea in Britaniis vel Scottiis prædicaverunt, quod vita Germani episcopi Antisiodorensis et vita beati Lupi adfirmat qui beatum Patricium spiritaliter litteras sacras docuerunt atque enutrierunt et ipsum Episcopum (perhaps *ipsi Episcopi*) per eorum prædicationem Archiepiscopum in Scottiis et Britanniis posuerunt, qui vixit annos centum quinquaginta tres et ipsum cursum ibidem decantavit.

Et post ipsum beatus Wandilochus senex et beatus Comgallus qui habuerunt in eorum monasterio monachos circiter tria millia.

Inde beatus Wandilochus in prædicationis ministerium ab Abbate Comgallo missus, et beatus Columbanus partibus Galliarum destinati sunt Luxogilum monasterium et ibidem ipsum cursum decantaverunt. Et inde postea percrebuit fama sanctitatis eorum per universum orbem terrarum, et multa cœnobia ex eorum doctrina tam virorum quam puellarum congregata sunt.

Et postea inde sumpsit exordium sub beato Columbano, quod ante beatus Marcus Evangelista decantavit, et si nos non creditis inquirite in vita beati Columbani et beati Eustasii abbatis, plenius invenietis,

the blessed Eucherius, who was abbot in the same monastery, continued to use this liturgy, and they had as monks in their monastery the blessed Lupus and Germanus. These, too, under the guidance of their rule, chanted there the same liturgy, and subsequently, in the episcopal dignity, were regarded with the greatest respect, through reverence for their sanctity.

Afterwards they preached in Britain or Ireland, as is commemorated in the lives of blessed Germanus, bishop of Auxerre, and of Lupus: these were the spiritual masters of blessed Patrick in sacred literature; and the same bishops, by their commendation, had him appointed archbishop of the Irish and Britons: he lived cliii. (probably a mistake for cxxii.) years, and chanted there the same liturgy.

And after him the aged and blessed Dichnill and blessed Comgall used it, who had in their monastery about three thousand monks.

Then the blessed Dichnill* and Columbanus sent by abbot Comgall to Gaul, built the monastery of Luxeu and chanted there the same liturgy. The fame of their sanctity spread far and wide throughout the whole world, and many convents for men, and many, too, for virgins, were formed according to their rule.

Thus was restored, under blessed Columbanus, that liturgy which, at first, was chanted by the blessed Mark the Evangelist; and should you not believe my statement, you will find it registered in the lives

---

* We have adopted the translation Deicolus or Dichnill, as this is the only name amongst the companions of Columbanus, as given by Jonas and others, that at all approaches the Wandilochus of the text.

et dicta, beati Atthcleti abbatis, Ebovensis.

Est alius cursus orientalis a sancto Cromacio et Eliodoro, et beato Paulino sed et Athanasio episcopo editus, qui in Gallorum consuetudine non habetur, quem sanctus Macharius decantavit, hoc est, per duodenas, hoc est, unaquaque hora.

Est et alius cursus quem refert beatus Augustinus Episcopus quod beatus Ambrosius propter hæreticorum ordinem dissimilem composuit qui in Italia antea decantabatur.

Est et alius cursus beati Benedicti, qui ipsum singulariter pauco discordante a cursu Romano, quem in sua regula reperis scriptum: sed tamen beatus Gregorius urbis Romæ Pontifex quasi privilegium monachis ipsum sua auctoritate in vita S. Benedicti in libro Dialogorum adfirmavit, ubi dixit: "*non aliter sanctus vir docere, nisi sicut ipse beatus Benedictus vixit.*"

of blessed Columbanus and blessed Eustatius, and in the *Dicta* of blessed Attala, abbot of Bobbio.

There is another oriental liturgy composed by St. Cromacius, and Eliodorus, and blessed Paulinus, and also Athanasius, the bishop; it is not in use in the French churches, but it was chanted by St. Macarius: it has twelve parts, one for each hour.

There is also another liturgy, commemorated by St. Augustine, which was composed by St. Ambrose on account of the conflicting order of the heretics; it was formerly chanted in Italy.

There is, moreover, the liturgy of St. Benedict, who drew it up, differing but little from the Roman liturgy, and you will find it inserted in his rule: however the blessed Gregory, bishop of the city of Rome, approved of it as a special privilege for the monks, in his Life of St. Benedict, in the 'Book of Dialogues,' where he says, "the holy man could not have thus taught, unless he himself had thus lived."*

From this tract it would appear that the faithful were accustomed to recite aloud, during the holy Sacrifice, the *Gloria in excelsis*, and other prayers. We shall present a few of these every-day devotional anthems, that the reader may form an idea of the peculiarities which characterized, in some churches at least, the Irish liturgy.

The Pater Noster.

The *Our Father* as recited in the liturgy was identical with that which is used at the present day. It is thus given in the Leabhar

---

* It is deserving of remark, that this ancient tract speaks of Saint Patrick as if he were *archbishop of Ireland and Britain*. The same title is given to our apostle in his life by Probus; and the archbishop of Armagh, Torbach, in the synod of 807, was styled in like manner, *archbishop of the Irish and English.*—(See above, p. 180.)

Breac, in alternate Latin and Irish, which we add as translated by O'Donovan:—

"*Sic ergo orabitis.* Thus then ye shall make prayer. *Pater noster qui es in coelis, sanctificetur nomen tuum.* O Father, who art in the heavens, sanctified be thy name. *Adveniat regnum tuum.* May thy kingdom come. *Fiat voluntas tua sicut in coelo et in terra.* May thy will be in earth as it is in heaven. *Panem nostrum cotidianum da nobis hodie.* Give us this day our day's sufficiency. *Et dimitte nobis debita nostra sicut et nos dimittimus debitoribus nostris.* And forgive to us our debts as we forgive to our debtors. *Et ne nos inducas in temptationem.* And let us not into intolerable temptation. *Sed libera nos a malo.* But free us from every evil. *Amen.* May it be true."*

The Book of Dimma, in Trinity College Dublin, written in the beginning of the seventh century, gives the *Pater Noster* with the sole peculiarity *et ne patiaris nos induci in temptationem.*

The evangelistarium of St. Moling, which was written towards the close of the same century, has some further particular phrases: "Panem nostrum *supersubstantialem* da nobis hodie ; et *remitte* nobis debita nostra sicut et nos *remittimus* debitoribus nostris et *ne patiaris nos induci in temptationem,*" etc.†

Gloria in Excelsis.

This hymn, as used in the liturgy, agreed in every respect with that of the Roman liturgy: as chanted, however, by the faithful, it assumed some peculiar formulas. It is thus given in the Roman MS. of the Liber Hymnorum.‡

"Gloria in excelsis Deo et in terra pax hominibus bonæ voluntatis. Laudamus te, benedicimus te, adoramus te, glorificamus te, magnificamus te. Gratias agimus tibi propter magnam misericordiam tuam. Domine Rex cœlestis Deus pater omnipotens. Domine fili unigenite Jesu Christe, sancte Spiritus Deus et omnes dicimus, Amen. Domine fili Dei Patris, agne Dei qui tollis peccata mundi miserere nobis. Suscipe orationem nostram qui sedes ad dexteram Dei Patris, miserere nobis, Domine. Quoniam tu solus sanctus, tu solus Dominus, tu solus gloriosus, cum Spiritu sancto in gloria Dei Patris. Amen."

---

* Leabhar Breac, fol. 124.
† See fac-similes in Curry's Lectures, page 651, seqq. ‡ Fol. 12.

The Apostles' Creed.

At the end of St. Columbanus's Missal, there is a short but curious tract on the Creed, which assigns to each apostle the portion composed by him in their common symbol of faith :—

"Petrus dixit: Credo in Deum Patrem omnipotentem. Johannes dixit: Credo in Jesum Christum filium ejus unicum, Deum et Dominum nostrum. Jacobus dixit: Natum de Maria virgine per Spiritum sanctum. Andreas dixit: Passum sub Pontio Pilato, crucifixum et sepultum. Philippus dixit: Descendit ad inferna. Thomas dixit: Tertia die resurrexit. Bartholomæus dixit: Ascendit in cœlos, sedet ad dextram Dei Patris omnipotentis. Matthæus dixit: Inde venturus judicare vivos et mortuos. Jacobus Alphæi dixit: Credo in Spiritum sanctum. Simon Zelotes dixit: Credo in Ecclesiam sanctam. Judas Jacobi dixit: Per Baptismum sanctum remissionem peccatorum. Matthias dixit: Carnis resurrectionem in vitam æternam. Amen."

The Antiphonary of Bangor gives also the symbol, in a somewhat peculiar form :—

"Credo in Deum Patrem omnipotentem invisibilem, omnium creaturarum visibilium et invisibilium conditorem.

"Credo et in Jesum Christum, filium ejus unicum Dominum nostrum, Deum omnipotentem, conceptum de Spiritu sancto, natum de Maria virgine, passum sub Pontio Pilato: qui crucifixus et sepultus descendit ad inferos, tertia die resurrexit a mortuis, ascendit in cœlos, seditque ad dextram Dei Patris omnipotentis, exinde venturus judicare vivos ac mortuos.

"Credo et in Spiritum sanctum Deum omnipotentem, unam habentem substantiam cum Patre et Filio. Sanctam esse Ecclesiam Catholicam: abremissionem peccatorum, sanctorum communionem, carnis resurrectionem. Credo vitam post mortem et vitam æternam in gloria Christi. Hæc omnia credo in Deum. Amen."

Hymnus Trium Puerorum.

This hymn seems to have been chanted after the manner of a litany in the early Church, the second hemistich of the first verse forming the response throughout the whole hymn. We give it from the Liber Hymnorum, fol. ii. a. :—

"Benedicite omnia opera Domini Domino, hymnum dicite et superexaltate eum in sæcula.

Benedicite cœli Domini Dominum,—hymnum dicite et superexaltate eum in sæcula.
Benedicite aquæ Domini Dominum,—hymnum, etc.
Benedicite aquæ omnes super cœlos Domini Dominum,—hymnum, etc.
Benedicite omnes potentiæ Domini Dominum,—hymnum, etc.
Benedicite sol et luna Domini Dominum,—hymnum, etc.
Benedicite stellæ cœli Domini Dominum,—hymnum, etc.
Benedicite imber et ros Domini Dominum,—hymnum, etc.
Benedicite omnes spiritus Domini Dominum,—hymnum, etc.
Benedicite ignis et calor Domini Dominum,—hymnum, etc.
Benedicite noctes et dies Domini Dominum,—hymnum, etc.
Benedicite tenebræ et lumen Domini Dominum,—hymnum, etc.
Benedicite frigus et æstus Domini Dominum,—hymnum, etc.
Benedicite pruina et nives Domini Dominum,—hymnum, etc.
Benedicite fulgura et nubes Domini Dominum,—hymnum, etc.
Benedicat terra Domini Dominum,—hymnum dicat et superexaltet eum in sæcula.
Benedicite montes et colles Domini Dominum,—hymnum dicite et superexaltate eum in sæcula.
Benedicite omnia animantia terræ Domini Dominum,—hymnum, etc.
Benedicite maria et flumina Domini Dominum,—hymnum, etc.
Benedicite fontes aquarum Domini Dominum,—hymnum, etc.
Benedicite beluæ et omnia quæ morantur in aquis Domini Dominum,—hymnum, etc.
Benedicite omnes volucres cœli Domini Dominum,—hymnum, etc.
Benedicite bestiæ et viventia Domini Dominum,—hymnum, etc.
Benedicite Israhelitæ Domini Dominum,—hymnum, etc.
Benedicite filii hominum Domini Dominum,—hymnum, etc.
Benedicite sacerdotes Domini Dominum,—hymnum, etc.
Benedicite servi Domini Dominum,—hymnum, etc.
Benedicite spiritus et animæ justorum Domini Dominum,—hymnum, etc.
Benedicite sancti et humiles corde Domini Dominum,—hymnum, etc.
Benedicite Ananias, Azarias, et Misael Domini Dominum,—hymnum, etc.
Benedicamus Patrem et Filium et Spiritum Sanctum Dominum, hymnum dicamus et superexaltemus eum in sæcula."

APPENDIX No. III.

ANCIENT IRISH PENITENTIALS.

A.—The Penitential of St. Cummian.

Penitential of St. Cummian.—Opinions of Dr. Lanigan, Theiner, Wasserschleben, as to the author, refuted.—St. Cummian Fota, who died about the year 662, is the author.—Great influence of his Penitential St. Theodore of Canterbury borrows many canons from it.—Extracts from it.

St. Cummian's Penitential is preserved in two MSS. of St. Gall,[*] of the ninth century; also in a Darmstadt Codex,[†] of the same century; and in a Vienna manuscript[‡] of the tenth century.

Its first printed edition was that of 1621. It was subsequently inserted by Fleming in Collectanea Sacra, printed at Louvain in 1667, and passed thence to the Bibliotheca Max. Patrum (vol. xii., p. 41, seqq.). A portion of it, too, was published amongst the spurious works of St. Jerome, in the edition of Martianay (vol. 1). Its last and best edition is that of the learned professor of Halle, Dr. Wasserschleben, who inserted it in his Bussordnungen der Abendländischer Kirche.[§]

As there were many saintly ornaments of our Irish Church known by the name *Cummianus*, it has long been a matter of controversy to which of them the present work should be referred.

Dr. Lanigan judged it to have been written, most probably, by St. Cummian, author of the Paschal Epistle.[||] Mone deemed it to belong to a still earlier period, and considered it to be the work of St. Columbkille, founder of Hy, whilst the name of Cummian remained attached to it from some additions made to the Penitential in later times by the biographer of St. Columbkille, who was also his successor in the government of Hy.[¶] Theiner refers the whole Penitential to the holy abbot of Iona, whose death, however, he

---

[*] Nos. 550 and 675.   [†] No. 91.   [‡] Codex Theolog. No. 651.
[§] Halle, 1851, pp. 460, 493.   [||] Ec. Hist. vol. iii. p. 401.
[¶] See Mone's "Quellen und Forschungen," etc. p 494.

erroneously assigns to 661. The Annals of the Four Masters, Tighernach, and the Annals of Ulster fix his death on 25th February, 669.*

Wasserschleben, in the work above referred to, embraced a quite different opinion. He remarked that it was principally preserved in the manuscripts that once belonged to the monastery of Bobbio; and that it was well known to the French and Italian compilers of the ninth and tenth centuries. He hence concluded that its author might probably be a *Cummian* who, during the reign of Luitprand,† acquired great fame for his sanctity and penitential life in Bobbio. As this holy man is but little known in his native island, we give the following extract from the ancient Bobbio chronicle, preserved to us by Ughelli in his Italia Sacra :‡

"Sanctus Cumianus Episcopus in Scotia 75um annum jam agens, Dei amore ignitus ad fines Italicos devenit, locatus in monasterio Bobbio, id est S. Columbani. In quo quidem monasterio sub dogmate id est constitutionibus S. Columbani, annis xx. et plus strenue ministravit: fuit enim mitis, prudens, pius fratribus, atque pacificus; moritur ibi ætatis suæ annis completis 95 mensibusque quatuor, temporibus Luitprandi Regis Longobardorum qui fabricari fecit in honorem ipsius notabile monumentum inscriptos hos versus continens.

"Hic sacra beati membra Cumiani solvuntur cujus cœlum penetrans anima cum angelis gaudet—iste fuit magnus dignitate, genere, forma.—Hunc misit Scotia fines ad Italicos senem.—Locatus Ebobio, Domini constrictus amore—ubi venerandi dogma Columbani servando—vigilans, jejunans indefessus sedulo orans—olympiades quatuor, uniusque curriculo anni—sic vixit feliciter, ut felix modo credatur—mitis, prudens, pius, fratribus pacificus cunctis.—Huic ætatis anni fuerunt nonies deni—lustrum quoque unum, menses quatuor simul.—At Pater egregie, potens intercessor existe—pro gloriosissimo Luitprando rege, qui suum—prætioso lapide tymbum decoravit devotus.—Sit manifestum almum ubi tegitur corpus—opus, est hic domnus Cumianus Episcopus—xiv. kal. Septemb. fecit Joannes."

The Penitential itself presents but one characteristic of the age to which it belongs, viz.: the warm condemnation of the quartodeciman celebration of Easter, which is introduced in the eleventh chapter in the 21st and 31st canon.

* Theiner "Disquisitiones Criticæ in Præcipuas Canonum Collectiones," 1836, p. 280.
† An. 711–744.   ‡ Vol. iv. p. 956.

The penitential treatises of the eighth, ninth, and tenth centuries often cite the canons of St. Cummian; but for the most part with the simple title *Judicium Cummeani*. Some documents, however, are more explicit in their reference, and whilst giving to St. Cummian the title of *Archimandrita*, they sufficiently exclude the holy monk of Bobbio. This title is added when citing the canons of St. Cummian, in the Vatican MS. collection of canons, (No. 1339, sæc. x^{mi}); also in the famous Collectio Canonum of St. Anselm of Lucca (xi. 38), and again in the Madrid MS. Collectio Canonica (A. 151.)

Of the various manuscripts which contain the Penitential itself, there is only one that throws any light on the history of its author. It is the St. Gall MS., (No. 675),[*] which describes St. Cummeanus, "*Abbas, in Scotia natus.*"

There is one MS., however, which gives a decisive testimony in regard to the author of our Penitential. It is a collection of canons preserved in the Vatican Archives, (No. 1349), and written towards the close of the ninth or the beginning of the tenth century.[†] Indeed, as Cardinal Mai remarks, the writing of this manuscript is so barbarous, that it remained unnoticed by the various writers on the Canonical Collections, although one of the most interesting that the Vatican Archives present. It was probably made by an Irishman, as it introduces into its text almost the whole of the "Collectio Hibernensis Canonum," of which we shall speak just now, and makes frequent references to Irish synods and the canons of St. Patrick. It is at fol. 193, a.b., that a long extract is given from the Penitential of St. Cummian, whilst it is expressly cited as "inquisitio Acumiani Longii," thus fixing as its author St. Cummian Fota (*i.e.*, the Tall) of whom we have more than once spoken in the preceding pages.—(*Vide* p. 174).

Indeed, the various facts connected with this Penitential all agree with the history of this saint: for instance, the decrees regarding the quartodecimans, since St. Cummian Fota lived at a time when that controversy raged with special ardour. On the

---

[*] Sæc. xi. 38.
[†] Conf. Mai, Spicilegium Romanum, tom. vi. p. 396, seq.

other hand, St. Cummian Fota was remarkable for his learning, and being styled the 'Gregorius moralium' of our Irish Church, may easily be supposed the author of some such penitential code. The ancient list often referred to by Colgan and the martyrology of Donegal, as "*preserved in the old parchment-book*," indicating the chief Irish saints in parallel with the great saints of the continent, whose prerogatives they seemed to share, is printed as follows from a Burgundian MS. by Dr. Todd.*

"Hi sunt sancti qui erant unius moris et vitæ, ut dicunt:—

Johannes Baptista,	Episcopus Ibair.
Petrus Apostolus,	Patricius.
Paulus Apostolus,	Finnan Cluain-iraird.
Andreas Ap.	Colum-cille.
Jacobus Ap.	Finnian Magh-bile.
Joannes Ap.	Ciaran Cluana.
Philippus Ap.	Cainnech.
Bartholomeus Ap.	Brendanus senior.
Thomas Ap.	Brendain Cluana-ferta.
Mattheus Ap.	Colum Tir-de-glass.
Jacobus Ap.	Comgall Bennchair.
Simon Ap.	Molaisi Daimh-insi.
Tatheus Ap.	Sinchellus, junior.
Mathias Ap.	Ruadhan Lothra.
Maria,	Brigita.
Martinus,	Caembgin Glendaloch.
Antonius Monachus,	Feichin Fobhair.
Augustinus sapiens,	Lonngaradh.
Ambrosius hymnodicus,	Mac Indecis.
Job patiens,	Munna mac Tulcain.
Hieronimus sapiens,	Manchan Leith.
Clemens Papa,	Ciaran Saighre.
Gregorius Moralium,	Cummini Fota.
Laurentius Diaconus,	Decoin Nesan.
Beda sapiens,	Buite mac Bronaigh.
Hilarius Epus. et sapiens,	Sechnall Episcopus.
Cornelius Papa,	Maedog Ferna.
Silvester Papa,	Adamnan Episcopus.
Bonifacius P.	Molaisi Lethglinne.
Pacomius Monachus.	Caimin Innsi-cealtra.
Benedictus caput Monachorum Europæ,	Fintan Cluana eidnech, caput monachorum totius Hiberniæ.
Augustinus Epus. Angalorum,	Bairre Episcopus Mumhain agus Conacht."

* Lib Hym. p. 69.

The scholiast on the Felire of Aengus, after commemorating the Feast of St. Caimin of Iniskeltra, on the 25th of March, gives the following note, which preserves to us a somewhat similar characteristic trait of our great saint:—

"Once upon a time that Guaire Aidhne, and Cumain Fota, and Caimine of Inis-Cealtra, were in the church of Inis-Cealtra, in Loch Deirgheire, namely, the great church that was built by Caimine there; they were then giving spiritual counsel to Guaire. 'Well, O'Guaire,' said Caimine, 'what wouldst thou wish to have this church, in which we are, filled with?' Guaire answered him, and said: 'I would wish to have it full of gold and silver; and not from covetousness of this world, but that I might give it for my soul to saints and churches, and in like manner to every one that would ask for it.' 'God will give thee help, O'Guaire,' said Caimine, 'and will grant thee the expectation thou hast formed for the good of thy soul; and hereafter thou shalt possess heaven.' 'We are thankful,' said Guaire. 'But thou, O Cumain,' said Guaire, 'what wouldst thou wish to have in it?' 'I would wish,' said Cumain, 'to have it full of books to instruct studious men and to disseminate the word of God into the ears of all, to bring them from following Satan, unto the Lord.' 'But thou, O Caimine,' said they, 'what wouldst thou wish to have in it?' Caimine answered them, and said: 'I would wish to have the full of it of disease and sickness to be on my body, and myself to be suffering my pain.' And so they obtained their wishes from God, viz., the earth to Guaire, wisdom to Cumain Fota, and sickness and disease to Caimaine, so that not one bone of him remained united to the other on earth, but his flesh dissolved, and his nerves with the excess of every disease that fell upon him. So that they all went to heaven, according to the wishes which they expressed in the church."[*]

Little more is known for certain regarding St. Cummian Fota. His death is registered by Tighernach, in the year 662, in the seventy-second year of his age. His Church of Killcummin, where he was interred, gave its name to a parish in the district of Tirawley, county of Mayo, on the western side of the bay of Killala.[†]

It is only within the last few years that writers on the early mediæval discipline of the Church have begun to appreciate the influence exercised by the Penitential of St. Cummian in the for-

---

[*] This passage is given in Latin by Colgan, Acta SS. p 746: and in the original Irish with the above translation by Todd, Liber Hymn. p. 87.
[†] See for this church and the genealogy of our saint, the tribes and customs of Hy-Fiachrach, edited by O'Donovan for I A.S., p. 9, and 44 seq.

mation of the disciplinary code in England and western Europe. No fewer than six Penitentials, drawn up before the tenth century, are given by Wasserschleben, having for their groundwork the canons of St. Cummian. Thus the Codex Alveldensis of the Escurial Library,* contains a Spanish Penitential, almost all whose canons are taken from our saint; so, too, the famous "Rheims" Penitential. Another Penitential, known by the name of *the thirty-five chapters*, written towards the close of the eighth century,† cites our Penitential fourteen times as *Judicium Canonicum ;* and on one occasion cites twenty-five of its canons under the one title of *Judicium Canonicum Cummeani*. The Parisian Penitential of the eighth century adopts nearly all St. Cummian's decrees, merely adding some extracts from the French councils and from St. Theodore. The Collectio Pœnitentialis, published by Martene, and drawn up about the year 730, inserts the greater part of the Penitential; and what is still more curious, the "Pœnitentiale" which bears the name of pope Gregory the Third, and was composed in the ninth century,‡ takes many of its canons *ad litteram* from St. Cummian.

St. Theodore of Canterbury has long been famed as the great founder of the penitential code of the Western Church in the eighth and succeeding centuries. His early connection with Rome—his being sent directly by the Holy See to Canterbury—the lustre of the Anglo-Saxon Church during the eighth century, served to render his name illustrious on the continent. On the contrary, the humble monk of Ireland was forgotten, and few cared to call to mind that St. Cummian's work was the basis of Theodore's Penitential, and that many of the decrees referred to the great archbishop of Canterbury were adopted *verbatim* by him from the Penitential of our Irish saint. Kunstmann, in his Lateinischen Pœnitentialbüchern der Angelsachsen (page 22), was one of the first to assert that Cummian's work was "the chief source of Theodore's Penitential." Theiner, in his dissertation

---

* Sæc. x.   † Wasserschleben, p. 36.
‡ Ib. pp. 84, 85.

above referred to,* repeats the same statement, and styles the Penitential of St. Cummian, "fundamentum celebris Pœnitentialis Theodori."

The ancient Pœnitentiale Theodori, published with great accuracy by the modern German editor, reveals to us its connection with the work of St. Cummian. In the very outset it refers to a "*libellus Scottorum*," as one of the chief sources from which its enactments are derived; and though the writer of that *libellus* is not named, it is added that he was eulogised by Theodore as an *ecclesiasticus homo*, a holy man imbued with the spirit of God.†

To one who has diligently examined the Penitentials of Theodore and Cummian, there can be but little doubt as to the *libellus Scottorum* to which the former refers; for, many of its canons are found to agree even verbally with those of St. Cummian. For instance, the fifth chapter of Theodore, entitled, "De his qui per hæresim decipiuntur," consists of fourteen canons, and all agree *ad verbum* with those of St. Cummian,‡ which we shall just now cite. It is still more clear in the seventh chapter, in which, after a series of canons agreeing with St. Cummian's, and as an introduction to six other canons taken literally from our Irish saint, the following remark is inserted:

"Ista testimonia sunt *de eo quod in præfatione diximus libello Scottorum*, in quo ut in cæteris aliquando, inibi firmavit de pessimis, aliquando vero lenius ut sibi videbatur, modum imposuit pusillanimis."§

Thus, then, to St. Cummian Fota‖ was the Anglo-Saxon Church indebted for the penitential code which rendered it illustrious on

---

* Page 279.

† Penit. Theod. ap. Wasserschleben, loc. cit. p. 183.

‡ Chap. xi. 19. seqq.

§ Ibid. p. 191. Were any further evidence required, we would find it in the annotation of the ancient collector of St. Theodore's decrees, who, after two of the canons agreeing literally with St. Cummian's, added the remark that they were not "consonant to the teaching of Theodore."—See cap. v. canons 2 and 6.

‖ St. Cummian Fota flourished about thirty years earlier than Theodore. In some MSS. of the Penitential of St. Cummian, the name of *Theodore* is prefixed to the decrees in which both Penitentials agree; but as Dr. Wasserschleben remarks, and the titles themselves clearly prove, these are merely additions made by a modern and inexpert scribe.

the continent, and in the monasteries of Ireland were first drawn up those disciplinary canons which, in a short time, were adopted throughout the greater part of Western Europe.*

We now give a few extracts from St. Cummian's great work, that the reader may the better appreciate its interest and importance.

Its proemium is cited in the Vatican MS.,† the text of which, now published for the first time, will be found to correct in many places manifest errors of Wasserschleben's text:

"Diversitas culparum diversitatem facit pœnitentiarum: nam et corporum medici diversa medicamenta componunt diversis morborum generibus. Aliter enim vulnera, aliter morbum, aliter tumores, aliter putredines, aliter caligines, aliter confractiones, aliter combustiones curant. Ita igitur et spiritales medici diversis curationum generibus, animarum vulnera, morbum, culpas, dolores, ægritudines, infirmitates sanare debent. Sed quia hæc paucorum sunt, ad purum scilicet cuncta cognoscere et curare atque ad integrum salutis statum debeant revocare, ideoque vel pauca juxta seniorum traditiones et juxta nostram ex parte intelligentiam (ex parte namque prophetamus et ex parte cognoscimus) aliqua proponamus, quæ ad remedium animæ pertinent. Et de remediis vulnerum secundum priorum Patrum definitiones dicturi, sacri tibi eloquii, fidelissime frater, antea medicamina compendii ratione intimemus.

"1. Itaque est remissio qua baptizamur in aqua, secundum illud: nisi quis renatus fuerit ex aqua et Spiritu Sancto, non potest videre regnum Dei. 2. Caritatis affectus, ut est illud: Remittuntur ei peccata multa, quia dilexit multum. 3. Eleemosynarum fructus, secundum hoc: sicut aqua extinguit ignem, ita eleemosyna extinguit peccatum. 4. Perfusio lachrymarum, Domino dicente: quia flevit in conspectu meo et ambulavit tristis coram me non inducam mala in diebus ejus. 5. Criminum confessio, psalmista teste: dixi confitebor adversum me injustitias meas Domino et tu remisisti impietatem peccati mei. 6. Afflictio cordis et corporis, apostolo consolante et dicente: dedi hujuscemodi hominem in interitum carnis satanæ ut spiritus salvus fiat in die Domini nostri Jesu Christi. 7. Emendatio morum, hoc est abrenunciatio vitiorum dicente Domino: ecce sanus factus es, noli ultra peccare, ne aliquid tibi deterius fiat. 8. Intercessio Sanctorum, ut est illud: si quis infirmatur inducat presbyteros ecclesiæ ut orent pro eo: et multum valet apud Dominum deprecatio justi assidua. 9. Misericordiæ meritum, ut est illud: beati misericordes quoniam ipsi misericordiam consequentur. 10. Conversio et salus alienorum, Jacobo confirmante: qui converti fecerit peccatorem

---

* Dr. Wasserschleben remarks, at p. 63, that the Penitential of St. Cummian is also "manifestly used in the penitentials of Ven. Bede and Egbert."
† No. 1,349, sæc. ix.

ab errore viæ suæ, salvavit animam suam a morte et operuit multitudinem peccatorum: sed melius est tibi, infirmum esse et vitam solitariam ducere quam perire cum plurimis. 11. Indulgentia et remissio nostra, veritate promittente et dicente: dimittite et dimittetur vobis. 12. Passio martyrii, spe unica salutis indulgente et latroni crucifixo Domino respondente: amen, dico tibi, quia hodie eris mecum in paradyso.

"His ergo de canonum auctoritate probatis, patrum etiam statuta Domini ore subrogatorum, investigare te convenit, secundum illud: interroga patrem tuum et adnunciabit tibi, seniores tuos et dicent tibi: istæ causæ deferantur ad eos. Statuunt ergo ut octo principalia vitia humanæ saluti contraria his octo contrariis sanentur remediis. Vetus namque proverbium est: contraria contrariis sanantur, qui enim illicita licenter commisit, a licitis coercere se debet," etc.

The decrees regarding the use of animals are very curious: they occur in the first chapter, can. 19, seqq.:—

"Si ceciderit sorix in liquorem, tollabur foras, et hoc potum aspergatur aquâ sanctificata et sumatur si vivens sit; si autem mortua inventa fuerit, omnis liquor projiciatur foras et mundetur vas.

"Animalia quæ a lupis seu canibus lacerantur, non sunt comedenda nisi forte ab hominibus adhuc viva prius occidantur sed porcis et canibus dentur: nec cervus nec capra si mortui inventi fuerint.

"Aves vero et animalia cætera si in retibus strangulentur, non sunt comedenda hominibus. . . .

"Pisces licet comedere quia alterius naturæ sunt.

"Equum non prohibemus, tamen consuetudo non est.

"Leporem licet comedere.

"Apes vero si occidant hominem, ipsæ quoque occidi festinanter debent: mel tamen manducetur.

"Si casu porci vel gallinæ sanguinem hominis comedant, non abjiciendos credimus sed manducandos.

"Sed qui cadavera mortuorum lacerantes manducaverint, carnem eorum manducare non licet, usquedum macerentur et post anni circulum."

The 23rd canon of the 2nd chapter illustrates the course of penance inflicted for heinous crimes:—

"Presbyter aut diaconus fornicationem faciens, prælato ante monachi voto, tres annos pœniteat, veniam omni hora roget, superpositionem faciat, in unaquaque hebdomada exceptis quinquagesimis diebus post superpositionem pane sine mensura utatur, et ferculo aliquatenus butiro impinguato, hoc est quadrante, et die Dominica sic vivat. Cæteris vero diebus paxmati panis mensura et misso parvo, impinguato horti oleribus, ovis paucis, formatico, hemina lactis pro fragilitate corporali, tenucla vel batuti lactis sextario pro sitis gratia et aquatili potu, si operarius est, lectumque non multum fœno habeat instratum. Per tres quadragesimas anni addit aliquid prout virtus ejus admiserit, semper ex intimo corde defleat culpam suam, obedientiamque præ omnibus libentissime exhibeat: post annum et dimidium Eucharistiam sumat et ad pacem veniat, et psalmos cum fratribus canat, ne penitus anima tanto tempore cœlestis medicinæ jejuna intereat.

"Si inferiore gradu positus sit monachus tres quidem annos pœniteat, sed mensura non gravetur panis, si operarius est, sextarium de lacte Romanum et aliam tenuelam et aquam, quantum sufficit pro sitis ardore sumat."

The fourth chapter regards the sin of robbery, and some of its enactments will illustrate the customs of our island at that early period:—

"Si pecunia Ecclesiastica furata sive rapta fuerit reddatur quadruplum; popularia dupliciter.

"Si quis aliquid de ministerio sanctæ Ecclesiæ furaverit aut neglexerit, septem annos pœniteat, tres ex his in pane et aqua, et reddat integrum quod abstulit. . . . .

"Si laicus semel furtum fecerit, reddat quod furavit et in tribus quadragesimis cum pane et aqua pœniteat. Si sæpius fecerit et non habet unde reddat, annos duos in pane et aqua pœniteat et in alio anno tribus quadragesimis, et sic postea in Pascha reconcilietur.

"Qui sæpe furtum faciebat, septem annos pœniteat, vel ut sacerdos judicat, juxta quod componi potest, quibus nocuit, et semper debet reconciliari ei quem offendebat, et restituere juxta quod ei nocuit et multum breviabit pœnitentiam ejus. Si vero noluerit aut non potest, constitutum tempus pœnitere debet per omnia. . . . .

"Si laicus monachum furtim abduxerit, aut intret in monasterium Deo servire, aut humanum subeat servitium.

"Si quis servum aut quemcumque hominem quolibet ingenio in captivitatem duxerit aut transmiserit, tres annos in pane et aqua pœniteat.

"Si quis patrem aut matrem expulerit, impius vel sacrilegus judicandus est et pœniteat æquali tempore, quamdiu in impietate extiterit.

"Qui præbeat ducatum barbaris si basilicas incenderint et si clericum vel sanctimonialem bonos occiderint, et innocentes ab Ecclesia traxerint, ductor quatuordecim annos pœniteat.

"Pecunia quæ in aliena Provincia ab hoste rapta fuerit, i. e. rege alio superato, tertia pars ad Ecclesiam tribuatur, vel pauperibus. . . . .

"Si quis domum vel aream cujuscumque igne concremaverit, tres annos pœniteat, unum ex his in pane et aqua."

In the eleventh chapter St. Cummian treats of pride and blasphemy and heresy:—

"Qui superbiæ cæteros qualibet despectione arguit, primo satisfaciat eis, deinde jejunet judicio sacerdotis.

"Contentiosus etiam alterius sententiæ se subdat, sin autem anathematizetur, et regno Domini sit alienus.

"Jactans in suis beneficiis se humiliet, alioquin quidquid boni fecerit humanæ gloriæ causa perdet. . . . .

"Qui aliquam novitatem extra Scripturas vel hæresim præsumpserit, alienetur: si autem pœniteat, suam publice sententiam damnet et quos decepit ad fidem convertat, et jejunet ad judicium sacerdotis . . . .

"Si quis laicus per ignorantiam cum hæreticis communicaverit stet inter catechumenos, i.e., separatus ab Ecclesia quadraginta dies et alios xl in extremis pœniteat et sic culpam suam diluat. Si vero postquam illi sacerdos prædicaverit ut cum hæretico non communicaret, et iterum fecerit, uno anno pœniteat, et tribus quadragesimis ; et tres annos abstineat se a vino et carne. . . . .

"Si quis a Catholica Ecclesia ad hæresim transierit et postea reversus, non potest ordinari nisi post longam abstinentiam aut pro magna necessitate. Hunc Innocentius Papa nec post pœnitentiam clericum fieri canonum auctoritate adserit permitti.

"Si quis contempserit Nicænum concilium et fecerit Pascha cum Judæis xiv. luna, exterminabitur ab omni Ecclesia nisi pœnitentiam egerit ante mortem.

"Si quis autem oraverit cum illo quasi cum clerico Catholico, septimanam pœniteat, si vero neglexerit xl. dies pœniteat prima vice.

"Si quis hortari voluerit hæresim eorum et non egerit pœnitentiam, similiter et ille exterminabitur Domino dicente : *qui mecum non est contra me est.*

"Si quis baptizatur ab hæretico qui recte Trinitatem non crediderit iterum baptizetur.

"Si quis dederit aut acceperit communionem de manu hæretici et nescit, quod Catholicæ Ecclesiæ contradicat, postea intelligens annum integrum pœniteat. Si autem scit et neglexerit et postea pœnitentiam egerit, decem annos pœniteat : alii judicant septem (annos) ; et humanius quinque annos pœniteat.

"Si quis permiserit hæreticum missam suam celebrare in Ecclesia Catholica et nescit quadraginta diebus pœniteat ; si pro reverentia ejus anno integro pœniteat ;

"Si pro damnatione Ecclesiæ Catholicæ et consuetudinis Romanorum, projiciatur ab Ecclesia sicut hæreticus, nisi habeat pœnitentiam, si habuerit decem annos pœniteat.

"Si recesserit ab Ecclesia Catholica in congregationem hæreticorum et alios persuaserit, et postea pœnitentiam egerit, xii. annos pœniteat, quatuor extra Ecclesiam, et sex inter auditores et duos adhuc extra communionem. De his in canone dicitur : decimo anno communionem sive oblationem recipiant.

"Si Episcopus aut Abbas jusserit monacho suo pro hæreticis mortuis missam cantare, non licet et non expedit obedire ei.

"Si Presbytero contigerit ut missam cantaverit et alius recitaverit nomina mortuorum et simul nominaverit hæreticos cum Catholicis ; ubi post missam intellexerit, hebdomadam pœniteat ; si frequenter fecerit, integrum annum pœniteat

"Si quis autem pro morte hæretici, missam ordinaverit et pro religione sua reliquias sibi tenuerit, quia multum jejunavit et nescit differentiam Catholicæ fidei et quartadecimanorum et postea intellexerit pœnitentiamque egerit, reliquias debet igne cremare et uno anno pœnitere Si autem scit et negligit pœnitentia commotus, decem annos pœniteat.

"Si quis a fide Dei discesserit sine ulla necessitate et postea ex toto animo pœnitentiam accipit, tres annos extra Ecclesiam sit, id est, inter audientes juxta Nicænum Concilium et septem annos in Ecclesia inter pœnitentes, et duos annos adhuc extra communionem"

The whole thirteenth chapter treats of the holy sacrifice of the altar, and assigns the various penances for the different degrees of irreverence or neglect in regard to it:—

"Pro bonis regibus offerre debemus, pro malis nequaquam.
"Presbiteri vero pro suis Episcopis non prohibentur offerre.
"Qui communicaverit nec ignorans excommunicato ab Ecclesia, xl. dies pœniteat.
"Si quis errans commutaverit aliquid de verbis sacrorum, ubi periculum adnotaverit, tres superpositiones faciat.
"Si sacrificium terratenus negligendo ceciderit, superponat.
"Qui sacrificii aliquid perdit, relinquens illud feris devorandum, si excusabiliter tres quadragesimas, sin vero unum annum.
"Qui non bene custodierit sacrificium, et mus comederit illud xl dies pœniteat.
"Qui autem perdiderit in Ecclesia et pars ceciderit et non inventa fuerit xx. dies pœniteat.
"Qui perdiderit suum crismal * aut solum sacrificium in regione qualibet et non inveniatur tres quadragesimas vel unum annum pœniteat.
"Perfundens aliquid de calice super altare, quando aufertur linteamen, septem dies pœniteat, aut si abundantius superpositionibus septem pœniteat.
"Si accidentis de manu acciderit † in stramen, vii. dies pœniteat is a quo ceciderit.
"Qui autem infuderit calicem in fine solemnitatis missæ xl. dies.
"Si vero neglexerit quis accipere sacrificium et non interrogat nec aliqua causa excusabilis extiterit, superponat.
"Diaconus obliviscens oblationem adferre donec auferatur linteamen quando recitantur nomina pausantium similiter pœniteat.
"Qui negligentiam erga sacrificium fecerit aut siccans vermibusque consumptum ad nihilum devenerit tres quadragesimas cum pane et aqua pœniteat. Si integrum inventum fuerit ita, ut sint in eo vermes, comburatur et cinis sub altare abscondatur, et qui neglexerit cl. dies suam negligentiam solvat.

---

* This name is derived from the Greek χαρισμα, by which the blessed Eucharist was often designated.
† This canon seems to imply that the blessed Sacrament was placed on the hand of the communicant.

"Si cum amissione saporis decoloratur sacrificium, xx. diebus expleatur jejunium, conglutinatum vero, viii. diebus ; qui autem mergit sacrificium, continuo abluat et bibat aquam, quæ in crismal fuerit, sumatque sacrificium et emendet per x. dies culpam solus.*

"Si ceciderit sacrificium de manu offerentis terratenus, et non invenitur, omne quod circa eum inventum fuerit in loco, in quo ceciderit, comburatur et cinis ut supra abscondatur, sacerdos deinde medio anno damnetur. Si vero inventum fuerit sacrificium, locus scopa mundetur et stramen ut supra ignetur et sacerdos xx. dies pœniteat ; si usque ad altare tantum lapsum fuerit superponat.

"Si vero per negligentiam de calice aliquid stillaverit in terra, lingua lambatur, tabula radatur, et si non fuerit tabula, mittat ut non conculcetur, igne consumatur ut supra et sacerdos xl. dies pœniteat.

"Si supra altare stillaverit calix, sorbeat minister stillam, ternis diebus pœniteat, et si in linteo ad aliud linteum transierit viii. diebus, si usque tertio, viii. diebus, si usque ad quartum, xv. diebus et linteamina, quæ tetigerit stilla, tribus abluat vicibus, calice subter posito et aquam ablutionis sumat.

"Si quando interluitur calix stillaverit, prima vice xii. canantur psalmi a ministro.

"Si titubaverit sacerdos super orationem dominicam, quæ dicitur periculosa, si una vice 4 plagas ; secunda centum, tertia superponat.

"Qui evomuit sacrificium et a canibus sumitur, anno uno pœniteat, sin autem, xl. diebus. Si in die quando communicaverit sacrificium, evomuerit, si ante mediam noctem, iii. superpositiones faciat ; si post mediam noctem ii. si post matutinas, i. superpositionem faciat.

"Si vero sacrificium evomuerit, xl. dies, si infirmitatis causa, vii. dies, si in ignem projecit, c psalmos cantet, si vero canes lambuerint talem vomitum, c. dies qui evomuit, pœniteat

"Qui communicaverit sanguinem inconscius, vii. dies pœniteat.

"Quicumque alicui capitale crimen admittenti per ignorantiam communicaverit, vii dies pœniteat."†

From the fourteenth and concluding chapter, we select a few canons illustrative of the matter treated of in the preceding extracts :—

"Si quis presbiter pœnitentiam morientibus abnegaverit, reus erit animarum quia Dominus dixit : *quacumque die conversus fuerit peccator vita vivet et non morietur.* Vera enim conversio in ultimo tempore potest esse quia Dominus non solum temporis sed etiam cordis inspector est, sicut

---

* The Vat. MS. has xl. dies.

† The Codex Vindobonensis, 651, adds another canon : "Si quis audenter sacerdos quando missas celebrat super sacro altario incumbit brachiis vel ulnis, si ignoranter fecit, vii. dies, si per industriam xl. dies pœniteat, et si iteravit dejiciatur." In the text of the above chapter xiii. we have adopted many corrections from the Vatican MS., No. 1339, of the tenth century.

latro unius momenti pœnitens meruit esse in Paradiso in hora ultima confessionis.

"Sacrificium non est accipiendum de manu sacerdotis qui orationes et lectiones secundum ritum implere non potest. . . .

"Pœnitentes secundum canones non debent communicare ante consumationem pœnitentiæ: nos autem pro misericordia post annum vel sex menses licentiam damus.

"Pro defuncto monacho missæ agantur in die sepulturæ ejus et tertio die et postea quantum voluerit Abbas.

"Pro laico bono, tertio die vel septimo post jejunium; pro pœnitente xxx. die vel vii. et propinquos ejus oportet jejunare vii. die et oblationem offerre ad altare, sicut in Jesu fili Sirach legitur, et pro Saul filii Israel jejunaverunt, postea quantum voluerit presbyter.

"Mulieres possunt sub nigro velamine accipere sacrificium Basilius hoc judicavit.

"Episcopis licet in campo confirmare.

"Presbytero in uno altari duas facere missas conceditur uno die.

"Omne sacrificium sordida vetustate corruptum igne comburendum est.

"Confessio autem Deo soli ut agatur si necesse est licebit.

"Missas sæcularium mortuorum tres in anno, tertio die et nono die et xxx. die, quia surrexit Dominus 3tio die et hora nona emisit spiritum et triginta dies Moysen filii Israel planxerunt.

"Presbytero licet solo missam cantare et crucem sanctificare.

"Qui acceperit sacrificium post cibum vii. dies pœniteat.

"Qui non communicat, non accedat ad Altare usque ad osculum; et qui prius manducat ad hoc osculum non admittitur.

"Ecclesiam licet ponere in alium locum, si necesse est, et non debet iterum sanctificari, tantum presbyter aqua spargere debet et in loco altaris crux debet componi.

"Ligna Ecclesiæ non debent ad aliud opus jungi nisi ad Ecclesiam aliam, vel igni comburantur; vel ad profectum in monasterium fratribus, coquere cum eis panem licet, sed talia in laicali opera non debent procedere.

"Presbyter si responsoria cantat in missa vel quacumque, cappam suam non tollet sed Evangelium legens super humeros ponat.

"Benedicens infantem vice baptismi annum extra numerum pœnitentiæ suæ cum pane et aqua expleat."

Thus terminates the Penitential of St. Cummian. These concluding canons attest that the kiss of peace was given in the early Irish Church during the holy Sacrifice, but only to those who intended to communicate. We also learn from them that the *cappa*, or hood, was a part of the ecclesiastical dress, and was worn on the head during the minor parts of the Mass: during the Gospel, however, the priest let it fall back on his shoulders.

B.—Penitential of St. Finnian.

We have already remarked, that St. Finnian of Maghbile was rendered illustrious in our early Church by certain penitential decrees which he enacted, based on the discipline of the Roman Church, and which were commonly styled "the Canons of St. Finnian." These *canons* were happily discovered by the learned German editor, Dr. Wasserschleben, and published in his Bussordnungen, etc. The only other writer in modern times that seems to have been acquainted with this penitential code was Mabillon, who makes incidental reference to it in his Analecta.* It is, nevertheless, preserved in the St. Gall MS. (No. 150) of the ninth century; also in a Viennese MS. of the ninth century;† and in part in the St. Germain MS. written before the year 800 (No. 121), and in another Parisian codex of the eleventh or twelfth century (No. 3182).

One of its canons is expressly cited in the Collectio Hibernensis, made about the year 700; it is the twenty-fifth canon in the printed penitential, and is quoted with the heading, *Finnian enacts* etc.‡ Almost the whole of St. Finnian's canons were introduced into the Penitential of St. Columbanus; and the authentic Penitential of Ven. Bede§ gives six canons from the work of our saint. We have also just now seen that St. Cummian composed his penitential "juxta seniorum traditionem;" and one of these spiritual masters was certainly St. Finnian, many of whose canons are adopted by that great ornament of our Church in the seventh century. It was also used by Egbert of York, and other penitential compilers of the eighth century.

In the conclusion of his work, St. Finnian acquaints us with the motives which induced him to compile this penitential code:—

"Hæc, amantissimi Fratres, secundum sententiam scripturarum vel opinionem quorundam doctissimorum, pauca de pœnitentiæ remediis vestro amore compulsus supra possibilitatem meam, potestatemque temptavi scribere: sunt præterea alia vel de remediis, aut de varietate curandorum

---

* Paris, 1723, p. 17. † Codex Th.; Latin, 725.
‡ Collect. Hib. xxviii. 7. § Ap. Wasserschleben.

testimonia, quæ nunc brevitatis causa, vel situs loci, aut penuria ingenii non sinit nos ponere, sed si quis divinæ lectionis scrutatus ipse magis inveniat aut si proferet meliora vel scripserit, et nos consentimus, et sequemur."

To which words is added by the scribe in the ancient text:

"Finit istud opusculum quod coaptavit Finnianus suis visceralibus filiis dilectionis vel religionis obtentu de scripturarum venis redundans ut ab omnibus omnia deleantur hominibus facinora."

This Penitential is not divided into chapters; neither does it present that clear methodical arrangement that characterizes the penitentials of the age of Cummian and Theodore. His canons are only fifty-three in number, and we now present a few of them, which may suffice to convey some idea to the reader of the wisdom that guided the author of the penitential code of the monastery of Moville in the sixth century:—

Can. 5. "Si quis rixam faciat de clericis aut ministris Dei, hebdomadam dierum pœniteat cum pane et aqua et petat veniam a Deo suo et proximo suo plena confessione et humilitate, et sic potest Deo reconciliari et proximo suo."

Can. 6. "Si quis ad scandalum surrexerit et disposuit in corde suo proximum suum percutere aut occidere, si clericus fuerit dimidium annum pœniteat cum pane et aqua per mensuram et annum totum abstineat se a vino et a carnibus et sic altario reconcilietur."

Can. 7. "Si autem laicus fuerit, hebdomadam dierum pœniteat quia homo sæculi hujus est et culpa levior in hoc mundo et præmium minus in futuro."

Can. 8. "Si autem clericus fuerit et percusserit fratrem suum aut proximum aut sanguinem effuderit, unum est ut occiderit eum, sed non eadem pœnitentia, annum integrum pœniteat cum pane et aqua et sine ministerio clericatus et orare pro se debet cum fletu et lachrymis ut misericordiam a Deo consequatur, quia dicit scriptura: qui odit fratrem suum, homicida est, quanto magis, qui percutit."

Can. 22. "Si quis juraverit juramentum falsum, magnum est crimen aut vix aut non potest redimi: sed tamen melius est pœnitere et non desperare, magna est enim misericordia Dei. Pœnitentia ejus hæc est: imprimis numquam in vita sua jurare debet, quoniam vir multum jurans non justificabitur et plaga de domo ejus non discedet, sed in præsentia celeri medicina pœnitentiæ prævenire oportet pœnas perpetuas in futuro, et agere pœnitentiam septem annorum et de reliquo vitæ suæ bene facere et non jurare et ancillam sive servum liberare sive prætium ejus pauperibus aut egentibus dare."

Can. 23. "Si quis clericus homicidium fecerit et occiderit proximum suum et mortuus fuerit, decem annis extorrem fieri oportet et agat pœnitentiam vii. annorum in alio orbe (perhaps *urbe*) et tribus quadragesimis jejunet cum pane et aqua per mensuram et iii. abstineat se a vino et a carnibus et sic impletis x. annis si bene egerit et comprobatus fuerit testimonio Abbatis seu sacerdotis cui commissus fuerat, recipiatur in patria sua et satisfaciat amicis ejus quem occiderat et vicem pietatis et obedientiæ reddat patri aut matri ejus si adhuc in corpore sunt et dicat: Ecce ego pro filio vestro quæcumque dixeritis mihi faciam. Si autem non satis egerit, non recipiatur in æternum."

Can. 29. "Si quis clericus iracundus aut invidus aut detractans aut tristis aut cupidus, magna sunt peccata hæc et capitalia et occidunt animam et demergunt in profundum inferni; sed pœnitentia eorum hæc est, donec evellantur et eradicentur de cordibus nostris per auxilium Domini et per studium et exercitium nostrum petimus Domini misericordiam et de his victoriam et tamdiu in pœnitentia constituti in fletu et lachrymis die ac nocte quamdiu versantur hæc in corde nostro sed e contrariis ut diximus festinemus curare contraria et vitia mundemus de corde nostro et virtutes insinuemus pro illis; et patientia pro iracundia, mansuetudo vel dilectio Dei et proximi pro invidia, pro detractione continentia cordis et linguæ, pro tristitia gaudium spiritale, pro cupiditate largitas nasci debet, dicit enim scriptura: ira viri justitiam Dei non operatur, et invidia lepra esse in lege judicatur. Detractio anathema in scripturis dicitur; qui detrahit proximo suo eradicabitur, scilicet de terra viventium: Tristitia comedit vel consumit animam: Cupiditas radix omnium malorum est, sicut ait Apostolus."

Can. 31. "Captivis redimendis communicandum esse præcipimus et exhortamur ecclesiastico dogmate, egenis et pauperibus fœnerandum."

Can. 33 "Basilicis sanctorum est ministrandum facultatibus nostris et omnibus qui sunt in necessitatibus constituti compatiendum et peregrini in domibus nostris suscipiendi sunt sicut scriptum est a Domino: infirmi sunt visitandi; et in vinculis constitutis ministrandum est et omnia Christi mandata a majoribus usque ad minora implenda sunt."

Can. 34. "Si quis in ultimo spiritu constitutus vel si qua sit licet peccator vel peccatrix fuerit et exposcerit communionem, Christi nomen non negandum ei esse dicimus, si promiserit votum suum et bene agat et recipiatur ab eo, si conversus fuerit, in hunc mundum impleat, quod Deo voverit. Si autem non impleat quod voverit Deo, in caput suum erit, et nos quod debemus non negamus ei: non est cessandum eripere prædam ex ore leonis vel draconis, i. e. de ore diaboli qui prædam nostræ animæ deripere non desinit; hinc in fine extremo vitæ hominis adsectandum et uitendum.

Can. 35. "De laicis si quis ex malis actibus suis conversus fuerit ad Dominum et ab omni malo quod antea egerit, tribus annis pœniteat et inermis existat, nisi virga tantum in manu ejus," etc.

In the extracts given above from St. Cummian's Penitential, we have seen how he states that the discipline of the Irish Church, in admitting penitents to the holy communion, had been relaxed from the severity practised by their fathers; and precisely in the fifty-third canon, which concludes the penitential of St. Finnian, we find that the rigorous disciplinary law of our early apostles is expressly laid down : "Non intrandum ad altare donec pœnitentia expleatur."

C.—Penitentials of St. David and St. Gildas.

The names of SS. David and Gildas are intimately connected with the early Irish Church. Though natives of Wales, they visited the Irish schools, to learn there the science of the saints; whilst at the same time they reflected on our Church the lustre of their own virtues and holiness.

The penitentials of these saints were published by Martene in his Thesaurus Nov. Anecdot. (tom. iv.), and are reprinted, with many corrections, by Wasserschleben. They are both drawn up in the same style and order as the Penitential of St. Finnian; and, that of Gildas was more than once followed in his penitential enactments by St. Cummian Fota.

The first canon of Gildas prescribes that a priest or deacon, whilst performing the term of penance, should incessantly weep for his fault; and adds :

"Post annum et dimidium Eucharistiam sumat et ad pacem veniat, psalmos cum fratribus canat, ne penitus anima tanto tempore cœlestis medicinæ (jejuna) intereat."*

The seventeenth canon enacts :

"Qui iram corde multo tempore retinet, in morte est. Si autem confitetur peccatum quadragesimam jejunet, et si ultra in peccato persistet, duas quadragesimas : et si item fecerit, abscidatur a corpore sicut membrum putridum, quia furor homicidium nutrit."

Nineteenth canon : "Qui non occurrit ad consummationem, canat octo in ordine psalmos : si excitatus veniat post missam, quidquid cantaverunt fratres, replicet, ex ordine. Si vero ad secundam venerit, cœna careat."

Twentieth canon : "Si quis errans commutaverit aliquid de verbis

* Edit. Wasserschleben, p. 105.

sacris ubi periculum adnotatur, triduanum aut tres superpositiones faciat."

Twenty-first canon: "Si sacrum terratenus, negligendo ceciderit, cœnâ careat."

In the Penitential of St. David, we meet with the phrase, "mulier desponsata Christo;" and its concluding canon enacts, that when once guilty of a capital crime, "presbytero offerre sacrificium vel diacono tenere calicem non licet, aut in sublimiorem gradum ascendere."

D.—Penitential of St. Columbanus.

The penitential drawn up by St. Columbanus, chiefly for the use of his religious companions, is better known to the generality of readers than those penitential treatises of which we have hitherto spoken. It has more than once been printed, and in the last edition occupies from page 353 to 360 of Wasserschleben's work.

Some have supposed that this penitential belonged to an earlier period of our Church, and was only brought by Columbanus to France and Italy from the Irish monasteries. However, one of its canons, which we will just now cite, proves that it was drawn up in a country infested with the Bonosian heresy, which could be true only of Luxeu or Bobbio. That it was composed in the former monastery is rendered probable by the fact shrewdly remarked by Dr. Wasserschleben, that, forsooth, this penitential of Columbanus forms the basis of nearly all the penitentials which in after ages were used in the French Church.*

We may hence conclude that the work now before us belongs to the latter years of the sixth century. It holds a sort of intermediate place between the two great works of Finnian and Cummian, and it manifestly reveals the use of the former in its compilation; for, no fewer than twenty-three of St. Finnian's canons are adopted by Columbanus. On the other hand, St. Cummian, when compiling his penitential code, seems not to have been acquainted with the enactments of Columbanus, for there is scarcely

* Loc. cit. p. 57, seq.

a trace of similarity between their works, except when both alike adopt the code of St. Finnian. St. Columban's Penitential consists of forty-two canons; there is no division of chapters, but the canons are so arranged that the first twelve are general enactments for all: then follow twelve others, " de clericis et monachis mixtim:" thirteen others regard the laity; and the concluding five canons contain rules for the minor faults of the religious, "*de minimis monachorum sanctionibus.*"

The penitential thus begins:

" Pœnitentia vera est, pœnitenda non admittere sed admissa deflere. Sed quia hanc multorum fragilitas, ut non dicam omnium, rumpit, mensuræ noscendæ sunt pœnitentiæ quarum sic ordo a sanctis traditur Patribus ut juxta magnitudinem culparum etiam longitudo statuatur pœnitentiarum."

The thirteenth canon enacts :

" Si quis clericus homicidium fecerit et proximum suum occiderit decem annis exul pœniteat : post hos recipiatur in patriam si bene egerit pœnitentiam in pane et aqua, testimonio comprobatus episcopi vel sacerdotis cum quo pœniteat, et cui commissus fuit, ut satisfaciat parentibus ejus quem occidit, vicem filii reddens et dicens : quæcumque vultis faciam vobis, si autem non satisfecerit parentibus illius, numquam recipiatur in patriam sed more Cain vagus et profugus sit super terram."

The penance for a layman guilty of the same crime is assigned in the twenty-fifth canon :

" Tribus annis inermis exul in pane et aqua pœniteat et post tres annos revertatur in sua reddens vicem, parentibus occisi, pietatis et officii et sic post satisfactionem judicio sacerdotis jungatur altario."

The thirty-second canon prescribes for the crime of perjury :—

" Si per cupiditatem hoc fecerit, totas res suas vendat et donet pauperibus et convertatur ex integro ad Dominum et tondatur omni dimisso sæculo et usque ad mortem serviat Deo in monasterio. Si autem non per cupiditatem sed mortis timore hoc fecit tribus annis inermis exul pœniteat in pane et aqua et duobus adhuc abstineat se a vino et carnibus et ita animam pro se reddens, id est, servum aut ancillam de servitutis jugo absolvens et eleemosynas multas faciens per duos annos in quibus illi licito uti facile est cibis cunctis excepta carne : post septimum annum communicet."

We shall conclude our extracts with the thirty-seventh canon, which regards the *Bonosiaci* and other heretics:—

"Si quis laicus per ignorantiam cum Bonosiacis aut cæteris hæreticis communicaverit, stet inter catechumenos idest ab aliis separatus Christianis, xl. diebus et duabus aliis quadragesimis in extremo Christianorum ordine id est inter pœnitentes insanæ communionis culpam diluat. Si vero per contemptum hoc fecerit id est postquam denunciatum illi fuerit a sacerdote ac prohibitum ne se communione sinistræ partis macularet anno integro pœniteat et tribus quadragesimis; et duobus aliis annis abstineat se a vino et carnibus et ita post manus impositionem Catholici Episcopi altario jungatur."

E.—CANONS OF ADAMNAN.

The chief facts connected with St. Adamnan's life, have been collected by the learned Dr. Reeves, in the Introduction to his edition of the Life of St. Columba. At page 51 of this Introduction are commemorated some canons which were enacted by St. Adamnan, in the year 697, and which are supposed by Reeves to be the same with the eight canons published by Martene, under the title Canones Adamnani.* Tighernach expressly records that Adamnan brought with him a law from Hy to Ireland in that year; and the Ulster Annals further particularize it "Adamnanus ad Hiberniam pergit et dedit *legem innocentium populis*" (ad. an. 696). The Origines Parochiales Scotiæ,† also commemorate this law, but give it a different title: "legem morientium."

Only a few of these canons of St. Adamnan, were published by Martene: Dr. Wasserschleben, however, published them in full from two Parisian manuscripts of the eighth and eleventh centuries. They are twenty in number, and lay down rules regarding the use of the flesh of deceased animals, and other articles food defiled by them:—

Can. 1. "Marina animalia ad littora cadentia quorum mortes nescimus sumenda sunt sana fide, nisi sint putrida.

Can. 2. "Pecora de rupe cadentia si sanguis eorum effusus sit, sumenda sunt, sin vero, sed fracta sunt ossa eorum et sanguis foras non venerit, refutanda ut *morticina* essent.

---

* Thes. Nov. Anecd. iv. 18, 19. † Vol. ii. p. 288.

Can. 3. "In aquis extincta, morticina sunt, quorum sanguis intrinsecus latet.

Can. 6. "Caro suilla morticinis crassa vel pinguis, ut morticinum quo pinguescit refutanda est. . . . .

Can. 8. "Gallinæ, carnem hominis vel sanguinem ejus gustantes, multum immundæ sunt et ova earum immunda sunt, pulli tamen observandi sunt.

Can. 9. "Puteus in quo invenitur morticinum seu hominis, sive canis sive animalis cujuslibet primo evacuandus est et humus ejus quam aqua putei madefecerat foras projicienda, et mundus est, etc."

As these canons, for the most part, regard what by Adamnan and other contemporary writers was styled *morticinum*, it seems not improbable that the title, as given in the Origines Parochiales Scotiæ, is the right one; or, perhaps, more correctly this should be styled "*lex de morticinis.*"

F.—SYNODUS SAPIENTIUM.

Several penitential canons are introduced in the treatises of the eighth and ninth centuries, under the heading of "Synodus Sapientium," or again of "Canones Sapientium." Many of these were printed by Martene in the Thesaurus Novus Anecdotorum, already referred to: but they are more complete in the Parisian MS. (No. 3182) of the eleventh century, and in the St. Germain (Paris MS., No. 121) of the eighth century. They are comprised under five distinct heads.

1. The first bears the general title "Canones Hibernenses"; it comprises twenty-nine canons. The first four will give a sufficient idea of the whole:—

"Pœnitentia parricidii xiv. annis, vel semis si ignorantiæ causa, in pane et aqua et satisfactione.

"Hæc est pœnitentia homicidii, septem annis in pane et aqua agitur.

"Pœnitentia homicidii septem anni in pane et aqua vel decem ut dicit *Monochema.**

"Hæc est pœnitentia magi vel votici mali si credulus *id dem ergach* vel præconis, vel cohabitatoris vel hæretici vel adulteri, septem anni in pane et aqua."

---

* Perhaps this is *Mainchin* the *Wise*, who, as we have seen, died in 652.

Here the reference to an early Irish writer *Monochema*, and the Irish gloss of the fourth canon, are especially interesting.

2. "De Arreis" consists of twelve canons, all of which are so peculiar, and as they more than once introduce Irish phrases, we present them in full to the reader :—

"Arreum superpossitionis, centum psalmi et centum flectiones genuum vel ter quingenta et cantica septem.

"Arreum triduani nox et dies in statione sine somno nisi parvum, vel tres, quinquaginta Psalmi cum canticis, et cum Missa xii. horarum et xii. flectiones in unaquaque hora et manus sopinatæ ad orationem.

"Arreum anni, triduum cum mortuo sancto in supulchro sine cibo et potu et sine somno, sed cum vestimento circa se et cantatione Psalmorum et oratione horarum per confessionem et votum sacerdoti.

Arreum anni, triduum in Ecclesia sine cibo et potu et somno et vestitu sine sede et canticum psalmorum cum canticis et oratione horarum et in eis xii. geniculationes post confessionem peccatorum coram sacerdote et plebe post votum.

"Arreum anni xii. dies et noctes super duodecim bucellos de tribus panibus qu' efficiuntur de tertia parte *coaid seir troscho*.

"Arreum anni, xii. triduani.

"Arreum anni, mensis in dolore magno ut dubius sit de vita.

"Arreum anni quadraginta dies in pane et aqua et superpossitio in singulis hebdomadibus et xl. psalmi et flectiones lx. et horarumque (sic) oratio.

"Arreum anni quinquaginta dies in longa superpossitione et lx. psalmi et flectiones, horarum oratio.

"Arreum anni xl. dies *fordo borfiit* et superpossitiones duæ omnis hebdomadis, xl. psalmi et flecti nes et oratio omnis horæ.

"Arreum anni centum dies in pane et aqua et oratio omnis horæ.

"Hæc omnia jejunia sine carne et vino nisi parvum de herbisa in cella aliena per tempus."

3. The third division is entitled *de jectione;* and prescribes penalties for refusing hospitality. It consists of the six following canons :—

"Qui ejicit pauperem occidit cum, et sexta aut septima aut octava aut n. na pars occisionis ejus *jectio*. Item qui succurere perituro valet et non succurrit, occidit eum : primum jugulum hospitis esurientis quando ei cibus denegatur: quia non plus quam octo dies esuriens sine cibo potuque vivere potest: ideo autem octava pars occisionis de sua jectione exquiritur et aliquotiens pro dignitate jecti quinta pars accipitur.

"Si quis jecerit Episcopum et si mortuus fuerit accipiatur ab eo pretium sanguinis ejus, quinquaginta ancillas reddat, id est, septem ancillas uniuscujusque gradus :* vel quinquaginta annis pœniteat et ex his accipiuntur vii. ancillæ de jectione ejus.

"Ita et reliqui usque ad hostiarium, quantum judices prætium sanguinis uniuscujusque gradus de his vii gradibus, judicaverint, septima pars occisionis ejus de sua jectione redde ur.

"Si epus. eporum. (sic) jectus fuerit quinta pars occisionis ejus jectio, i. e. octo ancillæ et duæ partes ancillæ unius.

"Si quis de minimis sine gradu, de Ecclesiastico ordine in nomine Dei ambulantibus non susceptus fuerit in hospitio, nona pars occisionis ejus jectio.

"Quicumque excelsum principem aut scribam aut auctoritatem, aut judicem non susceperit, quamdiu judices judicaverint qui judic buut in illo tempore debitum occisionis ejus hoc est septima pars in jectione ejus accipietur."

From these canons we might conclude that the word *jectio* in the early Irish Church corresponded in part with the system of *ejection* or *eviction* of modern times.

4. *De Canibus.* This division comprises four canons, and presents many curious details connected with the daily usages of our fathers in the first century :—

"Canis catenæ (*i. e.* a chained dog) quidquid in nocte mali fecerit, non reddetur. Canis vero pecorum quodcumque mali fecerit in bovello vel in pascuis suorum pecorum, non reddetur : si autem extra fines exierit reddetur quod mali fecerit.

"Item canis quod ibet manducet, prima cu'pa nihil reddatur, nisi ille solus. Si vero secundo vel tertio iteraverit reddetur quod fecerit vel comederit.

"De his qui canem occident, qui custodit pecora vel in domo manet Prudentes dicunt : qui occidit canem qui custodit pecora, quinque vaccas reddat pro cane, et canem de genere ejus reddat et quodcumque bestiæ comedent de pecoribus usque ad caput anni.

"Item statuta Prudentium : qui canem quatuor ostiorum, id est *domus* ubi habitat dominus ejus et *caulæ* ovium, et *vitulorum* et *bovum*, occidit, decem vaccas reddat, et canem de genere ejus opera ipsius facientem restituat."

5. The fifth section is entitled *de Decimis*, and consists of eight canons. We shall have occasion in the next part to cite some of these canons : for the present the *second* will suffice, which commemorates an ancient authority of our Church :—

---

* In the early Irish Church the bishop alone was looked upon as endowed with the seven ecclesiastical orders.

"Item: omnia præter fruges terræ quibus decima semel offeretur Domino, ut dicitur; quidquid consecratum fuerit semel Deo, sanctum sanctorum erit Domino, non iterum debet de illis offerri decimam, *ut Columnanus Doctor docuit*. Frugum vero terræ in unoquoque anno decima pars offerri debet, quia in unoquoque anno nascuntur."

As regards the age of these synodical canons, they certainly date back to the seventh century. One of the MSS. which preserves a portion of them belongs to the eighth century: and they are repeatedly cited in the Irish Collection of Canons, made, as we will see, about the year 700. Two of the canons, *De Arreis*, are, moreover, cited in St. Theodore's Penitential.* On the other hand they are not cited by St. Cummian, and hence it seems probable that the "Synodus Sapientium" was held in the latter half of the seventh century, and was, perhaps, the famous ecclesiastical assembly commemorated by our annalists as held during the episcopate of Flan Febhla about the year 694, and at which forty bishops and abbots assisted.† The fact of the canons being referred to in the Penitential of St. Theodore, who died about 690, is no argument against this conjecture, as Dr. Wasserschleben has proved that that Penitential, though bearing the name of Theodore, was composed some years after the death of that saint. The ancient preface to St. Theodore's Penitential expressly remarks: "Horum (canonum) *maximam partem* fertur famine veriloquo beatæ memoriæ Eoda presbyter cognomento Christianus a ven. antistite Theodoro sciscitans accepisse."‡

G.—Irish Penitential of the Eighth Century.

The Penitential published by Martene, in Thes. Nov. Anecd. (tom. iv. page 22-30), is preserved in the Parisian MS. No. 3,182, and being anonymous, received from its former proprietor the name Pœnitentiale Bigotianum. It is published in full by Wasserschleben.§

---

* Theodori Penitent. vii. 5, edit. Wasserschleb. page 191.
† See Reeves' Adamnan, p. 178, and Colgan, in Trias Thaumat. p. 503, *a*.
‡ Ap. Wasserschl. loc. cit. page 182, seqq.
§ Loc. cit page 441-60.

It is almost wholly taken from SS. Cummian, Finnian, and Theodore. We conclude that its origin must be referred to Ireland rather than to the sister island, from the fact of its canons in chap. i. sections 5 and 6, being styled *canones sapientium* and *canones Patrum*, whilst they are taken from the Synodus Sapientium of which we have just spoken. Again, in chap. iv. sec. 6, a series of decrees *de clamore*, are styled *canones Patrum*, and are all derived from Irish sources.

We refer it to the eighth century, as it shows no trace of the Penitentials of Ven. Bede and Egbert, and other disciplinary codes, which became so general after the middle of that century.

A few extracts from its preliminary discourse will, for the present, suffice to give some idea of this treatise:—

"Hieronymus vir beatæ memoriæ Ecclesiæ Pastores et doctores ut qualitates vitiorum in peccantibus animadvertant diligenter, admonuit dicens; tanto major fiat potentia medici quanto magis crevit morbus ægroti. . . . . Cor contritum et humiliatum Deus non spernit: et hoc sapientibus in pœnitentia moderanda intuendum est, ne dignum scelus gladio ferulâ vindicent, et dignum peccatum ferulâ gladio percutiant. Et secundum Gregorium magnopere Pastoribus procurandum ne incaute alligaverint, quod non alligandum est, et non solverint quod solvendum. His itaque de pœnitentia expressis, fateor, quod si in hoc pœnitentiæ temperamento plus minusve ante oculos creatoris videatur, non nostræ audaciæ culpa est; majorum enim decreta non nostra exposuimus. . . . . De remediis variis vulnerum prout antiquorum auctorum approbatio tulit, compendiosas carptim caraxamus eglotas. . . . . Sicut sementibus, naturam certis legibus creator, ita et omnibus secundum virtutum seu qualitatum discrepantiam indulgebit secundum illud Prophetæ: non enim in serris triturabitur neque rota plaustri super cuminum circumiet," etc.

APPENDIX No. IV.

MISSAL OF ST. COLUMBANUS.

First published by Mabillon.—Dr. O'Conor and Dr. Lanigan prove that it contains the Irish Liturgy.—Dr. Todd holds the contrary opinion.—His opinion refuted.—Proof that the Missal is Irish.—Agrees with the Stowe Missal.—Extracts from it.

MABILLON was the first to publish a very ancient Missal which, for centuries, had been preserved in the famous monastery of Bobbio, and thence passed to the Ambrosian Library of Milan. Writing in 1724, the learned Benedictine judged the manuscript from which this Missal was published to be more than one thousand years old: " Scriptus est codex ante annos mille."*

The question was at once raised, to what liturgy should this newly-discovered text be referred; and Mabillon found it no easy matter to give a satisfactory reply. He proved, indeed, that it was not the liturgy of Rome, nor the Ambrosian liturgy, nor the Mozarabic, nor the liturgy of the African Church; and his conclusion was a natural one, that, forsooth, it was " a Missal of the Gallican rite," for he was ignorant of the existence of any other liturgy to which it could be referred. Whilst, however, he thus asserted the claim of the Gallican Church to the old manuscript of Bobbio, he candidly acknowledged that in many important points it was entirely at variance with every text known to represent the Gallican liturgy. This was an important concession from such a writer as Mabillon, and even prescinding from other arguments, any one acquainted with the liturgical tract published in our second appendix, would be tempted to conclude that, perhaps, the Bobbio Missal did not present the true Gallican liturgy, but one which had a certain affinity with it, and which, though little known on the continent, was well known to our fathers as *the Irish liturgy*, or "Cursus Scottorum."

---

* Museum Italicum, vol. i. p. 275.

The Rev. Charles O'Conor, and after him Dr. Lanigan, entered into a minute examination of this Missal, and they unhesitatingly concluded that it was a fragment of our scattered literature, preserving to us an ancient text of the liturgy as used by the first fathers of our Church. Their learning and research seemed to set the matter at rest for ever; but Dr. Todd, in 1856, when treating of the Stowe Missal, entered into a lengthened discussion to prove that such a conclusion was grounded on erroneous or insufficient data; nay, more, that there was not "*the slightest reason*" for questioning the decision of Mabillon, and, hence, that the Bobbio MS. belonged to the Gallican liturgy.*

To proceed with order in our inquiry as to the genuine origin of this remarkable Missal, we shall first propose the general arguments which identify it with the Irish liturgy; secondly, we shall examine the "Penitential" which is appended to it; thirdly, to the reasoning of Dr. Todd we shall devote a few remarks; and, fourthly, in fine, we shall present a brief analysis of the Missal itself.

A.—The Bobbio Missal presents an Irish Liturgy.

Dr. O'Conor, who was a competent judge of Irish manuscripts, pronounced the MS. from which Mabillon printed his text, to belong to the Irish school.† Before him, the Benedictine editors of the great work "Nouveau Traité de Diplomatique"‡ had pronounced the same opinion; "its writing," they say, "is that of the British islands before the conversion of the Angles;" and, they add, "Mabillon was of opinion that it was brought by Columbanus from Luxeu to Bobbio; we may, with the same certainty, affirm that it was brought by the saint from his native Britain to France." We cannot be surprised at Ireland being comprised in

---

* See the paper of James Henthorn Todd, D.D., read before the Royal Irish Academy, June 23, 1856, entitled: On the Ancient Irish Missal and its Silver Box, etc., p. 29.

† Dr. Todd, who is also well versed in our ancient manuscripts, asserts, on the contrary, "that the writing does not belong to the Scotic or Irish school" (p. 26); his opinion is grounded on the wood-cut imitation of one sentence of the original, which Mabillon gives at p. 276. However, Mabillon does not profess to give a *fac-simile*; but merely to let the reader understand that the text was written in uncial letters—litteris majusculis. ‡ Paris, 1752.

the generic name of Britain, nor at the writing being styled that of the early Anglo-Saxon school; for, as Reeves has justly remarked, such is the common continental name for all the ancient monuments of Ireland.*

Zeuss and Mone, some years ago, called the attention of the learned to the important fact, that a characteristic orthography marked all the ancient Latin MSS. that came from the Irish school;† and Reeves, in his magnificent edition of Adamnan's Life of Columbkille, placed beyond all doubt this distinctive feature of our Irish writers.‡ Now, in the missal preserved to us in the archives of Bobbio, we meet at every page with examples of the distinctive characteristics thus assigned to the Latin monuments of our early Church. We give a few examples from the very first Mass that occurs, occupying from 278 to 282 in Mabillon's work. Thus, *stilla* for *stella*, *Cornili* for *Cornelii*, *discipolis* for *discipulis*, *optulit* for *obtulit*, *Eogenia* for *Eugenia*, *saciasti* for *satiasti*, *postolamus* for *postulamus*, *precium* for *prætium*, *malibolis* for *malevolis*, *homenibus* for *hominibus*, *volumtas* for *voluntas*, *ampotes* for *amputes*, *famolatus* and *famolus* for *famulatus*, etc.; *inpetrare* for *impetrare*, *exorcidio* for *exorcizo*, *de inferna* for *de inferno*, *oportuna* for *opportuna*. Mabillon, moreover, remarks that continually the *b* is exchanged for *v*, as *baptizavit* for *baptizabit*, *acervis* for *acerbis*, *sivilantes* for *sibilantes*, etc.§ In like manner, we frequently find *Josep* for *Joseph*, *exsecuntur* for *exsequuntur*, *expectacolum* for *spectaculum*, etc. These few examples embrace almost all the special rules which are laid down for determining the ancient Latin manuscripts of Ireland; and hence we may safely conclude that the missal of which we treat came from the schools of our early Church.

Though there are but scanty records to illustrate the ancient liturgy of the Irish Church, still the few incidental facts which we

* Reeves On Early Irish Caligraphy, in Ulster Journal of Archæology, July, 1860.
† See especially the Grammatico Celtica of J. C. Zeuss, Leipzic, 1853, præf. xxi. in nota, where a long list of examples is given.
‡ See Adamnan's Columba, printed for I.A.S., Dublin, 1857, præf. pp. 16-19.
§ Page 285 not. and also page 319.

glean from the acts of our first saints, and from the Stowe Missal, so ably illustrated by Dr. Todd, afford sufficient evidence for determining that the Missal of Bobbio belongs to our liturgy.

In Adamnan's Life of St. Columbkille, mention is made of his having recited the name of St. Martin in the Communicantes:

"When that prayer was being chanted, in which the name of St. Martin is commemorated, and when the chanters had arrived at that name, St. Columba said to them: To-day another holy bishop is to be named," etc.*

The Roman liturgy terminated its list of commemorations with the names of SS. Cosmas and Damian; the Irish, through reverence for the holy bishop of Tours, adopted his name from the Gallican liturgy; and not only was it recited by St. Columba, but it is also still found in the ancient portion of the Stowe Missal. In the Bobbio Missal, the name of St. Martin forms part of the Communicantes;† and we may add, that with it, after SS. Cosmas and Damian, are united the names of SS. Augustine, Hilary, Gregory, and Jerome, which are *also added in the Stowe Missal;* but for which, with the exception of St. Hilary, we shall seek in vain in the Gallican liturgy.‡

The history of the monks of St. Columbanus presents another interesting fact, illustrative of the same subject. The monastery of Luxeu continued, after the departure of our saint, and in opposition to some of the French clergy, to observe the rites and customs of the Irish Church, and even its peculiar tonsure from ear to ear. In 623, a synod was held at Matiscon, to examine into these peculiarities of the monks of Columbanus. Agrestius appeared as their accuser, whilst Eustasius, who describes himself as "the disciple and successor" of the founder of Luxeu, undertook their defence. One of the accusations urged by Agrestius was precisely regarding their liturgy:

"Quod a cæterorum ritu ac norma desciscerent, et sacra missarum solemnia orationum ac collectarum multiplici varietate celebrarent."§

---

* Reeves' Adamnan, p. 211.   † Ap. Mabillon, p 281.
‡ See Mabillon's work, De Liturgia Gallicana, lib. 1. cap. 5, p. 43.
§ Annales Benedict. by Mabillon, vol. i. p. 320.

To this Eustasius replied, acknowledging that such was the Irish practice, but contending that this multiplicity of prayers should be rather a subject of eulogy than of censure:

"Orationum multiplicationem in sacris officiis multum prodesse quis neget. Cum nihil cuivis Christiano et maxime pœnitentibus salubrius sit quam Deum multiplicatione precum et orationum assiduitate pulsare."*

In conformity with this special feature of the Irish liturgy, the Stowe Missal, as O'Conor and Dr. Todd remark, has in its *Missa Cotidiana* a variety of prayers after the *Gloria in excelsis*, and not merely one, as was usual in the Roman and Gallican liturgy. Now, this same characteristic marks the Bobbio Missal; and in its *missa cotidiana* no fewer than five prayers are assigned to be recited after the *Gloria in excelsis*.

To any one that reflects on the origin of the Irish liturgy, as described in the ancient liturgical tract which we published in our second appendix, it will seem most natural that a close affinity should subsist between the liturgies of Ireland and Gaul. It was through SS. Germanus and Lupus that the "Cursus Scottorum" was communicated to St. Patrick. They were bishops of important sees in France, and were chosen by the assembled bishops of the French Church as their representatives in the cause of Pelagianism. Their liturgy, therefore, must be supposed closely allied with that followed by their Gaulish brethren. On the other hand, the same bishops, as we have seen, were closely connected with Rome; St. Patrick, too, and his first associates, Auxilius, Secundinus, Augustinus, and Iserninus, were in great part identified with that central see of the Catholic Church. Now, the liturgy of Bobbio is precisely such as we should expect to arise from this combination of Gaul and Rome—retaining the chief prayers and the *canon* of Rome, and adopting from the Gallican liturgy all that it had most beautiful in its outward arrangement of the sacred festivals. Independent of every other argument, this was a stumbling-block to the defenders of Mabillon's opinion. Although the Missal of

---

* Annales Benedict. by Mabillon, vol. i. p. 320.

Bobbio had many parts fully agreeing with the Gallican liturgy, yet how could the *canon of the Mass* which it presents be that not of France, but of Rome? This one fact is of itself conclusive against the claim of the French Church to the Bobbio Missal. We have still preserved to us many monuments of the French liturgy of the same age, but not one of them that does not present the French peculiarities of the canon of the Mass; on the contrary, in the missal of which we speak there is not, in the canon of the Mass, even one of these Gallican peculiar features; and with the exception of some verbal differences (such as are often found in different missals of the Roman liturgy), it perfectly and fully coincides with the canon of the Mass as used in the Roman Church. The researches of O'Conor and Todd regarding the Stowe Missal enable us to give additional force to this argument. The greater part of its *canon*, too, corresponds accurately with the Roman canon; and in one of the peculiar verbal differences which it presents, we find precisely the same peculiarity in the Bobbio Missal: it is in the beginning of the Memento:

STOWE MISSAL.	BOBBIO MISSAL.
"Memento etiam Domine *et eorum nomina*, qui nos præcesserunt cum signo fidei et dormiunt in somno pacis."	"Memento etiam Domine et *eorum nomina* qui nos præcesserunt cum signo fidei et dormiunt in somno pacis."*

Indeed the coincidence of the Bobbio Missal with that of Stowe is so frequent and so striking, that it supplies a clear solution for the question which we are examining. The Bobbio Missal gives in the end the *Ordo Baptismi*, and the same is added in the Stowe manuscript: Mabillon styles the Bobbio Missal a *sacramentarium*, rather than a mere liturgy, and this same title is given to the Stowe Missal by Dr. Todd.†

The Bobbio *Missa Cotidiana*, is so different from any monument of the Gallican liturgy, that Mabillon was compelled to assign the part which follows it as the commencement of the Gallican rite: "*ab hoc maxime loco*," he writes in his note to the second Mass,

---

* Todd, loc. cit. p. 33; Mabillon, p. 281. † Page 29.

"*ab hoc maxime loco incipit Missale Gallicanum nam quæ præcedunt fere ex ordine Romano desumpta sunt.*"* Now, whilst this every-day Mass, with its Roman Ordo, is thus repugnant to the Gallican liturgy, the Stowe Missal gives us precisely an every-day Mass, and it, too, closely copied from the Roman *Ordo*.

The *Collect* of this *Missa Cotidiana* is the beautiful prayer still used in the Roman liturgy, beginning "Deus qui culpa offenderis, pœnitentia placaris," etc., and this same prayer, as we learn from Dr. Todd, is a *collect* in the Stowe Missal.† Another prayer referred to in the Stowe Missal is that of St. Gregory's Sacramentary: "Quæsumus omnipotens Deus, ne nos tua misericordia derelinquat quæ et errores nostros semper amoveat et noxia cuncta depellat."‡ And although this prayer is unknown in the ancient Gallican liturgy, it precisely is found with many others of the prayers of the same sacramentary, holding its place in the Bobbio manuscript.§

The Stowe text of the Nicene Creed is somewhat peculiar, and omits the celebrated formula *filioque*. Dr. O'Conor gives a fac-simile of this portion of its creed, which runs as follows:—

"Et in spiritum sanctum, dominum et vivificatorem ex Patre procedentem, cum patre et filio coadorandum, et conglorificandum."

The Bobbio Missal, expressly indeed, does not recite the Nicene Creed, but only that styled "the Apostles' Creed," in which this passage does not occur, but on two occasions, the formula of the former symbol regarding the Holy Ghost is introduced, and in such a way (as Mabillon remarks) as sufficiently proves that it, too, wanted that celebrated addition. Thus, at p. 376, the doctrine of the Blessed Trinity is fully explained, and of the Holy Ghost it is said: "Spiritus sanctus unus est ex Patre procedens, Patri et Filio coæternus;" and the same expression is used at p. 313, where the priest expounds the doctrines of faith to the catechumens.

Whilst speaking of the Creed, there is a peculiar formula added, in the interrogatories which are addressed to the catechumen, in

---

* Page 283. † Loc. cit. p. 20.
‡ Ibid. p. 23. § Ap. Mabillon, p. 382.

the Bobbio Missal. After reciting the various formulas of the Apostles' Creed in the preceding interrogatories, the concluding interrogatory is thus made:—

"Credit in spiritum sanctum, sanctam Ecclesiam Catholicam, sanctorum communionem, remissionem peccatorum, carnis resurrectionem vitam habere post mortem, in gloriam Christi resurgere?"[*]

Now it is remarkable that this most peculiar addition is, in part at least, found in the formula of faith preserved to us in the Antiphonary of Bangor. This ancient Irish monument presents a profession of faith "which, as it is founded on the Baptismal Creed, was probably used for the instruction of catechumens, not recited or chanted in the Mass."[†] Immediately after the formulas "Sanctorum communionem, carnis resurrectionem," is added the following concluding passage: "Credo vitam post mortem, et vitam æternam in gloria Christi. Hæc omnia credo in Deum. Amen."

Whilst these arguments render it manifest that the Bobbio Missal belongs to the Irish Liturgical School, there are many other arguments which should refute its Gallican origin. Thus in the Gallican liturgy there were numbered ten fruits of the Holy Ghost, whilst in the Bobbio text only nine are reckoned in conformity with the Greek liturgy.[‡] In the Gallican Church, the Feast of St. Eugenia, the illustrious Roman virgin and martyr, is nowhere alluded to, and as far as Mabillon could discover, no where celebrated;[§] on the contrary, in the Bobbio canon of the Mass, her name is added to the other virgin-saints, Agatha, Lucy, etc.; and again in the Mass on the vigil of Christmas, we have a special commemoration of St. Eugenia, the 25th of December being the day of her martyrdom. The fact of a special devotion to this holy martyr was a puzzle to the learned French liturgical writer; the Irish pilgrims, however, brought her veneration with them from Rome, and none can be more diffuse in her praise than St. Aldhelm who had studied under Irish monks in the monastery of Malmesbury,

---

[*] Ibid. p.324. [†] Todd, loc. cit. p. 26.
[‡] Ap. Mabillon, loc cit. p. 365. [§] Ib. 277.

and who, in his Eulogy of Virginity, presents St. Eugenia as a model of Christian heroism.* Other points of difference between the Bobbio text and the Gallican rite, will be found indicated at almost every page in the notes of Mabillon.

There is another argument, the grounds of which we shall just now more fully explain. At the end of the Bobbio Missal is added a *Penitential*, which is a fact unique as regards the Gallican liturgy. This Penitential, too, is an *Irish Penitential;* and thus the Missal of St. Columbanus once more proclaims its Irish origin. Another tract appended to it, assigns the division of the "Cursus Ecclesiasticus," by which name, too, the Irish treatise, published in the second appendix, designates the sacred liturgy. In fine, even the *benedictiones variæ*, which the Bobbio Missal adds in the end, sufficiently reveal the Irish source from which they proceed. One of them is entitled "Benedictio ubi aliquid immundum ceciderit in vas," and prays that the blessing of God may purify the vessel that was contaminated, and also the wine, oil, honey, or water, which it contained. Now, it is one of the peculiar canons of our Irish Penitentials, that declares such articles of food to be contaminated, "si aliquid immundum ceciderit in vas," and prescribes that they should be purified by blessing before being used by the faithful.

B.—The Penitential of the Bobbio Missal.

It is only since the publication of the various Western penitentials, by the learned professor of Halle, that a judgment could be pronounced with certainty as to the penitential which is added to the Bobbio Missal. A comparison of it with the other Irish penitentials must now, however, convince every unprejudiced mind that it is a monument of our Irish Church, bringing us back, also, to the earliest period of its history.

This Bobbio Penitential consists of forty-seven canons, without any division of chapters, or any trace of that methodical arrange-

---

* See Aldhelm, De Virginitate: in Thesaur. Monument. Canisii, edited by Basnage, vol. 1. p. 475.

ment which characterizes the age of SS. Cummian and Theodore. In this respect it is almost identical with the Penitential of St. Finnian of Maghbile. Of its forty-seven canons there is not one that is not purely Irish; and it may be affirmed, without fear of contradiction, that it was used by our great saints, Columbanus and Cummian, when compiling their penitentials. Compare, for instance, its three first canons with the three first decrees of the second division of Columbanus:

BOBBIO PENITENTIAL.	ST. COLUMBAN'S PENITENTIAL.
"Si quis clericus homicidium fecerit et proximum suum occiderit, decem annos exul pœniteat. Post hos recipiatur in patriam, etc.	"Si quis clericus homicidium fecerit et proximum suum occiderit decem annis exul pœniteat. Post hos recipiatur in patriam, etc.
"Si quis ruina maxima ceciderit et filium genuerit, septem annis pœniteat.	"Si quis ruina maxima ceciderit et filium genuerit, septem annis peregrinus in pane et aqua pœniteat.
"Si quis autem fornicaverit sicut Sodomitæ fecerunt, decem annos pœniteat, tres in pane et aqua," etc.	"Si quis autem fornicaverit sicut Sodomitæ fecerunt, decem annis pœniteat tribus primis cum pane et aqua," etc.

A similar identity runs through many of its subsequent decrees; thus, its sixth canon:

BOBBIO.	COLUMBANUS.
"Si quis perjuraverit septem annos pœniteat tres in pane et aqua et numquam juret postea."	"Si quis perjuraverit septem annis pœniteat et numquam juret postea."

Again, its twenty-fourth canon:

BOBBIO.	COLUMBANUS.
"Si quis clericus proximum suum percusserit, et sanguinem fuderit, uno pœniteat anno."	"Si quis clericus per rixam proximum suum percusserit, et sanguinem fuderit, annum integrum pœniteat."

St. Cummian, in his Penitential, adopts, in like manner, about thirty of the canons of our Bobbio text; one or two instances will suffice:

BOBBIO.

IV. "Si quis homicidium casu fecerit non volens, quinque annos pœniteat, tres in pane et aqua."

XXI. "Si quis usuras undecumque exegerit tres annos pœniteat, unum in pane et aqua."

XXIII. "Si quis sacrilegium fecerit, quod aruspices vocant, si per aves aut aguria colunt vel ad divinationes eorum vadunt, quinque annos pœniteat, tres in pane et aqua."

XXV. "Si quis malo ordine cupidus, aut avarus aut superbus, aut ebriosus, aut fratrem suum odio habuerit tres annos pœniteat."

XXVI. "Si quis sortes sanctorum contra rationem invocat, vel alias sortes habuerit, tres annos pœniteat, unum in pane et aqua."

XXVII. "Si quis ad arbores vel ad fontes aut cancellos vel ubicumque nisi in ecclesia, votum voverit, aut solverit, tres annos pœniteat unum in pane et aqua, quia hoc sacrilegium est: et qui ibidem comederit aut biberit, unum annum pœniteat."

CUMMIANUS.

"Si quis homicidium casu fecerit non volens quinque annos pœniteat, tres ex his in pane et aqua."*

"Si quis usuras undecumque exegerit, tres annos pœniteat, unum ex his in pane et aqua."†

"Si quis sacrilegium fecerit, id est, quod aruspices vocant qui auguria colunt per aves aut quocumque auguriaveriat, iii. annos pœniteat, i. ex his in pane et aqua."‡

"Si quis cupidus aut avarus aut superbus aut ebriosus aut fratrem suum hodio habuit, vel alia his similia quœ dimumerare longum est tres annos pœniteat," etc.§

"Si quis, ut vocant, sortes sanctorum, quas contra rationem vocant, vel alias sortes habuerit, vel qualicumque ingenio sortitus fuerit iii. annis pœniteat, i. ex his in pane et aqua."∥

"Si quis ad arbores vel ad fontes aut ad angulos vel ubicumque nisi ad ecclesiam Dei vota voverit aut solverit, tres annos pœniteat, unum ex his in pane et aqua: et qui ibidem ederit aut biberit unum annum pœniteat."¶

It is not, however, this agreement alone with SS. Columban and Cummian that proves the Irish origin of the Bobbio Penitential. The very words which are used, and its forms of expression, as, for instance, "*exsol pœniteat;*" "*si ruina maxima ceciderit,*" etc., are peculiar to the Irish Penitentials. Some of its canons, too, are those which are found only in the Irish documents. Compare the following as given in our Bobbio text and in the Penitential of St. Cummian:—

---

* Cum. Pœnit. vi. 13.   † Ibid. viii. 1.   ‡ Ibid. vii. 3.
§ Ibid. viii. 6.   ∥ Ibid. vii. 4.   ¶ Ibid. vii. 6.

MISSAL OF ST. COLUMBANUS.

BOBBIO.	CUMMIAN.
XII. "Si quis clericus vel superioris gradus qui uxorem habuit et post honorem iterum eam cognoverit, sciat se adulterium commisisse."	"Si clericus vel superioris gradus qui uxorem habuit et post confessionem vel honorem clericatus iterum eam cognoverit sciat sibi adulterium commisisse."†
XXXI. "Si quis kalendas Januarias in cervolo vel vicola vadit tres annos pœniteat."*	"Si quis kalendis Januarii aut in vecola aut in cervolo vadit, tribus annis pœniteat, quia hoc dæmonum est."‡
XXXII. "Si quis mulier avorsum fecerit voluntarie, tres annos pœniteat, unum in pane et aqua."	"Si mulier abortum fecerit voluntarie, tres annos pœniteat in pane et aqua."§
XIX. "Si quis maleficus immissor tempestatis (fuerit) septem annos pœniteat."	"Si quis emissor tempestatum fuerit, septem annos pœniteat tres ex his in pane et aqua."‖
XXXIII. "Si quis per invocationem dæmonum hominum mentes tulerit quinque annos pœniteat."	"Si quis matimaticus fuerit et per invocationem dæmonum mentes tulerit, quinque annos pœniteat," etc. ¶
XXXV. "Si quis dilaturas fecerit, quod detestabile est tres annos pœniteat, unum in pane et aqua."	"Si quis dilaturas fecerit, quod detestabile est, tres annos pœniteat, in pane et aqua."**
XXXVI. "Si quis servum vel qualemcumque hominem in captivitatem duxerit, tres annos pœniteat unum in pane et aqua."	"Si quis servum aut quemcumque hominem quolibet ingenio in captivitatem duxerit aut transmiserit, tres annos pœniteat," etc.††
XXXVII. "Si quis domum vel aream cujuscumque igne cremaverit tres annos pœniteat, unum in p. et a."	"Si quis domum vel aream cujuscumque igne concremaverit, tres annos pœniteat, unum in pane et aqua."‡‡

All the canons regarding the blessed Eucharist should be also cited: their parallel is only to be found in the various Irish Penitentials, and even their phrases "*si titubaverit sacerdos in oratione Dominica*," "*qui communicaverit inconscius*," etc., are found only in the documents connected with our early Church.

C.—Dr. Todd's Remarks.

We have more than once referred to an interesting paper of Dr.

---

* The word *vicola* was unknown to Mabillon. Now it not only occurs in Cummian's Penitential but also in Adamnan's Vita S. Columbæ, edit. Reeves, pages 64 and 114.

† Ibid. iii. 2.   ‡ Ibid. vii. 9.   § Ibid. vi. 21.   ‖ Ibid. vii. 8.
¶ Ibid. vii. 7.   ** Ibid. xi. 17.   †† Ibid. iv. 9.   ‡‡ Ibid. iv. 13.

Todd, read before the Royal Irish Academy in 1856, in which much valuable information is given regarding the Stowe Missal. Incidentally, however, he enters into an examination of the Bobbio manuscript, and candidly asserts: "I cannot subscribe to Dr. O'Conor's opinion, that the Sacramentarium of Bobbio, published by Mabillon, was an Irish MS."*

The only argument which he advances to support this opinion is one apparently of some weight, but in reality of no importance whatever. "The entire absence of any allusion to the name of an Irish saint, ought at once to decide the question: compare it in this respect with the Stowe Missal and the Antiphonary of Bangor, both of which exhibit, beyond the possibility of doubt, their Irish origin."† We shall not now make any inquiry as to the Antiphonary of Bangor, as our question only regards the *missals* of the early Irish Church. The Stowe Missal, indeed, in its *Memento*, gives the names "SS. Patrick, Ailbe, Finnian of Maghbile, Finnian of Clonard, Keiran of Saighir, Keiran of Clonmacnois, Brendan of Clonfert, Brendan of Birr, Columbkille, Columbanus, Comghill, Canice, Findbarr, Nessan, Fachtne, Lugid, Lacten, Ruadhan, Carthage, Kevin, Mochonna, Brigid, Ita, Scetha, Suinecha, and Samdine." Again, after the *Agnus Dei* is found another sort of litany, in which, to the apostles and martyrs, etc., is added a host of Irish saints, forty-six in number. These are the only places in which Irish saints are commemorated in the Stowe Missal. Now, at first sight, it seems rather strange indeed that the Irish saints should be so fully commemorated in the Stowe Missal, *undoubtedly an Irish one*, and yet not one of them should find a place in the Bobbio Missal. This difficulty occurred to Dr. Lanigan—and his reply might have been attended to by Dr. Todd: "This difficulty," he says, "can be easily removed by observing, that the respect paid by the Irish clergy to St. Patrick prevented them from adding any Mass to those contained in the missal brought by him."‡

It is, however, to Dr. Todd himself that we are indebted for a clear and irrefragable reply to the statement which he makes in

---

* Page 26.   † Ibid.   ‡ Eccl. Hist. iv. 372.

the preceding extract. This skilful antiquarian had very well remarked (at page 18 seqq.) that the Stowe Missal was written "in two different hands;" and that whilst "*the older writing is certainly not later than the sixth century, the more recent hand is probably of the tenth.*" Now, when speaking of the Irish saints who are commemorated, Dr. Todd expressly attests, that they are added by the more recent hand. He even makes this a matter of accusation against Dr. O'Conor, that he had not remarked the different date which should thus be assigned to the original missal and to the Irish Litany. Thus, in regard to the saints commemorated in the *Memento*, he writes:

"Dr. O'Conor has omitted to notice the fact that this litany is not in the original hand of the MS., but in the later hand-writing of which I have several times spoken."*

And after referring to the other saints who are mentioned in the litany after the *Agnus Dei*, he again remarks:

"Here again Dr. O'Conor omits the fact that this second enumeration of Irish worthies is also in the more recent hand, which is thus again referred to the same period as before."†

Thus, then, it results from Dr. Todd's own antiquarian researches, that in the *undoubtedly Irish missal* of Stowe, the mention of Irish saints was introduced in later times, whilst no trace of them is found in the earlier text of the sixth century. We may, therefore, conclude that the absence of Irish names from the Bobbio Missal nowise proves that it was not of Irish origin; but that it serves wonderfully to corroborate more and more the conclusion which we have deduced from other sources that, viz., it was an Irish missal, which dates from the very earliest period of our Church.

The second argument of Dr. Todd is still more amusing than the former one. In the Bobbio Missal, he says:

"No allusion occurs to Bobbio, Columbanus, or anything that could even indirectly connect it with Ireland, except that in the *Judicius Pœni-*

* Page 34. † Ibid.

tentialis, with which the volume concludes, the twenty-eighth canon seems to have been taken from the Mensura Pœnitentiarum of the Irish St. Cummian."

And then he gives, as follows, the two parallel texts of this canon:

BOBBIO.	ST. CUMMIAN.
XXVIII. "Si quis clericus postquam se Deo voverit iterum ad saeculum reversus fuerit vel uxorem duxerit duodecim annos pœniteat, sex in pane et aqua, et numquam in conjugio copuletur. Quod si noluerint, sancta sedes apostolica separavit eos a communione sanctorum: similiter et mulier postquam se Deo vovit et tale scelus admiserit, similiter faciat."	"Si clericus aut monachus postquam se Deo voverit ad saecularem habitum iterum reversus fuerit, aut uxorem duxerit, decem annis pœniteat, tribus ex his in pane et aqua et numquam postea in conjugio copuletur; quod si noluerit, sancta synodus vel sedes apostolica separavit eos a communione et convocationibus Catholicorum. Similiter et mulier, postquam secundo voverit, si tale scelus admiserit, pari sententiæ subjacebit."*

From these texts, Dr. Todd triumphantly concludes:

"This is the only contact of the Bobbio Missal *with anything Irish;* and yet, even here, we have not an identity of context."

It is painful to find the learned writer led away into so many and such palpable errors.

1. How could we expect to find mention of Bobbio and Columbanus in a missal which was probably brought by St. Columbanus himself or his companions to the hallowed retreat of Bobbio?

2. Dr. Wasserschleben's work on the Penitentials of the Western Church, was published in 1851, and how then could Dr. Todd, in 1856, assert that the Penitential of St. Cummian was the only Irish one known to the learned?†

3. We have given above many canons in which the Bobbio text perfectly coincides with the Penitential of St. Cummian: why then does Dr. Todd place as the groundwork of all his reasoning, that there was only the twenty-eighth canon in which they were sup-

---

* Chap. iii. 4. † See loc. cit. p. 27-8.

posed to agree? Dr. O'Conor had clearly stated, in general, that both texts agreed; for, when speaking of the Bobbio Penitential, he expressly says, "*in quo ipsa verba Pœnitentialium Cummeani et Columbani occurrunt.*"* Lanigan had also written "this Missal is accompanied with a Penitential, and what is exceedingly remarkable, one that agrees in very great part with that of St. Columbanus, and in some points with the Penitential of Cummian."† Is it then a fair exposition of his adversary's opinion to limit its coincidence with other Irish monuments to one mere canon, in which, too, it is supposed to agree only with the Penitential of St. Cummian?

4. After the many canons which we cited from the Bobbio Penitential, agreeing perfectly with the Penitentials of St. Columbanus and Cummian, it would be unnecessary to make any remark on the discrepancy which Dr. Todd points out between the text of St. Cummian and the twenty-eighth canon of Bobbio. However, we have here again an example of how every new discovery and careful research serves to confirm truth. Fleming, when publishing the text of St. Cummian's Penitential, had lamented that in many parts the manuscript was almost illegible, and the words well nigh effaced. This should have made the learned professor of Trinity somewhat cautious in asserting that the text of St. Cummian was in reality quite different from that of the twenty-eighth canon of Bobbio. However, what removes for ever all doubt on this head is that Dr. Wasserschleben, in his edition of 1851, restored from various MSS. the correct reading in various canons, and these corrections are invariably found to bring St. Cummian's text in closer connection with that of Bobbio. In the very canon of which we speak, the latter portion is thus given by this laborious editor:—

"Quod si noluerit, sancta synodus atque sedes Apostolica separavit eos a communione et convivio Catholicorum: similiter et mulier post quam se Deo voverit, si tale scelus admiserit, pari sententiæ subjacebit."

This corrected reading of St. Cummian's text is corroborated

* Rer. Hib. Script. 1, p. cxxxviii. † Ecc. Hist. iv. 372.

by the famous Vatican MS. (No. 1339, sæc. x.) in which this canon is cited under St. Cummian's name, and is given precisely as published by Wasserschleben.* The same ancient Vatican manuscript elsewhere affords another proof of the remark which we made just now, and of how incomplete is the present printed text of St. Cummian's Penitential. The thirty-fourth canon of Bobbio was one of the few canons that seemed not to have been adopted by St. Cummian, for no trace of it was found in Fleming's text. Now at fol. 257 of the Vatican MS. this canon is precisely quoted as a decree from the Penitential of St. Cummian: "Judicium Commeani: si quis virginem vel viduam rapuerit, v. annos cum pane et aqua pœniteat."

Thus, then, it is not merely one point of contact that the Bobbio Penitential has with the writings of St. Cummian: this contact is found in almost every one of its forty-seven canons. So much so, that we may unhesitatingly conclude that this very Penitential is to be reckoned amongst those "*Scripta Patrum*," which St. Cummian describes as the source of the Penitential code which he enacted. And yet, as we have seen, the work of St. Cummian is far from being the only one of our Irish monuments with which the Bobbio text has a close and undeniable affinity. It has a clear connexion with the Penitential work of Columbanus: it presents a striking affinity even with the Stowe Missal, so ably illustrated by Todd himself; and in fine, in each and all its parts it is a valuable monument of our early Church, closely allied with every fragment of our ancient liturgy that has come down to us.

D.—Extracts from the Bobbio Missal.

We may now add a few extracts from this ancient Irish Missal, that those readers who have not access to it may form some idea of the precious details regarding the faith of our fathers which it has preserved to us.

Its first Mass is the every-day Mass; then follow the special

---

* Lib. 2, chap. 116, fol. 96-b. This portion of the Vatican MS. was published as far back as 1836, by the indefatigable Prussian, F. Theiner, in his Disquisitiones Criticæ, p. 294.

Masses for Advent, and the Nativity, and subsequent festivals. On the vigil of the Nativity, we meet the following prayer:—

"Deus cujus nativitate filii tui Domini nostri gloriosa nativitas et Mariæ partum et Eogeniæ triumphum (sacravit); hodie quippe Maria Christum genuit; hodie Eogenia ad Christum vadit: hodie illa generat ad quem ista festinat; hodie Christus in mundum venit: hodie virginem in cœlo Christus suscepit: hodie nascendo virginem matrem fecit, qui hodie perficiendo martyrem coronavit," etc.

In the Preface of the same day we read:—

"Caro est quod involvitur; divinitas cui ab Angelis ministratur. Erat positus in præsepio, sed virtus ejus operabatur in cœlis. In cunabulis jacebat et regnum cœleste donabat. Natus est nobis Christus, inluminatus est mundus. Innupta peperit, et virgo concepit: de viro pura, de filio gloriosa, accepit nomen matris sed non habuit thronum uxoris. Per cujus nativitatem indulgentia criminum conceditur et resurrectio non negatur," etc.

In the Mass for the feast of St. Stephen (p. 292), the following beautiful prayer occurs:—

"Deus omnipotens qui Ecclesiæ tuæ sanctum Stefanum martyrem primum messis tuæ manipulum dedisti et primitivam oblationem novellæ confessionis ostendisti præconem, quod fructus maturescentes exhibuit; præsta universo cœtui intercessione Martyris meriti ut Ecclesiam tuam juvet suffragio quam ornavit ministerio."

The next page gives us the Mass of the Holy Innocents, and the sweet prayer:—

"Deus lactentium fides, spes infantium, caritas puerorum, qui per innocentium laudem cunctos provocas ad salutem, infunde in nobis puritatem lactentis infantiæ, concede doctrinam."

In the Mass of the *Cathedra Sancti Petri*, the following prayers occur:—

"Beatissimi Petri Apostoli solemnissimum diem in quo omne jus gentium Judæorumque sortitus est, quem diem ipsa divinitas consecravit delegando cœlorum claves, vel pontificalis cathedræ contulit dignitatem, fratres carissimi, exultantes in Domino celebremus, deprecantes ejus misericordiam; ut sicut beato Petro principalia munera contulit, ita et nobis peccatorum commissa concedat.

"Deus qui hodierna die beatum Petrum post te dedisti caput Ecclesiæ, cum te ille vere confessus sit et ipse a te digne prælatus sit, te supplices exoramus, ut qui dedisti Pastorem, ne quid de ovibus perderes (et) ut grex effugiat errores; ejus intercessione quem præfecisti, salvifices.

"Deum qui beato Petro tantam potestatem discipulo contulit, ut si ipse ligaverit non sit alter qui solverit; et quæ in terra solverit, item cœlo, soluta sint, precibus imploremus; ut eductis a tartaro defunctorum spiritibus, non prævaleant sepultis inferni portæ per crimina, quas per Apostoli fidem vinci credit Ecclesia."

In the Preface, too, of the same festival, we read:—

"Vere dignum et justum est, omnipotens Deus, qui dives infinitæ clementiæ copioso munere plasmam tuæ creaturæ in tantum dignaris erigere ut vernaculo limi compatiens homini de terrena compage claves cœli committeres, et ad judicandas tribus solium excelsæ sedis in sublimi conponeres. Testis est dies hodierna beati Petri Cathedra Episcopatûs exposita, in qua fidei merito revelationis mysterium fidei, Filium Dei confitendo, prælatus Apostolus ordinatur, in cujus confessione est fundamentum Ecclesiæ nec adversus hanc Petram portæ inferi prævalent, nec serpens vestigium exprimit, nec triumphum mors obtinet. Quid vero beato Petro diverso sub tempore accessit laudis et gloriæ quæ vox, quæ lingua, quis explicet. Hinc est quod mare tremulum fixo calcat vestigio et inter undas liquidas pendula planta perambulat," etc.*

The Mass "for the festival of Holy Mary" (*Missa in Sanctæ Mariæ solemnitate*) immediately follows in the Bobbio text. We give in full the prayers and preface of this ancient Irish Mass:—

"Omnipotens sempiterne Deus qui terrenis corporibus, Verbi tui veritatem per venerabilem Mariam conjungi voluisti; petimus immensam clementiam tuam, ut quod in ejus veneratione deposcimus, Te propiciante mereamur consequi.

"Exaudi nos Domine, sancte Pater, omnipotens Deus, qui beatæ Mariæ uteri obumbratione cunctum mundum inluminare dignatus es: majestatem tuam supplices deprecamur ut quod nostris meritis non valemus ejus adipisci præsidiis mereamur. Te quæsumus Dne. famulantes, ut beatæ Mariæ nos gaudia comitentur, cujus meritis nostra deleantur chirographa peccatorum.

"Offerimus Dne. preces et munera in honore sanctæ Mariæ gaudentes; præsta quæsumus, ut et convenientur hæc agere, et remedium sempiternum valeamus adquirere.

"Altario tuo, Dne. proposita munera Spiritus Sanctus benignus adsumat qui beatæ Mariæ viscera splendoris sui veritate replevit.

* Page 298.

"Vere dignum et justum est omnipotens Deus. Qui nos mirabile mysterium et inenarrabile sacramentum per venerabilem Mariam servare docuisti in qua manet intacta castitas, pudor integer, firma conscientia. Nam in hoc matrem Domini sui Jesu se esse cognovit, quia plus gaudii contulit quam pudoris. Lætatur ergo quod virgo concepit, quod cæli Dominum clausis portavit visceribus, quod virgo edidit partum. O magna clementia Deitatis! quæ virum non novit et mater est, et post filium virgo est. Duobus enim gavisa est muneribus: miratur quod virgo peperit; lætatur quod edidit Redemptorem Dominum nostrum Jesum Christum. Per quem," etc.

A Mass for the feast of the Assumption next follows:

"Generosæ diei, dominicæ Genitricis inexplicabile sacramentum, tanto magis præconabile quantum inter homines adsumptione virginis singulare, apud quam vitæ integritas obtinuit filium et mors non invenit par exemplum ... fratres carissimi deprecemur ut ejus adjuti muniamur suffragio, quæ beata Maria de partu clara, de merito felix prædicatur post transitum.

"Deus universalis, qui in sanctis spiritaliter, in Matre vero virgine etiam corporaliter habitasti; quæ, caritate decens, pace gaudens, pietate præcellens; ab Angelo gratia plena, ab Helizabet benedicta, ab gentibus prædicatur beata: cujus nobis fides mysterium, partus gaudium, pacem quam in adsumptione matris tunc præbuisti discipulis, nobis miserere supplicibus.

"Vere dignum et justum est omnipotens Deus per Jesum Christum, Dominum nostrum. Quo fidelis Israel egressa est de Egypto; quo virgo Dei genitrix Maria de mundo migravit ad Christum, germine gloriosa, adsumptione secura, Paradisi dote prælata, damna de cœtu, sumens vota de fructu; non subdita labori per partum, non dolori per transitum; speciosus thalamus, de quo decorus procedit sponsus, lux gentium, spes fidelium, prædo dæmonum, confusio Judæorum, vasculum gloriæ, templum cœleste; cujus juvenculæ melius prædicantur merita cum veteris Evæ conferentur exempla. Siquidem ista mundo vitam protulit; illa legem mortis invexit: illa prævaricando nos perdidit; ista generando servavit: illa nos pomo arboris in ipsa radice percussit; ex hujus virga flos exiit, qui nos odore refecerit, et fruge curarit: illa maledictione in dolore generat; ista benedictione in salute. Recte ab ipso suscepta es in adsumptione feliciter quem pie suscepisti conceptura per fidem ut qui terræ non eras conscia, te non teneret rupis inclusa. Vere diversis infulis anima redimita, cui Apostoli sacrum reddunt obsequium, Angeli cantum, Christus amplexum, nubes vehiculum, assumtio Paradisum, in choris virginum gloriâ tenens principatum," etc.

Then follow some Masses for Lent and Easter, for "the finding of the Holy Cross," and other festivals, amongst which we must remark that of St. Sigismund, king of Burgundy, who died in

515, and who was numbered amongst the chief patrons of Luxeu. This Mass was added immediately before the general Mass for the festivals of martyrs. There are also Masses for the Dead, and one in particular "for a deceased priest." To some passages in these various Masses we may have occasion to refer hereafter. The reader, however, must not expect to find rigorously exact the statement made by Dr. Todd, that forsooth the Bobbio Missal, in Mabillon's edition, "contains epistles and gospels for all the Sundays and festivals."* This statement has no foundation in the missal itself, and must be supposed to have proceeded from an oversight of the learned writer.

The missal has, in the end, various exorcisms and blessings, the penitential of which we have spoken above, a short treatise on the hours for chanting the ecclesiastical office, the Apostles' Creed as given in our second appendix, and a list of the sacred canonical books.

APPENDIX No. V.

THE "PROFESSION OF FAITH" OF ST. MOCHTA.†

This valuable treatise was first published by Muratori, in the second volume of his Anecdota, under the name of Bachiarius; which, as Colgan proves, was nothing more than a corruption of the Irish name of our saint.‡ Muratori styles it, "prætiosum opusculum, cui hucusque cum blattis ac pulvere secretissimum bellum fuit." He adds that he discovered it in "antiquissimo Ambrosianæ Bibliothecæ codice, olim Bobiensi ante annos mille

---

* Page 30. † For St. Mochta see ante, p. 92.
‡ See Acta SS. p. 731.

conscripto."* A few years later it was noticed by Montfaucon in his Museum Italicum,† who describes the manuscript in which it is preserved as belonging to the eighth century.

St. Mochta more than once refers to the fact of *one individual* having given the evil fame of heresy to our country; and thus he gives us a key to the statements of early writers concerning the faith of our island in the fifth century. On the one hand, we know that no heresy infected the Irish Church; whilst on the other hand, many ancient writers unite Ireland with England when treating of the spread of Pelagianism. Thus, the letter of the Roman clergy, written in 639, speaks of the *Pelagianæ hæreseos virus*, as if it had, in a preceding age, infected Ireland. The tract on the liturgy published in our second appendix, also eulogises St. Germanus for having expelled Pelagianism "from Britain and Ireland;" and similar phrases are met with in many other writers. Thus, what was the guilt of one individual, Celestius, was imputed to his country; and hence the evil fame of heresy was for a time attached to our sainted island. St. Mochta, in his Profession of Faith, alludes to no heresy; he had none to abjure; he and his countrymen had retained untainted and unchanged the profession of faith which they had made at the baptismal font; and hence, in the present treatise, we have little more than a running commentary on the Apostles' Creed, whilst he especially dwells on those precise points of doctrine which are characteristic of the early Irish writers:

1. "*Omne, quod fuit, ipsum, quod erit; et non est omne recens sub sole.* (Eccle. i. 9.) Et iterum Apostolus: *Omnia hæc in figuram nostri contigerunt:* (1 Corinth. x. 6) quod præsentis rei probatur effectu; cum gesta olim evangelici sacramenta mysterii, iterum ætatis nostræ temporibus renovata celebrentur. Ecce nunc, quantum intelligimus Christus a Samaritana aquam postulat, cum Beatitudo tua Fidem a nobis requirit. Suspectos nos, quantum video, facit, non sermo, sed regio; et qui de fide non erubescimus, de Provincia confundimur. Sed absit, beatissime, ut apud viros sanctos macula nos terrenæ nativitatis inficiat. Nos Patriam etsi secundum carnem novimus, sed nunc jam non novimus: et desiderantes

---

* Anecdota Ambrosiana, tom. ii. Milan, 1698, p. 1, seqq.
† Page 18.

Abrahæ filii fieri, terram nostram, cognationemque relinquimus. Hoc autem ideo dicimus, quia sicut Samaritanis, sic nobis non creditur a Judæis, eo quod cuiusdam hæresis macula solum nostrum originale perstrinxerit; sic præsidentium quorumdam sententia judicamur, quasi liberi esse ab erroris deceptione nequeamus. Dictum est similiter quondam ab incredulis: *A Nazareth potest aliquid boni esse?* et tamen inde Christus processit. Numquid, rogo, Apostolorum merita unius perfidia, avaritiaque mutavit, qui, non dicam de eadem regione, sed eorum processit e latere? Numquid Patriarcharum vitam fratrum culpa turbavit? Numquid Prophetarum oracula, Pseudoprophetarum commenta falsarunt? Core illo Levitico in hæresim declinante, numquid reliqua cognatio ex hac stirpe descendens, maculam ex propinquitate contraxit? Pontificis filiis ignem offerentibus alienum, germani eorum sacerdotali funguntur officio, et inculpatos se a crimine fratrum ministerii sui honore testantur. Nicolao Diacono in hæresim declinante, gloriosa collectorum fratrum in virtutibus Dei opera refulserunt. Crimen nobis regionis intenditur. Quisquis hoc dicit, legat Christum *Samaritanum*: in qua Provincia, non solum hæresis, sed idololatriæ criminibus servierunt. In domo profani et sceleratissimi Achab Abdias servus Domini inventus est, qui corporibus Prophetarum meruit copulari. In Sarepta Sidoniæ, inter Chananæorum scelestissimum genus, vidua fidelis reperitur, et Prophetarum hospita eligitur. Magister idololatriæ, et caput hæresis Balaam, ut Christum prædicaret, admissus est: Job ex Esau profani et infidelis stirpe descendit. Ruth cognata generis Christi Moabitis esse describitur, cujus origo in æternum ab Ecclesiæ foribus abdicatur. Abraham caput fidei de Chaldæorum stirpe descendit, quibus vernacula et naturalis magicæ artis impietas est. Magis Christum adorantibus, vetera errorum non imputantur opprobria. Moysi Ægyptiorum artibus erudito prophetalis spiritus gratia condonatur. Jam in Christo renatis terrenæ provinciæ error adscribitur?

2. "Si agnoscimus Patriam, erubescamus et culpam; mihi enim civitas, cui renovatus sum, regio effecta vel Patria est. Nihil mihi de terrenis affinitatibus adscribatur, quibus renuntiasse memini. Quis quis est, qui me de Provinciæ cognatione æstimat infidelem, ipse infidelem se esse noverit; quia aut oblitus est aut lubricum putat, quod in baptismo confessum esse cognoscit; sine dubio enim non relinquit terrenam cognationem, qui me de patrio errore confutat. Certe secundum institutionem actus humani Pater patriam facit. Qualiter mihi Patria in terra esse dicitur, cui ex præcepto cœlesti Patrem in terra vocare, aut habere non sinitur. Vis enim, ut evidentibus tibi per me hoc probetur exemplis, qui Patriæ culpas errorem? Nonne Novatiani hoc genere a Catholicis dissidentes, probrosæ hæresis lepram iudicio contraxere perverso, eo quod anteactam culparum seriem crediderunt etiam posteris adscribendam, et non tam hæresim odere quam plebem? Si pro culpa unius, totius Provinciæ anathematizanda generatio est, damnetur et illa beatissima discipula, hoc est Roma, de qua nunc non una, sed duæ vel tres, aut eo amplius hæreses pullularunt; et tamen nulla earum Cathedram Petri, hoc est sedem Fidei, aut tenere potuit, aut movere. Damnentur postremo et omnes Provinciæ, de quibus diversi erroris rivuli manavere. Ille vas

electionis, et Gentium Doctor lapso Eutycho de tertio tecto, credo, aliquid de Triuitate erranti, restituit calorem fidei, et vitam reddidit, hoc est, veniam relaxavit. Nos fortasse adhuc in fenestra id est, in lucis via, et fidei splendore residentes severi nimium judices, non ex discussione, sed ex suspectione condemnant: nescientes, quia *quo judicio judicaverint, judicabitur de eis*; *et qui fratri suo dixerit Racha, reus erit gehennæ ignis*. Racha enim, vacuus interpretatur. Et quis est vacuus, nisi cuius interiora carent fidei veritate, et est *velut æramentum sonans, aut cymbalum tinniens?* Ille, qui una tantum nocte Christum viderat, ait contribulis suis: *Numquid lex nostra judicat hominem, nisi prius audiat, quæ agit?* Et hi, qui tot annorum Domini sectatores sunt, prius judicant, quam id, unde judicant audiant, atque cognoscant? Si ante cognitionem promenda est sententia, cur Legislator præcepit, ne antequam introeat sacerdos, et videat domum quæ cariosæ vel tinnientis lepra hæresis scindatur, immunda judicetur? Ne, quæso, Beatissime frater, male de Provincia sentiatur. Non latet enim perspicaciam tuam, quia cum in adventu arcæ Dominicæ Dagonis caput in centum partes cum utrisque pedibus comminutum sit, spina ejus integra superfuisse describitur. Nos enim Dagonis caput, sive pedes, membra mundi, id est, orientem, et occiduum esse sentimus, in quibus partibus sub præsentia legis omnis errorum nutrita perversitas est. Tuum sit enim judicare, quæ sit medietas spinæ, in qua adhuc nodorum compago dissoluta perdurat. Ut quid, rogo, quæritur Provincia mea? *Peregrinus ego sum, sicut omnes Patres mei.* Verumtamen si magnopere quæritur, ubi natus sim, accipiatur confessio mea, quam in Baptismi nativitate respondi; non enim mihi Patria confessionem, sed confessio Patriam dedit; quia credidi, et accepi. Nec me offuscet Samaritana conditio, quia Christum, interrogatus ad puteum, credidi, et purgatus a lepra infidelitatis agnovi. Verumtamen quia apostolicæ eruditionis instituta nos commovent, ut omnibus poscentibus nobis rationem de fide et spe, quæ in nobis est, proferamus; non movemur Fidei nostræ regulam Beatitudini tuæ, qui artifex es ipsius ædificii, demonstrare.

3. "Sed ne forte hoc ipsum suspicionem infidelitatis incutiat, quod tardius ad interrogata respondeo; credimus Deum esse: quod fuit, erat; quod erat, erit, nunquam aliud, semper idem: Pater Deus, Filius Deus, Spiritus Sanctus Deus: unus Deus, et unus Filius de Patre, Spiritus Sanctus Patris et Filii. Unius Trinitatis ista substantia, et tria ista unam habentia voluntatem. Nec communicans major, nec accipiens minor: nec est secundus a primo, nec tertius de secundo; quia sic nos prophetica instituta docuerunt dicendo: *Non ascendes per gradus ad altare meum.* Altare enim velut quamdam basim Fidei suspicamur, unde vitalis cibi participantur alimenta; quia *altare* ex proprietate nominis sui nonnisi sublimium rerum alta cognitio est. Divisum enim per sillabas nomen altaris, inchoatumque de fine, *res alta* significatur et sonat. Ad hanc Fidem per gradus ascendere non debemus, ne inæqualiter sentiendo, de inferiore ad superiorem transitum faciamus; sed æquali gradu nostri cordis intrare, ut unius substantiæ, unius potestatis, unius virtutis, et Patrem, et Filium et Spiritum Sanctum sentiamus. Pater enim principale nomen Divinitatis per se, quod creditur, et dicitur Pater Deus, Filius

Deus ex Patre non ex se, sed Patris. Pater Deus, et Filius Deus sed non idem Pater, qui Filius; sed idem esse creditur Pater quod Filius, et Spiritus Sanctus non Pater ingenitus, sed Spiritus ingeniti Patris. Filius genitus, non Spiritus Filius, sed ipse Filius super quem a Patre missus est Spiritus. Itaque, cum ingenitus Pater sit, cuius est Spiritus, incaute Spiritus Sanctus dicitur ingenitus, ne duo ingeniti, aut duo Patres ab infidelibus æstimentur. Filius Patris ante sæcula genitus a Patre, non potest alium genitum habere consortem; ut credatur unigenitus et duo geniti non dicantur. Pater enim unus ingenitus, Filius unus est genitus, Spiritus Sanctus a Patre procedens, Patri et Filio coæternus, quoniam unum opus, et una in Patre et Filio et Spiritu Sancto voluntatis operatio est. Pater ingenitus, Filius genitus, Spiritus Sanctus a Patre procedens, Patri et Filio coæternus; sed ille nascitur hic procedit sicut in Evangelio Beati Johannis legitis: *Spiritus, qui a Patre procedit ipse vobis annunciabit omnia.* Itaque Spiritus Sanctus nec Pater esse ingenitus, nec Filius genitus aestimetur; sed Spiritus Sanctus, qui a Patre procedit. Sed non est aliud quod procedit quam quod unde procedit. Si persona quæritur, Deus est. Hæc per hoc tripartita conjunctio, et conjuncta divisio, et in personis, excludit unionem, et in personarum distinctione obtinet unitatem. sicque credimus beatissimam Trinitatem, quod unius naturæ est, unius deitatis, unius ejusdemque virtutis atque substantiæ: nec inter Patrem et Filium et Spiritum Sanctum, sit ulla diversitas, nisi quod ille Pater sit, et hic Filius, et ille Spiritus Sanctus, Trinitas in subsistentibus personis, unitas in natura atque substantia. Filium quoque credimus in novissimis diebus natum esse de virgine, et Spiritu Sancto, carnem naturæ humanæ, et animam suscepisse. In qua carne et passum et sepultum, resurrexisse a mortuis credimus et fatemur; et in eadem ipsa carne in qua jacuit in sepulcro, post resurectionem ascendisse in cœlum, unde venturum expectamus ad judicium vivorum et mortuorum: virginem quoque de qua natum scimus, et virginem ante partum, et virginem post partum, ne consortes Elvidiani erroris habeamur. Carnem quoque nostræ resurrectionis fatemur integram atque perfectam, hujus, in qua vivimus in præsenti sæculo aut bonis artibus gubernamur, aut malis operibus subjacemus; ut possimus in ipsa, aut pro malis pœnarum tormenta sustinere, aut pro bonis bonorum præmia adquirere: neque, ut quidam absurdissime, aliam pro hac resurcituram dicimus, sed hanc ipsam, nullo omnino ei vel membro amputato vel aliqua corporis parte defecta. Hic est nostræ Fidei thesaurus, quem signato Ecclesiastico symbolo, quod in Baptismo accepimus, custodimus. Sic coram Deo corde credimus sic coram hominibus labiis confitemur; ut et hominibus cognitio sua fidem faciat, et Deo imago sua testimonium reddat. Hic est baculus defensionis nostræ, quo murmurantium adversus nos ora feriamus, qui nos per viam hujus sæculi transeuntes iugo consuetudinis, non studio rationis oblatrant. Hoc scutum Fidei nostræ, quo obtrectantium verborum, et venenata suspicionum spicula repellimus, ac vitamus, ne aliquod in nobis patens membrum, et de protectione Fidei nudum, sermo inimici, qui ad feriendum destinatur inveniat. Sed sileamus de his quia nobis nunc, non repercutiendi, sed vitandi tantum hostis cura suscepta est.

4. "Jam vero, si etiam illud a nobis quæritur, qualiter de anima en-

tiamus, factam credimus esse, sicut legimus in Hieremia Propheta per Regem Sedeciam dicentem : *Vivit Dominus qui fecit nobis animam istam.* Si autem quæritur, unde sit facta, nescire me fateor, quia nec usquam legisse cognosco : et ideo nec de imperitia erubesco, quia lectione non doceor ; neque periculum formido, quia quæ non lego non præsumo, ne transgressor propheticorum inveniar præceptorum, qui mandat sanguinem non manducari adjiciens quia, *omnis carnis sanguis anima est.* Quid enim est sanguinem manducare, nisi de anima disputare ? et ideo carnem, quæ nobis in Adam fundata est, possumus dicere ex mundi qualitatibus substantiæ Deo artifice et auctore compactam ; sanguinem enim ad basim fundamus altaris, id est ut ipsi qui creavit, scire unde creaverit, relinquamus. Basis enim altaris velut quædam radix profunditatis est, cujus secreto etiam rationem animæ jungamus de qua disputare non possumus. Et ideo nec partem dicimus Dei animam, sicut quidam asserunt, quia Deus impartibilis, et indivisus, et impassibilis est, anima vero diversis passionibus manicipata, sicut quotidianus rerum exitus probat. Nec de creatura aliqua factam dicimus, ne eam faciamus viliorem reliquis creaturis, quibus domina, si bene egerit, constituta est ; sed ex Dei tantum voluntate formari, cuius potentiæ non necessaria est materia, ex qua quod voluerit operetur, sed ipsa voluntas eius materia eorum, quæ fieri aut esse mandaverit. Sed nec illi assertioni tradimus manus, qua quidam superfluo delectantur, ut credant animas ex transfusione gen.rari ; quia contradicit huic suspicioni beatus David dicendo : *Scitote, quoniam Dominus ipse est Deus : ipse fecit nos, et non ipsi nos.* Et alibi : *Qui finxit singillatim corda eorum.* Ubi hæc transfusio inveniet locum, ubi aut singillatim corda finguntur, aut dicitur : *ipse fecit nos, et non ipsi nos ?* Qui ergo ex transfusione dicunt animas generari, id asserere dicuntur, quia ipsi nos faciamus. Sed hoc præscientia prophetalis objurgat dicendo : *ipse fecit nos, et non ipsi nos.* Absque sola igitur Trinitate, omne quod in cœlis, sive in terris, et mari potentatur, agitur, movetur, creaturam esse credimus et fatemur.

5. "Diabolum non ita factum sentimus, ut diabolus est, nec proprium habuisse naturæ suæ genus, ut diabolus nasceretur, et hoc cognomen meritum dedisse, non Deum : nec ingenitum esse, quia deus non est ; nec factum esse diabolum, quia Deus malum non fecit, sed Angelum bonum factum, sicut Scriptura demonstrat : *Per bonum operatum est mihi omnem concupiscentiam.* Malum enim Angelum fuisse sic credo, ut apostolus dicit : *Datus est mihi stimulus carnis meæ, Angelus Satanæ, qui me colaphiset.* Et alibi : *Nisi venerit refuga et discessio.* Ergo qui nunc refuga est, fuit aliquando in intuitu Creatoris, et in illa gradus sublimitate descripta a prophetis, cum dicitur : *Et tu eras consignatio similitudinis, et corona decoris,* et reliqua ; et alibi : *Quomodo de cœlo cecidit Lucifer, qui mane oriebatur ?* Hunc boni et mali capacem dicimus accepisse ex factore naturam, immortalitatis gloria et honore circumdatum ; accepisse etiam scientiæ dignitatem, qui elatus in superbiam, suum credidit esse, quod non erat ; quoniam qui eum fecerat, Dominum non videbat. *Ego sum,* inquit, *et non est alius præter me.* Inde terræ deputatus est et cineri, ut scriptum est : *Quid superbis terra et cinis ;* et *Initium peccationis superbia.* Qui tartaro et igni perpetuo deputatus, perennis est pœnæ, non immortalis vitæ. Credimus omnem creaturam Dei, quæ ad usus ciborum a conditore concessa est,

bonum esse, sicut et factum est : *Et vidit Deus, quia bona sunt valde.* Sed ab his ad tempus abstinere, non pro superstitione religionis, neque abominatione creaturæ Dei, sed pro continentia carnis, utile esse sentimus secundum Apostoli consilium, qui dicit : *Bonum est non manducare carnem, neque bibere vinum*; atque cum libuerit, uti, et cum delectaverit, abstinere, in hominis potestate consistere. Conjugia probamus, quæ Deo auctore concessa sunt : continentiam in ipsis prædicamus; virginitatem, ut pote egregium germen, et ex effœta trunci radice procedens, extollimus et miramur. Justorum peccatorumque distantiam, non ex conditione Creatoris, sed arbitrio credimus accedere voluntatis. Pœnitentiam peccatorum plenissima fide suscipimus, ac veluti secundam gratiam suspicamur, sicut Apostolus ad Corinthios dicit : *Volui per vos venire, ut secundam gratiam habeatis.*

6. "Vetus et novum Testamentum aequali fidei lance suscipimus, ac veluti currentis per signa ponderis libra, sic testimoniorum gesta mobili meditatione pensamus. Nec evacuantes historiæ fidem, credimus universa gesta esse, quæ legimus : sed juxta doctrinam apostolicam sensum in his spiritualem, prout Dominus dederit, perscrutamur : qui tamen sensus ad typum Christi Ecclesiæque pertineat, aut in morum emendationem correctionemque proficiat. Et hoc ipsum juxta illud, quod Apostolus ait : *Omnia hæc in figuram nostri contigerunt.* Et alibi beatus Petrus : *Omnis sermo interpretatione indiget.* Omnem scripturam, quæ Ecclesiastico canoni non congruit, neque consentit, non solum non suscipimus, verum etiam velut alienam a Fidei veritate damnamus. Peregrinis atque ignotis fabulis de scripturarum continentia, non facile accommodamus assensum ; neque cito nova doctrina aurium nostrarum intrat cavernas, quia legimus Virginem novam aliam in secreto, quam rudem vel secretam suspicamur esse doctrinam, quæ ob hoc prohibetur inspici, ne hominum corda, commentitia sub specie veritatis, sermonum pulchitudine, suavitateque decipiat. Virgo est illa doctrina, quæ nulli viro Ecclesiastico vel Catholico cognita est; sed inter mulieres semper adolevit, id est, animas, quæ semper discentes, omni spiritui deceptionis credula se facilitate commiscent, non curæ habentes unde concipiant; cum Dominus in Lege mandaverit, ne nonnisi de tribu sua in conjugio copuletur, id est, illi fidei intellectus, qui ex Patrum semine, hoc est, doctrina descendit, et Abrahæ, qui primus in præputio credidit, prosapia nobilitatur et genere. Virgo est illa doctrina quæ tantum in secreto sibi placet, et in publicum erubescit exire. Hanc talem, non solum fugimus, verum etiam publica voce damnamus, stultum docentes hoc credere, quod aut ipsi defendere non possumus, aut ad aures publicas non debeat pervenire.

7. "Jejunia attentiora secundum Ecclesiasticam regulam disciplinamque servamus, ut *tribus temporibus anni masculinum nostrum* hoc est, opus virtutis, quod cætero operi præcellat, *appareat;* ac si quando jejunia indicta Ecclesiæ tunc nos cupimus, non solum de usu consuetudinari, verum etiam a conversatione, fabulis, salutationibus, quæ fabulas interserunt, jejunare. Et cum hoc teste Deo, ita, ut scribimus, sentiamus, tamen non sic nobis de veritate blandimur, ut si forte sacerdotes, sive Doct res, qui sunt capita populi, et columnæ Ecclesiarum, quodlibet ex his, quæ professi sumus, probantes (aliquid) rectius quid dixerint, pigri simus in eorum sententiam

transire; præceptumque meminimus Scriptum: *Interrogate Patres vestros et dicent vobis*. Neque enim tam stulti sumus, ut quibus capita pro sanctificatione summittimus, his corda nostra humiliare nolimus. Pastor est: quo vocaverit, sequar: quod dixerit, ruminabo; quia ipse scit sibi pro custodia mea reddendam esse rationem. Hæc sint, de quibus interim vobis ad præsens occurrere potui; si qua enim sunt, quæ aut studio præteriisse aut te adhuc titillare videantur, sine verecundia interrogare dignare, ut sine cunctatione respondeam, et aut emender de errore, aut confirmer in fide. Testor enim legenti verba professionis hujus, quoniam si quis dempserit de his, demet Deus de libro vitæ partem ejusdem. Etenim ille, qui nos crediderit aliud labiis loqui, aliud corde tenere; sicut superius dixi, cor nostrum Deus potest inspicere. Ipsi obtulimus labia ad confessionem: de quibus p. ssunt homines judicare satisfecimus; ac sic duobus testibus stabit omne verbum nostrum, id est, Deo, cujus judicium in nos, si fallimus, invocamus; et hominibus, quorum suspiciones nostra confessione corrigimus, ne amplius in nobis velit male sentiendo peccare. Si quis his auditis in incredulitate perstiterit, ut non nobis fidei assensum tradat, non dubito quin in die judicii partem aut inter incredulum populum, aut inter falsos testes habiturus sit, et secundum judicium legis Moysi, iniquitatem, quam in fratre suo meditatur, sit recepturus.

8. "Nos enim, etsi peccatores sumus, tamen propter illa trecenta aurea scuta, quæ Solomon fabricavit, ærea facere non debemus. Scutum enim fidei forma est secundum Apostolum, qui dicit: *Accipientes Scutum Fidei*. Et ille pro aureis ærea facit, qui subtracta Fidei veritate, solum degenere reddit ex confessione tinnitum et cum devotus videatur in numero, tamen reus invenitur ex voto, id quod non credit, confitendo. De quibus quidem dixisse beatus Apostolus suspicandus est: *Habentes speciem pietatis et virtutem ejus abnegantes*. Nonne videtur virtus in auro, et species in ære posse sentiri? Sed optamus assertionem propheticam custodire, ut ante pedes equorum Regis qui nisi Episcopi, aut Doctores sunt, quorum pedes veloces sunt super montes, evangelizantes pacem, fidei nostræ scuta ponamus. Trecenta enim aurea scuta, sive Beatæ Trinitatis Fides sive omnium creaturarum factio, cœli, terræ, et maris; cursores enim, qui ante pedes equorum ponent ea, illi credendi sunt, qui potuerunt dicere; *Cursum Consummavi*: qua instituti lege hucusque ad finem servare possimus, ne illa Saracim Rex Ægypti, hoc est, Diabolus, a templo nostri cordis abripiat. Excubent suffragia orationum tuarum ad Jesum Christum Dominum nostrum, cui gloria in sæcula sæculorum. Amen.

APPENDIX No. VI.

DR. TODD'S REMARKS ON THE SIXTH CANON OF ST. PATRICK'S SYNOD.

Dr. Todd refers that canon to ninth or tenth century—his arguments have no solidity.—The canon does not refer to the tonsure, but to the clipping of the hair and beard according to the Roman custom.—Druidical verse about St. Patrick.—The canon is found in MSS more ancient than the period to which it is assigned by Dr. Todd.—The canon from ancient MSS —Dr. Todd following Spelman, has not given it correctly.—The words referred to a cleric's wife by Dr. Todd, refer to married women in general.—The canon about offerings does not prove the synod to be of a late period.

DR. TODD, in his work on St. Patrick, displays an unmistakeable anxiety to refer to a much later period than the age of our apostle, the decrees of the synod which bears the name of SS. Patrick, Auxilius, and Iserninus. This synod was first published by Spelman, in 1639, and his edition was copied by Wilkins, Ware, and Villanueva. It is on the sixth canon of this synod that Dr. Todd chiefly rests his argument for referring its decrees to *the ninth or tenth century.** His reasoning is as follows :—

"The following canon, the sixth of this synod, is evidence of a very rude state of society. It seems to have been enacted before the celibacy of the clergy was enforced in Ireland, but after the adoption of the Roman tonsure : '*what cleric soever, from an ostiarius to a priest, who shall be seen without a tunic, or who does not cover his nakedness, or if his hairs are not tonsured after the Roman manner, or if his wife does not walk with her head veiled, let them* (*i.e.* the clerk and his wife) *be despised by the laity, and also separated from the Church.*' This allusion to the Roman tonsure, clearly indicates that the canon was as late as the eighth century, and probably not earlier than the tenth."†

The Latin text of this canon, as given by Dr Todd in his notes, is :—

" Quicumque clericus ab ostiario usque ad sacerdotem sine tunica (Martene adds, *femorali*) visus fuerit, atque turpitudinem ventris et

---

* Page 486-9. † Loc. cit.

nuditatem non tegat: et si non more Romano capilli ejus tonsi sint, et uxor ejus si non velato capite ambulaverit; pariter a laicis contempnentur, et ab Ecclesia separentur."

1. That this canon has reference to the Roman tonsure, is gratuitously supposed by the learned librarian of Trinity College; and yet this supposition is the whole groundwork of his argument. The words of the original canon literally mean, that " the hair should be cut after the Roman manner"—*Romano more capilli ejus tonsi sint.* Now it may, perhaps, be reasonably doubted whether the ecclesiastical tonsure was introduced as early as the year 430; but there can be no doubt that it was prescribed long before that period in the Roman Church, that the clergy should not wear long flowing hair, but keep it closely clipped. Hence, in the pontifical of pope Damasus, it is described as a law long observed in Rome, that " clerici juxta Apostolum, comam non nutriant."* Moreover, we learn from St. Paulinus, bishop of Nola, who died in the year 431, that it was customary with some monks of his time to closely clip their hair in front, and hence they are described by him as " casta informitate capillum ad cutem cæsi et inæqualiter semitonsi et destituta fronte prærasi."† Thus, then, we may suppose that St. Patrick's canon referred to the clipping of the hair by the clergy, as was customary in Rome, without at all alluding to the angry controversies of the seventh and eighth centuries.

We may further remark that this canon, regarding the clipping of the hair, is probably only a compendious expression of the original decree of our apostle. It is thus the decree of St. Patrick regarding Rome, though preserved in full in the Book of Armagh, is concisely expressed in all the other records that have come down to us, in the well known formula " si quæ quæstiones in hac insula oriantur ad Sedem Apostolicam referantur." Now the full decree of our apostle regarding this sort of tonsure has fortunately been preserved to us, in an ancient collection of canons of the tenth century, in the Vatican Archives, and we now present it in full to the reader:—

---

* Ap. Labbé, Concil. i. 581.   † Opp. S. Paulini, epist. 7.

"*Patricius: quicumque clericus ab ostiario usque ad sacerdotem, si more Romano capillos suos aut barbam ab anno pubertatis suæ tondere contempserit, a cœtu Christianorum et ab Ecclesia separetur, donec cum satisfactione emendetur. Ad Ezechielem Dominus dicit: sume tibi gladium acutum et duc per caput tuum et barbam."**

Here reference is made to the custom of Rome, *Romano more*, and yet the canon nowise relates to the ecclesiastical tonsure, as *the clipping of the beard* sufficiently proves. It is a striking coincidence, that if we suppose this complete canon to be rigorously carried out, we should have precisely such a picture as that given above in the words of St. Paulinus.

Amongst the most ancient fragments of our Celtic literature, must be ranked a celebrated druidical verse relative to our apostle, which is recorded in all the various lives of St. Patrick, as, for instance, in the Scholiast of Fiacc's hymn, the Leabhar Breac, Probus, etc. What is still more important for determining its age is the fact of its being prefaced by Muirchu-Maccu-Mactheni, in the Book of Armagh, with the following words: " Hæc autem sunt versiculi verba pro linguæ idiomate non tam manifesta :"† that is, even when he was writing before the year 690, the idiom of this ancient verse rendered it difficult to be understood, and as Eugene Curry remarks, " the Latin translation given by Muirchu clearly shows that he did not understand it."‡ This verse is thus translated by Mr. Curry :—

> "A Tailcenn will come over the raging sea,
> With his perforated garment, his crook-headed staff,
> With his table at the east end of his house;
> And all his people will answer, Amen, Amen."§

All the old scholia agree in referring the *perforated garment*, or, as Dr. Todd translates it, *his garment pierced at the neck*, to the chasuble used in the holy Sacrifice; the crook-like staff, to the episcopal crozier; the east-end table, to the altar. In like manner, the name *Tailcenn*, as Dr. Todd writes, is "the well-known

---

* Codex Vatican. 339, Collect. Can. Sæc. x$^{mi.}$
† Lib. Armac. fol. 2, b. col. 1.   ‡ Lectures, page 397.
§ Lectures, p. 397.

name of the apostle Patrick;* and means, literally, "one with a shorn crown." Colgan translates it, *tonsus in vertice;* and Muirchu, in the Book of Armagh, gives as its equivalent the name *Lasciciput;* which, as Dr. Todd ably illustrates, indicates *a shaven head,* this being the usual manner of tonsure at the time that Muirchu was writing. From all this we may conclude, that from the very earliest ages of faith in our island, a peculiar form of *shorn head* was attributed to our apostle; and hence the words of the sixth canon above-cited involve nothing requiring *the probable date* of the tenth century.

2. Indeed, this *probable date*† is so absurd, that it is not easy to conceive anything more improbable. The very canon of which we treat is expressly cited as a decree of St. Patrick in the Collectio Hibernensis Canonum, drawn up about the year 700. Even in the extracts given by D'Achery from this ancient collection, and cited by Dr. Todd himself,‡ the first portion of the canon is thus given:

"Patricius: si quis clericus, cujus capilli non sunt tonsi Romano more, debet excommunicari."§

And yet, it is from a MS. of the eighth century that D'Achery published these extracts. There is at least no excuse for our learned author's not referring to the famous Cottonian MS. cited by Usher, which also contains these canons, and nevertheless belongs to the eighth century.

It is not only the sixth canon of the synod that is cited in this old Collectio Hibernensis Canonum, but almost all the canons of the synod are introduced into it, and many of them with the name of our apostle prefixed. This surely affords sufficient evidence of the antiquity of the synod of which we treat.

3. We shall for the present dismiss, with a few words, the other point of Dr. Todd's remarks. He supposes that the second part of the sixth canon above cited has relation to *the clerk's wife;* the

* Page 435. † See Todd, p. 487.
‡ Page 145. § Ex Lib. 1. cap. 7.

original words, as quoted by him, of the text seem, indeed, to leave no doubt on this head: since after speaking of *quicumque clericus*, it adds *et uxor ejus*. However, to say the least, Dr. Todd does not display his usual candour in this argument. When citing the original Latin text, he refers to Martene's edition;* and yet he forgets to mention that the word *ejus* (on which his own argument entirely rests) is omitted in Martene's text.

If this word were supposed to form part of the original text, it would supply an additional argument for the antiquity of these canons, as we should suppose this decree to have been enacted at a time when very many were assumed from the marriage state to the sacerdotal dignity, and when, consequently, a special enactment was required regarding the wives from whom the clergy should separate themselves, according to the disciplinary law of celibacy rigorously observed in our early Church. However, this formula, *uxor ejus*, occurs only in the text of Spelman, from whose edition it was copied by Ware and some others. The MS. from which Spelman took this text seems to have been of the eleventh century; and he himself assures us that it was corrupt in many places, *pluries malesanum*, and standing in absolute need of critical correction, *et in locis quibusdam criticorum implorans sagacitatem*. On the other hand, we have an accurate text of this ancient decree, viz , as it is recorded in the Collectio Hibernensis Canonum, one of the most authentic of our ecclesiastical monuments, and dating from the year 700. Now, in this invaluable record, the canon of our apostle is thus quoted:

"Patricius: quicumque clericus ab ostiario usque ad sacerdotem, si non tunica usus fuerit, quæ turpitudinem ventris tegat et nuditatem, et si non more Romano capilli ejus tonsi sint: et uxor si non velato capite ambulaverit, pariter a laicis contemnentur et ab Ecclesia separentur."†

"Patrick decreed: Whatsoever cleric, from an ostiarius to a priest, who shall not wear a tunic to cover his nakedness, and whose hair is not shorn according to the usage of Rome; and a wife appearing in public with an unveiled head, shall be alike despised by the laity, and separated from the Church."

---

* Page 486.   † Lib. v. can. 5.

Thus, then, there is nothing in the ancient canon of St. Patrick about the "*clerk and his wife;*" but whilst the first part of the canon presents an enactment regarding the clergy, the second part prescribes that married women too should adopt the law of Rome, and that only when veiled should they be permitted to appear in public. In the Roman Church, as we learn from St. Jerome, the veil was worn by virgins consecrated to God, as a sign of their being espoused to Christ, and by married females, *in signum obedientiæ viro suo.* Thus our apostle, whilst sanctioning the Roman usage in regard to the ordinary dress of the clergy, wished, too, to introduce the veil as worn by the married females in Rome. This is the only meaning which can be attached to the second part of the sixth canon. Wearing the hair unshorn was considered equivalent to wearing the veil: and in the Collectio Hibernensis Canonum, almost immediately after the canon just cited, is added another chapter: "De eo quod non oportet mulieri tonderi," in which occurs the following extract from an ancient writer:—

"Duo abusiva vidi, viros comam enutrientes, et sacerdotem panem Domino offerentem albis non indutum ; tertium autem detestatum mihi et Deo, mulierem crines tondere qui pro velamine ei dati sunt."

In conclusion, we must remark, that the famous Vatican MS., No. 1349, written in the beginning of the tenth century, also cites this sixth canon of our apostle, and omits the *ejus* precisely as in the Collectio Hibernensis Canonum.*

4. The other canons which Dr. Todd refers to, in order to fix their date in the ninth or tenth century, will not detain us long.

The thirty-third canon enacts as follows:—" Clericus qui de Britannis ad nos venit sine epistola, etsi habitet in plebe, non licitum ministrare." Dr. Todd remarks: "It is possible that this may have been suggested by the similar canons made in England in the ninth century, to restrain the wandering bishops of the Scoti."† The canons, however, made in England, to which the learned author refers, have no similarity with that which is now

---

* Lib. vi. cap. 3, fol. 123.   † Pag. 488.

before us. They, for peculiar reasons, enacted that *nullus ex genere Scotorum* be allowed to assume the exercise of the sacred ministry.* On the other hand, the thirty-third canon of St. Patrick implies that Britain was infected with Pelagianism, and hence, every cleric coming from its shores to Ireland, whether he was Briton, or Scot, or Frank, should produce his letters of communion with the Catholic Church before being allowed to exercise his sacred ministry in Ireland. The first council of Carthage, held in the year 410, decreed, in its seventh canon: "Clericus vel laicus non communicet in aliena plebe sine litteris Episcopi sui." The same decree was repeatedly enacted at Antioch, and in other councils. It is therefore nowise necessary to look to the ninth century, when this canon might perhaps be dictated by a spirit of hostility to Britain: we find a more Christian motive for its enactment in the fifth century, when, forsooth, it merely re-echoed on the shores of Ireland the canonical decrees and the disciplinary laws of the whole western world.

Dr. Todd concludes his remarks on this synod with the following words:—

"We have already noticed the twenty-fifth canon, in which offerings made to the bishop are mentioned as *an ancient custom, mos antiquus*. This could not possibly have been written by St. Patrick: there could have been no such *ancient* custom in Ireland in the fifth century."†

The weak point in this argument of Dr. Todd is, that he gratuitously supposes *the ancient custom* to refer to Ireland. St. Patrick, however, only declares that such was an ancient custom in the Church; and we find precisely that custom which he thus declares to be an ancient one, confirmed in express terms in the council of Antioch, in 341. Thus, then, the gratuitous supposition of Dr. Todd would bring these decrees to a late date; but the words of the *canons* themselves have nothing to imply such a modern origin. They all, without exception, conspire in pointing to the very period of our apostle; and many of them which have reference to pagan-

---

* See Concil. Celichyth. can. 5, cited by Todd, pag. 43.   † Pag. 488.

ism and slavery, would be quite out of place in any other period of the history of our Church.

When we come to speak of the law of celibacy, as observed in the early Irish Church, we shall have occasion to further illustrate the second part of the sixth canon referred to in the present Appendix.

APPENDIX No. VII.

COLLECTIO HIBERNENSIS CANONUM.

Extracts from this collection by the Benedictines, D'Achery, etc.—Dr. Todd and Dr. Graves treat of it.—Usher refers it to the year 700.— The Cottonian MS. of it.—Cambray MS.—Other MS.—Two Vatican MSS.—Extracts.—Vallicellian MSS.—Extracts.

A DISCIPLINARY code, drawn up from various ecclesiastical sources for the use of the Irish Church, as early as the year 700, must be a subject of interest to every student of our antiquities. Though as yet unpublished, it has been long known to the literary world. Usher, in his Essay on the Religion of the Early Irish Church, more than once speaks enthusiastically in its praise. Spelman, Ware, and Wilkins make frequent reference to it. On the continent, the learned Benedictine D'Achery, in his Spicilegium, culled from it a long series of canons specially connected with Ireland. Two other members of the same order, Durand and Edmund Martene, continued the literary researches of their colleague; and in their Thesaurus Anecdotorum, published many additional extracts from our Irish collection. Later still, it was commemorated by Fabricy and Cardinal Maj. Dr. Todd, in his Memoir of St. Patrick,* laments that as yet no complete edition of this invaluable document has been made ; and Dr. Graves, towards the close of 1851, called the attention of the Royal Irish Academy to the importance of this ancient Collectio Canonum, and to the

* Page 145.

valuable authentic evidence which it supplied in proof of "the genuineness and antiquity of the Brehon laws."*

Usher referred this Collectio Hibernensis Canonum to "*about the year* 700." It was known to him through the famous Cottonian Manuscript (marked, *Otho, E.* xiii.), which even in his time was supposed to have passed unharmed through the vicissitudes of little less than 900 years. Reeves, in his edition of Adamnan, informs us that this precious manuscript was "one of those which suffered by the fire of 1731, and were lately restored under the care of Sir F. Madden."† The same skilful editor favours us with an extract from folio 142, which had already been incorrectly published by Usher. It assigns the origin of St. Peter's tonsure:

"Ut a Simone Mago Christianos discerneret, in cujus capite cæsaries ab aure ad aurem tonsæ anteriore parte, cum antea Magi in fronte cirrum habebant."

And adds:

"Romani dicunt tonsuram a Simone Mago sumpsisse initium, cujus tonsura de aure ad aurem tantum contingebat; pro excellentia ipsa *magorum tonsura*, qua sola frons anterior tegi solebat. Auctorem autem hujus tonsuræ in Hibernia subulcum regis Loigeri filii Nailis extitisse, Patricii sermo testatur: ex quo Hibernenses pene omnes hanc tonsuram sumpserunt."

Dr. Reeves remarks that the word *mael*, in Irish, means tonsured; and that one of king Leoghaire's magi is called, in our early records, *Lucet-mael*. Also the charioteer of St. Patrick is designated, in the Book of Armagh, by the names *Tot-mael* and *Bodmailus*.

Another manuscript containing this collection is marked No. 619 in the library of Cambray. O'Donovan, in the Introduction to his Irish Grammar, judging from the dialect of the Irish extracts inserted in the MS., concluded that it should be assigned to

---

* Proceedings of Royal Irish Academy, December 8, 1851. See above, p. 126.
† Preface, p. xlvii.

the eighth century; and a colophon added to the collection of canons confirms his opinion. It is as follows:—

"Explicit liber canonum quem Dominus Albericus Episcopus urbis Camaracensium et Adrabatensium fieri rogavit. Deo grâtias. Amen."*

Thus, then, this MS. was transcribed for Bishop Alberic, who governed the dioceses of Cambray and Arras from 763 to 790; and, in conformity with this colophon, the manuscript is registered in the Catalogue of Cambray as an "*écriture minuscule du huitième siècle.*" An Irish fragment from this manuscript was published by Zeuss, with a Latin translation, in the Appendix to his Celtic Grammar,† in 1853, it was also translated into English by the late lamented O'Curry,‡ in 1852. It is a sermon on the Gospel text, "Si quis vult post me venire tollat crucem suam et sequatur me," and thus begins:—

"These words are an invitation of Jesus to embrace self-denial, to banish from our hearts evil deeds and sin, to pursue good works, and to embrace the reproach and sign of the cross for Christ's sake, whilst we are in the subjection of the body and soul, that thus we may holily walk in the footsteps of the Redeemer: therefore, he says, *Si quis vult,*" etc.

It then gives the following extract without indicating the author:—

"Et nomen crux quippe a cruciatu dicitur et duobus modis crucem Domini bajulamus cum aut per abstinentiam, carnem afficiamus aut per compassionem proximi necessitatem illius nostram esse putamus; qui enim dolorem exhibet in aliena necessitate crucem portat in mente ut Paulus ait, portate onera vestra invicem, sic adimplebitis legem Christi."

It subsequently says:

"There are three sorts of martyrdom which are reputed as a cross unto man, white martyrdom, blue martyrdom, and red martyrdom. It is *white martyrdom* when, through love for God, man separates himself from all in which there is voluptuousness; it is *blue martyrdom* when he renounces his pleasures and embraces suffering in penance and mortification; it is *red martyrdom* when death is endured for Christ," etc.

---

* Pertz Archiv. etc. tom. 8, pag. 432; Zeuss Gram. Celt Introduct. xxxiii.; Proceedings of R. I. A. 1851, page 223.
† Vol. II. page 1003.   ‡ See his Lectures, etc. page 28.

The last words of this curious Irish fragment are :—

"There are, moreover, three sorts of martyrdom, for whose torture we return thanks, and great is our remuneration if we endure them, viz., *castitas in juventute ; continentia in abundantia ; et,*"

the sentence thus breaking off incomplete. This manuscript does not give the entire collection of canons, but only its first thirty-eight divisions.

D'Achery availed himself of two other MSS. when preparing his extracts from our Collectio Hibernensis. One belonged to the monastery of Corbey,* the other is now in the Imperial Library, Paris, amongst the St. Germain manuscripts, No. 121,† and belongs to the eighth century. The learned editor assigns two reasons why he published only extracts instead of the entire collection. 1st. That many of the passages from the fathers, and the decrees of the continental synods, which are introduced, were already well known to the public. 2nd. That such was the obscurity of the style, the peculiarity of the Latin construction, and the carelessness of the copyists in some passages, that he shrunk from the labour of editing them, *summum refugi laborem.* He tells us that at the end of the Corbey Manuscript the scribe added the following note:

"Arbedoc clericus ipse has collectiones conscripsi, laciniosæ conscriptionis, Haelhucar Abbate dispensante quæ de Sanctis Scripturis vel divinis fontibus hic in hoc codice glomeratæ sunt, sive etiam decreta quæ Sancti Patres et Synodi in diversis gentibus vel linguis construxerunt."

This *Haelhucar* is styled by Fabricy, *an Irish Abbot:* it is probable, however, that the name is a miss-print for Maelhucar, or some other similar word.

Martene added several canons to those edited by D'Achery, using a manuscript of the eleventh century, which he discovered in the Bigotian Library in Rouen. This MS. formerly belonged to the monastery of Fescamp, in Normandy, and is now preserved

---

* See Mabillon De Re Diplomatica, pag. 360.   † Olim, 572.

in the Parisian Library, No. 3182. It contains, in addition to this *collection of canons*, a fragment of an Irish synod, the penitential canons of St. Adamnan, and many other records connected with our early Church. In its sixty-fourth division, chapter v., we find the following passage:—

"De quatuor petitionibus Patricii, Hibernenses dicunt: sed Deo tuo gratulare nunc quia tuæ datæ sunt tibi quatuor petitiones quas petisti. Prima petitio est, ut in Ardmach ordinatio tuæ fiat gratiæ. Secunda petitio est ut quicumque hymnum qui tibi compositus est in die exitus de corpore cantaverit tu ejus pœnitentiam judicaveris. Tertia petitio est: ut nepotes Dichuin qui te benigne susceperunt misericordiam consequantur hic et in futuro et non pereant. Quarta petitio est: ut Hibernenses omnes in die judicii a te judicentur sicut dicitur ad Apostolos, *et vos sedentes judicabitis duodecim tribus Israel;* ut eos, quibus Apostolus fuisti, judices."

It is a striking confirmation of the authenticity of our early records, that these four petitions are found almost word for word in the Book of Armagh (fol. 8), from which they were translated by Todd, in his Memoir of St. Patrick (pag. 490-1). There is another and distinct heading amongst the extracts of D'Achery: "De tribus petitionibus Patricii," which must not be confounded with the one just cited. It is as follows:—

"Tres petitiones Patricii sunt; quarum prima est ut bipartitæ vel tripartitæ regionis pars Ecclesiæ propinquorum detur ei. Secunda ut non per juramentum ab aliquo firmetur super Ecclesiam infirmam. Tertia, ut clericus similis quæratur a laico."

This passage is, to say the least, very unintelligible; to render its meaning somewhat clear, we add it as given in the Vallicellian Manuscript, to which we shall just now refer:—

"Prima est ut bipartitæ regionis vel tripartitæ pars, Ecclesiæ detur, quæ ei vicinior cæteris. Secunda: ut non per juramentum mundiales subtrahant jus Ecclesiæ. Tertia: ut in judicio cum inter clerum et laicum orta fuerit contentio, quærat laicus clericum qui cum clerico contendat."

The Vatican MS. No. 1339, (sæc. x^{mi}) contains a collection of canons made in North Italy about the year 920. The Ballerinii, in their learned treatise On the Ancient Canonical Collections, enter into a full examination of this important manuscript, and Theiner, in his later disquisition, eulogizes it: "Hæc pro critica fontium disquisitione maximi momenti esse dignoscitur."[*] It adopts many canons of our apostle, and also introduces passages from the life of St. Furse and other Irish records. What is of most importance for our present purpose, it inserts almost the entire of the Irish collection now before us. "Utramque collectionem despiciens," writes Theimer, "valde miratus sum quod totam collectionis Hibernensis materiam in nostra collectione excerptam ac tractatam viderim."[†] Hence it must be regarded as a distinct text for determining the accurate reading of the decrees of our Collectio Hibernensis. It may not be uninteresting to give a few examples: at folio 20 is given the decree regarding the *Ostiarius*, "Hostiarium decet percutere *cloccas* et aperire Ecclesiam, et sacrarium, et codicem quo prædicatur et legitur?" and the marginal note is added in the original hand-writing, "Cloccas: signa quæ nos dicimus campanas." At folio 124: "Patricius; si quis clericus acceperit permissione Abbatis, collatum prætium de artificio suo, non plus exigat quam necessitas poposcit; si qua usura remanserit, detur indigentibus et captivis; non tradat aliis, nam si tradiderit peccatum facit." Subsequently we have: "Synodus Hibernensis; sors inter dubia, aut inter duo æqualia aut inter duo Catholica mitti debet." Again: "Synodus Hibernensis; Hi sunt modi excommunicationis hominis mali; a celebratione Missarum, a communicatione mensæ, a cohabitatione, a colloquio pacifico, a benedictione, a comitatu et muneribus." At folio 134 is the following curious extract from the fiftieth book of the Collectio Hibernensis:—

"De quinque causis quibus tonsuratus est Petrus. Romani dicunt: Petrus quinque causis tonsuram accepit; 1. Ut simularet spineam coronam Christi; 2. Ut clerici a laicis in tonsura discretionem haberent, ut in habitu sicut in operibus discernerentur; 3. Ut sacerdotes Veteris Testamenti reprobaret, suscipiendo tonsuram in illa parte capitis, supra quam

---

[*] Disquisitiones Criticæ in præcipuas Canonum Collectiones. Romæ, 1836 (pag. 271).
[†] Ib. page 278.

Columba descendit; 4. Ut derisionis ganuituram suscepturus pro Christo sustineret; 5. Ut a Symone Mago Christianorum discerneret tonsuram in cujus capite arula ab aure ad aurem ducta per frontem tonsurando pendebat."

To the word *arula* is added the marginal note *areola quadrangula*.

The Vatican Manuscript, No. 1,849, is also a collection of canons, and is referred by Cardinal Mai to the close of the ninth or the beginning of the tenth century. It was made for the use of some religious in Rome, and several Irish documents, especially the Penitential of St. Cummian, are repeatedly referred to. Many extracts from our Collectio Hibernensis Canonum are also introduced. Its sixth book, divided into twenty-five chapters, each of which has several sub-divisions, is wholly taken from our Irish collection, and even the preface or prologue prefixed to the Irish collection is introduced as a prologue to this sixth book. Amongst the extracts from our Collectio Hibernensis we find in book iii. can. 5 :—

"De modis quibus nunc immolat Ecclesia. Synodus Hibernensis: Ecclesia multis modis offert: 1. pro se ipsa; 2. commemoratione Jesu Christi qui dixit hoc facite in meam commemorationem; 3. Pro animabus defunctorum."

Again, in book viii. can. 22 :—

"De Sedacio communionis. Sedacium (that is, *the alms*) communionis si modicum fuerit respui non debet, et si magnum, accipiendum sed prætium vaccæ non excedat. Hoc sedacium aufugit reges et episcopum cui monachus est et fratres. Quidem autem Hibernensium in hoc sedacium, ovem aut prætium ejus statuta dimensione tribui censuerunt."

We may add the *prologue*, which was already, indeed, printed by D'Achery, from the Corbey MS., but with many errors. It is thus in the Vatican MS. :—

"Synodicorum exemplarium innumerositatem conspiciens, ac plurimorum ex ipsis obscuritatem rudibus inutilem prævidens necnon cæterorum diversitatem inconsonam destruentemque magis quam ædificantem perspiciens, brevem plenamque ac consonam ex ingenti silva scriptorum in unius voluminis textum expositionem digessi, plura addens ut plura describerentur, singulorum nomina singulis testimoniis præscripta composui, ne quis velut incertum quid pro quo dicat, ut cum generales titulos quos necessario præposuimus percurrat, numeros diligenter observet; quibus observatis quæstionem quam voluerit sine ulla cunctatione reperiet."

We were happily able to avail ourselves of these two Vatican manuscripts, when referring in the preceding pages to the ancient Collectio Hibernensis Canonum. We were still more fortunate in having free access to a complete and elegant copy of the same Irish collection, which is carefully preserved in the Vallicellian Archives, Rome. This precious MS. was accurately described by the Ballerinii and Theiner in the treatises already referred to; it dates from the tenth century, and is numbered *xviii.* in the Vallicellian catalogue. The Ballerinii reckoned it more accurate than the MSS. consulted by D'Achery and Martene :* the scribe, however, seems to have found it difficult in some places to decipher the Irish text which he was engaged in copying; occasionally space is left for some words which he could not decipher; frequently he errs in reading the original contractions, and hence *Gil.* (*i.e.* Gildas) a name but little known to the Roman copyist, becomes *Gelasius; Hir.* (*i.e.* Hieronymus) is changed to *Hieremias;* and *Patrius* (the contraction used for our apostle's name in the Book of Armagh, O'Curry Lectures, pag. 653) is transformed into *Paterius*. What, however, renders it still more unsatisfactory is the occasionally recurring *reliqua* as a substitute for Irish canons, the peculiar construction of which was probably unintelligible to the copyist.

As regards the date of the Collectio Hibernensis, it is generally assigned to the close of the seventh century or the beginning of the eighth. No documents as late as the year 700 are introduced into it: even Theodore of Canterbury, whose Penitential decrees are continually referred to in the collections of the eighth century, is named but once. The delicacy with which the compiler speaks of the Paschal question shows that it had been but lately settled in our island: he refers the error solely to the Britons : " Pascha et tonsura Brittonum." How different is the English Penitential that was drawn up by the priest Eoda some years after the death of abp.

---

* See Appendix to opp. S. Leonis Magni. tom. 3tio. pag. cclxxiii. 5.

Theodore; it invariably links together *the Irish and Britons*;[*] and two other Penitentials[†] drawn up about the middle of the eighth century employ the same language.

The decrees of the Irish Synod, held in 694 or 695, are usually cited with the simple title *Synodus*, though in the later MSS. the word *Hibernensis* is often added. This manner of referring to that celebrated synod, which formed an epoch in the Irish Church, and, moreover, was celebrated for the precise purpose of restoring uniformity in the Paschal and Tonsure discipline, sufficiently proves that the Collectio Canonum was made immediately after its celebration; and, perhaps, was ordered by the assembled Fathers, that thus one common code of ecclesiastical and disciplinary laws might be within the reach of all.

At all events, more than one of the manuscripts which present the Collection to us belong, as we have seen, to the eighth century. There is, moreover, a very ancient Penitential which helps to fix its date. This Penitential was first published by Martene,[‡] and subsequently by Wasserschleben.[§] One of its decrees fixes its date, as, citing the council held in Rome in 721, by Gregory II., it adds regarding that pontiff: "qui *nunc* Romanam Catholicam gerit matrem Ecclesiam." Pope Gregory died in 731: so thus we may safely refer the date of the Penitential to about the year 730. Now, more than fifteen of its decrees are extracted from our Collectio Hibernensis Canonum; and so plainly are they copied from it, that one of the decrees (the thirteenth) inserts in the text the rubric of the canon in our Irish collection.

We may, therefore, without hesitation, acquiesce in the opinion of Usher, that the Collectio Hibernensis Canonum was drawn up towards the close of the seventh or the beginning of the eighth century.

We now add, as a specimen of this ancient record, its ninth book, which is one of the shortest of the whole Collection, as found in the Vallicellian manuscript:—

---

[*] Ap. Wasserschleben, p. 210.   [†] Ib.
[‡] In Nov. Thes. Anecd tom, iv. pag. 31, seqq.
[§] Loc. cit pag. 282, seqq.

"De Acolytho et Psalmista, capitula duo.

1. "*De acolythi ordinatione.*

"Acolythus accensor luminarium : is cum ordinatur, ab Episcopo quidem docetur qualiter se in officio suo gerere debeat. Sed ab Archidiacono accipiat trasorium cum cereis ut sciat accendere Ecclesiæ luminaria, eique ministerio mancipari : accipiat et urceolum vacuum ad suggerendum vinum in Eucharistiam Corporis Christi.

2. "*De Psalmistarum exordio et voce et usu et nomine.*

"Psalmistarum auctores David et Asaph extiterunt : mortuo enim Asaph filii ejus ad hanc ordinationem a David subrogati sunt erantque psalmistæ per successionem generis sicut ordo sacerdotalis. Ex hoc veteri more Ecclesia sumpsit exemplum ordinandi psalmistas quorum cantibus ad affectum Dei mentes audientium excitantur. Vox enim ejus non aspera vel rauca vel dissonans sed canora erit et suavis, lucida atque acuta habens sonum et melodiam sanctæ religioni congruentem neque musica vel theatrali arte redoleat sed quæ compunctionem cordis magis audientibus faciat. Psalmista potest absentiâ Episcopi sola jussione Presbyteri officium suscipere cantandi ; dicente presbytero, vide ut quæ ore cantas, corde credas ; et quæ corde credis, operibus impleas.

Psalmista Græce, cantor Latine ; psalmus, canticum ; sed psalmus divinus, canticum humanum."

APPENDIX No. VIII.

IRISH SYNOD OF THE YEAR 807.

"HIBERNENSIS SYNODUS SUB LEONE 3TIO."

FOR this synod see page 180, where we have referred to it. The two extracts here given are from the Vallicellian Archives, c. 24:

"Inter cætera quæ de ordine Sanctarum Ecclesiarum sancita sunt, Sancta Synodus Hibenensis, cui præfuit Leo Sanctæ Rom. Ecclesiæ Episcopus, tempore Karoli Regis Francorum cum Theodorico* (*i.e.* Torbach) Anglorum et Hibernensium Archiepo multisque aliis illarum regionum Episcopis de lapsu sacerdotum sic ait : si presbyter fornicationem fecerit quamquam secundum Apostolorum canones deponi debeat tamen juxta auctoritatem beati Silvestri Papæ si in vitio non perduraverit sed sua sponte confessus adjecit ut resurgeret, decem annis in hunc modum

---

* It is thus the Irish name Torbach, as also Turlogh, is Latinized by our writers.

pœniteat. Tribus siquidem mensibus privato loco a cæteris remotus solo pane et aqua a vespera in vesperam utatur: diebus autem Dominicis et præcipuis festis modico vino et pisciculis atque leguminibus recreetur, sine carne, sine sagmine, ovis et caseo: sacco indutus humo adhæreat; die ac nocte jugiter omnipotentis Dei misericordiam imploret. Finitis tribus continuis mensibus exeat, tamen in publicum non procedat, ne grex fidelis in eo scandalum patiatur. Nec enim debet sacerdos publice pœnitere sicut laicus. Postea aliquantisper resumptis viribus unum annum et dimidium in pane et aqua expleat, exceptis dominicis diebus et præcipuis festis, in quibus vino, sagmine, ovis et caseo juxta canonicam mensuram uti poterit. Finito primo anno et dimidio, corporis et sanguinis Domini Christi, ne indurescat, particeps fiat, et ad pacem veniat; cum fratribus psalmos in choro ultimus canat, ad cornu altaris non accedat: juxta B. Clementis vocem minora gerat officia. Deinde vero usque ad expletionem septimi anni omni quidem tempore exceptis Paschalibus diebus tres legitimas ferias in unaquaque hebdomada in aqua et pane jejunet. Expleto vii anni circulo, si sui confratres, apud quos pœnituit ejus condignam pœnitentiam conlaudaverint, Episcopus in pristinum honorem juxta B. Callisti Papæ auctoritatem eum revocare poterit. Sane sciendum quia secundam feriam unum psalterium canendo aut unum denarium pauperi dando si operarius est, redimere poterit. Finitis septem annis deinde usque ad finem decimi anni sextam feriam nulla interveniente redemptione observet in pane et aqua. Eadem quoque pœnitentia erit sacerdoti de omnibus aliis peccatis et criminibus, quæ eum in depositionem adducunt, neque hoc cuilibet videatur onerosum, si sacerdos post lapsum digne, ut supra dictum est, pœnitens ad pristinos redeat honores."

To this extract is added, with the heading *ex alio libro*, a somewhat similar decree of the same Irish synod, as follows:

"Ex Concilio Hibernensi.

"Inter cætera quæ de ordine etc. (as above) sic ait: Placuit ut deinceps nulli sacerdotem liceat quemlibet commissum alteri sacerdotum ad pœnitentiam suscipere sine ejus consensu cui se prius commisit, nisi per ignorantiam illius cui pœnitens prius confessus est: qui vero contra hæc statuta facere temptaverit, gradus sui ordinis periculo subjacebit. Sed et hoc in omni pœnitentia non solum laicali sed etiam sacerdotali sollerter est intuendum quanto quis tempore in delictis remaneat. Qua eruditione imbutus, quali impugnatur passione vel ætate, qualiter compulsus est peccare gravitate aut necessitate. Omnipotens etenim Deus qui corda hominum novit, diversisque gentibus quas creavit, diversas naturas indidit non æquali lance pœnitudinis pondera peccaminum pensabit: ut est illud propheticum. (Isai xxviii.) Non enim in serris triturabitur gith nec rota plaustri super cyminum circuibit: sed in virga excutietur gith, et cyminum in baculo: Panis autem comminuetur. Ac proinde considerata humanæ fragilitatis infirmitate, sacerdos si suggerente diabolo in fornicationem ceciderit, et Deo miserante ad pœnitentiæ remedia confugerit,

Y

quatuor annis in hunc modum expiabitur. In primis xl diebus et noctibus se purificet tuto remotus in loco in solo pane et aqua; Quibus exactis primo anno qui sequitur in pane et aqua similiter luat exceptis Dominicis et paschalibus et præcipuis festis, in quibus vino et omnibus pulmentis uti poterit excepta sola carne. Cæteris vero diebus solo pane et aqua sit contentus nisi considerata personæ qualitate in his etiam feriis indulgeatur, et de modico vino, legumine, lacte, pomis, pisciculis et oleribus sicut confessori suo visum fuerit. Decurso igitur primo anno statim sacrosancti corporis et sanguinis Domini particeps fiat; psalmos cum fratribus in choro ultimus canat et ad pacem veniat, minora gerat officia : in secundo anno tres legitimas ferias in unaquaque hebdomada expleat in pane et aqua. Expletis duobus annis si juxta præfixos gradus pœnituit, Episcopus eum in gradum unde excidit revocare poterit."

APPENDIX No. IX.

HYMNS FROM THE BANGOR ANTIPHONARY.

The Bangor Antiphonary.—Extracts from it.—Hymn of St. Comghill.—Hymn commemorative of the Holy Abbots of Bangor.—Hymn of St. Camelach.

THE following hymns, together with the extracts already given in the text,* will suffice to give some idea of the remarkable Irish MS. known as the Antiphonarium Benchorense. It was first published by Muratori, in his Anecdota Ambrosiana, vol. iv. Padua, 1713, and was inserted in the thirteenth volume of his complete works, printed at Arezzo in 1771. Lanigan writes of it, in the preface to his Ecclesiastical History :

"It was written in the seventh century, and originally belonged to the monastery of Bangor, in the now county of Down, whence it was removed to the monastery of Bobbio, in Italy, in the library of which latter place it was discovered by Cardinal Frederick Borromeo,† and from which it was transferred to the Ambrosian Library at Milan, where it is now to be found (No. 10, letter C). This curious and authentic

---

* See p. 164.
† This cardinal was titular of the church of St. Agatha, at present attached to the Irish College, Rome. See *Paneiroli*, Tesori Nascosti dell' Alma citta di Roma, p. 279.

document was shown by Muratori to Montfaucon—a competent judge of ancient manuscripts—who, after the closest inspection, pronounced it to be above one thousand years old."*

Dr. O'Conor has ably proved, from its intrinsic characteristics, the accuracy of the date thus assigned to the MS. by Montfaucon and Muratori. In the Commemoration of the Abbots of Bangor, he remarked that Cronan is described as still living and governing the monastery; and as St. Cronan died in 691, it necessarily follows that this MS. should be referred to an earlier period. The various saints referred to in the hymns are treated of by Colgan, Lanigan, and others:

A.

HYMNUS SANCTI COMGILLI ABBATIS NOSTRI.

1. "Recordemur justitiæ,
    Nostri patroni fulgidæ
    Comgilli Sancti nomine
    Refulgentis in opere.
    Adjuti Dei flamine
    Sancto claroque lumine,
    Trinitatis celsissimæ
    Cuncta tenentis regmine,
    Quem Deus ad ætherea
    Conduxit habitacula,
    Ab angelis custodita,
    Permansura in sæcula.

2. "Audite *pantes ta erga*,
    Allati ad angelica
    Athletæ Dei abdita,
    A juventute florida,
    Aucta in legis pagina,
    Alta sancti per viscera
    Affatim concordantia,
            Ab Angelis, etc.

3. "Bonam vitam, justitiam
    Benignitatem floridam,
    Caritatem firmissimam,
    Deo primo adhibitam,
    Juxta mandatum solidam
    In regno præstantissimam,

Proximis sæpe debitam,
Corde sereno placitam
Efficiebat cognitam,
In futuro fructiferam,
        Quem Deus, etc.

4. "Contemptum mundialium
    Voluptatum, præsentium
    Vitiorum firmissimum
    Infirmos devastantium
    Verborum cogitaminum
    Parte læva versantium,
    Continebat per viscerum
    Secreta vigilantium,
            Ab Angelis, etc.

5. "Doctus in Dei legibus
    Divinis dictionibus
    Ditatus sanctis opibus,
    Deo semper placentibus,
    Dedicatus in moribus,
    Dei Stephanus *agius*,
    Docebat sic et exeteros
    Dicta docta operibus,
            Quem Deus, etc.

6. "Elegit a primordio,
    Quod erat in principio,

* Page 8.

Æternum verbum paterno
Eructatum Sanctissimo
Corde verum altissimo
Carus eidem lucido
Pignus præclaro animo
Constans opere placido,
    Ab Angelis, etc.

7. "Fulgebat alti fulgore
Solis vice in vertice,
Rutilantis meridie
Fidei claritudine,
Confirmatus ex viscere
In Dei semper fidere,
Confidens sanctimoniæ
Præcipuo numine.
    Quem Deus, etc.

8. "Gaudium Sancti Spiritus
Habebat in visceribus
Regnum quod est sublimitus
Deo dignum, et fortius,
Gladium quoque spiritus
Levatum ad nequissimum
Quo prosterneret superbos
Tenens sanctis in manibus,
    Ab Angelis, etc.

9. "Humilis, sanctus, benignus
Probus in Dei legibus
Humanus, justus, commodus,
Laudabilis in moribus
Hilaris vultu, sobrius,
Caritatis in floribus,
Factus palam mortalibus
In scripturis eruditus.
Inspiratus divinitus,
In sacramentis providus,
Canonicis affatibus
Testamenti præfulgidus,
Fervens spiritu, placidus,
Deo carus, et piissimus :
    Ab Angelis, etc.

10. "Kalcavit mundum subdolum
Karitatis per studium
Kastitatis firmissimum
Contempnens omne vitium,
Inserens agrum floridum

Pectus adornans lucidum,
Divinum habitaculum,
Trino nomine sancitum.
    Quem Deus, etc.

11. "Lampadem sapientiæ
Constituit in pectore
In thesauro sapientiæ
Condito Dei munere
Inflammatus magnopere
Lucere veræ justitiæ,
Exaltatus munimine
Legis, spiritus, literæ,
    Ab Angelis, etc.

12. "Magnum adprehendit bravium
Æterna vita condignum,
Adeptus sanctum præmium
Post laborem firmissimum,
Cujus perfectum meritum
Vocamus in auxilium,
Ut mereamur omnium
Vitiorum excidium,
    Quem Deus, etc.

13. "Notus sanctorum cœtibus
Abbatum in ordinibus
Monachorum militibus
Anachoretarum sensibus
Synodum sanctis plebibus
Imo vir apostolicus
Clarus cunctis in sortibus,
Adauctus in sublimibus.
    Ab Angelis, etc.

14. "O petram solidissimam
In fundamento positam,
O contemptorem omnium
Rerum nequam præsentium,
O ducem sanctum militum
O Tyronem fortissimum,
Domino totum deditum.
    Quem Deus, etc.

15. "Positus muri ferrei
Vice in luce populi
Dissipare, disperdere,
Cuncta mala destruere,
Ædificare, plantare

Bona tota in commune
More sancti Hieremiæ
Constituti in culmine.
    Ab Angelis, etc.

16. " Quis contempsit presentia
Hujus ævi decidua?
Quis ascendit ad superna
Toto animo gaudia?
Quis volebat in æthera
Carne volare posita?
Qualiter iste talia
Adeptus sancta merita.
    Quem Deus, etc.

17. " Rexit Sanctam Ecclesiam
Catholicam per regulam,
Retinens fidem solidam
Malam contra nequitiam
Suam exercens animam
Sanctæ legis per paginam,
Cujus exopto gratiam
Mihi adornat animam.
    Ab Angelis, etc.

18. " Sapiens suos internos
Sanctos elevans oculos
Deducebat ad superos
Capite sancto intentos
Parte sancta in dextera
Collocans sua viscera,
Centurionis opera
Habens sancta per studia.
    Quem Deus, etc.

19. " Tulit suam memoriam
Ad mansionem supernam
Caram Deo, et floridam
Suam exercens animam,
Contempnens terram subdo-
  lam
Vanam omnem insaniam
Domans cum Abraham
Ad terram illam optimam.
    Ab Angelis, etc.

20. " Vitam æternam fulgida
Adeptus est sub corona
Ubi adsumet præmia
Permansura in sæcula
Comitaturus agmina
Angelorum præcipua
Inquirens semper talia
Vigilans in Ecclesia.
    Quem Deus, etc.

21. " Xristum orabat magistrum,
Summum ornans obsequium,
Christi gerens officium
Actum per apostolicum
Hujus sequens vestigium
Ducens Deo exercitum
In sanctum habitaculum
Trinitatis lectissimum.
    Ab Angelis, etc.

22. " Ymnum Deo cum cantico
Immolabat altissimo,
Diei noctis circulo
Orans sæpe cum triumpho
Nunc cantavit sub numero
Canticum novum Domino
Junctus choro angelico
Summo sanctis in jubilo
    Quem Deus, etc.

23. " Zona cinctus justitiæ
Castitatis eximiæ
Mundus opertus sindone
In signo castimoniæ
Fœminalia lucidæ
Habens toto ex viscere,
Cujus sancto pro opere
Reddetur merces condigne.
    Quem Deus ad æthera
    Conduxit habitacula
    Ab Angelus custodita
    Permansura in sæcula.

"Per merita, et orationes S. Comgilli abbatis nostri omnes nos Domine in tua pace custodi."

B.

MEMORIA ABBATUM NOSTRORUM.

" Sancta sanctorum opera
Patrum, fratres, fortissima
Benchorensi in optima
Fundatorum Ecclesia,
Abbatum eminentia
Numerum, tempora, nomina
Sine fine fulgentia,
Audite magna merita,
Quos convocavit Dominus
Cœlorum regni sedibus.

" Amavit Christus *Comgillum*,
Bene et ipse Dominum,
Carum habuit *Beognoum*,
Domnum ornavit ac Deum,
Elegit sanctum *Simlanum*,
Famosum mundi magistrum
Quos convocavit Dominus
Cœlorum regni sedibus.

" Gratum fecit *Fintenanum*
Heredem, almum, inclytum
Illustravit *Machlaisreum*
Kaput abbatum omnium
Lampadem sacram *Seganum*
Magnum scripturæ medicum
Quos convocavit Dominus
Cœlorum regni sedibus.

" Notus vir erat *Beracnus*,
Ornatus et *Cumnenus*,
Pastor *Columba* congruus,
Querela absque *Aidanus*,
Rector bonus *Bautherius*
Summus antistes *Cronanus*
Quos convocavit Dominus
Cœlorum regni sedibus.

" Tantis successit *Camanus*
Vir admirabilis omnibus
Christo nunc sedet supremus
Hymnos canens quindecimus
Zoen ut carpat *Cronanus*
Conservet eum Dominus,
Quos convocabit Dominus
Cœlorum regni sedibus.

" Horum sanctorum merita
Abbatum fidelissima
Erga Comgillum congrua
Invocamus altissima,
Uti possimus omnia
Nostra delere crimina
Per Jesum Christum æterna
Regnantem in sæcula.

C.

HYMNUS SANCTI CAMELACI.

" Audite bonum exemplum
Benedicti pauperis
Camelaci Cumiensis
Dei justi famuli.
Exemplum præbet in toto,
Fidelis in opere,
Gratias Deo agens,
Hylaris in omnibus,
Jejunus, et mansuetus ;
Kastus hic servit Deo,
Lætatur in paupertate,
Mitis est in omnibus,

Noctibus, atque diebus
Orat Dominum suum,
Prudens, justus, ac fidelis,
Quem cognati diligunt.
Regem Deum aspexit,
Salvatoremque suum
Tribuit huic æternam
Vitam cum fidelibus.
Christus illum insinuavit
Patriarchæ Abrahæ
In Paradiso regnabit
Cum sancto Eleazaro."

APPENDIX No. X.

HYMNS IN HONOUR OF ST. FOILLANUS.

We insert the following hymn, taken from a MS. in the Vallicellian library in Rome, regarding an Irish saint, Foillanus, whose festival is celebrated in Liege.* For the history of this saint, and his brothers, St. Furse and St. Ultan, see Lanigan's Ecclesiastical History of Ireland † (See also ante, page 145.) St. Foillanus was martyred in Belgium about the year 655 :

HYMNUS IN FESTO S. FOILLANI, EPI. ET MART.

Die 31 *Octob. ad* 1*as Vesperas.*

Novis hymnorum modulis Christo canamus gloriam
Foillani Pontificis venerantes memoriam.
Foillanus nunc sequitur agnum quocumque ierit
Et Præsuli conceditur quidquid Deum rogaverit.
Auctor nostri Collegii, gregisque Pastor crediti,
O Foillane, quæsumus, fer opem nobis omnibus.
Quondam refulgens nitoris Maris Hyberni sedibus
Procedens sol et aureus nostris ortus est finibus.
Vir doctrina clarissimus urbem Romanam adiit
Carnis fatiscens artubus Mortis futuræ præsciens
Martino tum Pontifice venit jubente in Galliam
Suæ virtutis lumine hanc ut bearet patriam.
Huc Ultanus comitatur; Gertrudis patrimonio
Fossis Doctor collocatur. Signorum fulgens radio
Cœleste tenens bravium Agnumque sequens prævium
Nostris peccatis poscimus medere sanctis precibus
Ave Pater Foillane, ave Martyr et Patrone
Tuo psallentes nomine, junge choris cœlestium
Ne nos illudat zabulus hac nocte suis fraudibus
Carnis utens illecebris vel somnii ludibriis.
Christo sit laus et gloria ac Foillano gaudia
Qui nobis cœli regia æterna donet prœmia. Amen.

---

* In Vallicellian Biblioth. *H.* 48. Codex MS. Offic. Eccles. Leodiensis.
† Vol. ii. p. 464.

Ad Completorium. Hymnus.

Respiremus in beati Foillani memoria
Et colamus ssmi præsulis solemnia
Exsurgamus excitati in ejus præconia.
Oriundus ex Hibernia sed regali prosapia
In ætate tenerrima crescens in sapientia
Florensque sanctimonia sprevit transitoria
Profectus in desertum sacro ducente spiritu
Fit Deo sacrificium manu peremptus impia
Delatus jussu Numinis ornat Fossas Reliquiis.
O Martyr nobilissime tua per suffragia
Foillane Deum flecte impetratâ venia
Ut æternæ conferatur vitæ nobis gloria. Amen.

Ad Laudes.

Clara prius Hyberniæ, lux Foillane patriæ
Densis tenebris obsitæ lumen dedisti Galliæ
In qua peractis omnibus quæ docuit Paraclitus
Quod summum vitæ decus est, beatus Martyr factus est.
Lucis compos æviternæ, nostras tenebras discute
Quos cultor stygis horridæ, densat multa caligine.
Hac nocte qua tartareum Jesus salvator januum
Rupit triumphans dæmonem, veram mentis confer pacem.
Ut cum corda discusserit et cum judex advenerit
Nos gaudentes efficiat, secumque cœlis inferat.
Deo Patri sit gloria, ejusque soli Filio
Cum Spiritu Paraclito et nunc et in perpetuum. Amen.

Ad Secundas Vesperas, in festis Inventionis et Translationis S. Foillani.

Exultet cœli Regia, tellus gaude Leodica
Quia regnat in patria præsul noster cum gloria,
Foillanus nunc sequitur Agnum quocumque ierit
Et Martyri conceditur quidquid Deum rogaverit.
Ignis in columna claruit solum tangens et sydera
Quæ luce signavit sua in nocte Divum corpora
Fons limpidus Martyrii demonstrat privilegium
Et Fossis sancto Corpori præstat undis obsequium
Sursum ferantur animi ad Præsulis præsidium
Nobis ut Deus conferat perennis vitæ bravium
Præsta Pater ingenite, Jesu cum sacro flamine
Ut Foillani precibus jungamur in cœlestibus. Amen.

INDEX.

	PAGE
Dedication	iii
Preface	v
Errata	viii

ESSAY

On the Origin of the Irish Church, and its connexion with Rome.

Part First.

CHAP. I.
MISSION OF ST. PALLADIUS.

Few Christians in Ireland before the arrival of St. Palladius: testimony of Prosper: Palladius sent from Rome in 431: Palladius as Deacon held a high post in Rome: Ireland known by the name *Scotia*: St. Palladius unsuccessful in his mission: account of his labours from the Book of Armagh: from the Scholiast of St. Fiacc and other sources 3-8

CHAP. II.
GENERAL SKETCH OF ST. PATRICK'S HISTORY.

Early life of St. Patrick: his captivity and subsequent liberation: he studies at Tours, Lerins, and Auxerre: visits Rome: accompanies St. Germanus into Britain: proceeds a second time to Rome, accompanied by Segetius: is consecrated by St. Amator: sets out for Ireland towards the close of 432 . 8-12

CHAP. III.
ST. PATRICK'S CONNEXION WITH ST. GERMANUS.

Testimony of Fiacc, Bishop of Sletty: Book of Armagh: Muirchu-Maccu-Mactheni: Cottonian Liturgical Tract of the 7th cent.: Eric of Auxerre: Irish Scholia on St. Fiacc's hymn: Irish *Nennius:* Lives of our Apostle 12-22

CHAP. IV.

ST. PATRICK'S MISSION FROM ROME.

Testimony from *Dicta S. Patritii*: St. Columbanus : St. Ultan, Bp. of Ard-Breccan : Tirechan : *Leabhar Breac*: St. Aileran : Scholiast on Fiacc : Probus : other Lives of St. Patrick : Life of St. Kieran : Eric of Auxerre : *historia Brittonum*: Annals of Four Masters ; of Innisfail ; of Ulster ; Maelbrighte : St. Prosper . 22-34

Part Second.

MODERN THEORIES REGARDING ST. PATRICK.

CHAP. I.

Theory of Ledwich : rejected by the tradition of Ireland : Aengus : Irish collection of Canons in 700 : St. Adamuan : Book of Armagh : Antiphonary of Bangor : St. Cummian Fota : St. Columba, Fiacc, Secundinus, etc. 35-38

CHAP. II.

Theories of Sir W. Betham and Usher : Betham's opinion contrary to the very documents which he cites : the formula *Scotos in Christo credentes*: the Irish Germanus. Usher's opinion contrary to our ancient annals: date of SS. Ailbe, Declan, Ibar, and Kieran: testimony of Prosper : of St. Patrick himself : origin of Irish Church from Rome 38-42

CHAP. III.

Dean Murray's theory : the Irish writers are not silent as to the mission of Palladius : foreign writers commemorate St. Patrick : Sigebert : Ricemarch : silence of Prosper and Bede : Fordun and the *Irish Nennius* 43-45

CHAP. IV.

Some opinions of Dr. Lanigan and Petrie : St. Sen-Patrick different from our Apostle : commemorated by Aengus, Annals of Connaught, etc. : corrected text of Marianus : Irish quatrain : Annals of Innisfail : Petrie's theory : distinctive features of St. Patrick's history : the Irish Augustine : St. Patrick not confounded with Palladius 46-50

CHAP. V.

Dr. Todd's opinion that St. Palladius was not a deacon of Rome; contrary to the testimony of Prosper: Mactheni and other writers: the Palladian family in Gaul and elsewhere: held high offices in Rome at this period 51-54

CHAP. VI.

Dr. Todd's opinion that St. Patrick did not commence his apostolate until 440: not supported by St. Patrick's writings: the *Irish Nennius: Synchronisms of the Irish Kings*: explicit testimony of the Annals of Ulster: Tirechan's statement: inconsistency of Todd's arguments: the Irish poet *Gilla-Caemhain*: not opposed to the common opinion: chronological Tract of Book of Lecan: true meaning of the passage cited by Dr. Todd: all our records conspire in referring the mission of St. Patrick to the year 432-3 55-66

CHAP. VII.

Dr. Todd's opinion that St. Patrick received no mission from Rome: the confession of our Apostle: why composed by him: why silent as to his mission from Pope Celestine: other writings of our Apostle: hymn of St. Sechnall: illogical reasoning of Dr. Todd: Muirchu-Maccu-Mactheni's Tract: titles of its lost chapters: his text coincides with Probus: reconstruction of his 5th and 6th chapters: conclusion 66-79

Part Third.

SENTIMENTS OF THE EARLY IRISH CHURCH REGARDING ROME.

CHAP. I.

Early Irish writers on the prerogatives of Rome: two hymns of the early Irish Church on the privileges of St. Peter: metrical translation of same: testimony of St. Cummian Fota: his Penitential: St. Sechnall's text mistranslated by Usher and Todd: St. Mochta of Louth: Irish profession of faith made in 460 (see Appendix V. page 296) 81-94

CHAP. I.—*Continued.*

Missal of St. Columbanus: His letters to Pope Boniface: objections drawn from them by Protestant writers: only serve to place in clearer light the Catholic teaching of the Irish Saint: letter to St. Gregory the Great 95-102

CHAP. I.—*Continued.*

The Irish Claudius: author of a commentary on the Gospels: passages cited by Usher: some passages carefully omitted by the Protestant Primate: Ancient Irish hymn: St. Cummian's Paschal letter: glimpse of Irish theology in the 7th century: St. Colman of Lindisfarne: the Whitby Conference: the Brehon Laws: Probus's life of Saint Patrick: St. Furse: Gillibert of Limerick 103-120

CHAP. II.

CANONICAL ENACTMENTS OF THE IRISH CHURCH REGARDING ROME.

Canon of St Patrick, that difficult cases are to be referred to Rome: Usher's remarks on this canon: it is found in the Book of Armagh: was acted on by the Irish synod of 630: is inserted in the Collectio Hibernensis Canonum: Dr. Todd's remarks on the published synod of SS. Patrick, Auxilius, and Iserninus: analysis of various decrees of the Irish collection of canons: incidental testimony of the same ancient monument: delusion of the late Protestant dean of Ardagh 120-131

CHAP. III.

IRISH PILGRIMAGES TO ROME.

Irish pilgrimages even in the time of our Apostle: *Germanus*, son of an Irish chieftain: St. Enna of Arrann islands: curious fact connected with his visit to Rome: St. Conlaedh, bishop of Kildare, brings vestments with him from Rome: St. Nennidh of the *pure hand*, and St. Brigid: St. Finnian of Clonard: St. Finnian of Moville devotes himself to sacred literature in Rome: was probably the same as the patron saint of Lucca: St. Gildas makes an offering on the altar of St. Peter: St. Molua: St. Flannan of Killaloe consecrated bishop in Rome: St. Carthage the elder: St. Laserian and Rome: SS. Wiro and Plechelm: St. Sylas: Irish bishops at Roman Council of 721; also in third Council of Lateran: St. Dichuill: St. Kilian and companions, etc. 131-144

CHAP. III.—*Continued.*

Pilgrimage of St. Canice to Rome: St. Foillan, patron of Brabant: St. Senanus of Inniscattery: Romans and other foreign religious seek a home in Ireland: St. Dagan: St. Gregory the Great sanctions Irish Rules: St. Cardoc and other pilgrims: Donogh O'Brien: St. Marianus: testimony of Ricemarch: Irish *hospitalia* in France: Irish expelled from them: St. Willibrord: St. Boniface: St. Witta 145-153

CHAPTER III.—*Continued.*

Appeals of Irish Saints to Rome : St. Columbanus : St. Virgilius the Paschal controversy: St. Cummian : Synod of Magh-lene attended by the bishops of Munster and Leinster : letter of the archbishop of Armagh and the northern bishops and clergy to Rome : reply of the Roman Church ; importance of this document: words of Dr. Lynch 153-160

ESSAY

On the Teaching of the Irish Church regarding the Blessed Eucharist.

CHAPTER I.

ANCIENT LITURGICAL TREATISES.

The Stowe Missal : its date : its doctrine regarding the Blessed Eucharist: the Bobbio Missal affords similar evidence : the Antiphonary of Bangor : the hymn Sancti Venite : remarks of the German hymnologist: old Gælic Tract from Leabhar Breac, on the Ceremonies of the Mass: Manuscript Treatise on the Mass-Vestments : catalogue of three classes of Irish Saints 161-173

CHAPTER II.

IRISH PENITENTIALS AND OTHER RECORDS.

Penitential of St. Cummian Fota : of St. Finnian : Bobbio Penitential : Pœnitentiale Bigotianum : beautiful canon of St. Columbanus : other facts connected with this saint and his disciples : ancient Irish collection of canons : decrees concerning the Viaticum, etc.: MS. Tract on the Ecclesiastical Orders : on the consecration of a church: the Brehon laws : on the rights of Church and Churchmen : Irish Synod in 807, held by Abp. Torbach (See Appendix VIII. page 320) . 174-182

CHAPTER II.—*Continued.*

Teaching of the Monastic or Cenobitical Rules : Rule of St. Mochuda or Carthage, patron of Lismore : duties of abbots and priests : St. Carthage receives the Holy Viaticum : St. Maelruan's Rule for the Céle Dei : extract from Curry MSS. in Catholic University : Feliré or Festology of Aengus . . . 182-187

CHAPTER III.

THE TEACHING AND PRACTICE OF THE IRISH SAINTS.

Facts connected with our Apostle: he instructs Fedhelmia and Ethne, daughters of King Leoghaire: his visit to Tirerrill: he receives the Viaticum from St. Tassach: St. Benignus: St. Brigid: her life by Cogitosus: her metrical life by St. Coellan of Inniskeltra: she receives the Viaticum from St. Nennidh: St. Columbkille's life by Adamnan: St. Columba at Maghbile: at Trevet, in Meath: in Iona: his life by Cumineus Albus: St. Canice: St. Furse: St. Colgu the Wise: Extract from his MS. Prayer: St. Kieran of Saigir: St. Munnu of Taghmon: St. Comgall: Bede's Life of St. Cuthbert: St. Fechin of Fore: St. Mida, *the Brigid of Munster*: St. Brendan of Clonfert: St Malachy punishes a monk for doubts regarding the Blessed Eucharist 187-201

CHAPTER IV.

TESTIMONY ON THE BLESSED EUCHARIST OF THE IRISH WRITERS APPEALED TO BY OUR ADVERSARIES.

The Poet Sedulius: Usher's extracts from the Carmen Paschale examined: other extracts from the works of Sedulius: the Commentator Sedulius: bears Witness to the Catholic teaching of our Church: the Irish Claudius, as cited by Usher: beautiful passages omitted by Usher 201-213

CHAPTER IV.—*Continued*.

Manuscript copy of the Gospel by Maelbrighte: Toland's theory: refuted as regards the age of the Manuscript: he, moreover, falsifies the text of Maelbrighte: St. Manchan: the Treatise de *Mirabilibus S. Scripturæ*: Analysis of this Irish document: John Scotus Erigena: Conclusion 213-221

ESSAY

On Devotion to the Blessed Virgin in the Ancient Church of Ireland.

CHAPTER I.

Ancient Irish Litany to the Blessed Virgin from Curry MSS. in the Catholic University: Hymn of St. Cuchumneus written in the seventh century, from the Liber Hymnorum in Rome:

Festivals of the Blessed Virgin in the Irish Church: Extracts from the Bobbio Missal: St. Brigid extolled as like unto the Mother of God: Extract from Leabhar Breac, etc. . 223-231

CHAPTER II.

Feliré of Aengus: Prayer of St. Colgu in the Eighth Century: Devotion of St. Columbanus to the Blessed Virgin: Irish Recluse in Austria: Sedulius's Poems in honour of the Mother of God: MS. fragment of Sedulius, Abbot of Kildare: Doctrine of Claudius Scotus: some ancient Irish Hymns: St. Mochta: St. Laurence O'Toole: Conclusion . . 231-240

APPENDIX No. I.

Testimony added to that of St. Mochta, given at p. 94 in the text: addition to p. 166, from the Bangor Antiphonary on Blessed Eucharist 241

APPENDIX No. II.

IRISH TRACT ON THE VARIOUS LITURGIES.

Conjectures as to sense of this tract, and version of it: the Pater Noster as used in the Irish liturgy: Gloria in Excelsis: the Apostles' Creed; the Hymn of the Three Children . 246-249

APPENDIX No. III.

ANCIENT IRISH PENITENTIALS.

A. *The Penitential of St. Cummian.*

Opinions of Lanigan, Theiner, Wasserschleben regarding this Penitential refuted: St. Cummian Fota, who died about 662, the author: great influence of this Penitential during the Middle Ages: St. Theodore of Canterbury borrows from it largely: extracts from it; introduction: general rules from Scripture: Canons on the use of animals: heinous crimes: robbery: pride and heresy: holy sacrifice of the Mass: regarding penance, the mass, churches, etc. . . . 250-263

B. *Penitential of St. Finnian.*

His Canons, published by Wasserschleben, more ancient than the year 700: extracts: Canon 31, regarding the redemption of captives, etc. 264

C. Penitentials of SS. David and Gildas.

Their Canons, published by Martene: extracts . . . 267

D. Penitential of St. Columbanus.

Drawn up in France or Italy: extracts: Canon 32 prescribes the liberation of slaves: communicating with heretics, etc. . . . 268-270

E. Canons of Adamnan.

Published in part by Martene—in full by Wasserschleben: extracts regarding flesh of deceased animals . . . 270-271

F. Synodus Sapientium.

Extracts: Canons de arreis: de jectione: the liberation of slaves prescribed: de canibus: great value of a sheep-dog: penalty for killing one: on tithes 271-274

G. Penitential of Eighth Century.

Taken from SS. Cummian, Finnian, and Theodore: extract from preliminary discourse 274-275

APPENDIX No. IV.

Missal of St. Columbanus.

Published by Mabillon: Dr. Lanigan and O'Conor prove that it contains the Irish liturgy: Dr. Todd's opinion refuted: proofs that it is Irish: agrees with Stowe Missal . . . 276-284

B. Penitential of the Bobbio Missal.

Extracts which show its connexion with the Penitentials of Columbanus and Cummian 284-287

C. Dr. Todd's Remarks on Bobbio Missal.

Dr. Todd endeavours to prove that this Missal is not Irish: his arguments refuted 287-292

D. Extracts from Bobbio Missal.

Prayer on the vigil of Christmas: regarding Blessed Virgin and St. Eugenia: preface: prayer from Mass of St. Stephen and Holy Innocents: of the chair of St. Peter: feasts of the Blessed Virgin, of the Holy Cross, etc. . . . 292-296

APPENDIX V.

PROFESSION OF FAITH OF ST. MOCHTA.

Referred to ante at page 92: first published by Muratori : given here in full 296-303

APPENDIX No. VI.

DR. TODD'S REMARKS ON SIXTH CANON OF ST. PATRICK'S SYNOD.

Dr Todd refers this Canon to ninth or tenth century : his arguments have no solidity : this Canon does not refer to the tonsure, but to the clipping of hair and beard in Roman fashion : Druidical verse about St. Patrick : this canon is found in MSS. more ancient than the period assigned to it by Dr. Todd: reading of Canon in ancient MSS: not given correctly by Spelman or Dr. Todd : the words referred to a cleric's wife by Dr. Todd regard married women in general : the Canon about offerings does not prove the synod to be of a late period . 304-311

APPENDIX No. VII.

COLLECTIO HIBERNENSIS CANONUM.

Extracts from this collection given by the Benedictines, D'Achery, etc. : Usher refers it to the year 700 : Dr. Todd and Dr. Reeves treat of it : the Cottonian MS. : Cambray MS. : other MSS. : two Vatican MSS. : extracts : Vallicellian MS. : extracts . 311-320

APPENDIX No. VIII.

IRISH SYNOD OF THE YEAR 807.

For this synod see page 180, where it is treated of : two extracts from the Vallicellian archives : Torbach of Armagh styled archbishop of the English and Irish 320-322

APPENDIX No. IX.

THE BANGOR ANTIPHONARY.

First published by Muratori: Lanigan refers it to the seventh century : in Ambrosian library at Milan : Hymn of St. Comghil : Hymn commemorative of the holy abbots of Bangor : Hymn to St. Camelach 322-326

APPENDIX No. X.

Hymns at vespers : complin : lauds and second vespers in honour of St. Foillanus (see p. 144), an Irish saint who, with his brothers SS. Furse and Ultan, is honoured in Brabant . . 327

2 A

www.ingramcontent.com/pod-product-compliance
Lightning Source LLC
Chambersburg PA
CBHW030323240426
43673CB00040B/1254